Symbols and Notations

♦	Any source of drinking water	⌂⌐	Post Office
◊	Seasonal water source	⊠	Will hold mail
⊏	AT Shelter	☽	Privy
◑	Camping, Tentsite	♀♂	Public restroom
⛺	Hostel	☎	Pay Phone
⛏	Hotel, Cabin or B&B	⚒	Laundry
☔	Shower available w/o stay	⛶	Computer available
🏃	Outfitter	⛳	Wireless (WiFi)
🚐	Shuttle, Bus or Taxi	🎋	Train Station
🍴	Any place that serves food	⚕	Pharmacy
🛒	Long term resupply	✚	First Aid
🏛	Short Term Resupply	🐕	Vet or kennel
🔨	Hardware store	✂	Barber
💲	Bank or ATM	⑂	Lounge
◎	View	ℹ	Info center
✿	Flora	+	Intersection

P Parking. Many have GPS coordinates that can be entered into a vehicle's GPS to navigate to trailhead parking lots. GPS systems are not always able to plot a course to remote locations.

⚠ Warning: watch for trail turn or heed special rule.

◀▶ Southbound / Northbound. Used to show distances to next shelter, and to show a transition of trails in the White Mountain National Forest.

■ Not cate~~~~~~~~~ ~~~~~~~~~~~~~~~~~~~~

(x.xE) Distance~ ~~~~~ to the n~ East (E) ~~~~~ left for a~ ~~~~~~~ or "W" m~~~~~~~~~~~~~~~~~~~~~~~~

(pg.xx) More information on page xx

B/L/D Breakfast/Lunch/Dinner

$nnS, $nnD, $nnPP, $nnEAP: Room prices: single, double, per-person, each additional person.

Contents

The A.T. Guide

Jerelyn Press
Titusville, FL
www.Jerelyn.com

Copyright © 2012 by David Miller
2012 Northbound Edition
ISBN 978-0-9797081-2-1

Contributors: Jim Austin (Skyline), Peter Barr (Whippersnap), Ken Bigelow, Grant Cibula (Fire Marshal), Tripp Clark, Ernest Engman (SGT Rock), John Gordon (Teej), Brad Horncastle (Chef), Jim Houck, Steve Huntress (Pilgrim), Rodney Ketterman (Rodman), Ray Klahne (RoCK), Allard Kremer, Wayne Krevetski (Mad Hatter), Dave Levy (Survivor Dave), Jessie, Juli, Lynn & Rene Miller, Raymond Myers (Rain Man), Pat Ohleger, Janet & Mike Pengelly (Purple and Carnivore), Bill Spach, John Stempa (Mechanical Man), Jeff Taussig, Rick Towle (AT Troll)

Maildrop Guidelines

► Use your real name (not a trail name), and include an ETA.
► FedEx and UPS packages cannot be addressed to PO boxes.
► Be prepared to show an ID when you retrieve your mail.
► Only send "General Delivery" mail to a Post office.
► The "C/O" name is essential when mailing to a business's PO Box; without it, they may not be able to retrieve your mail.
► Do not send maildrops to a lodging facility unless you plan to stay with them. If your plans change, offer to pay for the service of holding your mail.

Packages sent to post offices:

John Doe
C/O General Delivery
Trail Town, VA 12345

Please hold for AT hiker
ETA May 16, 2012

Packages sent to businesses:

John Doe
C/O Hiker Hostel
2176 Appalachian Way
Trail Town, VA 12345
Please hold for AT hiker
ETA May 16, 2012

Visit the Website: www.theATguide.com

The website contains the most recent updates, additions and corrections to the information contained in this book. Please let us know if there is anything we can do to improve the material or its presentation.

Directions

North/ South

At many points along the trail, a northbound hiker will be heading some direction other than compass north, but this book will always refer to "north" as the direction on the AT that ultimately leads to Katahdin. "South" means on the path leading to Springer Mountain. When reference is made to the true bearing, the word "compass" will precede the direction (e.g.: "compass south"). If the trail joins a section of road, enters a park, or enters a town, the "south" end is where a northbound hiker first arrives, and the "north" end is where he leaves.

East/West

Likewise, "east" is to the right of the trail for a northbound hiker and "west" is to his left, regardless of the compass reading. Most east-west directions are provided in shorthand notation along with a distance in miles. For example, three-tenths of a mile east is written "0.3E."

Left/Right

If a road leads to a town that is to the west, then a northbound hiker would go to his left, and the southbound hiker to his right. Once on the road both hikers are headed in the same direction, so any additional directions are given using the words "left" and "right." "Left" and "right" are also used to describe features near a shelter, from the perspective of a person outside, facing the front of the shelter.

Book Organization

A spread is the pair of pages seen when the book is laid open. *The A.T. Guide* contains trail data and services in alternating spreads; a spread containing trail data is followed by a spread detailing services available to hikers within that section. Occasionally the information is not distributed evenly and there are back-to-back spreads of data or services.

Data Spread

Data Spreads contain a table of landmarks, mileages and elevations. Every spread covers approximately 41 miles of trail (20.6 miles per page). An elevation profile is "watermarked" on the data. The lines of text that describe the landmarks are spaced so that they intersect the profile map at the approximate location of each landmark. Small triangular pointers below the profile line identify shelter locations. The vertical exaggeration of the profile maps is 5.6.

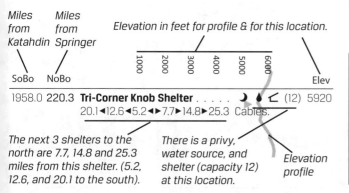

Miles from Katahdin
Miles from Springer

Elevation in feet for profile & for this location.

1000 2000 3000 4000 5000 6000

SoBo   NoBo   Elev

1958.0 220.3 **Tri-Corner Knob Shelter** . . . . . 🌙 ◊ ⊏ (12) 5920
                20.1◄12.6◄5.2◄►7.7►14.8►25.3 Cables.

The next 3 shelters to the north are 7.7, 14.8 and 25.3 miles from this shelter. (5.2, 12.6, and 20.1 to the south).

There is a privy, water source, and shelter (capacity 12) at this location.

Elevation profile

Services Spread

The Services Spreads tell where hikers can regroup and resupply. These mostly cover towns that the trail passes through or near. This book presents a limited view of trail towns. Businesses are selectively included, and maps may only show a portion of town closest to the trail.

When a map is provided, information presented in the map is not repeated in the text unless more elaboration about the service is needed. Post office information will be on the map and is not repeated in the text. Three features of the maps help in estimating distance around town; 1) the maps are proportionally scaled, 2) the width of the mapped area is at the bottom of the map, and 3) horizontal and vertical gridlines cross the map at one or one-half mile intervals. Keep in mind that places of business that appear to be adjacent may be separated by one or more unspecified buildings or roads.

Prices are listed as given in fall of 2011. **No establishment is obliged to maintain these prices.** Lodging prices are particularly volatile, but most facilities listed will do their best for hikers. Let them know if you are thru-hiking; there may be a "thru-hiker rate."

The A.T. Guide

Water Sources

Be aware of trail conditions before heading out, and tune in to advice from outfitters and other hikers. The trail gets re-routed, springs dry up, streams alter their course. Businesses come and go and prices change. Be prepared to deal with changes, particularly with respect to water sources. Never plan to carry just enough water to reach the next spring.

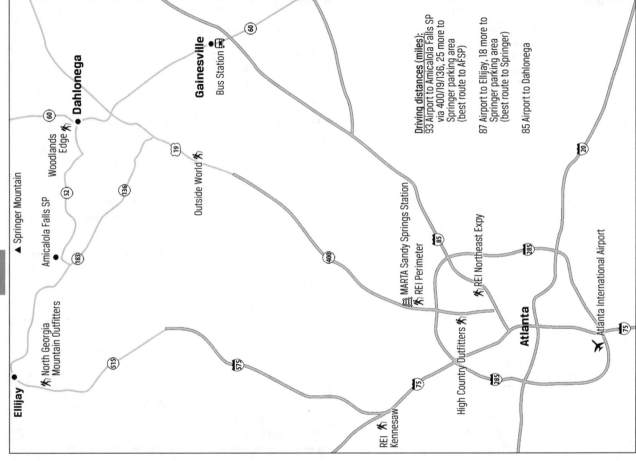

Driving distances (miles):
93 Airport to Amicalola Falls SP
via 400/19/136, 25 more to
Springer parking area
(best route to AFSP)

87 Airport to Ellijay, 18 more to
Springer parking area
(best route to Springer)

85 Airport to Dahlonega

Dahlonega

Gainesville
Bus Station

Springer Mountain

Woodlands
Edge

Amicalola Falls SP

Outside World

North Georgia
Mountain Outfitters

Ellijay

MARTA Sandy Springs Station

REI Perimeter

REI Northeast Expy

High Country Outfitters

Atlanta

Atlanta International Airport

REI
Kennesaw

Getting to Springer Mountain

The southern terminus of the trail is atop Springer Mountain, and is accessible only by foot. The 8.8-mile Approach Trail, originating at the Visitor Center in Amicalola State Park, is one means of getting there. An alternative is to drive to Big Stamp Gap via USFS 42, a dirt road passable by most vehicles. From the gap, hike one mile south to Springer Mountain. Your hike would begin by retracing your steps back to Big Stamp Gap. (See Start of Trail map on page 10)

The closest major city is Atlanta, GA, 82 miles south. If you fly or take AMTRAK into Atlanta, take the MARTA rail system to the North Springs Station, and a shuttle service can pick up from there. There is also Greyhound bus service to Gainesville, GA, 38 miles from the park.

🚐 **Hiker Hostel** Package deal including shuttle, see page 11.

🚐 **Survivor Dave's Trail Shuttle** 678-469-0978 ⟨www.atsurvivordave.com⟩ Shuttle service to/from Atlanta Airport, Gainesville Bus/AMTRAK Terminal, and North Springs MARTA Station to Amicalola, Springer, Woody Gap, Neel Gap, Unicoi Gap, Dick's Creek Gap and as far as Fontana Dam. Will stop at the outfitter and/or supermarket for supplies (time permitting). Reasonable rates. 24 hours notice please. Will respond promptly to phone messages.

🚐 **Wes Wisson** 706-747-2671, dwisson@alltel.net Based in Suches, GA. Will shuttle year-round, up to four hikers. MARTA to Amicalola or to Big Stamp Gap.

🚐 **Ron Brown** Home: 706-636-2825, Cell: 706-669-0919 hikershuttles@hotmail.com. Shuttle range Atlanta to Fontana.

Outfitters Near the Southern Terminus

🥾 **Mountain Crossings** 706-745-6095 (see page 11)

🥾 **North Georgia Mountain Outfitters** 706-698-4453 583 Highland Crossing, Suite 230, East Ellijay, GA 30540 Full service outfitter.

🥾 **Woodlands Edge** 706-864-5358 Open 10-6, 363 days a year (closed Easter and Christmas Day). Full service outfitter, fuel/oz, ask about shuttles. 36 North Park Street Dahlonega, GA 30533

🥾 **Outside World** 706-265-4500 471 Quill Drive, Dawsonville, GA 30534

🥾 **Half Moon Outfitters** 404-249-7921 1034 N. Highland Ave. NE, Atlanta, GA 30306

🥾 **High Country Outfitters** 404-814-0999 3906 Roswell Rd. #B, Atlanta, GA 30342

🥾 **REI** 3 Atlanta area stores:
1800 Northeast Expy NE, Atlanta, GA 30329, 404-633-6508
1165 Perimeter Ctr W Suite 200, Atlanta, GA 30338, 770-901-9200
740 Barrett Parkway Suite 450, Kennesaw, GA 30144, 770-425-4480

"Appalachee" is the name of an Indian tribe that once populated northwest Florida. Sixteenth century Spanish explorers used variants of the name to describe a region extending into the southern end of the mountain range. The place name, now morphed into "Appalachian," stuck to the mountains and moved north, leaving behind the flatlands where it originated.

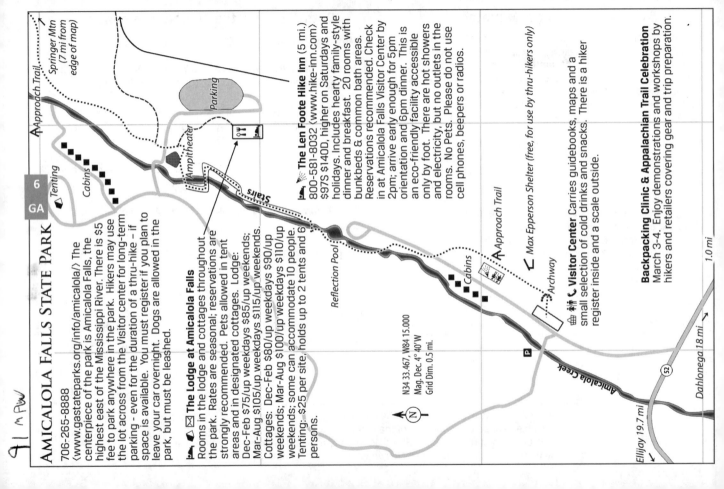

AMICALOLA FALLS STATE PARK

706-265-8888
<www.gastateparks.org/info/amicalola/> The centerpiece of the park is Amicalola Falls, the highest east of the Mississippi River. There is $5 fee to park anywhere in the park. Hikers may use the lot across from the Visitor center for long-term parking – even for the duration of a thru-hike – if space is available. You must register if you plan to leave your car overnight. Dogs are allowed in the park, but must be leashed.

The Lodge at Amicalola Falls
Rooms in the lodge and cottages throughout the park. Rates are seasonal; reservations are strongly recommended. Pets allowed in tent areas and in designated cottages. Lodge: Dec-Feb $75/up weekdays $85/up weekends; Mar-Aug $105/up weekdays $115/up weekends. Cottages: Dec-Feb $80/up weekdays $90/up weekends; Mar-Aug $100/up weekdays $110/up weekends; some can accommodate 10 people. Tenting: $25 per site, holds up to 2 tents and 6 persons.

N34 33.467, W84 15.000
Mag. Dec. 4° 40'W
Grid Dim. 0.5 mi.

The Len Foote Hike Inn (5 mi.)
800-581-8032 <www.hike-inn.com> $97S $140D, higher on Saturdays and holidays. Includes hearty family-style dinner and breakfast. 20 rooms with bunkbeds & common bath areas. Reservations recommended. Check in at Amicalola Falls Visitor Center by 2pm; arrive early enough for 5pm orientation and 6pm dinner. This is an eco-friendly facility accessible only by foot. There are hot showers and electricity, but no outlets in the rooms. No Pets. Please do not use cell phones, beepers or radios.

Max Epperson Shelter (free, for use by thru-hikers only)

Visitor Center Carries guidebooks, maps and a small selection of cold drinks and snacks. There is a hiker register inside and a scale outside.

Backpacking Clinic & Appalachian Trail Celebration
March 3-4. Enjoy demonstrations and workshops by hikers and retailers covering gear and trip preparation.

Springer Mtn (7 mi from edge of map)

Approach Trail

Parking

Tenting

Cabins

Ampitheater

Stairs

Reflection Pool

Cabins

Approach Trail

Archway

Amicalola Creek

N

Ellijay 19.7 mi

Dahlonega 18 mi

1.0 mi

The Approach Trail

SoBo	NoBo		Elev
8.8	0.0	**Amicalola Falls State Park,** archway behind Visitor Center	1800
8.7	0.1	**Max Epperson Shelter,** for thru-hiker use only	1858
8.4	0.4	Reflection Pond at base of falls	2003
8.1	0.7	Staircase - 604 steps to the top of the Falls	2216
7.7	1.1	Parking, side trail to Lodge	2639
7.6	1.2	Lodge Road (lodge to east)	2642
7.5	1.3	Trail to **Len Foote Hike Inn** (5.0E)	2656
7.3	1.5	USFS Road 46, steps on north side	2584
5.6	3.2	High Shoals Road	2841
4.0	4.8	Frosty Mountain. Spring (0.2E) is unreliable.	3384
3.7	5.1	Frosty Mountain Road, USFS Road 46.	3178
3.4	5.4	Trail to **Len Foote Hike Inn** (1.0E) blazed lime-green	3353
3.1	5.7	Woody Knob.	3406
2.8	6.0	Nimblewill Gap, USFS Road 28	3100
2.6	6.2	Spring (left of trail), unreliable	3419
1.5	7.3	**Black Gap Shelter** (0.1W). Spring is on opposite side of the Approach Trail (0.1E).	3300
0.0	8.8	Springer Mountain	3782

SoBo	NoBo	The A.T. Guide	Elev
2184.2	0.0	Springer Mountain southern terminus, register on back of rock with plaque.	3782
2184.0	0.2	**Springer Mountain Shelter** (0.2E).	3733
2183.2	1.0	0.0◀0.0◀0.0▶2.6▶7.9▶15.6 150 yards north, Benton MacKaye Trail to east. N34 38.257 W84 11.725	3350
		Big Stamp Gap, USFS 42	
2182.2	2.0	Benton MacKaye Trail.	3303
2181.5	2.7	Footbridge, stream	2950
2181.4	2.8	**Stover Creek Shelter** (0.1E).	2932
		0.0◀0.0◀2.6▶5.3▶13.0▶25.3	
2181.3	2.9	Footbridge, stream	2890
2180.8	3.4	Stream.	2709
2180.5	4.2	Benton MacKaye / Duncan Ridge Trail to east	2591
2179.9	4.3	Three Forks, USFS 58, footbridge	2530
2179.5	4.7	Campsites to west, between trail and creek	2564
2179.0	5.2	Benton MacKaye / Duncan Ridge Trail to west, Trail to Long Creek Falls	2800
2178.0	6.2	Dirt road, 0.2W to Hickory Flats Cemetery, pavillion	3000
2176.1	8.1	**Hawk Mountain Shelter** (0.2W) 0.0◀7.9◀5.3◀▶7.7▶20.0▶21.2. Water south on AT and 0.1 mile behind shelter.	3209
2175.7	8.5	Stream.	2979
2175.6	8.6	Hightower Gap, junction USFS 42 & 69. N34 39.809 W84 7.779	2854

✽ **Mayapple** – White flower ball dangling under an umbrella of broad leaves. Plant is about a foot tall.

SoBo	NoBo	The A.T. Guide	Elev
2173.6	10.6	Horse Gap.	2691
2172.6	11.6	Sassafras Mountain	3350
2171.8	12.4	Cooper Gap, USFS 15, 42 & 80	2946
2171.3	12.9	Justus Mountain	3224
2169.8	14.4	Campsites to west	2622
2169.2	15.0	Justus Creek, footbridge, campsites uphill	2648
2168.7	15.5	Blackwell Creek.	2674
2168.4	15.8	**Gooch Mountain Shelter** (0.1W). 15.6◀13.0◀7.7◀▶12.3▶13.5▶22.6 Water 100 yards behind shelter. Cables.	2821
2167.2	17.0	Spring to the east	2872
2166.9	17.3	Gooch Gap, USFS 42. N34 39.1256 W84 1.9402. **Suches, GA** (2.7W) (see town info on page 9)	2784
2165.6	18.6	Roadbed.	2962
2165.4	18.8	Liss Gap.	3061
2164.6	19.6	Ramrock Mountain	3260
2163.5	20.7	Springs (many).	3239

SoBo	NoBo	Feature	Elev
2163.0	21.2	Woody Gap, GA 60 . . . N34 40.659 W84 0.000 **P** ♦ (pg.11)	3256
		Suches, GA (2.0W); Hostel (6.0E); spring north of road 0.2W.	
2162.4	21.8	View .	3560
2162.1	22.1	Big Cedar Mountain, rock ledges and views.	3737
2162.0	22.2	Spring to west	3632
2161.1	23.1	Spring to west	3283
2160.4	23.8	Dockery Lake Trail	3100
2159.9	24.3	Lance Creek .	2880
2159.1	25.1	Henry Gap is 70 yards west on side trail, woods road to GA 180. **P**	3081
2157.5	26.7	Jarrard Gap . ♦ (0.3W) (pg.11)	3250
2157.3	26.9	Gaddis Mountain	3397
2156.2	28.0	Turkey Stamp	3751
2156.1	28.1	**Woods Hole Shelter** (0.4W) 25.3◀20.0◀12.3◀▶15.1	3688
2156.0	28.2	Bird Gap, Freeman Trail east bypasses Blood Mtn & rejoins AT at Flatrock Gap.	3724
2155.7	28.5	Slaughter Creek Trail 0.4W to campsite, spring on AT	3876
2155.3	28.9	Duncan Ridge Trail, Coosa Trail to west	4178
2154.9	29.3	**Blood Mountain Shelter** (1934)	4461
		21.2◀13.5◀1.2◀▶9.1▶13.9▶ 21.2 Privy 50 yards south on west side of AT. No fires.	
		Stream on trail to Slaughter Creek (0.8S)	
2153.6	30.6	Flatrock Gap, Freeman Trail east bypasses Blood Mtn; west. **P** ♦ (0.2W)	3479
		to Byron Reece parking area. Balance Rock 150 yards north.	
2152.5	31.7	Neel Gap, US 19 . N34 44.464 W83 55.237 **P** (pg.11)	3125
2151.3	32.9	Bull Gap, spring 0.1W .	3671
2150.7	33.5	Levelland Mountain, view	3825
2149.6	34.6	Swaim Gap, spring to west, campsites within 0.1 to north and south.	3518
2148.8	35.4	Wolf Laurel Top, campsite with views to east.	3759
2147.5	36.7	Cowrock Mountain	3842
2146.5	37.7	Tesnatee Gap, GA 348, Russell Hwy . N34 43.5708 W83 50.8453 **P**	3138
2146.0	38.2	Wildcat Mountain	3561
2145.8	38.4	**Whitley Gap Shelter** (1.2E) Spring 0.3 mile behind shelter.	3650
		22.6◀10.3◀9.1◀▶4.8▶12.1▶20.2 Campsite 0.1E with view just beyond.	
2145.6	38.6	Hogpen Gap, GA 348, Water south of rd. east of AT N34 43.351 W83 50.395 **P** ♦	3450
2144.7	39.5	White Oak Stamp	3470
2143.6	40.6	Poor Mountain .	3620

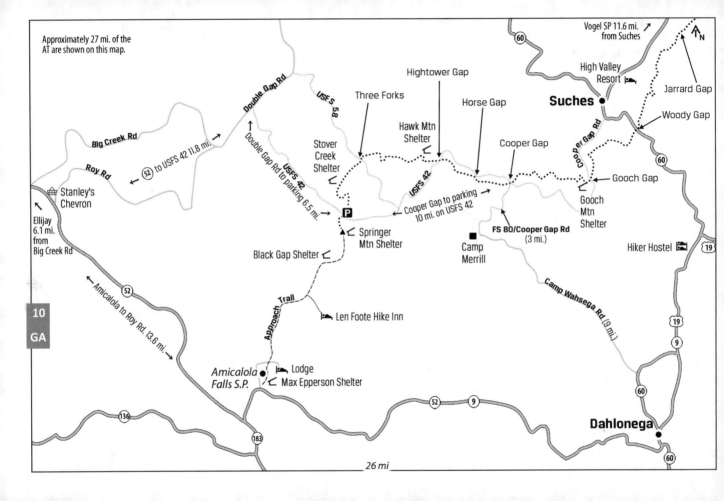

Approximately 27 mi. of the AT are shown on this map.

Vogel SP 11.6 mi. from Suches

High Valley Resort

Suches

Jarrard Gap

Woody Gap

60

Double Gap Rd

USF S 58

Hightower Gap

Three Forks

Horse Gap

Hawk Mtn Shelter

Big Creek Rd

52 to USFS 42 11.8 mi.

Double Gap Rd to parking 6.5 mi.

Stover Creek Shelter

USFS 42

Cooper Gap

Cooper Gap Rd

Gooch Gap

Roy Rd

USFS 42

Cooper Gap to parking 10 mi. on USFS 42

Gooch Mtn Shelter

Stanley's Chevron

P

FS 80/Cooper Gap Rd (3 mi.)

Hiker Hostel

19

Ellijay 6.1 mi. from Big Creek Rd

Springer Mtn Shelter

Camp Merrill

Black Gap Shelter

52

Approach Trail

Amicalola to Roy Rd. 13.6 mi.

Len Foote Hike Inn

Camp Wahsega Rd (9 mi.)

19

9

10
GA

Amicalola Falls S.P.

Lodge

Max Epperson Shelter

60

136

52

9

Dahlonega

183

26 mi

60

21.2   Woody Gap, GA 60

🛏 ⛺ 🚍 📶🖥 ✉ (6.0E) **Hiker Hostel** 770-312-7342
⟨www.hikerhostel.com⟩ hikerhostel@yahoo.com
Open year-round. $17PP Bunks $40 Private room for 2. Overnight stay includes breakfast, bed linens, towel & shower. Computer w/ internet & wireless available. Laundry $3. SPECIAL(Feb 20-Apr 20): $75 pickup from Atlanta North Springs MARTA Station or Gainesville, overnight stay in bunk, breakfast, shuttle to Amicalola or Springer, 8oz of white gas/alcohol. Canister fuel available for purchase. Mar 1-Apr 24 5pm daily pickup at Woody Gap. Shuttles from Atlanta to Dick's Creek Gap by reservation year round. Maildrops: (USPS) PO Box 802 or (FedEx/UPS) 7693 Hwy 19N, Dahlonega, GA 30533.

Suches, GA 30572 (2W)
🏤 M-F 7:30-11:30, 1-4:30, 706-747-2611
🏪 **Wolfpen Gap Country Store** 706-747-2271 M-Sat 7-6, Su 7-5:30
🛏 🔥 ⛺ 📶 **High Valley Resort** (0.7W) of Post Office, 706-747-2037
⟨www.highvalleyresort.com⟩ Camping $15PP, bunkhouse $45PP. Tenters and bunkhouse have access to bathhouse, showers and lodge with satellite TV. Winter special (until Apr 1); cabins $100/night, some sleep 4, some sleep up to 8 persons.
🚍 **Wes Wisson** 706-747-2671, Shuttles covering Atlanta the AT in Georgia.
➕ **Don Pruitt** 706-747-1421, M, Tu, Th, F 8-3, walk-ins 9-10.

26.7   Jarrard Gap
🔥 🍴 (1.0W) **Lake Winfield Scott Recreation Area** tent sites $12 for up to 5 persons, showers & bathrooms, leash dogs.
🛉 **180 Diner** 706-747-1018 On Rt. 180 0.2 mi. "left" (southwest) from Winfield Scott Rec Area. Open F 12-9, Sa 11-9, Su 11-2:30

31.7   Neel Gap, US 19

🚶 🛏 🚍 🍴 ⛺ 🚍 ✉ **Mountain Crossings** 706-745-6095
⟨www.mountaincrossings.com⟩ A full-service outfitter and gift shop operated by Winton Porter, bunk $15PP with towel and shower, sleeps 16. Shower without stay $3.50. No pets in hostel, kennels available. Denatured alcohol/oz. Mar-Oct hours Su-Sa 8:30-6, Nov-Feb hours Su-Sa 9-5. Ask about shuttles. Maildrops: (USPS/UPS) held for two weeks with $1 fee at pickup, 12471 Gainesville Hwy, Blairsville, GA 30512.
🛏 ⛺ 📶 (0.3E) **Blood Mountain Cabins** 800-284-6866
⟨www.bloodmountain.com⟩ Thru-hiker rate $60. Cabin with kitchen and satellite, holds up to 4 adults & 2 children under the age of 13. Laundry free w/stay, no pets.
🔥 🍴 ⛺ 🅿 (3W) **Vogel State Park** 706-745-2628
⟨www.gastateparks.org⟩ Tent sites with shower $19, cabins for 2 to 10 persons $85-$140, $2 shower w/o stay. Long term parking $5.
🛏 🔥 🍴 ⛺ 🚍 🅿 ✉ (3.5W) **Goose Creek Cabins** 706-745-5111
⟨www.goosecreekcabins.com⟩ goosecreek@alltel.net. $25PP/up, tent sites $10PP, shower/towel without stay $2, laundry $5 per load, pets allowed, includes lodge with game room, CATV, and shuttles from/to trail. Shuttle to Blairsville for dinner $25 for up to 6 persons. Parking for section hikers free with stay. $25 for shuttle to Hogpen Gap. Trout fishing on-site. Maildrops: (UPS) Goose Creek Cabins, 29 Goose Creek, Blairsville, GA 30512.
🚍 **Ron Hulbert and Sam Duke** 706-781-7641 or 706-745-1596 Centered in Blairsville, shuttle range Atlanta to Fontana.

Blairsville, GA 30514 (14W) All major services.
Dahlonega, GA 30597 (17E) All major services.

SoBo	NoBo	The A.T. Guide	Elev
2141.8	42.4	Sheep Rock Top.	3600
2141.0	43.2	**Low Gap Shelter** ☾●◁⌐(7)	3054
		15.1◀13.9◀4.8◀▶7.3▶15.4▶22.8 Water 30 yards in front of shelter. Cables.	
2140.6	43.6	Stream. ●	3214
2139.6	44.6	Poplar Stamp Gap ☾	3361
		spring 0.1E, gap and side trail unmarked.	
2138.9	45.3	Spring to west ●	3554
2137.6	46.6	Stream with cascade, several streams in area ●	3476
2137.1	47.1	Cold Springs Gap	3472
2136.0	48.2	Chattahoochee Gap, Jacks Knob Trail to west, spring 0.5E ●	3457
2135.3	48.9	Red Clay Gap (pg.14)	3485
2134.6	49.6	Site of former Rocky Knob Shelter ☾●	3621
2134.4	49.8	Spring west of trail down slope ●	3608
2133.7	50.5	**Blue Mountain Shelter** ☾●⌐(7)	3906
		21.2◀12.1◀7.3◀▶8.1▶15.5▶23.6 Spring on AT (0.1S)	
2132.8	51.4	Blue Mountain	4025
2131.3	52.9	Unicoi Gap, GA 75, **Helen, GA** (9.0E) . . . N34 48.101 W83 44.570 P (pg.14)	2949
2130.6	53.6	Stream. ●	3531
2130.4	53.8	Rocky Mountain Trail to west ●	3725
2129.9	54.3	Rocky Mountain, views from AT 0.1 north of summit 📷	4017
2128.6	55.6	Indian Grave Gap, USFS 283 . . . N34 47.563 W83 42.855 P	3113
		Andrews Cove Trail to east.	
2127.9	56.3	Tray Mountain Rd (gravel), USFS 79, piped stream east on road. ●	3580
2127.6	56.6	Cheese factory site, water (0.1W) on blue-blazed trail. ●◁	3585
2126.9	57.3	Tray Gap, Tray Mountain Rd, USFS 79 . . . N34 47.959 W83 41.461 P	3847
2126.1	58.1	Tray Mountain. 📷	4430
2125.6	58.6	**Tray Mountain Shelter** (0.2W) ☾●◁⌐(7)	4199
		20.2◀15.4◀8.1◀▶7.4▶15.5▶22.8 Spring 0.1 mile behind shelter. Cables.	
2124.4	59.8	Wolfpen Gap	3582
2123.9	60.3	Steeltrap Gap, water to east ●	3513
2123.3	60.9	Young Lick Knob	3790

SoBo	NoBo	Description	Elev
2120.9	63.3	Sassafras Gap, campsite and water to east	3500
2120.0	64.2	Addis Gap. Campsite 0.5E down old fire road, stream to right of campsite.	3304
2119.0	65.2	Kelly Knob, trail skirts summit, water 0.1E down steep trail	4191
2118.2	66.0	**Deep Gap Shelter** (0.3E), water 0.1 mile before shelter 22.8◄15.5◄7.4◄►8.1►15.4►20.3	3583 (12)
2117.3	67.1	"Vista" blue-blaze leads 0.1E to campsite.	3888
2116.8	67.4	Powell Mountain	3850
2115.6	68.6	Moreland Gap, water to east	2994
2114.6	69.6	Dicks Creek Gap, US 76 N34 54.728 W83 37.130 P (pg.14-15) Water, picnic tables at the gap, **Hiawassee, GA** (11.0W)	2675
2113.5	70.7	Campsite, water	3183
2112.8	71.4	Cowart Gap	2900
2111.5	72.7	Buzzard Knob	3708
2111.3	72.9	Bull Gap	3690
2110.6	73.6	Spring	3304
2110.1	74.1	**Plumorchard Gap Shelter** (0.2E) Privy 0.2 mile down steep trail 23.6◄15.5◄8.1◄►7.3►12.2►19.8 Creek on trail to shelter & spring (0.1W) of AT.	3165 (14)
2109.4	74.8	As Knob	3460
2108.9	75.3	Blue Ridge Gap, dirt road	3079
2107.9	76.3	Spring to west, campsite	3389
2107.2	77.2	Rich Cove Gap	3506
2107.0	77.0	Rocky Knob	3581
2105.7	78.5	**GA-NC border**	3836
2105.6	78.6	Bly Gap, spring west 30 yards / Old and twisted tree often photographed.	3840
2104.4	79.8	Couthouse Bald, summit 0.1W	4669
2103.7	80.5	Sassafras Gap	4300
2103.4	80.8	Piped Spring	4519
2102.8	81.4	**Muskrat Creek Shelter** 22.8◄15.4◄7.3◄►4.9►12.5►19.3	4580 (8)
2102.0	82.2	Whiteoak Stamp, old roadbed, Chunky Gal Trail to west	4620

48.9   Red Clay Gap

🛏 🏠 ⚓ ⛺ ⛪ **Enota Mountain Retreat** 706-896-9966, 1.5W from Red Clay Gap. No sign & trail not blazed; be certain of location if you walk. Marked on some maps by its previous name "Camp Pioneer." Trail is downhill to Joel's Creek and follows creek into camp. Driving from Unicoi Gap: 2.0W on Hwy 17, then left 3.0 mi. on Hwy 180. Tentsites, cabins, bunkrooms, laundry and store. Maildrops (guests only): 1000 Highway 180 Hiawassee, GA 30546

52.9   Unicoi Gap, GA 75
        Helen, GA 30545 (9E)

🏤 M–F 9–12:30 & 1:30–4, Sa 9:30–12:30, 706-878-2422
Tourist town with many hotels, restaurants, gift shops, ice cream shops, river rafting and tubing rentals. Visitor Center on Bruckenstrasse (near the PO) has information about places to stay and a free phone for making reservations.

🛏 ⛺ 🖥 **Helendorf River Inn** 800-445-2271 Prices are for 1 or 2 persons Su-Th; weekends are more: Dec-Mar $34, Apr-May $44, Jun-Sep $59, $5EAP, pets $10. Includes cont B. Visa/MC/Disc accepted.

🛏 **Super 8 Motel** 706-878-2191, ask for hiker room $35+tax for 1 or 2 persons, no pets.

🛏 **Econo Lodge** 800-443-6488   Weekdays $60, higher on weekends. Pets under 20 pounds allowed with $20 fee.

🛏 🖥 **Best Western Motel** 706-878-2111 Hiker rate $45 wkday, $71 wkend.

🏬 **Betty's Country Store** 706-878-2943 open 7 days 7am-9pm.

⛺ **laundromat**

69.6   Dicks Creek Gap, US 76

🏠 ⚓ ⛺ ✉ (W3.4) **Blueberry Patch Hostel** 706-896-4893
Christian ministry in its 20th season operated by Gary and Lennie Poteat. Gary is a 1991 thru-hiker. Open mid-February until the end of April. Bunks and tentsites; donations accepted. Please check in between 10am and 6pm. Shower, laundry, breakfast and 9:30 shuttle back to Dick's Creek Gap, white gas/alcohol/oz. No pets; no alcohol or drugs. Maildrops: 5038 Hwy 76 East, Hiawassee, GA 30546.

        Hiawassee, GA 30546 (11W) *(more services on map)*

🛏 🚶 ⛺ 🚌 📶 🖥 ✉ **Budget Inn** 706-896-4121 $39.99S, $5EAP, pets $10, coin laundry. For guests, free ride to/from Dick's Creek Gap or Unicoi Gap. Outfitter supply on-site. Accepts Visa/MC. Maildrops: 193 East Main Street, Hiawassee, GA 30546.

🛏 🚌 📶 ✉ **Mull's Motel** 706-896-4195 $45/up, no pets, shuttles by arrangement. Guest maildrops: 213 N Main St, Hiawassee, GA 30546.

🛏 ⛺ 📶 🖥 ✉ **Holiday Inn Express** 706-896-8884
⟨www.hiexpress.com/hiawasseega⟩ $72/up, accepts all major credit cards. Full hot breakfast included, free use of bicycles, indoor pool and hot tub, no pets. Maildrops: 300 Big Sky Drive, Hiawassee, GA 30546.

🛏 🍴 ⛺ 📶 🖥 **Ramada Lake Chatuge Lodge** 706-896-5253 $89/up includes continental breakfast. **Chophouse Restaurant** on site.

🚶 ⛪ **Buckhead House** 706-896-0028 Hiker friendly, carries boots, clothes and small gear, freeze-dried food, canister fuel, denatured/white gas/oz.

🚌 **Bill's Wheels of Georgia** 706-949-1976 (Cell)
BillsWheelsOfGeorgia@yahoo.com Shuttles to/from airports, bus & train stations and trailheads from Atlanta to NOC in Wesser, NC. Available 365 days a year at any hour, however extremely early or extremely late shuttles are price-adjusted accordingly. Advance notice appreciated.

■ **Goin' Postal** 706-896-1844 FedEx and UPS shipping 9-5 M-F.

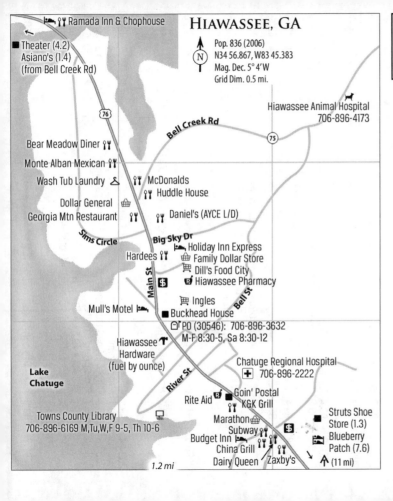

HIAWASSEE, GA

Pop. 836 (2006)
N34 56.867, W83 45.383
Mag. Dec. 5° 4'W
Grid Dim. 0.5 mi.

Ramada Inn & Chophouse

Theater (4.2)
Asiano's (1.4)
(from Bell Creek Rd)

Bell Creek Rd

Hiawassee Animal Hospital
706-896-4173

Bear Meadow Diner

Monte Alban Mexican

Wash Tub Laundry

McDonalds
Huddle House

Dollar General

Georgia Mtn Restaurant

Daniel's (AYCE L/D)

Sims Circle

Big Sky Dr

Hardees

Holiday Inn Express
Family Dollar Store
Dill's Food City
Hiawassee Pharmacy

Main St

Ingles

Mull's Motel

Buckhead House

PO (30546): 706-896-3632
M-F 8:30-5, Sa 8:30-12

Bell St

Hiawassee
Hardware
(fuel by ounce)

Chatuge Regional Hospital
706-896-2222

Lake
Chatuge

River St

Rite Aid

Goin' Postal
K&K Grill

Struts Shoe
Store (1.3)

Towns County Library
706-896-6169 M,Tu,W,F 9-5, Th 10-6

Marathon
Subway
Budget Inn
China Grill
Dairy Queen   Zaxby's

Blueberry
Patch (7.6)

(11 mi)

1.2 mi

At most post offices, postal workers are present before and after the window closes, and may retreive a package for you. Doing so is a courtesy not an obligation. Do not impose on them unnecessarily.

SoBo	NoBo	The A.T. Guide	Elev
2100.9	83.3	Wateroak Gap	4490
2100.6	83.6	Spring	4571
2099.4	84.8	Spring	4581
2098.8	85.4	Deep Gap, USFS 71, Kimsey Creek Trail. N35 2.3756 W83 33.1812 P ◆ (pg.18)	4341
2098.4	85.8	Spring to west, campsite	4560
2097.9	86.3	**Standing Indian Shelter,** creek 70 yards downhill	4757
		20.3◄12.2◄4.9▶7.6▶14.4▶16.2	
2097.6	86.6	Spring	4837
2096.4	87.8	Standing Indian Mountain, summit (0.1E) Campsites on side trail to summit. Lower Ridge Trail to west.	5498
2094.5	89.7	Spring.	4939
2093.5	90.7	Beech Gap Tenting area with water.	4460
2092.4	91.8	Stream.	4405
2091.8	92.4	Coleman Gap	4226
2090.8	93.4	Timber Ridge Trail to west	4635
2090.3	93.9	**Carter Gap Shelters,** newer shelter to north.	4520
		19.8◄12.5◄7.6◄▶6.8▶8.6▶12.1 Spring 100 yards downhill behind old shelter.	
2089.8	94.4	Stream.	4766
2089.2	95.0	Spring	4933

White blazes on the north side of trees are identical to the blazes on the south side. Make sure you are headed in the right direction, especially when sleepily leaving shelters in the morning.

SoBo	NoBo	The A.T. Guide	Elev
2086.6	97.6	Betty Creek Gap.	4300
2085.8	98.4	Mooney Gap, USFS 83, Ball Creek Rd, stream 0.1 north.	4496
2084.4	99.8	Albert Mtn bypass to west reconnects 0.4 north	4841
2084.1	100.1	Albert Mountain, fire tower.	5250
2083.9	100.3	USFS 67, Albert Mountain bypass, west 0.2 to parking.	5040
2083.5	100.7	**Big Spring Shelter.**	4973
		19.3◄14.4◄6.8◄▶1.8▶5.3▶13.3 Cables. Spring behind and to left of shelter.	
2082.2	102.0	**Long Branch Shelter** (2012) 16.2◄8.6◄1.8◄▶3.5▶11.5▶18.3	4503

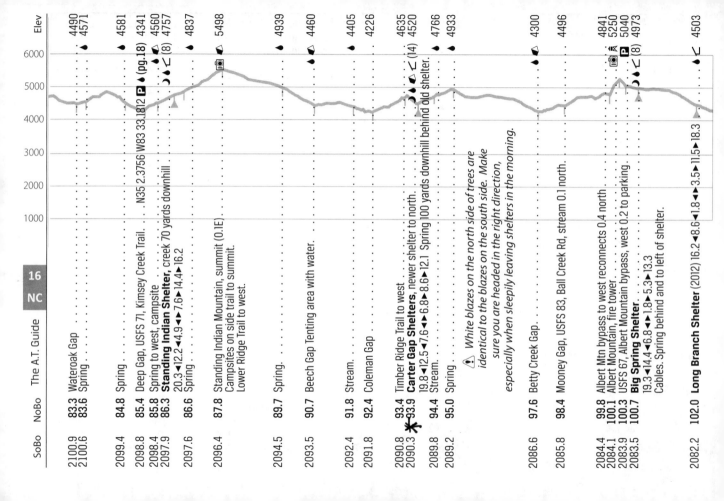

SoBo	NoBo	Description	Elev
2081.7		Glassmine Gap, Long Branch Trail 2.0W to USFS 67	4202
2078.2	✿106.0	**Rock Gap Shelter** ♪♦⊏ (8)	3787
		12.1◄5.3◄3.5▸►8.0►14.8►19.6 Cables.	
2078.1	106.1	Rock Gap, 0.7E to Wasalik Poplar and water. N35 5.6402 W83 31.3555 **P** (pg.18)	3757
2077.5	106.7	Wallace Gap, Old US 64, stream to north ♦	3738

✿ **Trillium** – Three-petal flower set upon three leaves. White and pink varieties are plentiful in the southern Appalachians.

SoBo	NoBo	Description	Elev
2074.4	109.8	Winding Stair Gap, US 64. N35 7.178 W83 32.878 **P** ♦ (pg.18-19)	3770
		piped spring east of steps, **Franklin, NC** (10.0E)	
2074.2	110.0	Forest Service road, waterfall ♦⊏	3749
2074.1	110.1	Stream, campsite. ♦	3814
2073.8	110.4	Logging road	4018
2073.3	110.9	Swinging Lick Gap	4100
2072.4	111.8	Panther Gap	4480
2070.2	114.0	**Siler Bald Shelter** (0.5E), south end of shelter loop trail ♪♦⊏ (8)	4786
		13.3◄11.5◄8.0▸►6.8►11.6►17.4	
2069.8	114.4	Siler Bald, summit (0.2W), shelter (0.3E), north end of shelter loop trail 📷	5012
2069.0	115.2	Piped spring ♦⊏	4477
2068.0	115.5	Footbridge, stream ♦	4366
2068.6	115.5	Wayah Crest Picnic Area (0.1W), trash cans **P**	4247
2068.5	115.7	Wayah Gap, Wayah Rd N35 9.237 W83 34.844	4180
2068.1	116.1	AT skirts USFS 69	4353
2067.7	116.5	USFS 69, meadow	4497
2067.3	116.9	Wilson Lick Trail, 0.2W to historic site	4659
2066.8	117.4	USFS 69, piped spring to east ♦	5036
2066.4	117.8	Bartram Trail to west ⊏	5290
2066.2	118.0	0.1E to Wine Spring Rd, meadow, campsites 0.1E, water on west side of AT	5290
2064.7	119.5	USFS 69	5213
2064.5	119.7	Paved footpath to latrines and parking N35 10.509 W83 34.845 ♪♦ **P** 👥	5315
2064.3	119.9	Wayah Bald, stone tower and paved footpath 📷♦	5342
2063.7	120.5	Bartram Trail, campsite, spring to west of trail ♦⊏	4902
2063.4	120.8	**Wayah Bald Shelter**, east to shelter, west 0.2 to water ♪♦⊏ (8)	4729
		18.3◄14.8◄6.8▸►4.8►10.6►15.5	
2062.1	122.1	Licklog Gap ♦ (0.5W)	4440
2060.7	123.5	Intersection with old roadbed and side trails, AT turns to east ⊏	4502

85.4   Deep Gap, USFS 71

106.1   Rock Gap

⬥ 🏠 🚻 ⚒ **Standing Indian Campground** 828-369-0442 3.7W from Deep Gap and 1.5W from Rock Gap. Campsites $16, open Apr 1 - Nov 30. Campstore with small selection of foods.

🛏 ⬥ 🍴 ⛺ 🚐 🛜 ✉ **Muskrat Creek Hostel** 828-389-4900 Shuttle to & from trailhead with reservations (Deep Gap, Wallace Gap or Winding Stair Gap). Cabin w/shower $20pp, tent sites $10 w/ shower. Meals by request, pets with prior arrangement.   Cabin has WiFi, nominal fee for laundry. Shuttles available to Franklin or Hiawassee $1.50 mi (one-way mileage).   Maildrops: P.O. 681 Hiawassee,Ga 30546, or 955 Muskrat Creek Rd, Hayesville, N.C. 28904.

109.8   Winding Stair Gap, US 64

          Franklin, NC (10E) *(more services on map)*

Hiker Fool Bash March 31 - April 1 at the Sapphire Inn at 5pm vendors, food, fun and games.

🚐 **Ron Haven**, owner of Budget Inn, Sapphire Inn and Franklin Motel, makes two trips at 9 & 11am Mar-Apr, and picks up at Rock Gap, Wallace Gap and Winding Stair Gap. Guests of Budget Inn, Sapphire Inn and Franklin Motel, call for free pick-up Mar-Apr.

🛏 ⛺ 🚐 🖥 ✉ **Haven's Budget Inn** 828-524-4403 ⟨www.havensbudgetinn.com⟩ $39.99S, $5EAP, $50 pet deposit, shuttles back to trail and around town. Internet and coin laundry on-site. Maildrops: 433 East Palmer Street, Franklin, NC 28734.

🛏 🖥 ✉ **Sapphire Inn** 828-524-4406, $39.99S, $5EAP Maildrops: 761 East Main Street, Bus 441, Franklin, NC 28734.

🛏 🛜 🖥 ✉ **Microtel Inn & Suites** 888-403-1700   Prices vary, continental breakfast, pet fee $20. Maildrops: 81 Allman Dr, Franklin, NC 28734

🍴 **Fun Factory** AYCE pizza lunch M-Sa.

🧗 ✉ **Three Eagles Outfitters** 828-524-9061 ⟨www.threeeaglesoutfitters.net⟩ Open M-Sa 10-6, Su 12-4. Full-service outfitter serving AT hikers for over 18 years. 10% discount for thru-hikers, white gas/alcohol/oz. Shuttle to store available. Maildrops: 78 Siler Road, Franklin, NC 28734.

🧗 🚐 🛜 🖥 ✉ **Outdoor 76** 828-349-7676 ⟨www.outdoor76.com⟩ Open M-Sa 10-7, extended hours in March & April. Filling all hiker needs including lightweight gear, footwear, food and all types of fuel. Gear shakedowns and 10% off for thru-hikers. Shipping services, free internet, ask about shuttles. Maildrops: 76 East Main Street, Franklin, NC 28734.

🔨 **Ace Hardware** Coleman/alcohol/oz

🚐 **City Taxi** 828-369-5042, until 6 pm.

🚐 **Roadrunner Driving Services** 706-201-7719 where2@mac.com Shuttle anywhere from Atlanta to Damascus.

✚ **Angel Urgent Care** 828-349-3114 M-F 9:30-5:30, Sa 9:30-2:30, Su 10-2

🐾 **Lenzo Animal Hospital** 828-369-2635 M-F 8:30-5:00, some Sa 8:30-noon. Emergency clinic 828-665-4399.

ℹ **Visitor Center** (Chamber of Commerce) 828-524-3161 M-F 9-5, Sa 10-4, closed Sunday. List of hiker services and shuttles.

✉ **UPS Store** 828-524-9800, M-F 8-6, Sa 10-3.

The A.T. Guide

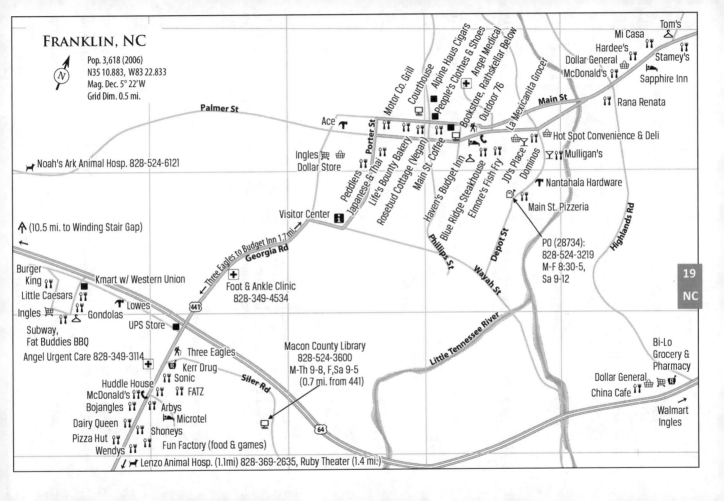

FRANKLIN, NC

Pop. 3,618 (2006)
N35 10.883, W83 22.833
Mag. Dec. 5° 22'W
Grid Dim. 0.5 mi.

Palmer St

Ace

Noah's Ark Animal Hosp. 828-524-6121

Ingles
Dollar Store

Peddlers
Japanese & Thai
Life's Bounty Bakery
Rosebud Cottage (Vegan)
Main St. Coffee
Haven's Budget Inn
Blue Ridge Steakhouse
Elmore's Fish Fry

Porter St

Motor Co. Grill
Courthouse
Alpine Haus Cigars
People's Clothes & Shoes
Angel Medical
Bookstore, Rathskellar Below
Outdoor 76
La Mexicanita Grocer

Main St

Tom's

Mi Casa
Hardee's
Dollar General
McDonald's
Stamey's
Sapphire Inn

Rana Renata

Hot Spot Convenience & Deli
Mulligan's

JD's Place
Dominos
Nantahala Hardware

Highlands Rd

Main St. Pizzeria

PO (28734):
828-524-3219
M-F 8:30-5,
Sa 9-12

Visitor Center

Three Eagles to Budget Inn 1.7 mi.

Georgia Rd

Phillips St

Depot St

Wayah St

(10.5 mi. to Winding Stair Gap)

Burger
King
Little Caesars
Ingles
Gondolas

Kmart w/ Western Union

Lowes

UPS Store

441

Foot & Ankle Clinic
828-349-4534

Macon County Library
828-524-3600
M-Th 9-8, F,Sa 9-5
(0.7 mi. from 441)

Little Tennessee River

64

Bi-Lo
Grocery &
Pharmacy

Dollar General
China Cafe

Walmart
Ingles

Subway,
Fat Buddies BBQ
Angel Urgent Care 828-349-3114

Three Eagles

Kerr Drug
Sonic
Huddle House
McDonald's
Bojangles
Dairy Queen
Pizza Hut
Wendys

FATZ

Arbys
Microtel
Shoneys
Fun Factory (food & games)

Siler Rd

Lenzo Animal Hosp. (1.1mi) 828-369-2635, Ruby Theater (1.4 mi.)

SoBo	NoBo	The A.T. Guide	Elev
2060.1	124.1	Stream.	4313
2059.8	124.4	Burningtown Gap, NC 1397.	4236
2059.4	124.8	Spring.	4513
2058.6	125.6	**Cold Spring Shelter.** 19.6◄11.6◄4.8◄►5.8►10.7►18.4 Trail to tentsites 0.1N on AT.	4945
2057.9	126.3	Copper Ridge Bald, views	5080
2056.7	127.5	Side trail 0.1E to Rocky Bald, views	5030
2055.0	129.2	Tellico Gap, NC 1365 Otter Creek Rd	3850
2053.6	130.6	Wesser Bald, east 40 yards to observation tower, panoramic views	4627
2052.9	131.3	Spring-fed stone cistern on blue-blazed trail (0.1W)	4276
2052.8	131.4	**Wesser Bald Shelter** (0.1W) 17.4◄10.6◄5.8◄►4.9►12.6►21.7 Spring 0.1S on AT (at switchback). Cables. Just north of shelter trail, Wesser Creek Trail to east.	4227
2051.2	133.0	The Jumpoff, views	4000
2049.5	134.7	Spring	3017
2047.9	136.3	**A. Rufus Morgan Shelter.** 15.5◄10.7◄4.9◄►7.7►16.8►22.9 Shelter in view to east, stream west of AT.	2201
2047.3	136.9	Multiple streams and footbridges	2013
2046.9	137.3	US 19 & 74, **Nantahala Outdoor Center** (pg.22)	1746
2046.7	137.5	Side trail to bunkhouse	1780
2045.3	138.9	Wright Gap, dirt road	2415
2044.5	139.7	Grassy Gap, Grassy Gap Trail to west	2980
2042.9	141.3	Spring	3575
2042.3	141.9	The Jump-up, views to Nantahala Gorge	3789
2041.1	143.1	Swim Bald	4710
2040.2	144.0	**Sassafras Gap Shelter** (0.1W) 18.4◄12.6◄7.7◄►9.1►15.2►21.8 Reliable spring front-right of shelter.	4400

Coordinates shown on profile:
N35 13.340 W83 33.734
N35 16.082 W83 34.353
N35 19.873 W83 35.529

SoBo	NoBo	Feature	Elev
2039.0	145.2	Cheoah Bald, Campsite at top of Cheoah Bald.	5062
2038.8	145.4	Bartram Trail to west	4919
2036.6	147.6	Locust Cove Gap, water to west	3690
2035.6	148.6	Simp Gap	3700
2033.5	150.7	Stecoah Gap, NC 143 . . . N35 21.494 W83 43.076 P (pg.22)	3165
		Sweetwater Creek Rd (paved) 100 yards west to picnic tables.	
2032.5	151.7	Sweetwater Gap, start of "Jacob's Ladder"	3270
2031.9	152.3	Cliff, west 20 yards to view.	3898
2031.1	153.1	**Brown Fork Gap Shelter**	3739
		21.7◄16.8◄9.1◄►6.1►12.7►23.7 Reliable spring to right of shelter.	
2030.9	153.3	Brown Fork Gap	3600
2030.5	153.7	Brushnell Knob	3681
2029.3	154.9	USGS survey marker	3681
2028.3	155.9	Cody Gap, water 0.2W	3600
2026.2	158.0	Yellow Creek Gap, stream	3267
2025.9	158.3	County Rd 1242, Yellow Creek Mountain Rd . . . N35 24.630 W83 45.942 P	2966
2025.0	159.2	**Cable Gap Shelter**	2905
		22.9◄15.2◄6.1◄►6.6►17.6►20.4 Stream in front of shelter.	
2023.6	160.6	Black Gum Gap	3490
2022.2	162.0	Walker Gap	3450
2022.0	162.2	Footbridge, stream	3289
2020.3	163.9	Spring	2305
2019.6	164.6	NC 28, **Fontana 28 AT Crossing** . . . N35 26.485 W83 47.806 P (pg.22-23)	1863
		Fontana Dam, NC (2.0W)	

137.3   US 19 & 74

🍴⛺🚐📞 Nantahala Outdoor Center
888-905-7238 ⟨www.noc.com⟩ Large complex at the intersection of the AT and the Nantahala River has lodging, food, gear and whitewater rafting. Coin operated showers available to non-guests.

🛏 There are 6 "cabin motel" rooms on-site for $54/ up. More rooms are available at their **Nantahala Inn** 1.5 miles away. For large groups, it can be economical to rent a cabin; ask about prices.

🏠 **Base Camp (hostel)** $17 includes shower and use of common area and kitchen. Check in at general store.

🍴 **River's End Restaurant** (B/L/D); **Slow Joe's/ Pourover Pub** Live music, opens mid-April. **Relia's Garden** (upscale);

🏃 🚐🚐 ✉ **NOC Outfitters** Full service outfitter, fuel/oz. Experienced staff, gear shakedowns, Full line of gear and trail food. Ask about shuttles. Maildrops: dated & marked "Hold for AT Hiker", 13077 Hwy 19W, Bryson City, NC 28713.

🏛 Wesser General Store

🚐 **Jude Julius** 828-488-6399, 828-736-0086 In Bryson City, NC. Shuttles from Springer Mtn, GA to Hot Springs, NC. Call for rates.

Events at NOC:

Southern Ruck Jan 13-16.

Founder's Bridge AT Festival Apr 6-7 Features live music, lightweight backpacking, cooking, and trail maintenance clinics. Support from local hiking clubs, sales at the Outfitter's Store, and lots of fun and giveaways along the Nantahala River. Gear reps on hand for support & repairs. Extended restaurant and store hours.

FONTANA VILLAGE, NC

N35 26.067, W83 49.500
Mag. Dec. 5° 6'W
Grid Dim. 0.5 mi.

PO (28733):
828-498-2315
M-F: 8:30-3

Fontana Rd

Visitor's Center

Fontana Hilton

Dam Rd

Fontana 28 A.T. Crossing

Fontana Rd

The Hike Inn (6.3 mi.)

Fontana Pit Stop

Grocery, Hazel Creek Outfitter, Ice Cream, Laundry

🍴 Wildwood Grill

Mountainview 🍴 🛏 Fontana Lodge Bistro

2.2 mi

150.7   Stecoah Gap, NC 143

🛏 🏠 🚐 **The Cabin in the Woods** Phil Capper 828-735-3368 ⟨www.thecabininthewoods.com⟩ Cabin & loft; both include a ride to/from the trail up to 15 miles each way. Cabin is often booked so reserve early. The loft accommodates 2 hikers; $15PP includes ride, shower, bathroom. Shuttles Georgia through Hot Springs; longer shuttles 50 cents per mile.

♛♛ Fontana 28 AT Crossing Bathrooms, vending machines, GSMNP maps ($1), and a house phone to call a $3 shuttle from Fontana Village. Northbound hikers get a backcountry permit here or at the Visitor Center.

Fontana Village, NC (2W) *(more services on map)*

Contact for all facilities: 800-849-2258 ⟨www.fontanavillage.com⟩

◄ ⊠ ⎕ 🛒 **Fontana Lodge** $59/room, after April 15 $109/room, no pets. Maildrops: P.O. Box 68, Hwy 28 North, Fontana Dam, NC 28733

⛪⎕ **General Store** Small grocery store, seasonal ice cream shop, Coleman/alcohol/oz, a small selection of major gear items (packs, tents, sleeping bags). 10% discount for thru-hikers. In winter (Nov 1 - March 1) the store is only open Friday, Saturday and Sunday.

🍴 **Mountainview Bistro** is pricey; the **Wildwood Grill** does not open until May 1; the **Fontana Pit Stop offers** hot dogs, nachos and microwave fare.

△ **Laundromat** 7 days

166.1   Fontana Dam Visitor Center

🚻 ⛪♛♛ 🚿 Sodas, snacks, camera supplies, free showers, GSMP self-registration permits. Open 9am-6pm daily May-Oct. Verizon and AT&T cell phones may get signal at the overlook near the shelter parking area.

◄ △ 🚐 (6.3E) **The Hike Inn** 828-479-3677 ⟨www.thehikeinn.com⟩ ⟨hikeinn@graham.main.nc.us⟩ A hikers only service open Feb 15 - Jul 10 and Sep 1 - Dec 1, other dates by reservation only. 5 rooms with max 2 per room. Thru-hiker/long distance hiker package: $60S, $75D rate includes shuttle to and from dam, 1 load laundry, evening (5-7pm) shuttle to Robbinsville for dinner and supplies. Check in by 4pm, check out by 9am firm. Reservations are required; NoBo call from NOC, SoBo call from Hot Springs to arrange pick-up. Section/day hikers $40S/D (room only). Mail accepted for guests only c/o Hike Inn 3204 Fontana Rd, Fontana Dam, NC 28733 ($20 service charge for non-guests includes delivery to dam area only.) NO credit cards or pets. Fuel/oz & canisters, shuttles, slack-packs, internet at Robbinsville public library. Has GSMNP permits.

Great Smoky Mountains National Park (GSMNP)

Backcountry Information: 865-436-1297

Reservations: 865-436-1231

A permit is required - There is no cost. NoBos can get one at 28 AT Crossing, Dam Visitor Center, Hike Inn or Fontana Lodge. SoBos get permit from Bluff Mountain Outfitters in Hot Springs, at Standing Bear Farm, or at Big Creek Ranger station.

Limited campsites - The only near-trail campsite is Birch Spring. Otherwise AT hikers must overnight at the shelters. Section hikers must make reservations. Four spaces set aside at each shelter for thru-hikers. If those spaces are taken, additional thru-hikers may tent in the vicinity of the shelter. Thru-hikers who want to ensure shelter space may reserve them. All hikers must use bear cables to secure food.

No pets - Dogs are not permitted inside the park. Below are options for kenneling:

🐕 **Standing Bear Farm** (see page 30)

🐕 **Rippling Water Kennels** 828-488-2091 ⟨www.ripplingwaterkennel.com⟩ Will pickup and kennel your dog for up to one week for $250 and a $50 deposit. Reservations and vaccination records required. Cash or check in advance. Owners David and Peggy Roderick.

🐕 ⊠ **Loving Care Kennels** 865-453-2028, 3779 Tinker Hollow Rd, Pigeon Forge, TN 37863. Pick up your dog at Fontana Dam and return him/her to Davenport Gap. $300 for one dog, $450 for two. Will also deliver maildrops at time of pickup or return. It is recommended that you call at least 2 days in advance.

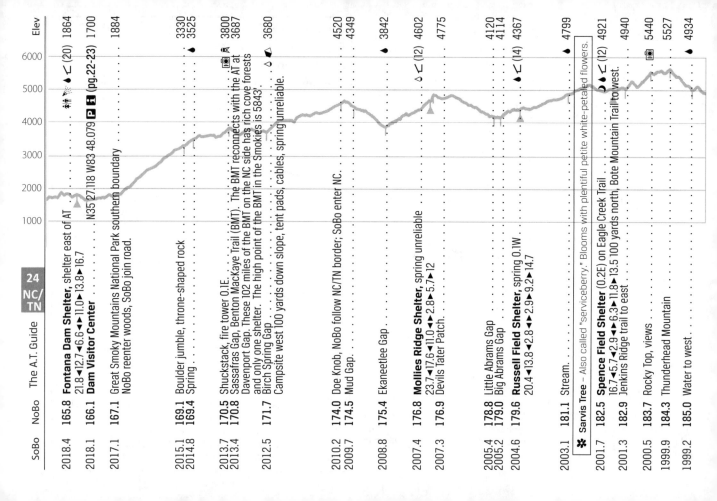

SoBo	NoBo	The A.T. Guide	Elev
2018.4	165.8	**Fontana Dam Shelter,** shelter east of AT 🕮⚡️✦⌐ (20)	1864
2018.1	166.1	**Dam Visitor Center** N35 27.118 W83 48.079 **P H** (pg.22-23)	1700
2017.1	167.1	Great Smoky Mountains National Park southern boundary NoBo reenter woods, SoBo join road.	1884
2015.1	169.1	Boulder jumble, throne-shaped rock	3330
2014.8	169.4	Spring	3525
2013.7	170.5	Shuckstack, fire tower 0.1E.	3800
2013.4	170.8	Sassafras Gap, Benton MacKaye Trail (BMT). The BMT reconnects with the AT at Davenport Gap. These 102 miles of the BMT on the NC side has rich cove forests and only one shelter. The high point of the BMT in the Smokies is 5843'.	3687
2012.5	171.7	Birch Spring Gap Campsite west 100 yards down slope, tent pads, cables, spring unreliable.	3680
2010.2	174.0	Doe Knob, NoBo follow NC/TN border; SoBo enter NC.	4520
2009.7	174.5	Mud Gap.	4349
2008.8	175.4	Ekaneetlee Gap	3842
2007.4	176.8	**Mollies Ridge Shelter,** spring unreliable ⌐ (12) 23.7◄17.6◄11.0◄▶2.8▶5.7▶12	4602
2007.3	176.9	Devils Tater Patch.	4775
2005.4	178.8	Little Abrams Gap	4120
2005.2	179.0	Big Abrams Gap	4114
2004.6	179.6	**Russell Field Shelter,** spring 0.1W ✦⌐ (14) 20.4◄13.8◄2.8◄▶2.9▶9.2▶14.7	4367
2003.1	181.1	Stream.	4799
		❀ **Sarvis Tree** – Also called "serviceberry." Blooms with plentiful petite white-petaled flowers.	
2001.7	182.5	**Spence Field Shelter** (0.2E) on Eagle Creek Trail ✦⌐ (12) 16.7◄5.7◄2.9◄▶11.8▶13.5 100 yards north, Bote Mountain Trail to west.	4921
2001.3	182.9	Jenkins Ridge trail to east	4940
2000.5	183.7	Rocky Top, views	5440
1999.9	184.3	Thunderhead Mountain	5527
1999.2	185.0	Water to west.	4934

SoBo	NoBo	Feature	Elev
1997.3	186.9	Starkey Gap	4560
1996.5	187.7	Sugar Tree Gap	4435
1995.4	188.8	**Derrick Knob Shelter** 12◄9.2◄6.3◄►5.5►7.2►13.5 Reliable spring near shelter. Cables.	4901
1995.1	189.1	Sams Gap, Greenbrier Ridge Trail to west	4779
1993.1	191.1	Cold Spring Knob	5218
1992.8	191.4	Miry Ridge Trail to west.	4965
1992.6	191.6	Buckeye Gap	4817
1989.9	194.3	**Silers Bald Shelter,** spring 75 yard to right of shelter. 14.7◄11.8◄5.5◄►1.7►8.0►15.5	5454
1989.7	194.5	Silers Bald, survey mark on boulder, AT turns to east	5607
1989.5	194.7	Welch Ridge Trail to east.	5454
1988.2	196.0	**Double Spring Gap Shelter** 13.5◄7.2◄1.7◄►6.3►13.8►21.2. Best water 15 yards from crest on NC side. Water is also 35 yards down TN side.	5511
1987.6	196.6	Goshen Prong Trail to west.	5755
1985.7	198.5	Mt Buckley	6527
1985.6	198.6	Trail 0.5E to Clingman's parking area (NoBo be careful at this fork).	6493
1985.3	198.9	Clingmans Tower Path, paved path between tower and parking area	6643
1985.1	199.1	Clingmans Dome, tower to east	6588
1984.1	200.1	Mt Love	6446
1983.0	201.2	Collins Gap	5738
1982.3	201.9	Mt Collins	6175
1981.9	202.3	Sugarland Mtn Trail, **Mt Collins Shelter** (0.5W) 13.5◄8.0◄6.3◄►7.5►14.9►20.1 Cables. Small spring 0.1 beyond shelter.	5970
1981.6	202.6	Fork Mountain Trail east ot Clingmans Dome Rd	5892
1980.8	203.4	Spring	5672
1979.1	205.1	Road Prong Trail, AT skirts Clingmans Dome Rd. N35 36.564 W83 26.799 P	5284
1978.7	205.5	Mingus Ridge, two wild hog containment bridges	5458

SoBo   NoBo   The A.T. Guide

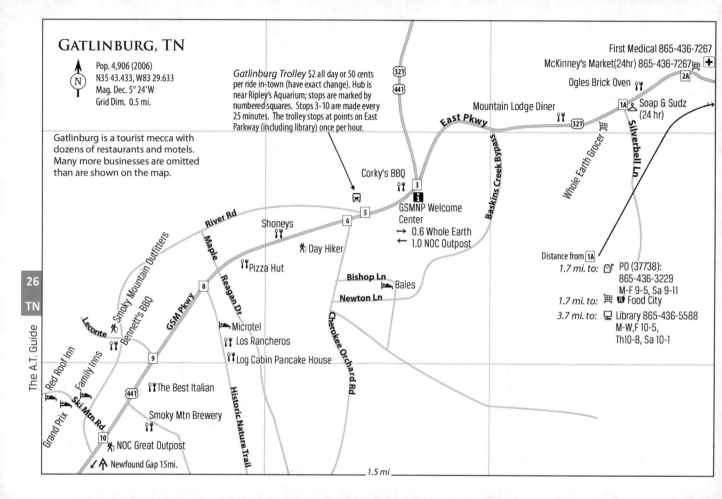

199.1   Clingmans Dome
N35 33.433 W83 29.634 🅿 🚻
This is the highest point on the Appalachian Trail. Parking lot and restrooms are 0.5E on a paved walkway. There are no sinks in the restrooms and outside water fountains are off in winter (until May 1). It is seven miles from the parking area to Newfound Gap along Clingmans Dome road.

206.8   Newfound Gap, US 441
Gatlinburg, TN (15W) *(more services on map)*
🛏⛺🚌🖥 **Grand Prix Motel** 865-436-4561, $29.95/up, coin laundry. Shuttle up to 4 persons to Newfound Gap or Clingmans Dome for $30. Maildrops: 235 Ski Mtn Rd, Gatlinburg, TN 37738.

🛏📶✉ **Microtel Gatlinburg** 865-436-0107 $44.95, cont B, pets $10. Call ahead if you'd like to send a maildrop: 211 Historic Nature Trail, Gatlinburg, TN 37738.

🛏📶✉ **Family Inns** 865-436-3300 Ask for hiker rate $49.77D, $10EAP, cont B, pets $10. Maildrops: 218 Ski Mountain Rd, Gatlinburg, TN 37738.

🛏📶✉ **Bales Motel** 865-436-4773 $30/up, ask for hiker rate, no pets. Maildrops: 221 Bishop Lane, Gatlinburg, TN 37738.

🛏📶✉ **Red Roof Inn** 865-436-7813
⟨www.redroofgatlinburg.com⟩ $45/up, cont B, pool, pets $10. Trolley stops at the front door. All major CC. Maildrops: 309 Ownby St, Gatlinburg, TN 37738.

🥾🚿🚌✉ **NOC Great Outpost** 888-905-7238, 865-277-8209
M-Sa 9-9, Su 10-6, free showers and pack storage, full line of gear and fuel/oz. Ask about shuttles Newfound-Gatlinburg; call for sched. Maildrops: 1138 Parkway, Gatlinburg, TN 37738.

🥾🚌✉ **Smoky Mountain Outfitters** 865-430-2267 Full service backpacking store, Coleman/alcohol/oz and other fuels, discount for thru hikers, gear repair, open 7 days, 8-6. Shuttles to all locations in the park. Maildrops: 206 Long Branch Rd, Gatlinburg, TN 37738.

🥾 **The Day Hiker** 865-430-0970 Small shop with shoes and fuel.
🚌 **A Walk in the Woods** 865-436-8283
⟨www.aWalkintheWoods.com⟩ GSMNP guides Vesna and Erik Plakanis shuttle anywhere from Springer to Damascus. Can help with resupply & dog shuttling while you are in the Smokies.
🚌 **Cherokee Transit** 866-388-6071 ⟨www.cherokeetransit.com⟩ Newfound Gap to Gatlinburg, TN or Cherokee, NC $5 one-way. Pickup at Visitor Center and Newfound Gap.
ℹ **Carol Capooth** 865-640-7653 Trail angel.
        Cherokee, NC (21E) Large town with many services.
🏨🐕🚌 **Appalachian Services** 828-507-5747 Bill (GryWolf) 24hr cell. Near Cherokee, NC ⟨www.appalachianservices.com⟩, grywolfshostel@hotmail.com. Full service hiker support since 2001. Open year round, bunks and tentsites, verify tenting availability. $15/night includes shower, laundry, one meal and shuttle to Cherokee Transit station next to GSMNP. Micro, frig, grill, fire ring, wi-fi, canine kennel and long term parking also available. Shuttle for up to 4 guests $35/trip to/from Newfound Gap or $45 to/from Clingmans Dome. Shuttles to/from most airport, bus, train stations between Atlanta, GA and Damascus, VA. No fee for transportation to urgent care facilities within 25 miles of GSMNP. Pay with cash or PayPal.
🛏⛺🚌📶🖥📞 **Microtel Inn & Suites** 828-497-7800 $65, higher on wkends, includes breakfast, free local/long distance phone. Shuttle guests to/from Newfound Gap $10 one way. Coin laundry, pool. Adjacent supermarket, fast-food, shoe store.

SoBo	NoBo	The A.T. Guide	Elev
1977.4	206.8	Newfound Gap, US 441 . . . . N35 36.669 W83 25.540 **P** ◉ **(pg.26-27)** Large parking area, restrooms. There are no sinks in restrooms, and water fountain is turned off in winter. **Gatlinburg, TN** (15.0W)	5045
1975.7	208.5	Sweat Heifer Creek Trail to east	5608
1974.7	209.5	0.2W to Mt Kephart, 0.6W to Jumpoff (views), Blvd. Trail 5.5W to Mt LeConte. ◉	6034
1974.4	209.8	**Icewater Spring Shelter** to east. . . . . ◉ ☽ ◖ ⊂ (12) 15.5◀13.8◀7.5◀▶7.4▶12.6▶20.3 Spring 75 yards north on AT.	5939
1973.5	210.7	South end of Charlies Bunion Loop Trail (0.1W)	5513
1973.4	210.8	North end of Charlies Bunion Loop Trail	5472
1973.1	211.1	Unmarked side trail 0.1W to original Charlies Bunion.	5425
1973.0	211.2	Dry Sluice Gap Trail to east	5431
1972.4	211.8	The Sawteeth	5395
1972.1	212.1	Porters Gap	5388
1969.3	214.9	View	5728
1968.3	215.9	Bradleys View	5469
1967.0	217.2	**Pecks Corner Shelter** (0.5E) on Hughes Ridge Trail . . . . ☽ ◖ ⊂ (12) 21.2◀14.9◀7.4◀▶5.2▶12.9▶20.0 Spring just south of shelter side trail.	5555
1966.1	218.1	Eagle Rocks, view.	5829
1965.3	218.9	Copper Gap	5513
1964.6	219.6	Mt Sequoyah, AT skirts summit	5941
1962.6	221.6	East ridge of Mt Chapman	6249
1961.8	222.4	**Tri-Corner Knob Shelter** 20.1◀12.6◀5.2◀▶7.7▶14.8▶25.3 . . . ☽ ◖ ⊂ (12)	5911
1961.7	222.5	Balsam Trail to east. . . . . . ◉	5986
1960.4	223.8	Guyot Spring, trail skirts Mt Guyot ◂	6330
1959.9	224.3	Spring . . . . ◂	6278
1958.9	225.3	Deer Creek Gap . . . . ◉	6081
1958.2	226.0	Yellow Creek Gap	5909
1958.1	226.1	Plane wreckage	5912
1958.0	226.2	Snake Den Ridge Trail, 5.3W to Cosby Campground	5796

NoBo		Elev	SoBo
228.5	Camel Gap, Camel Gap Trail to east	4692	1955.7
230.1	**Cosby Knob Shelter,** 100 yards east 20.3◄12.9◄7.7◄▶7.1▲17.6▶25.8	◖▶◆ ⊏ (12) 4791	1954.1
230.8	Low Gap, 2.5W to Cosby Campground.	4247	1953.4
232.9	Mt Cammerer Trail, 0.6W to summit, lookout tower.	📷 🔭 5000	1951.3
233.2	Spring	◆ 4740	1951.0
235.2	Lower Mt Cammerer Trail, Cosby Campground (7.8W)	3481	1949.0
236.2	Chestnut Branch Trail, 2.1E to parking at Big Creek Ranger Station.	N35 45.558 W83 6.412 P (2.0E) 2864	1948.0
236.4	Spring	◆ (12) 2822	1947.8
237.2	**Davenport Gap Shelter,** spring to left of shelter, cables. 20.0◄14.8◄7.1◄▶10.5▲18.7▶23.6	⊏ (12) 2572	1947.0
238.1	TN 32, NC 284, Davenport Gap. Great Smoky Mountains National Park northern boundary	(pg.32) 1975	1946.1
239.0	Stateline Branch, multiple crossings	◆ 1723	1945.2
239.6	Pigeon River Bridge.	1400	1944.6
240.0	I-40 underpass	(pg.32) 1500	1944.2
240.2	Stream	◆ 1592	1944.0
240.8	Green Corner Rd, hostel to west, AT to east (NoBo on road)	◆ (pg.32) 1807	1943.4
242.9	Painter Branch, cross branch to campsites. Blue-blazed trail east across Painter Creek to campsite and spring.	◆⌂ 2878	1941.3
243.2	Stream.	◆⌂ 3109	1941.0
243.8	Spanish Oak Gap, trail joins old roadbed	3483	1940.4
245.2	Snowbird Mountain, grassy bald, side trail 50 yards to FAA tower on summit.	📷 🔭 4263	1939.0
246.0	Wildcat Spring uphill from trail	◆ 4082	1938.2
246.7	Turkey Gap	3652	1937.5

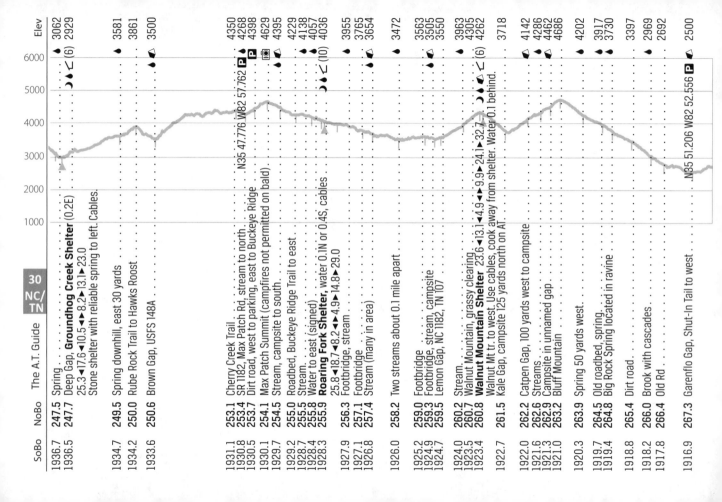

SoBo	NoBo	The A.T. Guide	Elev
1936.7	247.5	Spring	3062
1936.5	247.7	Deep Gap, **Groundhog Creek Shelter** (0.2E)	2929
		25.3◄17.6◄10.5◄►8.2►13.1►23.0	
		Stone shelter with reliable spring to left. Cables.	
1934.7	249.5	Spring downhill, east 30 yards	3581
1934.2	250.0	Rube Rock Trail to Hawks Roost	3861
1933.6	250.6	Brown Gap, USFS 148A	3500
1931.1	253.1	Cherry Creek Trail	4350
1930.8	253.4	SR 1182, Max Patch Rd, stream to north. N35 47.776 W82 57.762 P	4268
1930.5	253.7	Dirt road, west to parking, east to Buckeye Ridge	4398
1930.1	254.1	Max Patch Summit (campfires not permitted on bald).	4629
1929.7	254.5	Stream, campsite to south.	4395
1929.2	255.5	Roadbed, Buckeye Ridge Trail to east.	4229
1928.7	255.5	Stream.	4138
1928.4	255.8	Water to east (signed)	4057
1928.3	255.9	**Roaring Fork Shelter**, water 0.1N or 0.4S, cables	4036
		25.8◄18.7◄8.2◄►4.9►14.8►29.0	
1927.9	256.3	Footbridge, stream	3955
1927.1	257.1	Footbridge	3765
1926.8	257.4	Stream (many in area)	3654
1926.0	258.2	Two streams about 0.1 mile apart	3472
1925.2	259.0	Footbridge	3563
1924.9	259.3	Footbridge, stream, campsite	3505
1924.7	259.5	Lemon Gap, NC 1182, TN 107	3550
1924.0	260.2	Stream.	3963
1923.5	260.7	Walnut Mountain, grassy clearing	4305
1923.4	260.8	**Walnut Mountain Shelter** 23.6◄13.1◄4.9►9.9►24.1►32.7	4262
		Walnut Mt tr. to west. Use cables, cook away from shelter. Water 0.1 behind.	
1922.7	261.5	Kale Gap, campsite 125 yards north on AT	3718
1922.0	262.2	Catpen Gap, 100 yards west to campsite	4142
1921.6	262.6	Streams.	4286
1921.3	262.9	Campsite in unnamed gap.	4462
1921.0	263.2	Bluff Mountain	4686
1920.3	263.9	Spring 50 yards west.	4202
1919.7	264.5	Old roadbed, spring.	3917
1919.4	264.8	Big Rock Spring located in ravine	3730
1918.8	265.4	Dirt road.	3397
1918.2	266.0	Brook with cascades.	2969
1917.8	266.4	Old Rd	2692
1916.9	267.3	Garenflo Gap, Shut-In Tail to west. N35 51.206 W82 52.556 P	2500

SoBo	NoBo		Elev
1916.2	268.0	Taylor Hollow Gap, two footbridges, one over a stream.	2649
1913.5	270.7	**Deer Park Mountain Shelter** (0.2E). 23.0◀14.8◀9.9▶14.2▶22.8▶29.6	2339
		Gragg Gap 0.1 north on AT, water at gap west of AT. Cables.	
1912.7	271.5	Deer Park Mountain.	2589
1910.3	273.9	NC 209 + US 25/70 . . . . N35 53.371 W82 49.937 P (pg.32-33)	1326
		Hot Springs, NC	
1909.9	274.3	French Broad River, US 25/70 bridge	1350
		⚠ NoBo turn east (hop rail) immediately after crossing river.	
1909.4	274.8	50 yards east to campsite by river	1345
1909.0	275.2	Lovers Leap Rock, several rock outcroppings, Silver Mine Trail to west	1691
1908.3	275.9	Campsite to east	2209
1907.0	277.2	Pump Gap, trail crossing.	2130
1906.3	277.9	Springs	2287
1905.4	278.8	Campsite, north intersection with Pump Gap Loop Trail	2490
1905.1	279.1	Pond with boxed spring, campsite.	2469
1904.9	279.3	⚠ NoBo: AT 0.3W on dirt road. Cross Mill Ridge to gravel road.	2603
		(double-blazed oak tree). Go 0.1W on gravel road and reenter woods to east.	
1904.6	279.6	Stream. . . . . N35 54.597 W82 47.46i P	2441
1904.4	279.8	Tanyard Gap, US 25/70 overpass	2270
1903.1	281.1	Piped spring	3052
1902.6	281.6	Roundtop Ridge Trail west 3.5 miles to Hot Springs (former path of AT)	3253
1902.1	282.1	Side trail 0.1W to Rich Mountain Lookout Tower,	3600
		piped spring and campsite north on AT.	
1901.5	282.7	Spring.	3220
1901.0	283.2	Hurricane Gap, northmost of two gravel road crossings.	2900
1900.7	283.5	Grave stone.	3002
1899.3	284.9	**Spring Mountain Shelter** 29.0◀24.1◀14.2▶8.6▶15.4▶21.3	3556
		Water 75 yards down blue-blazed trail on east side of AT. Cables.	
1897.5	286.7	Deep Gap, Little Paint Creek Trail, west 200 yards to spring	2933
1896.1	288.1	Spring in ravine 30 yards west	2777

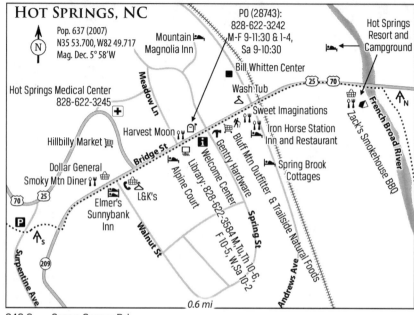

238.1   TN 32, NC 284, Davenport Gap
         Great Smoky Mountain National Park
(northern boundary)

(1.3E) **Big Creek Ranger Station** 828-486-5910
Self-registration backcountry permits.

(2.3E) **Big Creek Campground** $14 per site,
no showers. Open mid-March through October.
It is 2.0 miles to AT on Chestnut Branch Trail,
connecting 0.1 south of Davenport Gap Shelter.

240.0   I-40

Melissa Browning 423-623-7074 shuttles
from I-40 or Davenport Gap to Newport (a town
with hotels, restaurants and Walmart)

240.8   Green Corner Rd
Standing Bear Farm (0.1W) 423-487-0014
curtisvowen@gmail.com; Hosted by Maria & Curtis. $20PP cabin, $15 bunkhouse or
tenting; cooking facilities available. $1/15min internet use. Cook your own breakfast
sandwiches, hot dogs, and hamburgers. Enough resupply to get to Hot Springs
or through the Smokies. White gas/alcohol/oz, canister fuel. Daypack loaner for
slackpackers. Shuttles from Fontana to Hot Springs and to Asheville/Knoxville. Will
kennel your dog while you hike the Smokies; $220/dog for dropoff/pickup at Fontana.
Directions: Green Corner Road is a gravel road 0.9 mile north of I-40; go west 200 yards
to white farmhouse. Permits for GSMNP are available here. Maildrops: 4255 Green
Corner Rd, Hartford, TN 37753.

273.9   NC 209, US 25/70

Hot Springs, NC (more services on map)

Home to **Trailfest** on April 20-21, which includes a Friday night AYCE spaghetti dinner for a nominal fee at the Community Center. Southbound hikers can obtain permits for hiking through Smoky Mountain National Park from Bluff Mountain Outfitters.

🏠 ✉ **Elmers Sunnybank Inn** 828-622-7206 Long-distance hikers (100 miles or more) can stay for $20PP, includes linens, towel and shower. Guests only can purchase breakfast $6 and dinner $10; gourmet organic vegetarian meals. No credit cards. Historic Sunnybank Inn has offered hospitality to AT hikers since 1947. Staffed by former thru-hikers, the Inn offers an extensive library and a well-equipped music room. Work exchange possible. Maildrops: PO Box 233, Hot Springs, NC 28743.

🏠 🍽 📶 **Iron Horse Station** 866-402-9377 Hiker rate $55D. One pet room available. Restaurant, tavern and coffee shop. Serves L/D, and offers some vegetarian options. Live music Tuesday, Wednesday, Friday & Saturday.

🏠 ✉ **Alpine Court Motel** 828-622-3231, $44S, $66D/up, no credit cards. Maildrops: 50 Bridge St, Hot Springs, NC 28743.

🏠 🍴 🏛 🍽 📶 **Hot Springs Resort Cabins Campground & Spa** 828-622-7267 ⟨www.nchotsprings.com⟩ Tenting $10 (up to 4) and camping cabins $45 cabin sleeps 5 with common bath & hot showers, $65 cabin sleeps 8. $10 pet fee. Famous Hot Springs mineral water spa $27 before 6pm, $32 after 6pm. The Campstore carries snacks and some supplies. Also offers massage therapy. Accepts Visa/MC/Disc.

🏠 🍽 📶 **Mountain Magnolia Inn** 800-914-9306 Discount hiker rates when rooms available $65-$130 includes AYCE breakfast. Dinner served F-M open to all. Maildrops: 204 Lawson St, Hot Springs, NC 28743.

🏠 ⛺ 📶 **River Spirit B&B** 828-622-9568 $50-130D, some rooms can hold additional persons, free laundry and outdoor grill use, ask about shuttles. One mile North of main St. on River Road.

🍽 **Harvest Moon** Coffee, fresh-squeezed lemonade. Next to post office; feel free to spread out on lawn and sort through your maildrops.

🏃 🚍 💲 🖥 🖳 ✉ **Bluff Mountain Outfitters** 828-622-7162, Su-Th 9-5, F-Sa 9-6 ⟨www.bluffmountain.com⟩ Full service outfitter, fuel/oz. Natural foods grocery and other foods make this a one-stop location for complete resupply. Computer for internet access, free 30 min for hikers. ATM and scale inside. Shuttles Springer to Roanoke and to area airports. Maildrops: (USPS) PO Box 114 Hot Springs, NC 28743 or (FedEx/UPS) 152 Bridge St. Will also ship UPS packages.

290.2   Log Cabin Drive

🏠 🛏 ⚑ 🚍 🔧 🅿 🖳 ✉ (0.7W) **Hemlock Hollow Inn & Paint Creek Cafe** 423-787-0917 ⟨www.hemlockhollowinn.com⟩ At mile marker 288.1 west on dirt/gravel Log Cabin Drive to paved Viking Mountain Road, on right. Heated cabin $50/60 (double) with linens. Single $25 w/linens, $20 without. Tent site $12PP. Pets $2 extra. All stays include shower, free 30 min internet and return ride to trail. Non-guests can get shower & towel for $4 and for-fee internet. Camp store stocked with long term resupply, some gear, cold drinks, foods, fruit, stove fuels. Cafe open 7 days in hiker season. Shuttles available, slack-packing welcomed. Parking $2/day. Accepts Visa, M/C, Discover. Maildrops: 645 Chandler Circle, Greeneville, TN 37743.

SoBo	NoBo	The A.T. Guide	Elev
1895.5	288.7	NC 208, TN 70, Allen Gap, water 0.2W	2246
1894.5	289.7	AT skirts gravel road	2370
1894.0	290.2	Log Cabin Drive . . . .(pg.33)	2383
1890.7	293.5	**Little Laurel Shelter** 32.7◄22.8◄8.6◄►6.8►12.7►21.5 Boxed spring 100 yards down blue-blazed trail behind shelter. Campsites west side of AT, south of shelter. Cables.	3670 ⌒●△�ⵦ (5)
1889.4	294.8	0.1W to Camp Creek Bald Lookout Tower, Pounding Mill Trail to east.	4750 ⌖🀄
1888.6	295.6	Jones Meadow, campsites 0.2W, spring 100 yards south	4446 ●△
1887.6	296.6	Trail west to Jones Meadow, 30 yards east to Whiterock Cliff.	4461
1887.4	296.8	0.1W to Blackstack Cliffs.	4420
1887.2	297.0	Bearwallow Gap, Jerry Miller Trail to east, Firescald bypass to west reconnects with AT 1.5 miles north. At between bypass points is rocky and strenuous.	4435
1886.5	297.7	Big Firescald Knob	4546 ⌖
1885.6	298.6	Firescald bypass to west, reconnects with AT 1.5 miles south.	4191
1884.9	299.3	Round Knob Trail to west.	4293
1884.1	300.1	Fork Ridge Trail to east.	4290
1883.9	300.3	Chestnut Log Gap, **Jerry Cabin Shelter**. 29.6◄15.4◄6.8◄►5.9►14.7►24.8 Water opposite shelter. Cables.	4166 ⌒●⌇ (6)
1883.1	301.1	Bald Ridge	4561
1882.7	301.5	Sarvis Cove Trail to west	4587
1882.3	301.9	Howard C. Bassett Memorial, old roadbed before and after	4699
1882.0	302.2	Big Butt Mountain, summit to west, short bypass trail.	4750
		⚠ Squibb Creek Trail is "straight ahead," NoBo: AT east on gravel road for 1.5 mi.	
1880.4	303.8	Shelton Gravesite.	4490
1880.1	304.1	Green Ridge Trail to east.	4482
1878.7	305.5	Flint Gap.	3467
1878.0	306.2	**Flint Mountain Shelter**, water on AT 50 yards north of shelter. 21.3◄12.7◄5.9◄►8.8►18.9►29.5	3586 ⌒●⌇ (8)
1877.7	306.5	Spring.	3518
1876.8	307.4	Spring.	3392 ●
1876.4	307.8	AT + roadbed south end	3305
1876.2	308.0	Spring.	3296 ●
1875.8	308.4	AT + roadbed north end.	3424 ●
1875.3	308.9	Devil Fork Gap, NC 212	3100 P

N36 0.392 W82 36.422

SoBo	NoBo	Feature	Elev
1874.8	309.4	Rector Laurel Rd, Boone Cove Rd, spring north on AT.	2960
1874.4	309.8	Stream	3251
1874.1	310.1	Cascade	3436
1873.9	310.3	Stream	3596
1873.4	310.8	Sugarloaf Gap.	4073
1872.1	312.1	Lick Rock	4582
1871.4	312.8	Big Flat, campsite to east	4311
1870.4	313.8	Rice Gap, dirt road	3800
1869.2	315.0	**Hogback Ridge Shelter** (0.1E) 21.5◄14.7◄8.8▲►10.1►20.7►31.2 Spring 0.2 mile beyond shelter. Cables.	4332
1868.6	315.6	High Rock	4460
1866.8	317.4	Sams Gap, US 23, I-26, trash cans N35 57.175 W82 33.636 P **Little Creek Café** (2.8E) B/L/possibly D. **Wolf Creek Market** (3.3E) Open 7 days.	3850
1865.1	319.1	Meadow	4454
1864.5	319.7	Street Gap, gravel road.	4100
1864.3	319.9	Powerline	4189
1863.1	321.1	Low Gap, campsite downhill to west with piped spring	4300
1862.3	321.9	Spring	4653
1861.9	322.3	Powerline	4821
1860.8	323.4	Blue-blazed trail 100 yards west to water; bypass trail to east	5073
1860.7	323.5	Spring	5234
1860.5	323.7	Yellow-blazed trail to west	5377
1860.3	323.9	Big Bald, survey marker	5516
1860.0	324.2	Big Stamp, treeless saddle on ridge, bypass trail to east (0.3W)	5300
1859.5	324.7	Dirt road	5274
1859.1	325.1	**Bald Mountain Shelter** (0.1W) 24.8◄18.9◄10.1▲►10.6►21.1►33.9 Spring on side trail to shelter. Cables.	5096
1857.7	326.5	Little Bald	5220
1856.8	327.4	Spring	4391
1856.0	328.2	Whistling Gap, campsite	3888
1855.4	328.8	Trail 0.1E to High Rocks.	4100

SoBo	NoBo	The A.T. Guide	Elev
1854.1	330.1	Stream.	3581
1853.4	330.8	Spivey Gap, US 19W. . . . . N36 1.911 W82 25.209 P (0.5W)	3200
1852.9	331.3	Stream south of gap. Campsite 30 yards west of stream. Ogelsby Branch, cross twice on footbridge	3567
1852.1	332.1	Stream.	3839
1851.9	332.3	Devils Creek Gap, dirt road	3785
1849.7	334.5	Stream.	3068
1849.6	334.6	Stream.	3014
1848.8	335.4	Stream.	3065
1848.5	335.7	**No Business Knob Shelter** 29.5◄20.7◄10.6◄►10.5►23.3►32.5 Reliable water on AT 0.2S of shelter. Cables.	3190
1846.1	338.1	Temple Hill Gap, Temple Hill Trail	2850
1844.0	340.2	Views to Erwin	2665
1842.7	341.5	River Rd, Unaka Springs Rd, ... N36 6.254 W82 26.802 P (pg.38-39)	2022
1842.0	342.2	**Erwin, TN** (3.8W). AT to east, crossing Nolichucky River on bridge Railroad tracks	1712
1840.9	343.3	Side trail to Nolichucky Gorge Campground before footbridge (pg.38-39)	1746
1840.5	343.7	Footbridge, stream	1808
1840.2	344.0	Footbridge, stream	1928
1839.8	344.4	Stream	2026
1839.5	344.7	Footbridge	2132
1839.3	344.9	Footbridge, campsite to east	2235
1838.0	346.2	**Curley Maple Gap Shelter,** water south of shelter 31.2◄21.1◄10.5◄►12.8►22.0►29.2	3083
1837.5	346.7	Spring	3239
1836.9	347.3	Stream	3343
1836.7	347.5	Stream	3325
1835.4	348.8	Campsite	3170
1833.9	350.3	Indian Grave Gap, TN 395 . . . . N36 6.578 W82 21.696 P to USFS **Rock** Water 0.1E outside of curve in road, campsites south on AT 3.3W to USFS **Rock Creek Recreation Area** $10 tent sites, restrooms, showers.	3350

SoBo	NoBo	Description	Elev
1833.4	**350.8**	Survey marker (USFS 381-28)	3721
1833.2	**351.0**	Powerline	3762
1832.8	**351.4**	USFS 230, Red Fork Rd (gravel)	3779
1830.5	**353.7**	Beauty Spot Gap, clearing . . . N36 6.9796 W82 20.2321 **P**	4333
		Parking to west, trail parallel to USFS 230 from here north to Deep Gap.	
1830.0	**354.2**	Piped spring & campsites 100 yards west across USFS 230.	4135
1829.6	**354.6**	AT skirts Red Fork Rd	4567
1828.5	**355.7**	Unaka Mountain, dense spruce forest.	5180
1826.3	**357.9**	Low Gap, campsite, weak stream 0.1W	3900
1825.4	**358.8**	Footbridge, stream	4130
1825.2	**359.0**	**Cherry Gap Shelter** 33.9◀23.3◀12.8◀▶9.2▶16.4▶21.8 ⊆ (6)	4012
		Spring 120 yards on blue-blazed trail behind shelter to the left.	
1824.8	**359.4**	Unmarked trail crossing	3923
1823.7	**360.5**	Little Bald Knob, trail skirts summit	4292
1823.6	**360.6**	Stream.	4285
1822.1	**362.1**	Iron Mountain Gap, TN 107, NC 226 . . . N36 8.600 W82 13.990 **P** (pg.42)	3723
1820.8	**363.4**	Campsite, water 0.1W from signpost near north end of clearing	4022
1819.7	**364.5**	Rock pillar	4438
1817.9	**366.3**	Greasy Creek Gap, campsite at gap, water 0.2W, (pg.42)	4034
		Greasy Creek Hostel 0.6E	
1817.1	**367.1**	Campsite, weak spring 0.1W	4150
1816.0	**368.2**	**Clyde Smith Shelter** (1976) (0.1W) ⊆ (10)	4514
		32.5◀22.0◀9.2◀▶7.2▶12.6▶14.5 Water 0.1 left of shelter, tent sites behind.	
1815.1	**369.1**	Little Rock Knob, views to west, south of summit	4918
1814.8	**369.4**	Stream.	4742
		Here to north to Roan parking, nobo trail bearing is compass south.	
1814.0	**370.2**	Stream.	4393

✽ **Golden ragwort** – Small flower with yellow center and small floppy petals. "Field flower" that can create a sea of yellow.

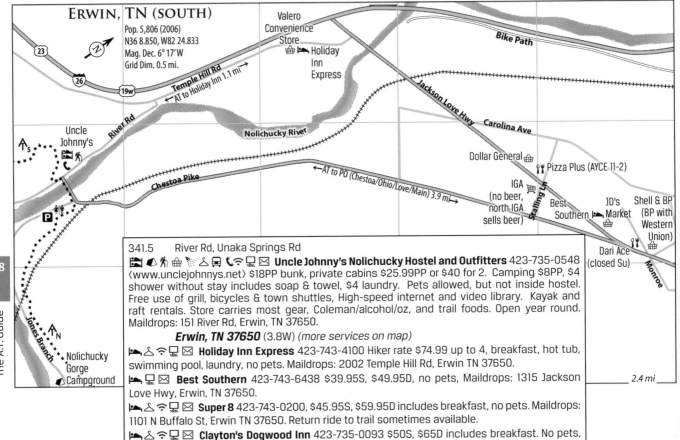

ERWIN, TN (SOUTH)

Pop. 5,806 (2006)
N36 8.850, W82 24.833
Mag. Dec. 6° 17'W
Grid Dim. 0.5 mi.

Valero Convenience Store

Holiday Inn Express

Bike Path

Temple Hill Rd

←AT to Holiday Inn 1.1 mi→

River Rd

Jackson Love Hwy

Carolina Ave

Nolichucky River

Uncle Johnny's

Chestoa Pike

←AT to PO (Chestoa/Ohio/Love/Main) 3.9 mi→

Dollar General

Pizza Plus (AYCE 11-2)

IGA (no beer, north IGA sells beer)

Stalling Ln

Best Southern

JD's Market

Shell & BP (BP with Western Union)

P

Dari Ace (closed Su)

Monroe

Jones Branch

Nolichucky Gorge Campground

2.4 mi

341.5   River Rd, Unaka Springs Rd

Uncle Johnny's Nolichucky Hostel and Outfitters 423-735-0548 ⟨www.unclejohnnys.net⟩ $18PP bunk, private cabins $25.99PP or $40 for 2. Camping $8PP, $4 shower without stay includes soap & towel, $4 laundry. Pets allowed, but not inside hostel. Free use of grill, bicycles & town shuttles, High-speed internet and video library. Kayak and raft rentals. Store carries most gear, Coleman/alcohol/oz, and trail foods. Open year round. Maildrops: 151 River Rd, Erwin, TN 37650.

Erwin, TN 37650 (3.8W) *(more services on map)*

Holiday Inn Express 423-743-4100 Hiker rate $74.99 up to 4, breakfast, hot tub, swimming pool, laundry, no pets. Maildrops: 2002 Temple Hill Rd, Erwin TN 37650.

Best Southern 423-743-6438 $39.95S, $49.95D, no pets, Maildrops: 1315 Jackson Love Hwy, Erwin, TN 37650.

Super 8 423-743-0200, $45.95S, $59.95D includes breakfast, no pets. Maildrops: 1101 N Buffalo St, Erwin TN 37650. Return ride to trail sometimes available.

Clayton's Dogwood Inn 423-735-0093 $50S, $65D includes breakfast. No pets, no credit cards. Maildrops: 430 Ohio Ave, Erwin TN 37650.

38

The A.T. Guide

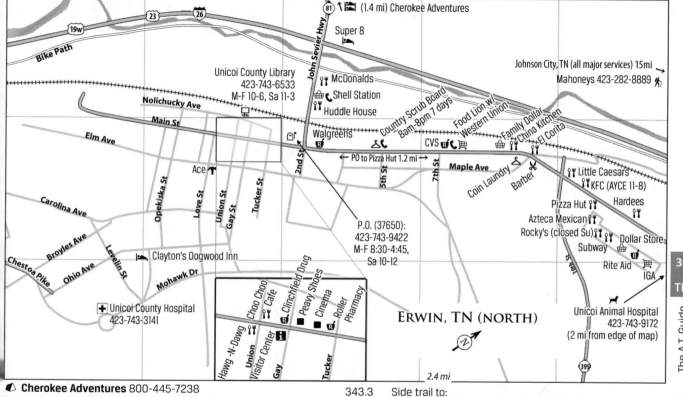

↑ (1.4 mi) Cherokee Adventures

Super 8

Unicoi County Library
423-743-6533
M-F 10-6, Sa 11-3

McDonalds
Shell Station
Huddle House

Johnson City, TN (all major services) 15mi →
Mahoneys 423-282-8889

Nolichucky Ave
Main St
Elm Ave

Walgreens

Country Scrub Board
8am-8pm 7 days
Food Lion w/
Western Union

Family Dollar
China Kitchen
El Corita

CVS

← PO to Pizza Hut 1.2 mi →

Ace

Opekiska St
Love St
Union St
Gay St
Tucker St

2nd St
5th St
7th St

Maple Ave

Coin Laundry
Barber

Little Caesars
KFC (AYCE 11-8)

Carolina Ave

Pizza Hut
Hardees

Broyles Ave
Levelin St
Ohio Ave
Chestoa Pike

Clayton's Dogwood Inn

Mohawk Dr

P.O. (37650):
423-743-9422
M-F 8:30-4:45,
Sa 10-12

Azteca Mexican
Rocky's (closed Su)
Subway

Dollar Store

Rite Aid

IGA

39
TN

Unicoi County Hospital
423-743-3141

Choo Choo Cafe
Clinchfield Drug
Peavy Shoes
Cinema
Roller Pharmacy

ERWIN, TN (NORTH)

Unicoi Animal Hospital
423-743-9172
(2 mi from edge of map)

Hawg-N-Dawg
Union
Visitor Center
Gay
Tucker

2.4 mi

The A.T. Guide

⚓ **Cherokee Adventures** 800-445-7238
⟨www.cherokeeadventures.com⟩ $8PP bunkhouse, $5PP camping.
Open Mar-Oct. Call ahead; rides sometimes available.

🍴 **Azteca** (north end of town) Serves beer.

343.3   Side trail to:

🛏 ⚓ **Nolichucky Gorge Campground** 423-743-8876, ⟨www.
nolichucky.com⟩ Tent site $10, cabin $80/up, primarily caters to river
recreation.

SoBo	NoBo	The A.T. Guide	Elev
1812.9	371.3	Hughes Gap, TN 1330, Hughes Gap Rd. N36 8.206 W82 8.457 P	4040
1812.4	371.8	Campsite 30 yards west	4453
1810.4	373.8	Ash Gap, campsite at gap, water 0.1E	5350
1809.5	374.7	Toll House Gap, saddle between Roan N36 6.238 W82 7.984 P	6217
		High Bluff & Knob, 0.1E to parking, picnic area, restrooms, trash cans.	
1809.3	374.9	Chimney (remnant)	6146
1808.8	375.4	**Roan High Knob Shelter** (0.1E).	6194
		29.2◀16.4◀7.2◀▶5.4▶7.3▶25.3 Piped spring, highest shelter on AT.	
1808.0	376.2	NoBo: watch for AT turning west, leaving wide treadway	5799
1807.4	376.8	Several footbridges, streams	5536
1807.3	376.9	Carvers Gap, TN 143, NC 261 N36 6.406 W82 6.633 P	5512
1806.6	377.6	Round Bald, 30 yards east to summit, views	5826
1805.8	378.4	Jane Bald, big rock slab, views back to Roan Mtn	5800
1805.2	379.0	Side trail 0.5E to Grassy Ridge Bald and views, AT to west.	5905
1805.0	379.2	Springs	5879
1804.1	380.1	Campsite to west.	5388
1803.4	380.8	**Stan Murray Shelter**	5063
		21.8◀12.6◀5.4◀▶1.9▶19.9▶29.5	
		Spring on blue-blazed trail opposite shelter.	
1801.5	382.7	**Overmountain Shelter** (0.3E) Yellow Mountain Gap	4654
		14.5◀7.3◀1.9◀▶18.0▶27.6▶35.5 Converted barn. Water on way to shelter.	
1800.5	383.7	Two intersections with old roadbed.	5179
1800.3	383.9	Side trail 0.1E to Big Yellow Mountain	5279
1799.9	384.3	Little Hump Mountain, clearing	5459
1799.0	385.2	Piped spring, campsites to north and south	5197
1798.6	385.6	Bradley Gap, spring east 100 yards	4950
1798.0	386.2	Fence	5403
1797.7	386.5	Hump Mountain, Stan Murray plaque, NoBo have several false summits	5587
1796.9	387.3	Fence	5169
1796.3	387.9	Spring	4986
1796.0	388.2	Spring	4845
1795.3	388.9	Doll Flats (unmarked), **NC-TN** border.	4600
1795.0	389.2	Stone steps, view.	4308
1794.7	389.5	Spring west of trail, massive stone wall.	4085
1793.1	391.1	Stream.	3266
1792.8	391.4	Former site of Apple House Shelter, to be removed in 2012	3000
		Piped spring 100 yards south on AT.	

NoBo	Feature	Elev	SoBo
391.9	US 19E **Elk Park, NC** (2.5E) **Roan Mtn, TN** (3.4W) N36 10.765 W82 0.767 (pg.42-43) P	2897	1792.3
392.1	Bear Branch Rd, streams north of road	2900	1792.1
392.9	AT + Jeep Path, south end, stream	3228	1791.3
393.3	AT + Jeep Path, north end	3448	1790.9
393.5	Barbwire fence	3560	1790.7
394.3	Open ridge with views to east and west	3765	1789.9
394.8	Isaacs Cemetery	3611	1789.4
395.2	Buck Mountain Rd, water at church 0.1E N36 12.240 W81 59.847 P	3515	1789.0
395.5	Campbell Hollow Rd, streams south of road	3330	1788.7
395.7	Footbridge at bottom of ravine	3433	1788.5
396.2	Footbridge, stream	3451	1788.0
397.3	Side trail 0.1E to Jones Falls	3013	1786.9
397.9	Campsite, Elk River 0.1E	2754	1786.3
398.4	Stream.	2718	1785.8
399.4	Stream (cross twice)	2851	1784.8
400.2	Footbridge, stream	3039	1784.0
400.6	Mountaineer Falls to west	3132	1783.6
400.7	**Mountaineer Shelter,** water 70 yards from shelter	3192	1783.5
	25.3◄19.9◄18◄▶9.6▶17.5▶26.1		
401.5	Campsite to east	3261	1782.7
401.9	Slide Hollow Stream, footbridge	3375	1782.3
402.1	Roadbed	3534	1782.1
402.3	Walnut Mountain Rd	3616	1781.9
403.2	Footbridge, stream (many in area)	3472	1781.0
404.0	Bench, view, unmarked side trail west to hostel 50' north of bench (pg.43)	3526	1780.2
404.6	Footbridge, stream	3335	1779.6
405.3	Upper Laurel Fork, 2 tent sites next to waterfall, side trail to hostel. (pg.43)	3466	1778.9
405.5	USFS 293 (gravel), campsite, waterfall south on AT	3475	1778.7
406.3	Spring	3363	1777.9
406.5	Spring	3393	1777.7
406.9	Footbridge, stream	3463	1777.3
407.3	Hardcore Cascades	3413	1776.9
408.1	Stream.	3648	1776.1
408.6	Campsite, several streams and footbridges	3581	1775.6
410.2	Rock outcropping, views.	3945	1774.0
410.3	**Moreland Gap Shelter**	3823	1773.9
	29.5◄27.6◄9.6◄▶7.9▶16.5▶23.7		
	Water source long way downhill across from shelter.		

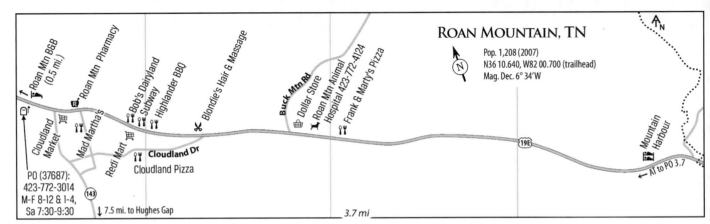

ROAN MOUNTAIN, TN

Pop. 1,208 (2007)
N36 10.640, W82 00.700 (trailhead)
Mag. Dec. 6° 34'W

Roan Mtn B&B (0.5 mi.)
Roan Mtn Pharmacy
Bob's Dairyland
Subway
Highlander BBQ
Blondie's Hair & Massage
Buck Mtn Rd
Dollar Store
Roan Mtn Animal Hospital 423-772-4124
Frank & Marty's Pizza
Cloudland Market
Mad Martha's
Redi Mart
Cloudland Dr
Cloudland Pizza

PO (37687):
423-772-3014
M-F 8-12 & 1-4,
Sa 7:30-9:30

↓ 7.5 mi. to Hughes Gap

19E

Mountain Harbour

← AT to PO 3.7

3.7 mi

362.1　Iron Mountain Gap, TN 107, NC 226
　　　　Buladean, NC (4.1E)

⌂ **Fox Den**

� **Mountain Grill** 828-688-9061 Large meals, cash only, closed Su.

366.3　Greasy Creek Gap
🛏🔥♨🍴🛒⚡⛺🏠🅿🖥✉ (0.6E) **Greasy Creek Friendly**
828-688-9948　All room prices include tax: $10PP bunkhouse,
$15PP/up indoor accommodations, $7.50PP tenting includes shower.
Shower without stay $3. Meals, including vegetarian options,
available except on the Sabbath (from sundown Friday to sundown
Saturday). Pets outside. Limited kitchen privileges, Well-stocked
store: Coleman/alcohol/oz.　Shuttles Hot Springs to Damascus.
Parking $2/night. Directions: take old jeep trail east, then take first
left.　You should be going downhill all the way.　Walk around metal
gate. Hostel is first house to your right. Maildrops: 1827 Greasy Creek
Rd, Bakersville, NC 28705.

391.9　US 19E
　　　　Roan Mountain, TN 37687 (more services on map)
🛏🏠♨🚿⚡🅿✉ (0.3W) **Mountain Harbour B&B/Hostel** 866-
772-9494 ⟨www.mountainharbour.net⟩ Hostel over barn overlooking
creek $20PP, semi private king bed $35, includes linens, shower,
towel, full kitchen, wood burning stove, and video library. Tenting
with shower $8, non-guest shower w/towel $3, guest laundry w/
soap $5 for guests, telephone w/calling card. Breakfast $9 available
during peak hiker season. B&B rooms $90-135 include breakfast,
separate shower & fireplace, AC, refrigerator, and cable TV/DVD.
Town shuttle free at 5pm. Complimentary white gas/denatured
alcohol. Sells fuel canisters. Slack pack/long distance shuttles
by arrangement. Secured parking $5/day or $2/day with shuttle.
Open year round. Maildrops: (non-guests $5) 9151 Hwy 19E, Roan
Mountain, TN 37687.

🛏🏕 **Roan Mountain B&B** 423-772-3207
⟨www.roanmountainbedandbreakfast.com⟩ $65S $85D
free pickup after 3:30, free return before 7am to trail at
Hwy 19E. Pets free. Free do-it-yourself laundry.
🍽 **Bob's Dairyland** 423-772-3641, closed Su.
🍽 **Frank & Mary's Pizza** 423-772-3083
🍽 **Cloudland Pizza** 707-304-2770 Wood fired pizza.
🍽 **Snack Shack** 423-772-4466 L/D M-Sa.

🛒 💲 **Redi Mart** 423-772-3032 M-Sa 8-10, Su 10-8
🛒 **Cloudland Market** 423-772-3201
🏕 **Laundromat**
       Elk Park, NC 28622 *(more services on map)*
🍽 (0.7E) **King of the Road Restaurant** 423-772-4968, B/L/D, Th-Sa 4-9, Su
11–8, Sunday lunch buffet 11-2.
🍽 **Around the Corner at Times Square** 828-733-5898, Lunch & dinner 7 days.
Buffets: Friday breakfast and dinner, Saturday breakfast, Sunday brunch (10-2).

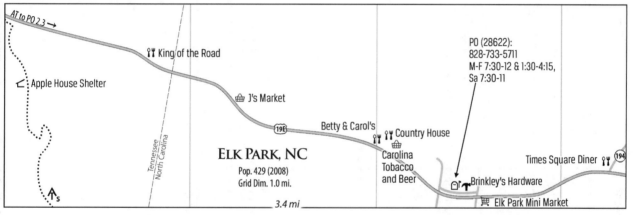

404.0   (0.3W) Side trail to hostel
405.3   (0.4W) Upper Laurel Fork
🏠 🔌 🚿 🏕 🚐 🖥 ✉ (0.2W) **Vango/Abby Memorial Hostel**
423-772-3450, vangoabby@gmail.com. ***Always*** open, private, quiet,
hiker-budget hostel run by "Scotty" who has over 14,000 trail miles.
Pets okay. Heated bunkroom w/stove & sink, LAN internet, library,
sleeps 6. Suggested donation $8/night w/o heat, $10 w/heat (limit
3 nights). Shower $3, wash $3, dryer $3. No credit cards. Hiker-
food resupply, beverages, pizza, ice cream, and stove fuels. Hike-
in/hike-out only; no yellow-blazers. Quiet hours 11pm-7am. Shuttles
$1.50/mile. Directions for NoBo: 2 miles north of Walnut Mtn Rd, on
AT there is a vista and bench. 200 ft farther, take trail at green/
white AT sign downhill (SW & SE) under powerline 0.3 mile to hostel.
SoBo: take blue-blazed trail from just before hand-railed Laurel Fork
bridge (requires fording creek), along mostly level ground 0.4 mile.
Maildrops must be mailed 2 weeks in advance: PO Box 185, Roan
Mtn, TN 37687

SoBo	NoBo	The A.T. Guide	Elev
1771.9	412.3	Spring	3827
1771.4	412.8	Forest Service road.	3790
1770.6	413.6	Trail skirts White Rocks Mountain	3993
1769.5	414.7	Trail to Coon Den Falls 0.8E downhill	3424
1768.5	415.7	Stream.	2888
1768.1	416.1	Barn.	2612
1767.9	416.3	Dennis Cove Rd, USFS 50 N36 15.858 W82 7.402 P (pg.47)	2550
1766.7	417.5	Laurel Falls	2120
1766.0	418.2	**Laurel Fork Shelter** 35.5◄17.5◄7.9◄▶8.6▶15.8▶22.6	2186
1765.7	418.5	Waycaster Spring, footbridge and campsite north on AT.	2048
1765.2	419.0	Side trail to **Hampton, TN** US 321 (1.0W) (pg.46-47) Hampton is west on 321.	1984
1762.6	421.6	Pond Flats, campsite, stream 0.1N on AT	3707
1759.3	424.9	NoBo: east on Shook Branch Rd	2039
1759.2	425.0	US 321, **Hampton, TN** (2.6W) N36 18.114 W82 7.738 P (pg.46-47) NoBo: turn west after crossing 321 **Shook Branch Recreation Area**, picnic area, sandy beach.	1990
1757.7	426.5	Griffith Branch	2100
1757.4	426.8	**Watauga Lake Shelter,** water south of shelter on AT 26.1◄16.5◄8.6◄▶7.2▶14.0▶21.6	2084
1756.2	428.0	Watauga Dam, AT on road for 0.4 mile south and north of dam, sparsely blazed.	1915
1754.9	429.3	Wilbur Dam Rd N36 19.726 W82 6.690 P	2250
1751.9	432.3	Spring	3400

NoBo		Description		Elev
1750.2	**434.0**	**Vandeventer Shelter,** views ▣ ● ⊂ (6)		3579
		23.7◀15.8◀7.2◀▶6.8▶14.4▶22.7		
		Water 0.3 mile down steep blue-blazed trail 0.1S of shelter.		
1746.4	437.8	Campsite 0.1N, piped spring 100 yards east beyond bog. ●		3872
1745.1	439.1	Turkeypen Gap		3980
1744.2	440.0	Powerline		4093
1743.6	440.6	Spring ●		4000
1743.4	440.8	**Iron Mountain Shelter,** spring 0.3S on AT ● ⊂ (6)		4118
		22.6◀14.0◀6.8▶7.6▶15.9▶35.5		
1742.1	442.1	Nick Grindstaff Monument		4090
1739.6	444.6	Footbridge, stream ●		3598
1739.3	444.9	Roadbed.		3601
1738.8	445.4	TN 91. N36 28.883 W81 57.619 **P** (pg.47) South end of handicap-accessible trail.		3525
		Shady Valley, TN (3.5E)		
1738.0	446.2	North end of handicap-accessible trail		3625
1735.8	**448.4**	**Double Springs Shelter** ⊂ (6)		4225
		21.6◀14.4◀7.6▶8.3▶27.9▶34.3 Spring about 0.1N of shelter.		
		Rich Knob to south, Holston Mtn Trail to north.		
1734.2	450.0	Locust Knob.		3635
1733.3	450.9	Campsite to west. ◁		3633
1732.3	451.9	Low Gap, US 421 N36 32.316 W81 56.933 **P** (pg.47) ●		3384
		Piped spring on south side of road.		
		Shady Valley, TN (2.7E)		
1730.9	453.3	Low stone wall on east side of AT		3575

To Elizabethton

91

McDonalds

Pizza Plus

Copper Kettle

Hampton Pharmacy

P.O. (37658): 423-725-2177
M-F 7:30-11:30 & 12:30-4, Sa 8-10

Brown's

Meme's

Ice House Saloon

321

N

Subway

Dollar Store

Hampton Trails
Bicycle Shop

Braemar
Castle
Hostel

P

Side trail 1.0 mi

Laurel Fork
Shelter

19E

To Roan
Mountain

HAMPTON, TN

N36 17.133, W82 9.139 (at parking area)
N   Mag. Dec. 6° 32'W
Grid Dim. 1.0 mi.

Dennis Cove Rd

Kincora   ← 0.3 mi →   ← 0.4 mi →

Black Bear
Resort

S

3.4 mi

416.3   Dennis Cove Rd, USFS 50

🛏🔥⛺🚐📞✉ (0.3W) **Kincora Hiking Hostel**
423-725-4409 Cooking facilities, laundry, $5 per night suggested donation. No dogs. Coleman/alcohol/oz, owner Bob Peoples will hold packages for hikers mailed to 1278 Dennis Cove Rd, Hampton, TN 37658.

🛏🔥⛺⛺✉ (0.4E) **Black Bear Resort**   423-725-5988 New, opening March 1, 2012 in location of former "Laurel Fork Lodge." Bunkroom $10, tentsite (up to 6) $20, cabin $15PP. Camp store with snacks, sodas, and food that can be prepared on-site with microwave or stove. Fuel/oz. Maildrops: 1511 Dennis Cove Road, Hampton, TN 37658.

419.0   Side trail to Hampton (1.0W)
425.0   US 321 (2.6W to Hampton)
         Hampton, TN 37658 *(more services on map)*
🕐 M–F 7:30–11:30 & 12:30-4, Sa 8–10, 423-725-2177

🚐🛏🚐📞 **Brown's Grocery & Braemar Castle Hostel**
423-725-2411, 423-725-2262. Both operated by Sutton Brown; check in at grocery to stay at the hostel or for shuttles. Store open M-Sa 8-6, closed Sunday.

🍴 **Copper Kettle** 423-725-4498, 7-3, 7 days.

🍴 **Pizza Plus** Has lunch buffet.

🍴 **Ice House Saloon** 423-725-5500

🚐 **Hampton Trails Bicycle Shop** 423-725-5000
⟨www.hamptontrails.com⟩ hamptontrails@embarqmail.com.

🛏⛺🚐📶🖥✉ **Iron Mountain Inn** 423-768-2446, 888-781-2399
⟨www.creeksidechalet.net⟩ 10 miles out of town, but you can call from Hampton for pickup, fee for pickup/return. $50PP/up. Log cabin with hot tub under the stars. Free laundry. Shuttles from Watauga Lake to Damascus. Maildrops: c/o Woods, 138 Moreland Dr, Butler, TN 37640.

445.4 TN 91

🛏🔥⛺ (2.0E) **Switchback Creek Campground** 407-484-3388
570 Wallace Rd, Shady Valley, TN 37688. 2-person cabin $40, campsite $12+tax. Showers, laundry, call for ride. 1.5 miles farther east to US 421 and Shady Valley (below).

451.9 Low Gap, US 421
         Shady Valley, TN 37688 (2.7E)
🕐 M–F 7:30–11:00 & 12-3:30, Sa 7:30–9:30, 423-739-2173

🏪 **S&S General Store**, open daily.

🏪🍴 **Shady Valley Country Store and Deli** M-Sa 6am-9pm. Coleman fuel.

🍴 **Raceway Restaurant**

🛏⛺📶 **Appalachian Folk School** 423-341-1843 ⟨www. warrendoyle.com⟩ Non-profit run by Warren Doyle offers work-for-stay (2-3 hrs/night) for all hikers who have a spiritual/poetic connection to the trail. Kitchen privileges, shower, wireless, laundry and rides to/from the AT between Rt. 321 (Hampton) and VA 603 (Fox Creek).

Elev	The A.T. Guide	NoBo	SoBo
3650	Double Spring Gap, campsite	453.8	1730.4
3649	Weak, muddy spring east side of AT	454.2	1730.0
3900	McQueens Knob, disused shelter 0.1N.	455.2	1729.0
3680	McQueens Gap, USFS 69 N36 34.460 W81 55.921 P	455.6	1728.6
3798	**Abingdon Gap Shelter** 22.7◄15.9◄8.3◄▶19.6▶26.0▶38.2 Piped spring 0.2 mile behind shelter on blue-blazed trail. ◆⊂(5)	456.7	1727.5
3688	Campsite, unnamed gap	460.7	1723.5
3598	Campsite to west.	461.6	1722.6
3497	Backbone Rock Trail leads 2.3E to USFS recreation area.	461.8	1722.4
3302	**TN-VA** border	463.2	1721.0
2776	Campsite, Spring 0.1E on blue-blazed trail	464.8	1719.4
1951	**Damascus, VA** (south), N36 38.162 W81 47.378 P (pg.50-51) Mercedes Street and welcome sign.	466.6	1717.6
1945	**Damascus, VA** (Laurel and Shady) (pg.50-51)	467.1	1717.1
2016	**Damascus, VA** (north), (pg.50-51) US 58, AT follows Virginia Creeper Trail for 0.4 mile.	468.0	1716.2
2392	Campsite to west.	468.5	1715.7
2557	Spring	468.9	1715.3
2964	Iron Mountain Trail to west.	470.4	1713.8
2366	Beech Grove Gap Trail to west, streams and footbridges in area	471.9	1712.3
2294	Feathercamp Trail to west, stream, campsite.	472.4	1711.8
2200	US 58, Feathercamp Branch N36 38.694 W81 44.197 P	472.5	1711.7
2236	Stream.	472.8	1711.4
2254	Stream.	473.3	1710.9

NoBo	Feature	SoBo	Elev
474.1	Footbridge, campsite.	1710.1	2335
474.8	Taylors Valley Trail	1709.4	2453
476.3	**Saunders Shelter** (0.2W) 35.5◄27.9◄19.6◄▶6.4▶18.6▶23.7	1707.9	3378
	Reliable spring on right behind shelter and down road.		
476.7	North shelter side trail	1707.5	3351
478.6	Beartree Gap Trail, 3.0W to Beartree Recreation Area	1705.6	3050
478.7	Pond, campsite.	1705.5	2988
479.3	Stream.	1704.9	2957
479.7	Footbridge, stream.	1704.5	2891
480.3	AT + Creeper Trail (south end)	1703.9	2680
481.0	Luther Hassinger Memorial Bridge, N36 38.965 W81 40.345	1703.2	2774
	AT + Creeper Trail (north end), VA 728, picnic tables.		
481.3	Stream.	1702.9	2820
481.5	VA 859, Grassy Creek Rd (gravel)	1702.7	2947
481.7	Streams	1702.5	3037
482.7	**Lost Mountain Shelter.** 34.3◄26.0◄6.4▶12.2▶17.3▶23.2 Water source on trail to left of shelter.	1701.5	3399
483.8	US 58, footbridge, stream N36 38.389 W81 39.926	1700.4	3160
484.1	Stream, campsite	1700.1	3253
484.5	Spring	1699.7	3373
484.7	Fence stile	1699.5	3464
485.0	VA 601, Beech Mountain Rd N36 38.235 W81 38.425	1699.2	3600
	Fence stile, 50 yards north of road is sign for spring to west.		
485.5	Spring	1698.7	3726
487.5	Buzzard Rock,	1696.7	5080
488.1	Side trail west to Whitetop Mtn Rd, summit of Whitetop Mountain.	1696.1	5107
488.1	Piped spring on east side of trail	1696.0	5150
488.2	Whitetop Mtn Rd, USFS 89 N36 37.921 W81 36.112		
488.9	Campsites just after road.	1695.3	5190
	Stream.		
490.6	VA 600, Elk Gardens, views, spring south on AT N36 38.769 W81 34.992	1693.6	4467
490.8	View, bench to west	1693.4	4600
491.1	Fence, enter Lewis Fork Wilderness	1693.1	4690
492.6	Deep Gap, spring 0.1 south and north.	1691.6	5033
493.6	Brier Ridge	1690.6	5234
494.1	Spring	1690.1	5210
494.5	Side trail 0.5W to Mt Rogers, Virginia's highest peak at 5,729 ft.	1689.7	5490

DAMASCUS, VA

Pop. 1,072 (2007)
N36 38.100, W81 47.350
Mag. Dec. 6° 49' W
Grid Dim. 0.5 mi.

Pizza Plus
Food City (M-Sa 6am-midnight, Su 8am-midnight)
Mtn Laurel B&B

Abingdon, VA 11 mi.

P.O. (24236): 276-475-3411
M-F 8:30-1 & 2-4:30, Sa 9-11

Old Mill

Imboden St

Dollar Store

Dave's

Montgomery Homestead

Lazy Fox B&B

Victorian Inn B&B

Town Hall

Quincey's Pizza

Adventure Damascus

Mt Rogers

Laurel Family Drugstore
Mountain Home Alliance
276-475-5116

Laurel Ave

Dairy King

Hiker's Inn

The Place

Cowboy's

Lorna's Laundry

Crazy Larry's

Library 276-475-3820
M-Th 11-7, Fr 11-5, Sa 9-1

Soothing Senses Massage

Pool

Mercedes St

Beaver Dam Creek

Water St

Shady Ave

Rock School

Country Corner

Subway

Mojoe's Coffeehouse

Sundog

Dots

In the Country

Douglas Dr

Laurel Creek

Whistle Pig Bistro

Tent City
(Trail Days only)

0.8 mi

466.6   Mercedes Street, *Damascus, VA* (more services on map)

467.1   Laurel and Shady

468.0   US 58

Trail Days ⟨www.traildays.us⟩ (May 18-20) is the largest event on the AT. Hiker reunion and talent show, presentations, music, contra dancing, and hiker parade. Many gear reps & retailers on-hand.

▦ ⚒ **Dave's Place** $10PP, private room $21, shower without stay $3, no alcohol. No pets. Check in at Mount Rogers Outfitters.

▙ ▦ ⚹ ⚘ **Hikers Inn** 276-475-3788, $25 bunks, hostel private room $35S, $45D. Rooms in house $65; $55/night for multi-night stays, Laundry $5. Run by Lee and Paul (2010 thru-hiker "Skink"). Open mid-March through October. A/C in all rooms. Smoking allowed outside, dogs allowed in hostel, cash or check. Maildrops: PO Box 396 or 216 Laurel Ave, Damascus, VA 24236.

▦ ◑ **The Place** 276-475-3441, Methodist Church-run bunkrooms and tenting. Please help to keep the bunkroom clean; there is no housekeeper. No pets, no alcohol, 2 night max unless sick/injured. Suggested donation $5. No vehicle-assisted hikers (except during Trail Days). Do not leave your gear unattended.

▙ ✉ **Montgomery Homestead Inn** 276-475-3053 $65/up. No smoking, no alcohol, no pets. Guest maildrops: (USPS) PO Box 12, (FedEx/UPS) 103 Laurel Ave, Damascus, VA 24236.

▙ ⚘ **Victorian Inn B&B** 276-475-5059, $65+tax, includes breakfast. Also, 2 bedroom cottage $110/night for 4 persons, $20EAP up to 7. Cottage room does not include breakfast. No pets.

▙ ✉ **Lazy Fox B&B** 276-475-5838, $65/up+tax. No pets. Maildrops: PO Box 757, 133 Imboden St, Damascus, VA 24236.

▙ **Mountain Laurel B&B** 276-475-5956

🛒 ⛟ **Food City** (0.5W on US 58) 276-475-3653, 7 days.

🚶 ⌂ ⚹ 🚌 🅿 ✉ **Mt. Rogers Outfitters** 276-475-5416 ⟨www.mtrogersoutfitters.com⟩ Full service backpacking store, fuel/oz. Shuttle service for the Appalachian Trail, parking for section hikers $2/day. Shower only $3. Maildrops: PO Box 546, 110 W Laurel Ave, Damascus, VA 24236.

🚶 ⌂ ⚹ 🚌 ✉ **Adventure Damascus** 888-595-2453 or 276-475-6262 ⟨www.AdventureDamascus.com⟩ Catering to thru-hikers with backpacking gear, a hiker-food section, denatured alcohol and Coleman/oz, other fuels, bike rentals, shuttles to area trailheads by arrangement, $2 showers ($4 includes a towel), open 7 days year-round. USPS and UPS Maildrops: PO Box 1113, 128 W. Laurel Ave. Damascus, VA 24236.

🚶 ⌂ 🚌 ✉ **Sundog Outfitter** 276-475-6252 ⟨www.sundogoutfitter.com⟩   Backpacking gear and clothing, repairs, hiker food, Coleman/alcohol/oz, other fuels, shuttles to area trailheads by arrangement, open 7 days a week. Maildrops: PO Box 1113 or 331 Douglas Dr, Damascus, VA 24236.

🍴 **Whistle Pig Bistro** Breakfast and lunch Wednesday-Sunday.

💻 **Library** 276-475-3820, M,W,F 9-5, T,Th 11-7, Sa 9-1, internet 1 hr.

SoBo	NoBo	The A.T. Guide	Elev
1689.3	494.9	**Thomas Knob Shelter** 38.2◀18.6◀12.2◀▶5.1▶11.0▶16.0. ⊙(16)	5430
1689.1	495.1	Campsite	5414
1688.5	495.7	Rhododendron Gap, Pine Mountain Trail to west	5415
1688.1	496.1	Wilburn Ridge Trail 0.1E to rock outcropping, view	5465
1687.9	496.3	Fatman Squeeze (rock tunnel)	5373
1687.4	496.8	Grayson Highlands State Park (south end), fence (pg.56) **Horse trail crosses AT**. No tenting in GHSP.	5017
1686.4	497.8	Massie Gap, 0.2E to parking area P	4800
1685.5	498.7	GHSP boundary, two fence stiles	4616
1684.5	499.7	Stream.	4450
1684.2	500.0	**Wise Shelter** 23.7◀17.3◀5.1◀▶5.9▶10.9▶20.0	4429
1684.1	500.1	East fork of Big Wilson Creek, footbridge, stream, fence stile	4410
		Grayson Highlands State Park (north end)	
1683.7	500.5	Horse trail	4374
1682.2	502.0	Bearpen Trail	4668
1681.7	502.5	Stone Mountain, views	4820
1681.0	503.2	The Scales livestock corral. First Peak Trail to east, Crest Trail to west. N36 40.182 W81 29.229 P	4662
1680.0	504.2	Fence stiles, Pine Mountain Trail to west	5000
1678.6	505.6	Spring	4261
1678.3	505.9	**Old Orchard Shelter** 23.2◀11.0◀5.9◀▶5.0▶14.1▶24.7 Water 100 yards on blue-blazed trail to right. Privy 50 yards behind shelter.	4084
1677.5	506.7	Old Orchard Trail	3789
1676.6	507.6	Fox Creek, VA 603. N36 41.795 W81 30.398 P Footbridges and streams 0.1 to north and to south. 100 yards east to parking and porta-potty.	3480
1674.3	509.9	Chestnut Flats, Iron Mountain Trail to west	4240
1673.3	510.9	**Hurricane Mtn Shelter** (0.1W) 16.0◀10.9◀5.0◀▶9.1▶19.7▶26.8 Creek and tentsites opposite side of trail.	3810
1672.7	511.5	Side trail 0.3W to USFS 84, AT to east	3472
1672.2	512.0	Spring	3161
1671.6	512.6	Powerline, stream just north on AT	3223
1671.0	513.2	Stream.	3018
1670.5	513.7	Stream.	2979
1670.2	514.0	Side trail to **USFS Hurricane Creek Campground** (0.7W) 276-783-5196 Tent site $16, shower $2. Open mid Apr-Oct. Restroom & shower open Memorial Day-Labor Day.	3090
1669.4	514.8	Comers Creek (drinking not advised), footbridge, cascades.	3316

SoBo	NoBo		Elev
1668.1	516.1	Dickey Gap, AT crosses VA 650 (gravel), 🛉 (pg.56)	3300
		VA 16 (paved Sugar Grove Hwy) to east, **Troutdale, VA** (2.6E)	
1667.3	516.9	Horse trail.	3485
1666.6	517.6	Campsite and spring on blue-blazed trail (0.2E) ● ◭	3706
1664.2	520.0	**Trimpi Shelter** (0.1E) ☾ ● ⌐ (8)	3029
		20.0◄14.1◄9.1◄►10.6►17.7►36.1	
1663.2	521.0	Fence stiles 0.2 apart, cattle graze in area, close gates behind you	2702
		Abandoned school bus.	
1662.7	521.5	VA 672 (gravel)	2700
1661.4	522.8	VA 670, South Fork Holston River. N36 45.784 W81 29.634 **P**	2450
1660.4	523.8	Stream, intermittent ◭	2613
1659.9	524.3	Campsite on west side of trail ● ◭	2872
1657.4	526.8	VA 601 (gravel), limited parking N36 47.963 W81 27.448 **P**	3280
1655.9	528.3	Powerline	3334
1655.0	529.2	Footbridge, stream ●	3022
1653.6	530.6	**Partnership Shelter**, showers ☾ ⚡ ● ◭ ⌐ (16)	3260
		24.7◄19.7◄10.6◄►7.1►25.5►34.6 Can call for pizza from Visitor Center.	
1653.5	530.7	VA 16, Mt Rogers Visitor Center N36 48.682 W81 25.224 **P** **H** ☾ (pg.56)	3220
		MRA HQ 276-783-5196 Permit for overnight long term parking required.	
		Sugar Grove, VA, 24375 (3.2E), **Marion, VA** 24354 (5.9W)	
1652.8	531.4	VA 622	3270
1649.4	534.8	USFS 86, Glade Mountain Rd. N36 50.089 W81 22.246 **P** ●	3650

SoBo	NoBo	The A.T. Guide	Elev
1648.1	536.1	Glade Mountain	4102
1647.0	537.2	Spring	3526
1646.7	537.5	Stream	3314
1646.5	537.7	Chatfield Shelter 26.8◄17.7◄7.1◄▶18.4▶27.5▶37.5 ☾ ♦ ⊏ (6)	3200
1646.2	538.3	USFS 644 (dirt), streams to north and south ♦	3065
1645.9	538.3	Footbridge, stream ♦	2949
1645.6	538.6	Stream ♦	2801
1644.9	539.3	Two powerlines	2714
1644.7	539.5	VA 615, Lindamood School	2650
		Settlers Museum 0.2E, parking available at farm. N36 52.246 W81 21.46I P	
1644.2	540.0	VA 729	2545
1643.4	540.8	Fence stile	2711
1642.8	541.4	Middle Fork of the Holston River, footbridge ♦	2444
1642.0	542.2	VA 683, US 11, I-81, **Atkins, VA** (pg.57)	2420
1641.6	542.6	I-81 underpass	2428
1640.8	543.4	VA 617, Davis Cemetery N36 53.840 W81 22.146 P	2462
1640.2	544.0	Fence stile, end of field ♦	2583
1640.0	544.2	Blue-blazed trail 0.1E to water at Davis Hollow	2561
1638.8	545.4	Davis Path campsite and privy ☾	2907
1636.8	547.4	Little Brushy Mountain	3300
1636.4	547.8	Virginia Horse Trail	3242
1635.7	548.5	Crawfish Trail to east, campsite and stream on AT south of here	2600
1634.8	549.4	Stream ♦	3078
1634.2	550.0	Spring ♦	3370
1634.0	550.2	Tilson Gap, crest of Walker Mtn	3500
1633.3	550.9	Spring, fence ♦	2945
1632.6	551.6	VA 610, fence stiles here and to south	2700
1631.8	552.4	Fence stile	2744
1631.2	553.0	VA 742, Holston River Bridge ♦	2458
1630.7	553.5	Stream ♦	2498
1630.2	554.0	VA 42, O'lystery Pavilion (private, do not use)	2650
		Campsite just north of trail to parking area. N36 58.995 W81 24.385 P	
1629.4	554.8	Brushy Mountain	3200
1628.1	556.1	**Knot Maul Branch Shelter**, water 0.1N on AT ☾ ♦ ⊏ (8)	2761
		36.1◄25.5◄18.4◄▶9.1▶19.1▶33.1	

SoBo	NoBo		Elev
1627.5	556.7	Footbridge, stream.	2614
1626.9	557.3	Lynn Camp Creek, footbridge, campsite	2400
1625.8	558.4	Lynn Camp Mountain.	3025
1624.7	559.5	Lick Creek, footbridge	2271
1623.6	560.6	Stream.	2322
1623.4	560.8	VA 625 (gravel) N37 1.358 W81 25.569 P	2334
1622.3	561.9	Stream.	3106
1621.1	563.1	Chestnut Ridge, south end, start of clearing	3793
1620.8	563.4	Pond, spring at north end, best water source for Chestnut Knob Shelter.	3908
1620.0	564.2	Views from open ridgeline	4194
1619.1	565.1	Spring 0.1E on unmarked roadbed	4334
1619.0	565.2	**Chestnut Knob Shelter** 34.6◄27.5◄9.1▶10.0▶24.0▶33.8 Concrete block shelter, fully enclosed with door.	4410
1617.7	566.5	Walker Gap, dirt road 100 yards south	3520
1616.7	567.5	Garden Mountain, rock outcropping.	3882
1613.0	571.2	VA 623 N37 4.622 W81 18.425 P	3906
1612.0	572.2	Davis Farm Campsite (0.5W)	3850
1609.8	574.4	Stream (unreliable).	2913
1609.0	575.2	**Jenkins Shelter,** creek 100 yards north on AT 37.5◄19.1◄10.0▶14.0▶23.8▶38.0	2421

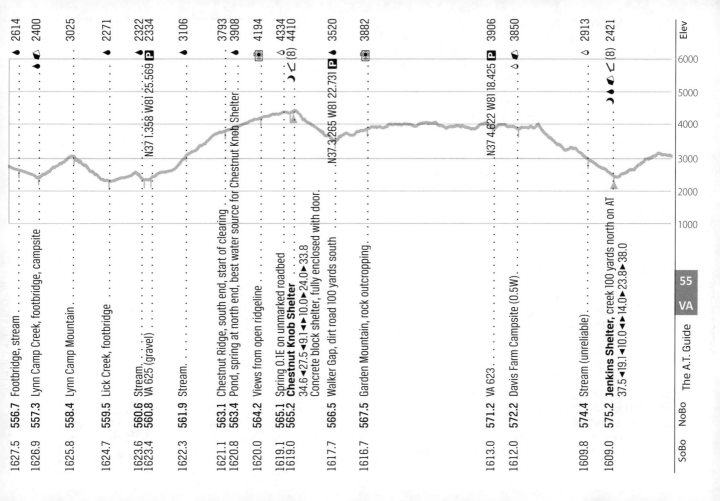

496.8   **Grayson Highlands State Park**

◐ 🏠 🚿 276-579-7092 Blue-blazed trail (0.5E) to parking area; campground 1.5 miles farther east down road. Park closed in cold weather, so call ahead if possible. Camp store with courtesy phone, tent site w/ shower $21, shower only $5. May 1 - Oct 31.

516.1   Dickey Gap, VA 650, VA 16, Sugar Grove Hwy
The AT crosses VA 16 fifty yards from a "T" intersection with VA 650 (Sugar Grove Hwy). Go east on VA 16 to VA 650, then right (compass south) to Troutdale.

     Troutdale, VA 24378 (2.6E) *(PO on map)*

🏠 ◐ (2.6E) **Troutdale Baptist Church Hostel** 276-677-4092 bunkhouse and campsites, restroom, showers with towel. Pets outside, no alcohol. Check in 8am-6pm, Mar15-Nov15, donations welcome. Hikers are welcome to church service in hiker attire. Pastor Ken Riggins.

🍴🏠🛜✉ (2.3E) **Jerry's Kitchen & Goods** 276-677-3010, B/L/D 7 days, shuttles sometime available, fuel/oz. Maildrops: (UPS, USPS) 10973 Troutdale Hwy, Troutdale, VA 24378

530.7   VA 16, Mt Rogers Visitor Center
     Sugar Grove, VA 24375 (3.2E) *(PO on map)*

🍴🏠 **Exxon Station** pizza and sandwiches
     Marion, VA 24354 (5.9W) *(PO on map)*
Lodging can be impacted by Bristol Motor Speedway races March 16-18 and Aug 24-25, 2012.

🛏✉ **Virginia House Inn** 276-783-5112, $39.99S $45.99D, fee for pets. Guest maildrops: 1419 N Main St, Marion VA 24354.

🏪 **Food Lion**, **Ingles Supermarket**, **Food City**, **Walmart**

⚲ **Cooks Laundromat**

🚌 **Marion Transit** 276-782-9300

🚌 **Greyhound** 276-783-7114 weekdays only, four buses/day.

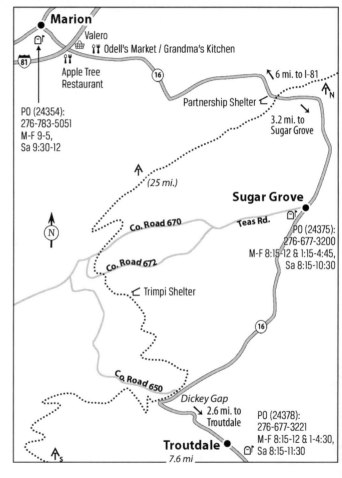

Marion

Valero

🍴 Odell's Market / Grandma's Kitchen

Apple Tree Restaurant

81

6 mi. to I-81

N

16

Partnership Shelter

3.2 mi. to Sugar Grove

PO (24354): 276-783-5051 M-F 9-5, Sa 9:30-12

(25 mi.)

N

Sugar Grove

Co. Road 670

Teas Rd.

PO (24375): 276-677-3200 M-F 8:15-12 & 1:15-4:45, Sa 8:15-10:30

Co. Road 672

Trimpi Shelter

16

Co. Road 650

Dickey Gap

2.6 mi. to Troutdale

PO (24378): 276-677-3221 M-F 8:15-12 & 1-4:30, Sa 8:15-11:30

Troutdale

S

7.6 mi

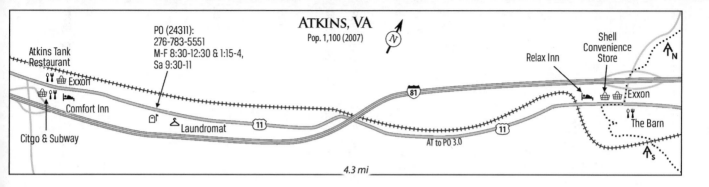

ATKINS, VA
Pop. 1,100 (2007)

PO (24311):
276-783-5551
M-F 8:30-12:30 & 1:15-4,
Sa 9:30-11

Atkins Tank Restaurant

Exxon

Comfort Inn

Citgo & Subway

Laundromat

11

81

11

AT to PO 3.0

Relax Inn

Shell Convenience Store

Exxon

The Barn

4.3 mi

542.2   VA 683, US 11, I-81

Atkins, VA 24311 (more services on map)

Upon reaching US 11, you are between Atkins and Rural Retreat in the township of Groseclose. There is a motel, restaurant and two convenience stores catering to hikers and traffic exiting from nearby interstate 81. The post office and laundry are 3 miles west. There is another hotel, service station and restaurants 3.7 west near another interstate 81 interchange.

Relax Inn 276-783-5811 $40S $45D, $5EAP, pets $5. Parking $3/day. Maildrops: (non-guests $5) Relax Inn, 7253 Lee Hwy, Rural Retreat, VA 24368. Shuttles when available from Damascus to Bland.

The Barn Restaurant 276-686-6222   16oz hiker burger, Sunday buffet 11-2, parking for section hikers.

Shell Convenience Store 24hr, Phone and ATM inside.

Exxon Convenience Store 276-783-5454 Open 24hr.

Rambunny & Aqua 276-783-3754

3.0 west on US 11:

Post Office

Laundry

3.7 west on US 11:

Comfort Inn 276-783-2144 Ask for hiker rate or get coupon from hotel discount book stand at Exxon station usually @ $60. Continental breakfast, sometimes ride. Maildrops: 5558 Lee Hwy, Atkins, VA 24311.

Exxon Convenience Store

Citgo

Atkins Tank Restaurant

Subway

SoBo	NoBo	Description	Elev
1604.2	580.0	Laurel Creek, VA 615 (gravel). N37 6.1414 W81 12.1399 [P] ♦ ◢ Intersection with Trail Boss Trail. Campsite just north of road.	2450
1602.0	582.2	Trail Boss Trail to west	3116
1600.1	584.1	Views to west. [◉]	2986
1599.2	585.0	Powerline	2739
1597.8	586.4	AT on gravel road from here north to US 52.	3095
1597.3	586.9	US 52 (North Scenic Hwy), **Bland, VA** (2.5E), **Bastian, VA** (3W) . . . (pg.60)	2923
1596.5	587.7	North end of VA 612, road walk over I-77. N37 8.335 W81 7.595 [P] ♦ Water near where the AT enters woods north of road.	2700
1595.0	589.2	**Helveys Mill Shelter** (0.3E) . . . ☾ ♦ ⊆ (6) 33.1◄24.0◄14.0◄►9.8►24.0►32.4 Water source 0.3 mile down switch-backed trail in front of shelter.	3139
1588.3	595.9	VA 611 (gravel). N37 8.7155 W81 0.561 [P] ◁	2820
1588.0	596.2	Stream, unreliable	2718
1586.9	597.3	Brushy Mountain	3101

SoBo	NoBo	Description	Elev
1585.2	599.0	**Jenny Knob Shelter,** spring near shelter. 33.8◄23.8◄9.8◄►14.2►22.6►37.6	2684 (6)
1584.5	599.7	Stream.	2338
1584.2	600.0	Stream, campsite.	2276
1584.0	600.2	Lickskillet Hollow, VA 608, footbridge. N37 9.415 W80 57.682 **P**	2200
1582.8	601.4	Powerline	2771
1578.8	605.4	Kimberling Creek, suspension bridge	2090
1578.7	605.5	VA 606, parking to east. N37 10.544 W80 54.500 **P** (pg.60)	2059
		Trent's Grocery (0.5W), **Nature's Way** (3.6E)	
1577.0	607.2	Dismal Falls Trail, 0.3W to waterfall, camping on side trail. Road on other side of falls sometimes brings visitors by car.	2364
1576.6	607.6	Stream, campsite.	2293
1575.9	608.3	Footbridge	2340
1575.4	608.8	Footbridge	2384
1575.1	609.1	Footbridge, stream	2410
1574.9	609.3	Two streams	2474
1574.3	609.9	Woods road	2601
1573.8	610.4	Streams	2545
1573.4	610.8	Footbridge, stream (2)	2471
1573.2	611.2	Dismal Creek, gravel road, campsite, footbridge to north	2465
1573.0	611.2	Ribble Trail 2.0W connects with AT near Big Horse Gap	2471
1572.4	611.8	Center of one-mile stretch with at least 6 stream crossings by footbridge.	2497
1571.8	612.4	Clearing, side trail to west	2531
1571.5	612.7	Footbridge, stream (2)	2535
1571.2	613.0	Dirt road	2599
1571.0	613.2	**Wapiti Shelter** 38.0◄24.0◄14.2◄►8.4►23.4►35.9	2622 (8)
1570.8	613.4	Stream.	2668
1570.5	613.7	Stream.	2824
1569.9	614.3	Spring	3361
1568.9	615.3	View	3903
1567.0	617.2	Side trail 0.1E to lookout tower, views	4030
1566.5	617.7	Ribble Trail west, reconnects with AT south of Wapiti Shelter	3800
1566.4	617.8	Big Horse Gap, USFS 103	3800

SoBo   NoBo   The A.T. Guide

586.9   US 52, North Scenic Hwy, *Bland, VA 24315* (2.5E)

⌂⛨ M-F 8-11:30 & 12-4, Sa 9 -11, 276-688-3751

🛏 ✉ **Big Walker Motel** 276-688-3331 $57.73 (1 or 2), 62.01 (3 or 4), pets okay. Guest maildrops: 70 Skyview Lane, Bland, VA 24315.

🍴 **Subway, Dairy Queen**

🛒 **Bland Grocery** Open 7 days, M-Th 7-10; F,Sa 7-11, Su 10-10, denatured alcohol $0.50/oz, can help with shuttle contacts.

⛽🍴 **Citgo, Bland Square Grill** 276-688-3851 groceries, fuel.

⛽ **Dollar General**

➕ **Mountain Medical Clinic** 276-688-4800   M-W 9-5, Th 9-12, 144 Seddon Street.

💻 **Bland County Library** 276-688-3737 M,W,F,Sa 9:30-4:30, T,Th 9:30-8, 697 Main Street.

Bastian, VA 24314 (3W)

⌂⛨ M-F 8-12 & 12:30-4, Sa 9:15-11:15, 276-688-4631

🍴 **Pizza Plus** 276-688-3332 Su-Th 11-9, F-Sa 9-10.

⛽💲 **Kangaroo Express** ATM

➕ **Medical Clinic** 276-688-4331 M, W 9-6, Tu, Th 8:30-8, F 8:30-5,

🚌 **Greyhound Bus Lines** 304-325-9442 Bluefield, WV, 18 miles north west of Bastian on US 52.

605.5   VA 606

♦⛽🍴🚿⛺🚃 **Trent's Grocery** (0.5W) 276-928-1349 Open M-Sa 7-8, Sun 9-8. Outside pay phone & soda machines. Deli includes pizza, hamburgers, hot dogs and more. Camping $6, shower $3, laundry $3. Coleman/alcohol/oz and canister fuel. Shuttles.

🛒🍴 **Nature's Way** (3.6E) 276-928-1349 Unique Amish-run grocery withorganic, locally grown foods. Dry goods, jerky, candy, produce, ice cream and sandwiches.

619.4   Sugar Run Gap, Sugar Run Rd

🛏🏠♦🍴🚿⛺🚌🛜💻✉ **Woods Hole Hostel** ⟨www.woodsholehostel.com⟩ 540-921-3444 Open year-round. A "Slice of heaven, not to be missed." The 1880's chestnut-log cabin was discovered by Roy & Tillie Wood, who opened the hostel in 1986. Their granddaughter, Neville, continues the legacy with her husband Michael, placing an emphasis on sustainable living through bee keeping, farming, organic gardening, yoga(free), & massage therapy. Directions: NoBo turn right on dirt road at Sugar Run Gap, SoBo turn left. Bear left at fork, and go downhill 0.5 mile to hostel on right. Offers massage, healing arts, & retreats. Bunkhouse has mattresses, electricity, and hot shower, $11 PP. Camping $6PP. Two indoor rooms: $50 private, $25PP shared room (thru-hiker rate). Guests often invited to share local/organic communal meals. Dinner $13, breakfast $8. Shuttles, WiFi internet, telephone (call limit 15 min), laundry, pizza, smoothies, snacks and drinks, Coleman/alcohol/oz, fuel canisters. Pet friendly. Accepts cash and credit cards. Maildrops: Woods Hole Hostel, 3696 Sugar Run Road, Pearisburg, VA 24134.

629.8   Lane Street, *Pearisburg, VA 24134* (more services on map)

🛏⛺🚗✉ **Rendezous Motel** 540-921-2636 $44S $50D. Larger room $60 for 4, $5EAP (up to 6). No pets, free long distance for guests, Coleman/alcohol/oz. Maildrops: 795 North Main Street, Pearisburg, VA 24134.

🛏⛺🛜✉ **Plaza Motel** 540-921-2591 $40S $50D plus tax, no pets, all credit cards except Disc. Maildrops: 415 Main Street, Pearisburg, VA 24134.

🛏💻✉ **Holiday Motor Lodge** 540-921-1551 $37.40S $46.76D $4EAP. Pets ok. Maildrops: 401 N Main Street, Pearisburg, VA 24134.

🏠♦ **Holy Family Hostel** 540-921-3547 Open early May to late Sept; if you arrive later, please call for availability. Please check in or call during daylight hours (8am-6pm). Bunks; tenting in designated areas, toilet, hot shower, refrigerator, 2 microwaves, grill. Keep hostel clean and noise down (church in residential area). Donation $10PP per night, 2 night max. No pets or alcohol.

⛺ **EZ Way Laundromat** M-Sa 6-9, Su 6-8

💊 **Rite Aid Pharmacy** 540-921-1284

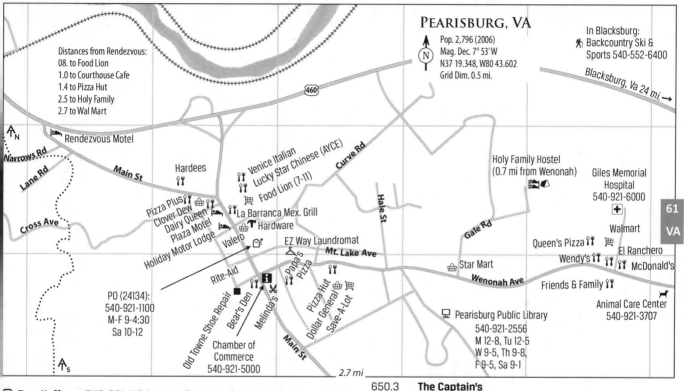

PEARISBURG, VA

N Pop. 2,796 (2006)
Mag. Dec. 7° 53'W
N37 19.348, W80 43.602
Grid Dim. 0.5 mi.

Distances from Rendezvous:
08. to Food Lion
1.0 to Courthouse Cafe
1.4 to Pizza Hut
2.5 to Holy Family
2.7 to Wal Mart

In Blacksburg:
Backcountry Ski & Sports 540-552-6400

Blacksburg, Va 24 mi →

Rendezvous Motel

Narrows Rd
Lane Rd
Cross Ave
Main St

Hardees

Venice Italian
Lucky Star Chinese (AYCE)
Food Lion (7-11)
Curve Rd

Holy Family Hostel
(0.7 mi from Wenonah)

Giles Memorial
Hospital
540-921-6000

Pizza Plus
Clover Dew
Dairy Queen
Plaza Motel
Holiday Motor Lodge
La Barranca Mex. Grill
Hardware
Valero

Hale St
Gale Rd

Queen's Pizza
Walmart
El Ranchero
Wendy's   McDonald's

EZ Way Laundromat
Mt. Lake Ave
Papa's Pizza

Star Mart
Wenonah Ave
Friends & Family

Rite-Aid

PO (24134):
540-921-1100
M-F 9-4:30
Sa 10-12

Old Towne Shoe Repair
Bear's Den
Melinda's

Pizza Hut
Dollar General
Save-A-Lot

Main St

Animal Care Center
540-921-3707

Chamber of
Commerce
540-921-5000

Pearisburg Public Library
540-921-2556
M 12-8, Tu 12-5
W 9-5, Th 9-8,
F 9-5, Sa 9-1

2.7 mi

61
VA

Tom Hoffman 540-921-1184 <gopullman@aol.com> mid-range shuttles centered in Pearisburg.
Don Raines 540-921-7433 Damascus to Troutville
Brenda 540-594-1850, 540-626-3105
Also: Old Towne Shoe Repair Open Wed & Sat, Warner Baker 540-230-6357

650.3   **The Captain's**
Camping available at 4464 Big Stony Creek Road, about 30 yards from trail. Use zip line to cross the creek. You may camp even when The Captain is not home. Dogs will bark but are friendly and are contained by an invisible electric fence. Hiker Feed two weeks after Trail Days. If it rains, you may stay on back porch.

SoBo	NoBo	The A.T. Guide	Elev
1565.2	619.0	Woods road	3513
1564.8	619.4	Sugar Run Gap, Sugar Run Rd (gravel), road fork in view to east (pg.60)	3450
1563.5	620.7	View, 30 yards east.	3925
1562.7	621.5	Roadbed, campsites 0.3W	3574
1562.6	621.6	**Docs Knob Shelter,** reliable spring to left of shelter 32.4◄22.6◄8.4◄▶15.0▶27.5▶31.4	3560
1561.5	622.7	Spring	3418
1559.9	624.3	Spring	3167
1559.3	624.9	Powerline, view	3450

❀ **Rhododendron** – 10-15 foot tall shrubs with broad waxy leaves. Grows in thick stands that the AT sometimes tunnels through. Flowers grow in large bouquets of ruffled pink flowers.

SoBo	NoBo	The A.T. Guide	Elev
1557.5	626.7	View	3694
1556.9	627.3	Angels Rest 0.1W to view	3550
1555.6	628.6	Roadbed.	2615
1554.8	629.4	Cross Ave (paved), VA 634	2025
1554.4	629.8	Lane St, **Pearisburg, VA** (pg.60-61)	1650
1553.9	630.3	US 460, Senator Shumate Bridge, New River, Circle under north end of bridge.	1600
1552.4	631.8	VA 641, Clendennin Rd	1750
1552.0	632.0	Gravel road, NoBo: turn right.	1661
1551.6	632.6	Unnamed paved road.	1699
1551.4	632.8	Powerline	1838
1550.6	633.6	Stream.	2470
1549.8	634.4	Spring, campsite	3075
1548.3	635.9	Powerline	3238
1547.6	636.6	**Rice Field Shelter** (0.1E) 37.6◄23.4◄15.0◄▶12.5▶16.4▶25.2 Stiles south & north. Unreliable water to left behind shelter 0.3 mile down hill.	3370
1547.0	637.2	Cell tower	3381
1546.5	637.7	Powerline, view	3460
1546.0	638.2	Campsite west, water to east	3300

Elev	NoBo	Feature	SoBo
3320	1542.5	Symms Gap, campsite to west.	
3394	1540.7	Campsite	
3300	1539.9	Dickenson Gap	
3743	1537.6	Allegheny Trail to west.	
2986	1535.7	Streams	
2549	1535.1	**Pine Swamp Branch Shelter** 35.9◄27.5◄12.5◄►3.9►12.7►18.5	
2399	1534.8	Stony Creek Valley, 0.1E to parking on VA 635. N37 25.146 W80 36.274 P	
2426	1534.3	Stream.	
2433	1533.9	Camping at "The Captain's" place 30 yards east (pg.61)	
2463	1533.7	Footbridge, stream	
2450	1532.7	Bridge over Stony Creek, VA 635	
2993	1531.8	Gravel road	
3380	1531.4	Spring to east.	
3531	1531.2	**Bailey Gap Shelter** 31.4◄16.4◄3.9►►8.8►14.6►21.0 Water 0.2S on AT, then east down blue-blazed trail.	
3744	1530.2	Spring	
3793	1528.6	Spring	
3950	1527.5	VA 613 (gravel), Mountain Lake Rd	
4100	1527.3	Wind Rock, view, campsite.	
4078	1526.5	Woods road	
4000	1526.0	Spring east in pipeline clearing	
4043	1524.9	Lone Pine Peak	

SoBo	NoBo	The A.T. Guide	Elev
1524.4	659.8	**War Branch Trail to east**	3530
1523.9	660.3	Spring	3290
1522.4	661.8	**War Spur Shelter,** spring north on AT ⊃●⊂ (6) 25.2◄12.7◄8.8◄►5.8►12.2►18.2	2377
1521.6	662.6	VA 632, cross Johns Creek on footbridge ●	2080
1521.5	662.7	Footbridge, stream, campsite	2086
1520.5	663.7	Spring ●	2659
1519.6	664.6	Rocky Gap, VA 601 (gravel)	3265
1519.0	665.2	Johns Creek Mountain Trail to west	3796
1517.8	666.4	Kelly Knob, view. [📷]	3750
1516.6	667.6	**Laurel Creek Shelter** 18.5◄14.6◄5.8◄►6.4►12.4►22.5 ⊃●⊂ (6) Water 60 yards north of shelter junction and west of AT.	2817
1516.4	667.8	Stream	2781
1516.0	668.2	Piney Ridge, abandoned house to west. ●	2633
1514.6	669.6	Pasture, several fence stiles.	2248
1514.2	670.0	Footbridge, Sinking Creek, VA 42, **Newport, VA** (8.0E) (pg.66) "trail east" (Nobo right, Sobo left) is compass west	2200
1513.3	670.9	VA 630 (paved), chimney, and footbridge close together ●	2166
1512.9	671.3	Keiffer Oak, largest oak tree on AT in south, over 18' around, over 300 yrs old Dover Oak along AT in NY is slightly larger.	2240
1512.5	671.7	Powerline	2543
1511.2	673.0	Powerline	3242
1510.4	673.8	Bruisers Knob	3434
1510.2	674.0	**Sarver Hollow Shelter** (0.4E) 21.0◄12.2◄6.4◄►6.0►16.1►29.7 ⊃●⊂ (6)	3418
1508.3	675.9	View [📷📷]	3375
1508.0	676.2	View	3350
1506.8	677.4	North end of ridge crest on Sinking Creek Mountain West is old route of AT, leading 2.5 miles to Old Hall Rd.	3383
1505.3	678.9	Stream. ●	2720
1504.2	680.0	**Niday Shelter,** water on opposite side of AT ⊃●⊂ (6) 18.2◄12.4◄6.0◄►10.1►23.7►24.7	2005

SoBo	NoBo		Elev
1502.8	**681.4**	VA 621, Craig Creek Rd	1556
1502.3	**681.9**	Many footbridges crossing Craig Creek and feeder streams, within a mile north of road.	1602
1499.9	**684.3**	Bench at southern crest of Brush Mountain	3056
1499.1	**685.1**	Audie Murphy Monument	3100
		Murphy was most decorated American soldier of World War II. Monument on blue-blazed trail to west.	
1495.4	**688.8**	Footbridge, Trout Creek, VA 620 (gravel)	1557
1495.0	**689.2**	Powerline	1760
1494.1	**690.1**	**Pickle Branch Shelter** (0.3E)	1921
		22.5◄16.1◄10.1◄▶13.6▶14.6▶17.0 Tenting along trail to shelter. Water on steep trail 0.2 mile downhill from shelter.	
1493.1	**691.1**	View	2393
1490.2	**694.0**	View	2962
1489.9	**694.3**	Cove Mountain	3020
		Trail 0.1E to Dragons Tooth (stone monolith), views.	
1488.9	**695.3**	Lost Spectacles Gap	2550
1488.5	**695.7**	Rawies Rest, view	2492
1488.4	**695.8**	View	2320
1487.7	**696.5**	Scout Trail west to Dragons Tooth Parking	2052
1487.4	**696.8**	VA 624, Newport Rd (pg.66)	1810
1486.6	**697.6**	Footbridge	1835
1486.1	**698.1**	Fence stile	1856
1485.8	**698.4**	VA 785, Blacksburg Rd	1790
1485.5	**698.7**	Footbridge, Catawba Creek, fence stile	1780

670.0   VA 42, Sinking Creek

        Note: An "east" or right turn for NoBo is compass west.

🛏 🚐 📶 ✉ (0.5E) **The Huffman House B&B** (540) 544-6942 ⟨www.thehuffmanhousebandb.com⟩, $129–$159 double, $20EAP, reservations required. Ask about shuttles. Owned by 1999 thru-hikers. Maildrops: 16 Huffman Store Dr., Newport, VA 24128.

        Newport, VA 24128 (8E)

 Store and post office are near intersection of 42 and 460.

📮 M-F 8:15-12 & 1-4:15, Sa 9-11, 540-544-7415

🏪 **Super Val-U**

696.8   VA 624, Newport Rd

🏨 🚐 ✉ (0.3E) **Four Pines Hostel**   Owner Joe Mitchell h: 540-384-7599, cell: 540-309-8615 Hostel is a 3-bay garage with shower; please leave a donation. Shuttles to/from The Home Place Restaurant (Thurs-Sun) and to Catawba Grocery. Maildrops: 6164 Newport Rd. Catawba VA 24070

🏪 🍴 **Catawba Grocery** 540-384-8050

West 0.3 mile to VA 311 and then left 0.1 mile to store, open 7 days 5am-11pm. Grill serves breakfast, pizza, burgers, ice cream. Keeps list of shuttlers.

702.7   VA 311, *Catawba, VA 24070* (1W)

📮 (1.0W) M-F 7:30-12 & 1-5, Sa 8-10:30, 540-384-6011

🍴 (1.4W) **Homeplace Restaurant** 540-384-7252 Th-Fr 4-8, Sa 3-8, Su 11-6, AYCE family-style meals including drink, dessert, and tax; $14 (2 meats) $15 (3 meats) kids (3-11) $8.

722.5   US 220, *Daleville, VA*

724.0   US 11, *Troutville, VA*

The adjoining towns of Daleville and Troutville have indistinct borders near the intersection of highways 220 and 11 and interstate 81, which is a major hub for truckers. The intersection is broad, busy and not at all pedestrian-friendly, which makes it a challenge to walk to services east of 81. The safer, but longer, route to these businesses is from the highway 11 trail crossing.

🛏 ♿ 📶 🖥 ✉ 💲 **Howard Johnson Express** 540-992-1234 $49.95 hiker rate, includes full hot breakfast. Pool table and pool. Maildrops: 437 Roanoke Road, Daleville, VA 24083.

🛏 ♿ 📶 🖥 **Super 8** 540-992-3000 Discounted rate for hikers, cont B, pool, accepts major credit cards.

🛏 📶 🖥 **Comfort Inn** 540-992-5600 hiker rate $49.99D, $10EAP, continental breakfast.

🛏 📶 🖥 **Quality Inn** 540-992-5335 $71/up, pets $25.

🛏 ♿ ✉ **Holiday Inn Express** 540-966-4444 $99-119. Maildrops: 3200 Lee Hwy, Troutville, VA 24175.

🛏 **Red Roof Inn** 540-992-5055

🛏 **Travel Lodge** 540-992-6700 $45 $6EAP.

🍴 **Three Li'l Pigs** 540-966-0165 Summer hrs M-Th 11-9:30, F-Sa 11-11, Su 11-9, Hiker friendly, hand-chopped BBQ ribs and wings, selection of micro-brewed beers.

🍴 **Bella Pizza** 540-966-5980 AYCE 11-1:30

🏪 🛒 **Kroger Grocery Store and Pharmacy** 540-992-4920 24hr pharmacy M-F 8-9, Sa 9-6, Su 12-6.

🥾 ✉ 🖥 **Outdoor Trails** 540-992-5850 full service outfitter, fuel/oz, one computer for internet use, ask about shuttles. Maildrops: Botetourt Commons, 28 Kingston Dr, Daleville, VA 24083.

🚐 **Del Schechterly** 540-529-6028 Shuttles from Pearisburg to Waynesboro.

        Roanoke, VA (13E)

A large city with an airport. Although the center of town is approximately 13 miles away, the town extends north. There are services at the next I-81 exit, 4 miles south, most notably Gander Mountain Sports.

🥾 **Gander Mountain** 540-362-3658

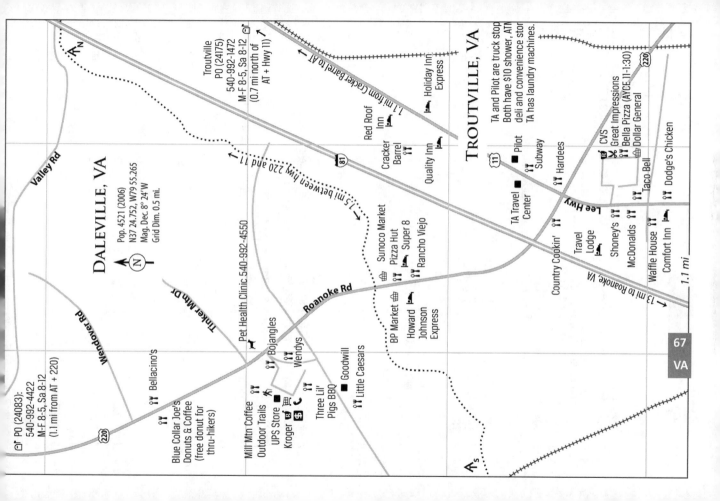

DALEVILLE, VA

N

Pop. 4521 (2006)
N37 24.752, W79 55.265
Mag. Dec. 8° 24'W
Grid Dim. 0.5 mi.

Valley Rd

Tinker Mtn Dr

Mendover Rd

220

PO (24083):
540-992-4422
M-F 8-5, Sa 8-12
(1.1 mi from AT + 220)

Blue Collar Joe's
Donuts & Coffee
(free donut for
thru-hikers)

Bellacino's

Pet Health Clinic 540-992-4550

Bojangles

Wendys

Mill Mtn Coffee
Outdoor Trails
UPS Store
Kroger

Three Lil'
Pigs BBQ

Goodwill

Little Caesars

Roanoke Rd

1.5 mi between hwy 220 and 11

Sunoco Market
Pizza Hut
Super 8
Rancho Viejo

BP Market

Howard
Johnson
Express

81

Troutville
PO (24175)
540-992-1472
M-F 8-5, Sa 8-12
(0.7 mi north of
AT + Hwy 11)

1.1 mi from Cracker Barrel to AT

Cracker
Barrel

Quality Inn

Red Roof
Inn

Holiday Inn
Express

TROUTVILLE, VA

TA and Pilot are truck stop.
Both have $10 shower. ATM
deli and convenience stor
TA has laundry machines.

11

Pilot

TA Travel
Center

Country Cookin'

Travel
Lodge

Lee Hwy

13 mi to Roanoke, VA

CVS
Great Impressions
Bella Pizza (AYCE 11-1:30)
Dollar General

Subway

Hardees

Taco Bell

Dodge's Chicken

Shoney's

McDonalds

Waffle House

Comfort Inn

1.1 mi

67
VA

N

S

SoBo	NoBo	The A.T. Guide	Elev
1481.9	702.3	Campsite	2096
1481.5	702.7	VA 311, **Catawba, VA** (1.0W) .... N37 22.808 W80 5.390 **P** (pg.66)	1990
1480.9	703.3	Footbridge	2034
1480.5	703.7	**Johns Spring Shelter** 29.7◄23.7◄13.6◄►1.0►3.4►9.4	1974
		Unreliable spring 25 yrds left front of shelter. Water 0.9N, just before next shelter.	
1480.1	704.1	Footbridge	2129
1479.5	704.7	**Catawba Mountain Shelter**	2220
		24.7◄14.6◄1.0◄►2.4►8.4►22.8 Piped spring just south on AT.	
1477.8	706.4	McAfee Knob; excellent views, no camping.	3197
1477.3	706.9	Powerline	2795
1477.2	707.0	Water to east, Pig Farm campsite	2694
1477.1	707.1	**Campbell Shelter**, water behind shelter	2649
		17.0◄3.4◄2.4◄►6.0►20.4►26.6	
1474.0	710.2	Brickeys Gap, Lamberts Meadow Trail to east	2250
1472.2	712.0	Tinker Cliffs, 0.5 mile cliff walk, views back to McAfee Knob.	3000
1471.7	712.5	Scorched Earth Gap, Andy Layne Trail to west	2600
1471.1	713.1	**Lamberts Meadow Shelter** 9.4◄8.4◄6.0◄►4.4►20.6►27.9	2143
1470.8	713.4	Lamberts Meadow Campsite, Sawmill Run	2000
		Footbridge, stream. Trail north of footbridge to east rejoins AT at Brickeys Gap.	
1468.6	715.6	Blue-blazed trail west to view	2244
1466.8	717.4	Angels Gap	1800
1466.4	717.8	Powerline	1853
1465.7	718.5	Hay Rock, view	1900
1464.5	719.7	Powerline, view	1936
1463.7	720.5	Powerline	1975

✿ **Fire Pink** – Scarlet-colored flower with five snake-tongued petals.

NoBo	Description	Features	Elev	SoBo
721.3	Powerline		1405	1462.9
721.9	Powerline, railroad tracks, bridge		1184	1462.3
722.5	US 220, **Daleville, VA** (pg.66-67)		1350	1461.7
723.7	I-81, trail passes under on VA 779		1400	1460.5
724.0	US 11, RR tracks, **Troutville, VA** (0.8W) N37 24.269 W79 53.369 **P** (pg.66-67)		1300	1460.2
724.3	Fence stile		1500	1459.9
724.5	VA 652, Mountain Pass Rd		1450	1459.7
724.8	Fence		1505	1459.4
727.5	**Fullhardt Knob Shelter** (0.1E) 22.8◀20.4◀14.4◀▶6.2▶13.5▶20.0 Treat water from cistern.	☾ ♦ ⊏ (6)	2651	1456.7
730.3	Salt Pond Rd, USFS 191		2260	1453.9
731.1	Curry Creek, Curry Creek Trail to west	♦	1680	1453.1
731.8	Stream.	♦	1695	1452.4
733.0	Wilson Creek, Colliers Pit historical marker to north		1690	1451.2
733.7	**Wilson Creek Shelter** 26.6◀20.6◀6.2◀▶7.3▶13.8▶20.8	☾ ♦ ◓ ⊏ (6)	1871	1450.5
734.1	Reliable stream 0.3 mile downhill in front of shelter. Spring	♦	2050	1450.1
736.1	Blackhorse Gap, dirt road, Blue Ridge Parkway (BRP) mile 97.7 to east.		2402	1448.1
736.8	BRP 97.0, Taylors Mountain Overlook	◉	2387	1447.4
738.6	BRP 95.3, Harveys Knob Overlook	◉	2550	1445.6
740.3	Hammond Hollow Trail to west.		2341	1443.9
741.0	**Bobblets Gap Shelter** (0.2W) 27.9◀13.5◀7.3◀▶6.5▶13.5▶18.4 If spring to left of shelter dry, look farther downstream.	☾ ♦ ⊏ (6)	2101	1443.2
741.8	BRP 92.5, Peaks of Otter Overlook	◉	2344	1442.4
SoBo	The A.T. Guide		Elev	NoBo

744.1   Bearwallow Gap, VA 43

🛏 🍴 ⛺ (4.4E) **Peaks of Otter Lodge** 540-586-1081, 800-542-5927 $95/up, Sa-Su breakfast buffet, B/L/D served daily May-Oct.

Buchanan, VA 24066 (5W on VA 43) Services more accessible from VA 614 listed below as "Buchanan (I-81 exit 168)."
📬 M-F 8:30-1 & 1:30-4:30, Sa 10-12, 540-254-2178

🍴 **The Rhein River German Restaurant** 540-254-2455 〈www.therheinriverinn.com〉 Open W-Su in the summer. There is no longer a B&B. Shuttles to/from trailheads sometimes available.

🍴 **Burger King**, **Old Buchanan Restaurant**, **Carini's Italian Restaurant**, **Subway** west of 81.

🛒 **Buchanan Supermarket** 540-254-2596, **Family Dollar**

💊 **Ransone's Drug Store**

💻 **Buchanan Branch Library**

750.7   Jennings Creek ♦ (0.3E), VA 614

🛏 🔋 🍴 ⛺ 🚿 ⛺ 🛰 ✉ (1.2E) **Middle Creek Campground** 540-254-2550 〈www.middlecreekcampground.com〉 cabins $65-75, $5EAP cabin sleeps 4-6, camping $20 (2 persons), showers $5, snack bar, Ask about shuttles, small amount of resupply, Coleman/alcohol/oz, and canister fuel. Laundry room (around back) is always open. Can also be reached on the northern side of Fork Mountain by taking VA 714 and VA 614 east 1.4 miles. Guest maildrops: 1164 Middle Creek Road, Buchanan, VA 24066.

Buchanan, VA (I-81 exit 168) (5W on VA 614)
🛏 🛰 **Wattstull Inn** 540-254-1551, $60/up, pets $10.

⛺ **Shell Convenience Store**

779.3   US 501, VA 130

⛺ 🏕 🏕 ✉ **Wildwood Campground** (5.0E) 866-883-5228 ⟨www.wildwoodcampground.com⟩ Hiker special $10 each on shared tent site. $60 cabins for 4. Camp store, Coleman/denatured/oz. Free showers, coin laundry. Ask about rides. Maildrops: 6252 Elon Road, Monroe ,VA 24574.

🚐 **Ken Wallace** 434-609-2704 Range is Waynesboro to Daleville.

Big Island, VA 24526 (5.6E)

📮 M-F 8:30-12:30 & 1:30-4:30, Sa 8-10, 434-299-5072

🏪 🍴 ✉ **H&H Food Market** 434-299-5153 7 days 5-9, B/L/D, Maildrops: 11619 Lee Jackson Hwy, Big Island, VA 24526.

➕ **Big Island Family Medical Center** 434-299-5951

Glasgow, VA 24555 (5.9W)

📮 M-F 8-11:30 & 12:30-4:30, Sa 8:30-10:30, 540-258-2852

⛺⛰🚿 Shelter & shower at pavillion behind laudromat under tower.

🚻 Public restrooms at Knick Field.

🏪 **Glasgow Grocery Express** 540-258-1818 M-Sa 6-11:30pm, Su 8-1130pm, Coleman/alcohol/oz.

🏪 **CC's Stop & Go** Convenience store with some hot foods.

🏪 **Dollar General**

🧺 **Lew's Laundromat**

💻 **Glasgow Public Library** 540-258-2509 M,Th 10-7, T,W 10-5:30, Sa 10-1, need ID for internet.

🐕 **Natural Bridge Animal Hospital** 540-291-1444 4.5W of Glasgow on VA 130. M,W,F 8-5:30, T,Th 8-7.

SoBo	NoBo	The A.T. Guide	Elev
1441.8	742.4	BRP 91.8, Mills Gap Overlook	2450
1440.1	744.1	Bearwallow Gap, footbridge, stream, VA 43, 0.2E to BRP 90.9 △ (pg.70) **Buchanan, VA** (5.0W)	2228
1438.5	745.7	Cove Mountain	2720
1438.1	746.1	Little Cove Mountain Trail to east	2600
1436.7	747.5	**Cove Mountain Shelter** 20.0◄13.8◄6.5◄▶7.0▶11.9▶17.2	1963
1436.5	747.7	View	1985
1435.0	749.2	Buchanan Trail	1790
1434.7	749.5	Water to east on blue-blazed trail	1572
1433.5	750.7	Jennings Creek, VA 614 N37 31.745 W79 37.350 P ♦ (pg.70) Swimming hole, campsites.	951
1431.9	752.3	Fork Mountain	2042
1430.7	753.5	Stream south of powerline	1258
1430.4	753.8	Stream	1290
1430.0	754.2	Stream	1213
1429.7	754.5	**Bryant Ridge Shelter** 20.8◄13.5◄7.0◄▶4.9▶10.2▶22.6 Stream on trail to shelter. Blue-blazed trail 0.1N of shelter leads 0.5E to VA 714.	1302
1426.6	757.6	Campsite, 0.1W to spring (signed).	2932
1425.4	758.8	Floyd Mountain	3560
1424.8	759.4	**Cornelius Creek Shelter** 18.4◄11.9◄4.9◄▶5.3▶17.7▶21.6 Water on trail to shelter. Privy 50 yards behind shelter	3126
1424.5	759.7	Stream.	3035
1423.9	760.3	Black Rock Overlook, view 200' west	3450
1423.6	760.6	Footbridge, stream.	3282
1423.3	760.9	Intersection with Cornelius Creek Trail	3204
1422.2	762.0	Apple Orchard Falls Trail 1.1W to 200' waterfall, 0.1E to Sunset Field, USFS 812 (Parkers Gap Rd) 0.1N on AT.	3339

SoBo	NoBo	Feature	Elev
1420.7	763.5	Apple Orchard Mountain, FAA tower, views	4225
1420.4	763.8	The Guillotine	4090
1419.8	764.4	BRP 76.3, spring 100 yards north, then east of AT	3900
1419.5	764.7	**Thunder Hill Shelter** 17.2◄10.2◄5.3►12.4►16.3►25.1	3934
		Poor water source, use spring south on AT.	
1418.5	765.7	Hunting Creek Trail, BRP 74.9	3607
1418.1	766.1	0.1E to BRP 74.7 Thunder Ridge Overlook	3501
1416.2	768.0	Harrison Ground Spring	3325
1415.7	768.5	Spring	2929
1414.8	769.4	Petites Gap, gravel road, BRP 71.0 to east.	2369
1412.6	771.6	Marble Spring, campsite, spring 100 yards west.	2367
1412.1	772.1	Sulphur Spring Trail south crossing	2400
1410.3	773.9	Gunter Ridge Trail, Hickory Stand	2650
1409.8	774.4	Sulphur Spring Trail north crossing	2588
1409.0	775.2	Big Cove Branch, stream.	1890
1407.1	777.1	**Matts Creek Shelter,** Matts Creek Trail 2.5E to US 501	869
		22.6◄17.7◄12.4►3.9►12.7►22.2	
1406.3	777.9	AT parallels James River from here north for 1.0 mile, no camping	706
1405.1	779.1	James River footbridge, longest foot-use-only bridge on AT	678
1404.9	779.3	US 501, VA 130, **Big Island VA** (5.6E), **Glasgow VA** (5.9W)	680
1404.7	779.5	Lower Rocky Row Run Bridge, stream.	696
		N37 36.286 W79 23.295	
1403.8	780.4	VA 812, USFS 36 (gravel)	818
1403.4	780.8	Stream.	939
1403.2	781.0	**Johns Hollow Shelter**	1036
		21.6◄16.3◄3.9►8.8►18.3►23.9	
		Springs to left and right of shelter.	
1401.3	782.9	Little Rocky Row Trail to west, view just north on AT	2394

P (pg.70)

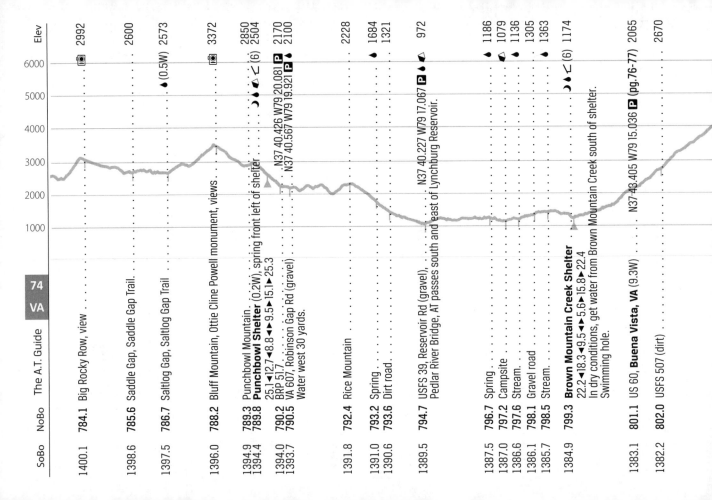

SoBo	NoBo	The A.T. Guide		Elev
1400.1	784.1	Big Rocky Row, view	回	2992
1398.6	785.6	Saddle Gap, Saddle Gap Trail.		2600
1397.5	786.7	Saltlog Gap, Saltlog Gap Trail.	● (0.5W)	2573
1396.0	788.2	Bluff Mountain, Ottie Cline Powell monument, views.	回	3372
1394.9	789.3	Punchbowl Mountain.		2850
1394.4	789.8	**Punchbowl Shelter** (0.2W), spring front left of shelter 25.1◄12.7◄8.8◄▶9.5▶15.1▶25.3	☽●◢⊏(6)	2504
1394.0	790.2	BRP 51.7	N37 40.426 W79 20.081 **P** ●	2170
1393.7	790.5	VA 607, Robinson Gap Rd (gravel) Water west 30 yards.	N37 40.567 W79 19.921 **P** ◆	2100
1391.8	792.4	Rice Mountain		2228
1391.0	793.2	Spring.	◆	1684
1390.6	793.6	Dirt road.		1321
1389.5	794.7	USFS 39, Reservoir Rd (gravel), Pedlar River Bridge, AT passes south and east of Lynchburg Reservoir.	N37 40.227 W79 17.067 **P** ●◢	972
1387.5	796.7	Spring.	◆	1186
1387.0	797.2	Campsite	●◢	1079
1386.6	797.6	Stream.	◆	1136
1386.1	798.1	Gravel road		1305
1385.7	798.5	Stream.	◆	1363
1384.9	799.3	**Brown Mountain Creek Shelter** 22.2◄18.3◄9.5◄▶5.6▶15.8▶22.4 In dry conditions, get water from Brown Mountain Creek south of shelter. Swimming hole.	☽◆⊏(6)	1174
1383.1	801.1	US 60, **Buena Vista, VA** (9.3W)	N37 43.405 W79 15.036 **P** (pg.76-77)	2065
1382.2	802.0	USFS 507 (dirt)		2670

NoBo	Feature	Elev	SoBo
803.9	Bald Knob	4059	1380.3
804.9	Hotel Trail, **Cow Camp Gap Shelter** (0.6E)	3487	1379.3
	23.9◄15.1◄5.6◄▶10.2▶16.8▶24.4		
	Water source on blue-blazed trail left of shelter before small stream crossing.		
806.1	Cold Mountain, views.	4022	1378.1
807.4	Hog Camp Gap, USFS 48 (gravel), Grassy meadow with many campsites.	3485	1376.8
	Signed spring just north of road crossing and 0.3 east.		
808.3	Tar Jacket Ridge, view	3847	1375.9
809.6	Salt Log Gap, USFS 63, two gravel road crossings	3257	1374.6
810.8	USFS 246	3500	1373.4
811.3	Greasy Spring Rd, Lovington Spring Trail to west.	3600	1372.9
	Spring 0.2E on woods road, then right 0.1 on old AT (look for double blaze)		
813.2	Piney River north fork.	3482	1371.0
814.4	Elk Pond Branch	3725	1369.8
815.1	**Seeley-Woodworth Shelter**	3822	1369.1
	25.3◄15.8◄10.2◄▶6.6▶14.2▶20.4		
815.3	Stream. Piped spring 0.1 mile downhill to right.	3741	1368.9
816.2	Porters Field, west 100 yards to campsite and spring	3540	1368.0
817.4	Spy Rock Rd (formerly Fish Hatchery Rd unpaved) . (pg.77)	3454	1366.8
817.8	Campsite, Spy Rock 0.1E, rock outcrop requiring scramble, view	3793	1366.4
820.0	Cash Hollow Rd	3280	1364.2
820.8	VA 826, (0.5W) to Crabtree Falls Trail, downhill 0.1 to major waterfall (pg.77)	3350	1363.4
	and 2.1 miles to VA 56 near **Crabtree Falls Campground.**		
821.7	**The Priest Shelter** (0.1E) 22.4◄16.8◄6.6◄▶7.6▶13.8▶29.6	3903	1362.5
822.0	The Priest, views on AT south of summit	4063	1362.0
823.7	View	2933	1360.5

BUENA VISTA, VA

Pop. 6222 (2009)
N37 44.045, W79 21.222
Mag. Dec. 8° 58'W

Glen Maury Park

Food Lion, Dollar Store, and CVS 0.9 mi.

Maury River

Todd's BBQ

10th

12th

Nick's Italian

Kenny's Burgers

Exxon

Burger King

Budget Inn
Subway
Ice Cream & More

Edgewater Animal Hospital

501

Bluedogart Cafe

Valley Cinemas
Don Tequilas

Family Dollar

Hardees

Uncorked Wine Shop

Canton Chinese Restaurant

Lewis Grocery

Frank's for the Memories

Original Italian Pizza

Magnolia Ave

60

Library
540-261-2715
M-W & F 10-5
Thurs 1-7
Sat 10-1

14th

15th

17th

18th

19th

20th

21st

22nd

23rd

PO (24416):
540-261-8959
M-F 8:30-4:30

Visitor Center

Buena Vista Motel

9.3 mi.

1.5 mi

801.1   US 60, **Buena Vista, VA 24416** (9.3W)
⌂ M-F 8:30-4:30, 540-261-8959

🛏 **Buena Vista Motel** 540-261-2138 $49-$79

🛏⚲ **Budget Inn** 540-261-2156 $44.95S $54.95D, pets $10 and must use smoking room. Continental breakfast on weekends.

◗ 🦃 **Glen Maury Park Campground** 540-261-7321 AT hiker special $5 tentsite. Free shower, even without stay, South end of town across river. Maury River Fiddlers Convention mid-June.

🍴 **Domino's Pizza** 540-261-1111

🍴📶 **Frank's for the Memories** Wifi, hiker friendly, live music on Fridays. Serves wide selection for lunch and dinner.

🛒 **Food Lion** 540-261-7672, 7 days

🐾 **Edgewater Animal Hospital** 540-261-4114 M-F 8-7, Sa 10-12

🛈 **Uncorked Wine Shop** 540-261-9463 Is instrumental in developing a trail angel network. Also sells wine in half-liter disposable cartons.

🛈 **Regional Visitor Center** 540-261-8004

Lexington, VA 24450 (15W of Buena Vista)

🛏⚲📶🖥📬 **Brierley Hill B&B** 540-464-8421 relax@brierleyhill.com Thru-hiker special $50 for any available room. Includes breakfast, free ride to/from the AT (Rt. 60), free use of laundry facilities, and internet. Credit cards okay. No Pets. Maildrops: 985 Borden Rd, Lexington, VA 24450.

🛏⚲📶📬 **502 South Main B&B** 540-460-7353 info@southmain.com. Mention "Thru-hiker special offer" to get $50pp for 2 or 3 persons, call for single rate. Free ride from/to AT (Rt. 60), free laundry, soaking footbath therapy, hearty breakfast, WiFi. Restaurants & shops nearby. No pets, No smoking. Maildrops: 502 S. Main St, Lexington VA 24450

🚶 **Walkabout Outfitter** 540-464-HIKE Full service outfitter owned by Kirk Miller (Flying Monkey '99). Fuel/oz, canisters.

817.4   Spy Rock Rd
1.1W to parking area, where the road is renamed to Fish Hatchery Road. You should be going downhill on a gravel road the entire way. Watch for right turn 0.5 from AT, and watch for blue blazes. It is another 1.5 to Dutch Haus; call to arrange pickup at the parking area if you plan to stay there.

🛏⚲🚌🖥📬 **Dutch Haus B&B** 540-377-2119 $30 for hikers arriving on foot (or picked up at trailhead) includes breakfast. Dinner extra. Free lunch is served to all thru-hikers (not just guests) during May and June-15 from 11am - 1pm. Clearly this is exceptionally generous; please be appreciative.   Maildrops: 655 Fork Mountain Lane, Montebello, VA 24464.

Montebello, VA 24464 (2.5W to VA 56, left 0.9 mile)
⌂ M-F 8-1 & 1:30-4:30, Sa 9-12, 540-377-9218

◗ 🏠⚲ **Montebello Camping & General Store**
540-377-2650 〈www.montebellova.com〉 Camping $10 site and $3EAP, coin laundry, Coleman/alcohol/oz. Open Apr 1 - Oct 31.

820.8   VA 826 (2.7 walking miles to campground)
826.5   VA 56, Tye River (4W to campground)
🛏◗🏠🦃⚲📬 **Crabtree Falls Campground**
540-377-2066 〈www.crabtreefallscampground.com〉 cfcg@ceva.net, cabins $50 six people, camping $26.50/site(2 tents). Coin laundry, free shower w/o stay. Maildrops: 11039 Crabtree Falls Hwy, Tyro, VA 22976.

The A.T. Guide

SoBo	NoBo	The A.T. Guide	Elev
1359.0	**825.2**	Cripple Creek	1869
1357.7	**826.5**	VA 56, Tye River suspension bridge 100 yards north, **Crabtree Falls Campground** (4.0W) N37 50.305 W79 1.387 **P** (pg.77)	970
1356.5	**827.7**	Roadbed.	1680
1356.0	**828.2**	Mau-Har Trail to west, southern intersection rejoins AT at Maupin Field Shelter	2090
1355.1	**829.1**	Stream.	1756
1354.9	**829.3**	**Harpers Creek Shelter** 24.4◀14.2◀7.6◀▶6.2▶22.0▶34.0 Harpers Creek in front of shelter. Privy up hill.	1910
1353.4	**830.8**	View	2784
1352.9	**831.3**	Chimney Rock, view	3190
1351.2	**833.0**	Three Ridges Mountain.	3870
1350.5	**833.7**	Hanging Rock Overlook, view	3514
1348.7	**835.5**	**Maupin Field Shelter** 20.4◀13.8◀6.2◀▶15.8▶27.8▶40.8 Piped spring behind shelter. Privy to right of shelter on unmarked path. Mau-Har Trail northern intersection.	2765
1347.0	**837.2**	Reeds Gap, BRP 13.6, VA 664. N37 54.097 W78 59.115 **P**	2650
1346.5	**837.7**	Three Ridges Overlook, BRP 13.1 N37 54.418 W78 58.77 **P**	2700
1344.3	**839.9**	Stream	2588
1343.5	**840.7**	Rock Point Overlook, view to west.	2792
1342.7	**841.5**	Cedar Cliffs, view.	2800
1342.2	**842.0**	Dripping Rock, BRP 9.6, spring N37 56.465 W78 56.214 **P**	2950
1341.9	**842.3**	Laurel Springs Gap, spring	2863
1341.0	**843.2**	Side trail 0.3W to Humpback picnic area	3227
1340.2	**844.0**	Campsite, view	3499
1339.4	**844.8**	Humpback Mountain.	3626

Elevation profile chart (elevations 1000–6000 ft)

NoBo	Description	Elev
845.8	Trail 0.2W to view at The Rocks	3286
847.5	Spring	2535
848.5	Spring	2353
848.6	Side trail 0.2W to Humpback Gap, BRP 6.0	2345
849.5	Glass Hollow Overlook, view to east	2271
849.9	Side trail 1.3W to Humpback Visitor Center N37 58.150 W78 53.846	2306
850.0	Albright Loop Trail to west	2242
851.3	**Paul C. Wolfe Shelter** 29.6◄22.0◄15.8◄▶12.0▶25.0▶38.2. (10)	1594
	Mill Creek 50 yards in front of shelter. Waterfall with pool 100 yards.	
852.1	Small cemetery	1879
852.8	Cabin ruins, chimney	2087
853.1	Spring	2061
854.4	Stream	1888
855.3	Stream	1751
856.5	US 250 + Blue Ridge Pkwy N38 1.864 W78 51.545 (pg.80-81)	1920
	Rockfish Gap, **Waynesboro, VA** (3.7W), I-64 overpass, south end of Skyline Dr.	
857.4	Shenandoah National Park (SNP) (pg.84)	2225
	Entrance station and self-registration for overnight permits.	
859.0	"Wrong Way" side trail to east	2584
860.2	Skyline 102.1, McCormick Gap	2458
861.3	Bears Den Mountain, communication towers	2885
861.8	Skyline 99.5, Beagle Gap, stream N38 4.373 W78 47.607	2550
862.1	Trail west to Little Calf Mountain	2802
862.7	Calf Mountain	2984
863.3	**Calf Mountain Shelter** (0.3W) (6)	2703
	34.0◄27.8◄12.0◄▶13.0▶26.2▶34.4 Spring on way to shelter. Bear pole.	
863.7	Powerline	2302
864.0	Spring	2315
864.3	Gravel road 0.1W to Skyline 96.9, Jarman Gap	2268
864.4	Spring, just south of woods road	2159

SoBo: 1338.4, 1336.7, 1335.7, 1335.6, 1334.7, 1334.3, 1334.2, 1332.9, 1332.1, 1331.4, 1331.1, 1329.8, 1328.9, 1327.7, 1326.8, 1325.2, 1324.0, 1322.9, 1322.4, 1322.1, 1321.5, 1320.9, 1320.5, 1320.4, 1319.9, 1319.8

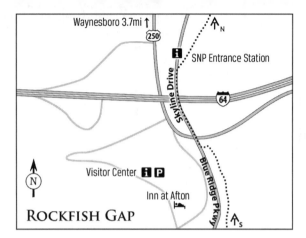

Waynesboro 3.7mi ↑
250
SNP Entrance Station
Skyline Drive
64
N
Visitor Center **i** **P**
Inn at Afton
Blue Ridge Pkwy
N
ROCKFISH GAP
S

856.5   US 250, Blue Ridge Pkwy

For NoBos, the AT intersects with the Blue Ridge Parkway just south of the I-64/US 250 interchange. The Visitor Center is west of the BRP and uphill. Continuing north, the AT goes over US 250 and I-64 alongside the BRP. The BRP becomes the Skyline Drive.

i ☎ P **Afton Mountain Visitor Center** 540-943-5187 Staffed by volunteers and open most days 9-5. Hiker information sheets offer the most current information about Waynesboro, town services, and trail angels. Many lodging facilities offer free pickup/return from this location. Long-term parking okay, please leave contact information and expected return date.

Inn at Afton 540-942-5201 Hiker rate $40+tax, pets allowed, pool, Dominos, Ming Garden, & Giovanni's deliver, located at top of hill west of I-64.

(0.5W on 250) Colony House Motel 540-942-4156 $49S, $59D+tax, pets $10, sells snacks, noodles, soup. Maildrops: 494 Three Notched Mtn Hwy, Waynesboro, VA 22980.

Waynesboro, VA 22980 (4.5W on I-64) *(more services on map)* A large town with all services.

Grace Hiker Hostel Supervised hostel at the Lutheran Church next to library, open May 21-June 24, closed Sunday nights, 2-night limit. Check-in 5-8pm, check-out 9am. Closed during day, but hikers staying over may leave packs. Cots in large, downstairs air-conditioned Fellowship Hall, 2 showers, internet, big-screen TV/DVD/VCR, kitchenette with snacks and breakfast foods in a separate hiker lounge. 15 hiker maximum. No pets, smoking, drugs or alcohol. Donations gratefully accepted. On Wednesday nights the congregation cooks a free dinner (limited to the 15 hostel guests) followed by an optional vespers service.

YMCA 540-942-5107 Free camping and showers. Use of YMCA facilities $10. Check-in at the front desk.

The Tree Streets Inn 540-949-4484, $75S/D, includes breakfast, pool, snacks, no pets. Call from Rockfish Gap for free pickup/return to trail with stay. Maildrops for guest: 421 Walnut Avenue, Waynesboro, VA 22980

Belle Hearth B&B 540-943-1910 ⟨www.bellehearth.com⟩ $75S, $95D, higher on weekends, includes breakfast, pool, pickup and return to trail, no pets, no smoking.

Quality Inn 540-942-1171 $54.99S $5EAP, continental breakfast, pets $10.

Green Leaf Grill Seafood gumbo, vegetarian meals, gourmet pizza, craft beer & wine

Kroger Supermarket 540-942-5100, 6-12

Rockfish Gap Outfitters 540-943-1461 full service outfitter, Coleman/alcohol/oz, other fuels, shuttle information. Located between town and the trail, so ask your ride to stop on the way.

Lyle Kirby 540-942-2413 Long distance shuttles. Charlottesville train and bus station.

Ace Hardware Coleman/oz.

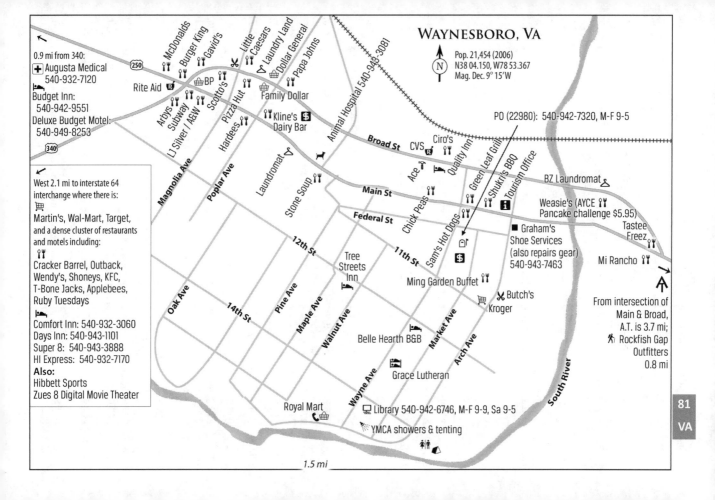

WAYNESBORO, VA

Pop. 21,454 (2006)
N38 04.150, W78 53.367
Mag. Dec. 9° 15'W

0.9 mi from 340:
✚ Augusta Medical
   540-932-7120
🛏 Budget Inn:
   540-942-9551
Deluxe Budget Motel:
   540-949-8253

McDonalds
Burger King
Gavid's
Little Caesars
Laundry Land
Dollar General
Papa Johns

250

Rite Aid
BP
Scotto's
Family Dollar

Arbys
Subway
LJ Silver / A&W
Hardees
Pizza Hut
Kline's Dairy Bar

340

West 2.1 mi to interstate 64
interchange where there is:
🛒
Martin's, Wal-Mart, Target,
and a dense cluster of restaurants
and motels including:
🍴
Cracker Barrel, Outback,
Wendy's, Shoneys, KFC,
T-Bone Jacks, Applebees,
Ruby Tuesdays
🛏
Comfort Inn: 540-932-3060
Days Inn: 540-943-1101
Super 8: 540-943-3888
HI Express: 540-932-7170
Also:
Hibbett Sports
Zues 8 Digital Movie Theater

Animal Hospital 540-943-3081

PO (22980): 540-942-7320, M-F 9-5

Broad St
CVS
Ciro's
Quality Inn
Green Leaf Grill
Shukri's BBQ
Tourism Office
BZ Laundromat
Weasie's (AYCE)
Pancake challenge $5.95)

Magnolia Ave
Poplar Ave
Laundromat
Stone Soup

Ace
Main St

Chick Peas
Federal St

Sam's Hot Dogs

Graham's
Shoe Services
(also repairs gear)
540-943-7463

Tastee Freez
Mi Rancho

12th St
11th St

Tree Streets Inn

Ming Garden Buffet

Butch's
Kroger

From intersection of
Main & Broad,
A.T. is 3.7 mi;
🚶 Rockfish Gap
Outfitters
0.8 mi

Oak Ave
14th St
Pine Ave
Maple Ave
Walnut Ave
Market Ave
Arch Ave

Belle Hearth B&B

Wayne Ave
Grace Lutheran

South River

Royal Mart

💻 Library 540-942-6746, M-F 9-9, Sa 9-5

YMCA showers & tenting

1.5 mi

81
VA

SoBo	NoBo	The A.T. Guide		Elev
1318.1	866.1	Skyline 95.3, Sawmill Run Overlook	🅿️	2200
1316.7	867.5	Turk Mountain Trail to west.		2628
1316.5	867.7	Skyline 94.1, Turk Gap.	N38 7.740 W78 47.092 P	2600
1314.5	869.7	Skyline 92.4.		3100
1314.1	870.1	Wildcat Ridge Trail east to Skyline 92.1	N38 8.904 W78 46.477 P	2915
1311.4	872.8	Skyline 90.0, spur trail to east leads to Riprap parking area.	P	2760
1311.0	873.2	Riprap Trail branches to west		2986
1310.3	873.9	Skyline 88.9.		2623
1308.6	875.6	Skyline 87.4, Black Rock Gap, Paine Run Trail.	N38 12.398 W78 44.974 P	2321
1308.4	875.8	Skyline 87.2.		2397
1307.9	876.3	**Blackrock Hut** (0.2E) 40.8◄25.0◄13.0◄►13.2►21.4►33.8.	☾♦⚲(6)	2758
1307.5	876.7	Trayfoot Mountain Trail to west		3092
1307.4	876.8	Blackrock, views from summit, which is skirted by the AT		3108
1306.8	877.4	Blackrock parking area.	N38 13.331 W78 43.992 P	2940
1306.3	877.9	Skyline 84.3.		2800
1306.2	878.0	Jones Run parking	N38 13.805 W78 43.577 P	2808
1305.6	878.6	Two trails west to Dundo Campground (primitive, reserved for group use)		2771
1304.9	879.3	Skyline 82.9, Browns Gap	N38 14.424 W78 42.653 P	2597
1304.3	879.9	Big Run Loop Trail to west		2843
1304.0	880.2	Skyline 82.2.		2791
1303.5	880.7	West to Doyles River Parking Overlook, Skyline 81.9	N38 14.806 W78 41.686 P	2853
1302.7	881.5	Doyles River Traill, west to Skyline 81.1, east to Doyles River Cabin (locked) and 0.1E to falls	N38 15.254 W78 40.982 P♦	2869
1301.9	882.3	Trail to Loft Mtn amphitheater.	◄(pg.85)	3188
1301.7	882.5	Trail to **Loft Mtn Campground** (go here if camping).	◄♦(pg.85)	3275
1301.2	883.0	Trail to **Loft Mtn Campground**	◄♦(pg.85)	3305
1300.8	883.4	Powerline		3248
1300.6	883.6	Trail to **Loft Mtn Store** (in view to west).	(pg.85)	3175
1299.4	884.8	Frazier Discovery Trail 0.3W to **Loft Mtn Wayside**	♦	3307
1299.3	884.9	Frazier Discovery Trail to west.		3314
1298.4	885.8	Trail to 0.5W to **Loft Mtn Wayside** (flatter than FDT), Ivy Creek spring 0.1W	♦	2991

SoBo	NoBo	Feature	Elev
1297.7	886.5	Cross Ivy Creek	2585
1297.1	887.1	View to west	2965
1296.3	887.9	West to Skyline 77.5, Ivy Creek Overlook	2893
1294.7	889.5	**Pinefield Hut** (0.1E), Skyline Dr (0.1W). 38.2◀26.2◀13.2◀▶8.2▶20.6▶32.1 Spring on trail to shelter and 50 yards behind. Both unreliable. Campsites uphill, beyond shelter.	2493
1294.5	889.7	Skyline 75.2, Pinefield Gap. N38 17.411 W78 38.511 [P]	2590
1293.7	890.5	Weaver Mountain.	2863
1292.6	891.6	Skyline 73.2, Simmons Gap Simmons Gap ranger station on paved road 0.2E from where AT crosses Skyline. Water available at pump outside buildings.	2250
1289.8	894.4	View east to Powell Gap Hollow	2605
1289.3	894.9	Skyline 69.9, Powell Gap	2294
1287.7	896.5	Skyline 68.6, Smith Roach Gap	2600
1286.5	897.7	**Hightop Hut** (0.1W), reliable spring 0.1 from shelter 34.4◀21.4◀8.2◀▶12.4▶23.9▶34.8	3200
1286.0	898.2	Spring east of AT	3536
1285.8	898.4	View to west from flank of Hightop Mtn	3526
1284.4	899.8	Skyline 66.7 N38 20.691 W78 33.183 [P]	2650
1283.1	901.1	Skyline 65.5, Swift Run Gap, bridge over US 33, **Elkton, VA** (6.4W) (pg.85) US 33 access rd north of bridge 0.1W to phone, water & SNP self-registration	2367
1281.5	902.7	Saddleback Mtn Trail to east.	3030
1280.5	903.7	Trail 0.1E to spring at former South River Shelter site	2967
1280.0	904.2	South River Picnic Area 0.1W. N38 22.904 W78 31.151 [P] (0.1W)	2895
1279.6	904.6	Falls Trail to east. South River Fire Road.	2891
1278.0	906.2	Baldface Mountain	3627

Backcountry Permits are required for overnight hikes within the park. There is no charge for the permit and there is a fine for not having one. Permits are available from self-registration sites at the south and north entrance of the AT into SNP, from any park visitor center, or by mail (see contact information above).

Concrete 4"x4" signposts are used to mark intersections. Information is stamped into an aluminum band at the top of the post.

What is known as a "shelter" on most of the AT is called a "hut" in Shenandoah, and three-sided day-use-only structures are called "shelters." When overnighting in the park, please use the huts or designated campsites, which are usually near the huts.

If you cannot tent in a designated campsite, seek a preexisting campsite; if one cannot be found, follow LNT principles of dispersed camping. Tenting at a new location is limited to one night. Backcountry stay is limited to 14 consecutive nights; two at any one location. Campsites other than those designated must be:

- One quarter mile from any park facility (roads, campgrounds, lodges, visitor centers, and picnic areas).
- 10 yards from any water source.
- 50 yards from other camping parties, building ruins, or "no camping" signs.
- Not within designated no camping locations.

Groups are limited to 10. Campfires are only permitted at pre-constructed fire rings at the huts. Pets must be leashed.

ARAMARK operates a number of lodges, camp stores and restaurants along the Skyline drive, many readily accessible from the trail.
Hiker discounts for lodging at Lewis Mt. Cabins, Big Meadows Lodge, and Skyland Resort are available at www.visitshenandoah.com/mvs or by calling 1-800-778-2871, (press option 1, then press option 2 and ask for code SHMVS).

The Park Service operates campgrounds. Call 877-444-6777 or visit ⟨www.recreation.gov⟩ to reserve campsites. All campsites accommodate 2 tents and up to 6 persons. All have coin operated laundry and showers except Mathews Arm. Many facilities are closed November-May and all are closed December-March.

Lodges and campgrounds are typically full on weekends. A small number of unreserved walk-in tentsites are available on a first-come, first-served basis at all campgrounds except Lewis Mtn.

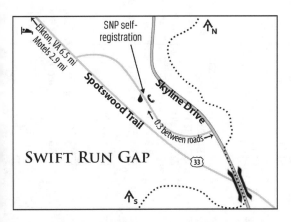

LOFT MOUNTAIN CAMPGROUND

Wayside

Skyline Drive

Approx. 4.4 miles of A.T. shown on map

Doyles River Cabin

Trail to ampitheater

Campstore

Trails to campground

2.0 mi

SWIFT RUN GAP

Elkton, VA 6.5 mi
Motels 2.9 mi

SNP self-registration

Spotswood Trail

Skyline Drive

0.3 between roads

33

| 882.5, 883.0 | Loft Mountain Campground |
| 883.6 | Loft Mountain Store |

Loft Mountain Campground Campsites $15. AT skirts the campground, and several short side trails lead to campsites and the camp store. Showers, laundry and long term resupply available from camp store. Open 5/13 - 10/30.

Loft Mountain Wayside 1.1 miles from camp store, serves B/L/D, short-order menu, 9-5:30, 7 days. Open 4/22 - 11/6.

901.1   US 33, Swift Run Gap. US 33 is also known as Spotswood Trail. The AT crosses over US 33 on the Skyline Drive. North of the bridge, take access road to the west to reach US 33.

(2.9W):

Country View Motel 540-298-0025 $50 most rooms hold 4. shuttle possible back to trail and to Elkton. Pets okay. Maildrops for guests: 19974 Spotswood Trail, Elkton, VA 22827.

Misty Mountain Motel 540-298-9771, $43–$53 1–4 people, no pets, all rooms nonsmoking.

(3.2W):

Swift Run Camping 540-298-8086, $20 campsite, laundry, pool, and snack bar.

Bear Mountain Grocery with deli, daily 6am–9pm.

(6.5W): *Elkton, VA 22827*

M-F 8:30-4:30, Sa 9-11, 540-298-7772

Food Lion, **O'Dell's Grocery**

several fast-food restaurants, pharmacy, ATM.

SoBo	NoBo	The A.T. Guide	Elev	
1276.8	907.4	Spring, Pocosin Cabin (locked), Parking on Skyline. .N38 24.813 W78 29.379	3150	P ♦
1276.7	907.5	Trail west to parking on Skyline	3159	P ♦
1274.9	909.3	West to **Lewis Mtn Campground & Cabins** (pg.88)	3448	
1274.8	909.4	West to **Lewis Mtn Campground**. N38 26.234 W78 28.737 (pg.88)	3396	P
1274.1	910.1	**Bearfence Mountain Hut** (0.1E), unreliable spring 33.8◄20.6◄12.4◄▶11.5▶22.4▶26.8	3212	P ⟩ ◊ ⌒(6)⊏(6)
1273.4	910.8	Bearfence Mountain Loop Trail, two intersections 0.2 mile apart, views 0.1E.	3529	
1272.9	911.3	Skyline 56.4, Bearfence Mtn Trail, parking 0.1W. N38 27.141 W78 28.015	3405	P
1271.5	912.7	Skyline 55.1, Bootens Gap N38 28.049 W78 27.440	3243	P
1271.0	913.2	Laurel Prong Trail to east.	3530	
1270.6	913.6	Hazeltop.	3812	
1268.7	915.5	Skyline 52.8, Milam Gap, parking to east. N38 29.928 W78 26.741	3300	P
1268.1	916.1	Spring, No camping in Big Meadows clearing within sight of Skyline Dr	3259	♦
1267.6	916.6	Tanners Ridge Rd (gravel), cemetery	3324	
1267.0	917.2	Lewis Spring & Road, Lewis Falls 0.5W N38 27.141 W78 28.015 (pg.88) Gravel road 0.2E to Skyline, then left 0.2 to **Big Meadows Wayside**	3340	P ♦
1266.5	917.7	Rock outcropping, view	3633	🛈
1266.1	918.1	Trail to **Big Meadows Lodge**, Lewis Falls 0.5W (pg.88)	3584	
1265.7	918.5	Trail east to **Big Meadows Campground** (pg.88)	3585	
1265.5	918.7	David Spring 20 yards west	3490	♦
1265.3	918.9	Stream.	3409	♦
1264.5	919.7	Fishers Gap, Skyline 49.3 to east, maintenance road	3050	🛈
1264.3	919.9	Franklin Cliffs, view.	3046	
1263.2	921.0	Trail to Spitler Knoll parking, 4 cars N38 32.892 W78 24.828	3246	P
1262.6	921.6	**Rock Spring Hut** (0.2W) 32.1◄23.9◄11.5◄▶10.9▶15.3▶28.4 Locked cabin in front.	3530	⟩ ♦ ◊ ⌒(9)⊏(8)
1262.3	921.9	Trail east to Hawksbill Mountain. No camping on summit (anywhere above 3600')	3644	
1261.3	922.9	Hawksbill Gap, parking to east. N38 33.776 W78 22.952	3361	P ♦
1260.8	923.4	Stream, trail to Crescent Rock Overlook, parking to east.	3444	P 🛈
1260.0	924.2	Spring	3337	♦
1259.1	925.1	Spring.	3458	♦
1258.8	925.4	Skyland stables, service road	3550	P
1258.2	926.0	Trail to **Skyland Resort & Restaurant** (0.1E) (pg.88)	3763	P P
1258.1	926.1	Skyland service road north.	3712	
1257.6	926.6	Trail to Stony Man Summit (0.2W)	3837	
1257.1	927.1	Little Stony Man Cliffs, overlook to west.	3561	🛈

NoBo	Feature	Elev
927.4	Passamaquoddy Trail	3417
927.7	Spur trail to parking	3236
928.1	Stony Man Overlook	3086
928.5	Nicholson Hollow Trail	3109
928.6	Crusher Ridge Trail	3188
929.2	Corbin Cabin Trail	3125
929.7	Powerline	3304
930.3	Pinnacles Picnic Area & Parking, restrooms, water from faucet. **P** 🏕♦	3381
930.5	East to Skyline 36.4, side trail to Jewell Hollow Overlook	3293
930.8	Leading Ridge Trail to west.	3364
931.5	The Pinnacle	3730
932.5	**Byrds Nest #3 Hut,** spring 0.4E on service road. ♦ ☽ ⊏ (8)	3279
	34.8◀22.4◀10.9 ▶4.4▶17.5▶28.0	
932.9	View	3344
933.2	Meadows Spring Trail to east ♦ (0.3E)	3376
933.8	Overlook, Mary's Rock to west	3478
934.7	Spring. ♦	2875
935.5	Trail to Panorama RR parking, powerline	2342
935.7	US 211, Thornton Gap, **Luray, VA** (9W). **P** 🏕♦	2307
935.8	Skyline 31.2 (pg.88-89)	2312
936.9	**Pass Mountain Hut** (1939) (0.2E). ☽ ♦ ⊏ (8)	2812
	26.8◀15.3◀4.4 ▶13.1▶23.6▶31.7 2 bear poles, 2 privies, and 8 tent sites.	
	Piped spring 15 yards behind shelter.	
937.7	Pass Mountain	3052
938.8	Beahms Gap Overlook, parking to east **P** 🖻	2490
939.2	Spring to west ♦	2453
940.1	Neighbor Mtn Trail, Byrds Nest #4 day use picnic area. ♦ (0.5E)	2681
940.9	Jeremys Run Overlook, parking to east **P** 🖻	2341
943.8	Stream, Jeremys Run Trail	2232
944.3	**Elkwallow Wayside** (and Gap) 0.1E on side trail or on Skyline 23.9 🏕 ☏ ⊁	2480
	Grill B/L/D, limited groceries, vending outside, 9-7 Early April-Early Oct.	
	Frost-free pump at picnic area south of wayside.	
945.0	Range View Cabin (locked) 0.1E ♦ (0.1E)	2984
945.8	Skyline 21.9, Rattlesnake Point Overlook 🖻	3104
946.1	Tuscarora Trail to **Mathews Arm Campground** (0.7W) ♦	3400
	Primitive campground; no services. Tent sites $14.	
946.8	Skyline 21.1, Hogback parking **P** 🖻	3350
947.1	Skyline 20.8, Hogback Overlook 🖻	3350

GPS coordinates:
- N38 36.354 W78 21.983 **P** (927.4)
- N38 36.735 W78 21.747 **P** (927.7)
- N38 39.627 W78 19.326 **P** (935.5)
- N38 42.747 W78 19.800 **P** (940.9)

SoBo: 1256.8, 1256.5, 1256.1, 1255.7, 1255.6, 1255.0, 1254.5, 1253.9, 1253.7, 1253.4, 1252.7, 1251.7, 1251.3, 1251.0, 1250.4, 1249.5, 1248.7, 1248.5, 1248.4, 1247.3, 1246.5, 1245.4, 1245.0, 1244.1, 1243.3, 1240.4, 1239.9, 1239.2, 1238.4, 1237.8, 1237.4, 1237.1

909.3, 909.4   Lewis Mountain Campground
🛏 🏕 ⚿ ⚿ ⛺ **Lewis Mountain Campground and Cabins**
(see page 84 for cabin discount) 540-999-2255, campsites
$16. Reservations, 800-999-4714, Lewis Mountain Camp
store, open 9-7 in summer. Open 4/8 - 11/6.

917.2   Lewis Spring Road (See map for easiest access.)
918.1   Big Meadows Lodge
🍴 🚉 **Big Meadows Wayside** B/L/D, Fuel/oz at gas station. Open 3/18 - 11/27.
🛏 🍴 **$** **Big Meadows Lodge** *(see page 84 for room discount)* There are lodge
rooms, cabins, suites, and motel-type rooms, reservations required. Some pet-
friendly rooms. B: 7:30-10, L: 12-2, D: 5:30-9. Open 5/19 - 11/6.

918.5   Big Meadows Campground
⛺ ♦♦ ⚿ ⛺ **Big Meadows Campground** Tentsites $20 for 2 tents and 6 persons,
self-register after-hours. Coin-op laundry and showers, Open 3/25 - 11/27.

926.0   Side trail to Skyland
🛏 🍴 **$** ♦♦ **Skyland Resort and Restaurant** 800-999-4714
(see page 84 for room discount) Rates seasonal, reservations required. Dining
room hours B: 7:30-10, L: 12-2, D: 5:30-9, nightly entertainment. Snack foods
and sodas sold at gift shop and vending machines. Open 3/31 - 11/27.

935.7   US 211, Thornton Gap
🛏 🍴 📶 (4.5W on US 211) to **Brookside Cabins and Restaurant** 540-743-5698
$85-$195, luxury cabins, Homestyle restaurant with AYCE L/D buffet daily,
weekend breakfast buffet. Closed Dec-early March, open 7 days 8am-8pm the
rest of the year. Open till 9pm in summer.
🛏 🏕 🍴 🏨 ⛺ 🍸 (5.3W) **Yogi Bear's Jellystone Park** 540-743-4002 ⟨www.
campluray.com⟩ cabins $55-$190, tent sites $37-59, two-night minimum on
weekends. Pets at tentsites only. Memorial to Labor Day snack shop serving
hamburgers, hot dogs, pizza on wkdays only; breakfast on wkends. Coin
laundry, campstore, pool.
🛏 ⛺ 📶 🖥 (6.9W) **Days Inn** 540-743-4521 $80-$300, pool, pets $10.
        Luray, VA 22835 (9W) Farmer's market held on Saturdays.
🛏 📶 🖥 **Budget Inn** 540-743-5176 $49.95S/up, $10EAP, pets $10.
🛏 **Best Value Cardinal Inn** 888-648-4633 Call for rates, no pets.
🛏 📶 **Luray Caverns Motels** East and West Buildings 540-743-4536, 888-941-
4531 ⟨www.luraycaverns.com⟩, 20% discount coupon on food/merchandise at

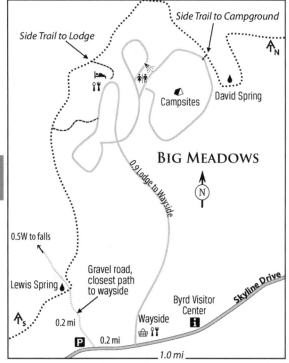

Side Trail to Campground

Side Trail to Lodge

N

Campsites

David Spring

BIG MEADOWS

N

0.9 Lodge to Wayside

0.5W to falls

Lewis Spring

Gravel road,
closest path
to wayside

Byrd Visitor
Center

Wayside

S

0.2 mi

0.2 mi

P

1.0 mi

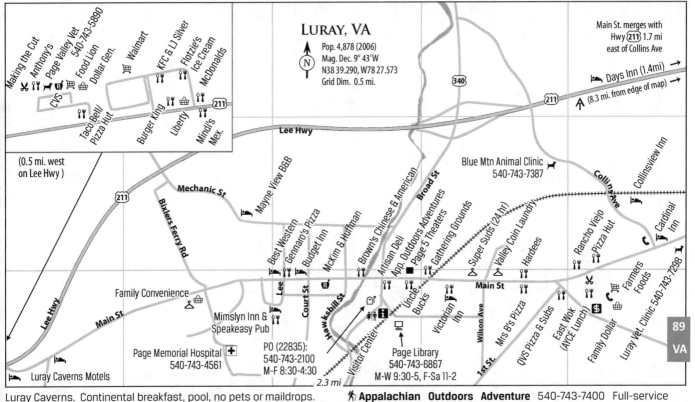

LURAY, VA

Pop. 4,878 (2006)
Mag. Dec. 9° 43′W
N38 39.290, W78 27.573
Grid Dim. 0.5 mi.

Main St. merges with Hwy 211 1.7 mi east of Collins Ave

Days Inn (1.4mi)
(8.3 mi. from edge of map)

Inset (0.5 mi. west on Lee Hwy): Making the Cut, Anthony's, Page Valley Vet 540-743-5890, Food Lion, Dollar Gen., CVS, Walmart, KFC & LJ Silver, Flotzie's Ice Cream, McDonalds, Taco Bell, Pizza Hut, Burger King, Liberty, Mindi's Mex.

Blue Mtn Animal Clinic 540-743-7387

Collinsview Inn

Cardinal Inn

Rancho Viejo, Pizza Hut

Luray Vet. Clinic 540-743-7298

Farmers Foods

Family Dollar

East Wok (AYCE Lunch)

QVS Pizza & Subs

Mrs B's Pizza

Lee Hwy

Mechanic St

Mayne View B&B

Best Western, Gennaro's Pizza, Budget Inn, McKim & Huffman, Brown's Chinese & American, Artisan Deli, App. Outdoors Adventures, Page 5 Theaters, Gathering Grounds, Super Suds (24 hr), Valley Coin Laundry, Hardees

Broad St

Main St

Wilson Ave

1st St

Hawksbill St

Court St

Lee

Bixlers Ferry Rd

Family Convenience

Mimslyn Inn & Speakeasy Pub

Page Memorial Hospital 540-743-4561

PO (22835): 540-743-2100 M-F 8:30-4:30

Visitor Center

Page Library 540-743-6867 M-W 9:30-5, F-Sa 11-2

Uncle Bucks

Victorian Inn

Luray Caverns Motels

Main St

Lee Hwy

2.3 mi

89
VA

Luray Caverns. Continental breakfast, pool, no pets or maildrops.
Best Western 540-743-6511 ⟨www.bestwesternvirginia.com/luray-hotels⟩ Prices vary, call for rates. Pool. Pets $22.
Woodruff Inns B&B 540-743-1494 $109/up, includes breakfast.
Skyline Inn & Suites 540-743-4575 $59.95D+tax, pets $10.

Appalachian Outdoors Adventure 540-743-7400 Full-service outfitter, Coleman/alcohol/oz. M-Th 10-6, F-Sa 10-8, Su 1-5.
Speakeasy at Mimslyn Inn Dinners 4-10pm, full bar and sometimes entertainment.
Visitor Center 540-743-3915 M-Sa 9-5, Su 12-4.

SoBo	NoBo	The A.T. Guide	Elev	
1235.9	948.3	Skyline 19.7, Little Hogback parking 50 yards east	3058	🅿
1235.8	948.4	Little Hogback Mountain, view	3050	📷
1235.3	948.9	Skyline 18.8	2843	
1234.2	950.0	**Gravel Springs Hut** (0.2E), spring en route to shelter. 28.4◄17.5◄13.1◄►10.5►18.6►24.1	2658	☽ ♦ ⌂ (8)
1234.0	950.2	Skyline 17.7, Gravel Springs Gap	2666	🅿 N38 46.068 W78 14.010
1233.2	951.0	View west	3077	
1232.9	951.3	South Marshall Mountain	3212	📷
1232.4	951.8	Skyline 15.9, parking to west.	3050	🅿
1231.7	952.5	North Marshall Mountain, view	3368	📷
1230.8	953.4	Hogwallow Flat	2966	
1230.2	954.0	Skyline 14.2, Hogwallow Gap	2739	🅿 N38 47.388 W78 11.319
1228.5	955.7	Skyline 12.3, Jenkins Gap, parking to east.	2400	🅿 N38 48.389 W78 10.846
1227.6	956.6	Compton Springs	2700	♦
1227.2	957.0	Compton Peak	2909	
1226.4	957.8	Skyline 10.4, Compton Gap parking	2425	🅿 N38 49.414 W78 10.234
1224.6	959.6	Compton Gap Trail, **Front Royal Hostel** (0.5E)	2350	(pg. 93)
1224.4	959.8	SNP permit self-registration station.	2332	
1223.7	960.5	**Tom Floyd Shelter** 28.0◄23.6◄10.5◄►8.1►13.6►18.1	1961	☽ ♦ ⌂ (6)
1223.6	960.6	Ginger Spring to west	1845	♦
1222.2	962.0	VA 602, stream	1150	♦
1220.8	963.4	US 522, small parking area, **Front Royal, VA** (4.0W)	950	🅿 (pg.92-93)
1220.0	964.2	Bear Hollow Creek	1099	♦
1217.4	966.8	Forest Service Rd	1849	♦
1217.2	967.0	Sealock Spring	1767	
1216.5	967.7	Powerline	1672	

SoBo	NoBo	Features	Elev
1215.6	968.6	**Jim & Molly Denton Shelter,** Spring on AT ☾ ☀ ◐ ◐ ⌂(8) 31.7◄18.6◄8.1◄►5.5►10.0►18.4 Excellent shelter, porch, chairs, solar shower.	1343
1214.5	969.7	Stream. ●	1059
1214.4	969.8	VA 638	1083
1212.6	971.6	VA 55, Manassas Gap. AT passes under I-66 on Tucker's Lane. N38 54.550 W78 3.199 P (pg. 93)	800
1212.4	971.8	Footbridge, stream ●	824
1211.1	973.1	Stone wall.	1433
1210.1	974.1	**Manassas Gap Shelter** ◐ ◐ ⌂(6) 24.1◄13.6◄5.5◄►4.5►12.9►19.8 Cables. Reliable spring downhill to right of shelter on side trail. Blue-blazed trail south of shelter leads 0.9W to VA 638.	1696
1208.8	975.4	Spring. ●	1736
1208.1	976.1	Trico Tower Trail 0.4W to tower.	2102
1205.6	978.6	**Dicks Dome Shelter** (0.2E) 18.1◄10.0◄4.5◄►8.4►15.3►29.4. ◐ ◐ ⌂(4) Whiskey Hollow Creek in front of shelter (treat water). Stream on AT 75 yards north of shelter side trail.	1409
1205.2	979.0	Powerline.	1632
1204.6	979.6	Spring.	1772
1204.4	979.8	Signal Knob parking on VA 638 / Fire Rd 0.1W. ● P N38 59.112 W77 59.980	1851
1203.5	980.7	Boundary to Sky Meadows State Park.	1851
1203.3	980.9	Bench, 1.7E to **Sky Meadows State Park Visitors Center** H 🛉 ⚐ ● ● 800-933-PARK Open W-Su, 8-5, restrooms, soda machine, 12 sites & primitive group camping, $9PP, reservation required, campers must arrive before dusk.	1821
1202.5	981.7	View 0.4E on Ambassador Whitehouse Trail ◉	1598
1200.9	983.3	Two footbridges, streams ●	914
1200.8	983.4	Ashby Gap, US 50/17	960
1200.6	983.6	Trail 0.1E to parking on VA 601, Blueridge Mtn Rd P N39 0.942 W77 57.718	1090
1199.4	984.8	Stream. ●	1142
1198.8	985.4	Stream. ●	1042
1198.5	985.7	Trail west to Myron Glaser Cabin (locked)	1122
1198.0	986.2	Stream. ●	1010
1197.6	986.6	Fishers Hill Trail to west	1107
1197.2	987.0	**Rod Hollow Shelter** (0.1W) 18.4◄12.9◄8.4◄►6.9►21.0►36.6. ● ◐ ◐ ⌂(8) Piped spring left of shelter. Stream on AT south of side trail.	917
1196.8	987.4	Stream, Fishers Hill to west, south end of The Roller Coaster 13.5 miles of tightly packed ascents and descents. ●	824
1195.5	988.7	Spring at Bolden Hollow	871

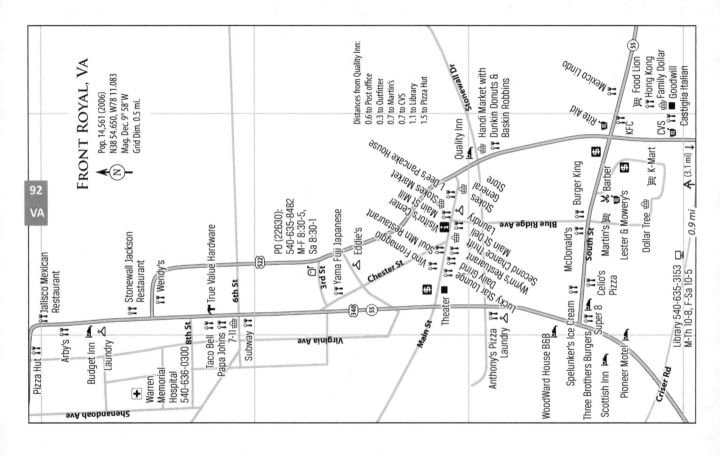

FRONT ROYAL, VA

Pop. 14,561 (2006)
N38 54.650, W78 11.083
Mag. Dec. 9° 58'W
Grid Dim. 0.5 mi.

Distances from Quality Inn:
0.6 to Post office
0.3 to Outfitter
0.7 to Martin's
0.7 to CVS
1.1 to Library
1.5 to Pizza Hut

PO (22630):
540-635-8482
M-F 8:30-5,
Sa 8:30-1

Library 540-635-3153
M-Th 10-8, F-Sa 10-5

Warren Memorial Hospital
540-636-0300

92
VA

Jalisco Mexican Restaurant
Stonewall Jackson Restaurant
Wendy's
True Value Hardware
6th St
522
3rd St
Yama Fuji Japanese
Eddie's
Vino Fromaggio
Soul Mtn Restaurant
Chester St
Main St Mill
Stokes Market
L Dee's Pancake House
Visitor's Center
Main St Deli
Second Chance Thrift
Wynn's Restaurant
Daily Grind
Stokes General Store
Blue Ridge Ave
Laundry
Quality Inn
Handi Market with Dunkin Donuts & Baskin Robbins
Stonewall Dr
Mexico Lindo
Rite Aid
55
Food Lion
Hong Kong
Family Dollar
Goodwill
Castiglia Italian
KFC
CVS
K-Mart
Burger King
Barber
Dollar Tree
Lester & Mowery's
Martin's
South St
McDonald's
Celio's Pizza
Super 8
Spelunker's Ice Cream
Three Brothers Burgers
Scottish Inn
WoodWard House B&B
Anthony's Pizza
Laundry
Lucky Star Lounge
Theater
340
55
Main St
Virginia Ave
Pioneer Motel
Criser Rd
(3.1 mi)
0.9 mi

Pizza Hut
Arby's
Budget Inn
Laundry
8th St
Taco Bell
Papa Johns
7-11
Subway
Shenandoah Ave

959.6   Compton Gap Trail

🏚 🏕 🚌 ✉ **Front Royal Terrapin Station Hostel** (0.5E)
540-539-0509, 540-631-0777 The Compton Gap Trail intersection is marked with a cement post labeled "VA 610/Chester Gap." Go east (straight ahead for NoBo) on the Compton Gap Trail 0.5 mile to paved road. Hostel is first house on the left. Enter around back through marked gate (residential neighborhood, please respect noise level). Open May 1-June 30, 2012, includes bunk with mattress & sheets, shower, soap, shower clothes, laundry, free morning shuttle to town for groceries, P.O. etc. Cost $19/night, $35/2nights, $50/3nights. Three night max unless trail injury. Fuel, snacks, sodas, ice cream & oven pizza on site. Free slackpacking for multi-night guests; shuttles available for all. Hikers only, picture ID required, reservations encouraged. Owned by Mike Evans (AT '95, PCT '98), ⟨gratefulgg@hotmail.com⟩. Guest maildrops: 304 Chester Gap Rd, Chester Gap, VA 22623.

963.4   US 522

Front Royal 22630 (4W) *(more services on map)*

🅷 🚻 **Visitor Center** 540-635-5788 7 days, 9-5pm.
Helpful and usually has hiker goodie bags. Restrooms, water.

🏨 🏕 ✉ **Quality Inn** 540-635-3161 $65 S/D, $10EAP (up to 4), pets $15. Pool, coin laundry, shuttle can be arranged back to trail. This is the first hotel you pass on the way into town, and may be the best choice considering location, services and price. Maildrops: 10 Commerce Avenue, Front Royal, VA 22630.

🏨 📶 🖥 **Woodward House B&B** 540-635-7010 $110D includes breakfast, pickup and return to trail.

🏨 📶 🖥 **Super 8** 540-636-4888 $56.65S, $5EAP, pets $10.

🏨 📶 **Pioneer Motel** 540-635-4784 $39S+tax

🏨 📶 **Scottish Inn** 540-636-6168 $50/up

🏨 📶 **Blue Ridge Motel** 540-636-7200 $38-45S, $45-55D, no pets.

🍴 **Lucky Star Lounge** L/D variety, some vegetarian, live music.

🏪 **Stokes Market** Wonderfully random selction of goods & foods.
🚌 **Mobile Mike's** 540-539-0509 shuttles and more.

971.6   VA 55, Manassas Gap, **Linden, VA 22642** (1.2W)
🏤 M-F 8-12 & 1-5, Sa 8-12, 540-636-9936, packages held only 15 days.
🏪 **Monterey Convenience Store**

996.9 Bears Den Rocks

🏚 🛶 🏠 🚿 🏕 🅿 🖥 ✉ **Bears Den Hostel and Trail Center** 540-554-8708 ⟨www.bearsdencenter.org⟩ The castle-like stone lodge is ATC owned and PATC operated. Bunk $15, tenting $10PP with full house privileges which include cooking & shower. Hiker Special: Bunk, laundry, pizza, ice cream, and a soda for $27.50 plus tax. Check in and store hours are from 5-9pm, but the hiker room with lounge, internet, phone, and sodas is open 24 hours/day. Short term resupply available and fuel/oz. Short-term secured parking $3/day. Accepts credit cards. Maildrops: Bears Den Hostel, 18393 Blue Ridge Mountain Rd, Bluemont, VA 20135. Hosts the **PA Ruck** Jan 27-29.

997.5   Snickers Gap, VA 7 & 679
The AT crosses VA 7 near its intersection with State Route 679, On the north of VA 7, 679 curves away on a westerly path. Take 679 west to reach the restaurants and store listed below. To reach the post office, take VA 7 0.8 mile east, then turn right on route 734 and go another 0.8 mile.

Bluemont, VA 20135 (1.7E)
🏤 M-F 8:30-12 & 1-5, Sa 8:30-12, 540-554-4537
🍴 (0.3W) **Horseshoe Curve Restaurant** 540-554-8291 M-Sa 12-9, good pub food.
🍴 (0.9W) **Pine Grove Restaurant** 540-554-8126 Su, M 7-1, W-Sa 7-8, closed Tuesday.
🏪 (1.1W) **The Village Market** 540-554-8422 M-Sa 7-7.

SoBo	NoBo	The A.T. Guide	Elev
		Elev	800
			1140
			1034
			1276
			836
			931
			1311
			752
			865
			1305
			1000
			872
			1140
			1166
			1264
			1387
			1200
			1380
			1650
			1472
			1537
			1438
			1334
1193.9	990.3	Footbridge, Morgan Mill Stream, campsite	800
1193.5	990.7	VA 605, Morgan Mill Rd (gravel)	1140
1192.8	991.4	Stream.	1034
1191.8	992.4	Buzzard Hill, AT east of summit	1276
1191.2	993.0	Two streams	836
1190.3	993.9	**Sam Moore Shelter** (1990) 19.8◄15.3◄6.9►14.1►29.7►33.8 ⟩ ◭ ⌂ (6) Springs in front of shelter and to the left. Several tent sites to left of shelter.	931
1189.8	994.4	Campsite	1311
1189.0	995.2	Spout Run Ravine, stream	752
1187.8	996.4	Footbridge, stream, campsite 60 yards north on AT	865
1187.3	996.9	Bears Den Rocks, **Bears Den Hostel** (0.2E), view north on AT ▣ (pg. 93)	1305
1186.7	997.5	Snickers Gap, VA 7 & 679, N39 6.919 W77 50.849 **P** (pg.93) **Bluemont, VA** (1.7E)	1000
1185.8	998.4	Stream.	872
1184.2	1000.0	**VA-WV** border	1140
1184.1	1000.1	Spring	1166
1183.9	1000.3	Raven Rocks, Crescent Rock 0.1E, view ▣	1264
1183.7	1000.5	Campsite, trail east to tower.	1387
1183.4	1000.8	The Roller Coaster (north end); 13.5 miles of ascents and descents Sand Spring to west, good water source, Devils Racecourse boulder field to north	1200
1180.6	1003.6	Wilson Gap	1380
1179.4	1004.8	Two trails 0.2E to N39 11.259 W77 47.866 **P** ⌕ ◭ 🚿 **Blackburn AT Center** 540-338-9028. PATC caretaker in main building. Free hiker hostel in small cabin near building. Wood-burning stove, solar shower on lawn, pay phone on porch, water from hose, picnic tables. Open year-round.	1650
1177.7	1006.5	Laurel Springs, campsite north on AT	1472
1176.7	1007.5	Buzzard Rocks	1537
1176.2	1008.0	**David Lesser Memorial Shelter** (0.1E) 29.4◄21.0◄14.1►15.6►19.7►24.7 Overflow camping area below shelter. Spring 0.2 mile downhill from shelter.	1438
1174.9	1009.3	Roadbed.	1334

SoBo	NoBo		Elev
1173.2	1011.0	Keys Gap, WV 9 ⛺🍴☎(0.3W) **Mountaineer Mini-Mart & Torlone's Pizza** ⛺ (0.3E) **Sweet Springs Country Store**	926
1171.6	1012.6	Powerline	923
1171.0	1013.2	Campsite ◨	1120
1169.3	1014.9	**VA-WV** border, Loudoun Heights, Loudoun Heights Trail to east	1134
1168.7	1015.5	WV 32, Chestnut Hill Rd	599
1167.8	1016.4	US 340, north end of Shenandoah River Bridge (pg.97)	336
1167.5	1016.7	Side trail to **Appalachian Trail Conservancy** (0.2W) (pg.97)	440
1167.1	1017.1	Jefferson Rock, view north to Potomac and Shenandoah Rivers 🖼	450
1166.9	1017.3	**Harpers Ferry, WV,** High Street N39 18.989 W77 45.350 **P** (pg.96-97)	297
1166.7	1017.5	Potomac River, Byron Memorial Footbridge, **WV-MD** border. North of river turn east on C&O Canal Towpath. No camping along AT section of towpath.	275
1165.5	1018.7	Pass under Sandy Hook Bridge, US 340. (pg.98)	289
1164.0	1020.2	C&O Canal Towpath north end, RR tracks, US 340 underpass. (pg.98)	266
1163.4	1020.8	From Keep Tryst Rd: **Knoxville, MD** (1.0W), **Brunswick, MD** (2.5E) **P** Weaverton Rd. N39 19.977 W77 40.993	392
1162.7	1021.5	Trail east to Weaverton Cliffs, view 🖼	880

❋ **Poison Ivy** – Vine that can grow as ground cover or that can cling to trees or other brush. Stems redden toward the end and terminate with 3 pointed-oval leaves.

SoBo	NoBo		Elev
1160.6	1023.6	**Ed Garvey Shelter** 36.6◄29.7◄15.6▼4.1▲9.1►16.6 Water on steep 0.4 mile trail in front of shelter. 2 tent sites north & south of shelter.)♦◨⊏(12)	1100
1158.8	1025.4	Brownsville Gap, roadbed	1080
1156.9	1027.3	Gapland Rd, Gathland State Park, War Correspondents Monument. Frost-free spigot by restrooms. Vending machines. No camping, no trash cans. 🏕♦	950
1156.5	1027.7	**Crampton Gap Shelter** (0.3E), intermittent spring 0.1S on AT 33.8◄19.7◄4.1▼5.0►12.5►20.7 NoBo: consider bringing water from Gathland SP in dry season.)♦◨⊏(6)	1185
1153.9	1030.3	Spring 0.5E, trail to Bear Spring Cabin (locked) ♦	1458

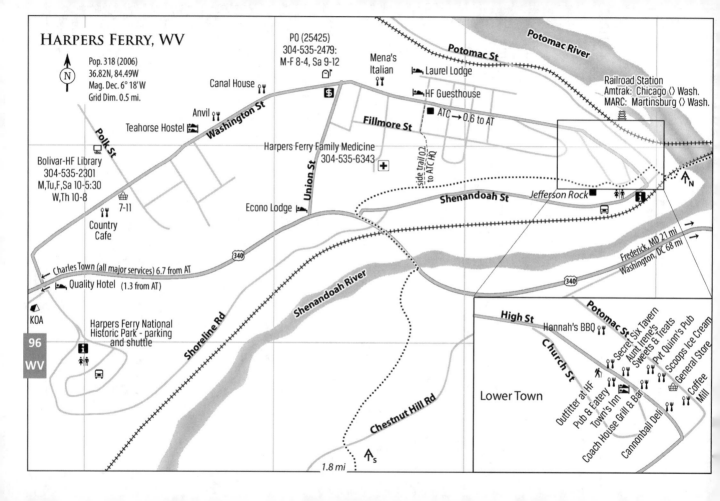

1016.4   US 340, Shenandoah River Bridge
For NoBos, this is the first of 3 opportunities to enter Harpers Ferry
Go west on 340 to the Quality Hotel, KOA, or to Charles Town; east to
Frederick. Stay on the AT for better access to Harpers Ferry.

🛏🏕📶🖥 **Econo Lodge** 304-535-6391 $70–$100, 10% thru-hiker
discount, cont B, one computer for guests, no pets.

🍺🛏🍴🚿🏕 (1.2W) **Harpers Ferry KOA** 304-535-6895 Hiker
discount 10% on camping rates that start at $36.50. One room cabin
for five $68/up. Shower only $5, coin laundry on-site.

🛏🍴🏕📶🖥 (1.3W) **Quality Hotel** 877-424-6423 or 304-535-6302
$88/up, pool, Vista Gourmet Restaurant.

Charles Town, WV 25414 (6W) All major services.
🏪🛒 **Walmart** with grocery and pharmacy 304-728-2720
➕ **Jefferson Urgent Care** 304-728-8533 M-F 9-7, Sa-Su 9-5
✈ **Jefferson Animal Hospital** 304-725-0428

Frederick, MD 21701 (20E) All major services.

1016.7   Side Trail to ATC HQ (0.2W)
✉ **Appalachian Trail Conservancy HQ** - 304-535-6331
⟨www.appalachiantrail.org⟩ Open year-round, 7 days a week 9-5,
closed Thanksgiving, Christmas and New Year's Day. If you're thru-
hiking or hiking the entire trail in sections, have your photo taken
for the album; a postcard version of this photo may be purchased
(first one is free for ATC members). Hiker lounge, register, scale, and
cold drinks inside, along with hats, shirts, maps, all ATC publications.
Coleman/denatured alcohol/oz for donation. There is an information
board on the front porch. Maildrops: (USPS) PO Box 807 or (FedEx/
UPS) 799 Washington St, Harpers Ferry, WV 25425.

1017.3   Harpers Ferry, WV 25425 (more services on map)
🏠🍴🏕🚌 **Town's Inn** 304-702-1872 ⟨www.TheTownsInn.com⟩ In
historic downtown building. Many options (hostel, private & semi-
private) ranging $30/up. Kitchen facilities with all rooms. Snack

shop: breakfast sandwiches, frozen pizza, ice cream. Laundry $5,
shuttles $1/mile, no maildrops, Visa/MC accepted. **Restaurant & PUB**
(adjacent) is open 6am-10pm every day.

🏠🏕🚌📶✉ **Teahorse Hostel** 304-535-6848
⟨www.teahorsehostel.com⟩ 0.5W of ATC. $28 per bunk plus tax
includes waffle breakfast. Laundry $5. Open 7 days Mar-Oct. No
pets, alcohol or smoking. Will deliver your pack to designated spots
to facilitate slackpacking. Coleman/white gas/denatured alcohol/oz.
Maildrops ($2 fee for non-guests): 1312 W. Washington St., Harpers
Ferry, WV 25425.

🛏📶 **Laurel Lodge** 304-535-2886 ⟨www.laurellodge.com⟩
$95-165 for 2 includes big breakfast, view overlooking Potomac.

🛏🏕📶🖥 **Harpers Ferry Guest House** 304-535-6955 Weekdays
$100, weekends $125 + tax for 2, includes breakfast and laundry.

🏃🏕 **The Outfitter at Harpers Ferry** 888-535-2087
Knowledgeable full service outfitter with good selection of shoes
and trail food. Shuttle referrals. Open daily 10–6.

🏕 **Harpers Ferry General Store** Hiker foods and bike rental.

🍴 **Stone Feather Farm** B/L/D Southwestern and American cuisine.

➕ **Foot and Ankle Care** Dr. Warren BeVards, 304-535-3040

🚻🅿 **Harpers Ferry National Historical Park** 304-535-6029 $6
entrance fee, long-term parking. Free shuttle bus to lower town.

🚌 **Pan Tran** 304-263-0876 Route to Charles Town M-Sa, $2.50.

🚆 **Amtrak** 800-USA-RAIL, "Capitol Limited" 10:55 and 4:05 every day
to Washington, DC Union Station. Rates vary with demand from $12
to $23. Departs for Washington at 11:25am, returns 4:05.

🚆 **Maryland Rail Commuter Service (MARC)** 410-539-5000 ⟨www.
mta.maryland.org⟩. "Brunswick Line" on weekdays to Washington DC
Union Station 5:51am and 6:56am, returns 4:55, 5:40 and 7:15pm.
Fares each way $12 + $2 surcharge paid in cash upon boarding.

The ATC works with the National Park Service, 31 volunteer maintaining clubs, and multiple other partners to engage the public in conserving this essential American resource.

Their website, www.AppalachianTrail.org, contains information about trail history and protection, hike planning, and trail conditions. If you hike all of the AT, you may complete a "2,000-miler" application and receive a certificate and patch from the ATC. You will also be added to their registry of 2,000-milers and your name will be printed in the March/April issue of ATC's member magazine, *AT Journeys* and on their website. The application is available from the website.

The ATC provided the bulk of the mileage data that appears in this book, and a portion of every book sold is donated to the organization. We encourage all AT hikers, particularly hikers who intend to hike all of the AT, to join or donate to the ATC.

1018.7   Sandy Hook Bridge, US 340
Sandy Hook Road is parallel to the towpath on the other side of the railroad tracks. It is illegal to cross RR tracks anywhere but at road crossings and designated locations. With that in mind, hikers should not take the short-cut side trail that crosses the tracks just south of the 340 overpass to get to Sandy Hook Rd, and then go right 0.3 mile to reach the Harpers Ferry Hostel.

1020.2   US 340, Keep Tryst Rd, *Knoxville, MD, 21758* (1W)
Motel, and convenience store 1.0 mile west; to get to the Hostel, go west 0.9 mile, then left 0.2 mile on Sandy Hook Road.
🏨 🍴 ⛺ 🏠 🚲 **P** 🛜🖥 ✉ **Harpers Ferry Hostel** 301-834-7652 ⟨www.harpersferryhostel.org⟩ Bunkhouse includes free pancake breakfast, shower, kitchen privileges, internet use, free coffee & tea. Thru-hikers ask for H.I. rate. Tenting $6PP. $5 shower w/towel for tenters and non-guests. Dogs on leash allowed if tenting. Laundry $4/load includes soap. Denatured alcohol/oz; please donate. Check in 3-10pm, check out by 11am. No drinking. Closed Aug 15–Apr 15. Shuttle service Apr-Aug, range includes Harpers Ferry, Washington D.C. BWI Airport, and Baltimore, parking $5/day. Maildrops: 19123 Sandy Hook Rd, Knoxville, MD 21758.
🛏 **Hillside Motel** 301-834-8144
⛺ 🍴 **⑤** **Hillside Station** 301-834-5300 Convenience store with pizza, wings, and more.

Brunswick, MD 21716
🏤 M-F 8:30-1 & 2-4:30, Sa 9-12, 301-834-9944 (2.5E)
🛏 🍴 ⛺ 🛜 ✉ (1.5E) **Green Country Inn and Green Country Diner** 301-834-9151 weekdays $59.39D, weekends $70.19D. Restaurant open 24/7 B/L/D. Credit cards accepted. Guest maildrops: 62 Souder Road, Brunswick, MD 21716.

Suggestions for Providing Trail Magic

The suggestions below incorporate Leave No Trace practices (www.LNT.org) to help those providing trail magic to have the most positive impact on hikers, the Trail, its plants and wildlife, and the volunteers who maintain and preserve it. The Appalachian Trail Conservancy and the Appalachian Long Distance Hikers Association endorse these suggestions.

Help conserve and maintain the Trail. The most essential service you can perform is to volunteer to maintain the Trail and overnight sites, or to monitor boundaries and resource conditions. To find out how or where you may assist, visit www.appalachiantrail.org or check with your local trail-maintaining club.

Locate events in developed areas on durable surfaces. Large gatherings in the backcountry can lead to the disturbance of wildlife habitat. Trail towns and local parks are better locations. Keep events small. Consider whether your event may be contributing to an overabundance of trail feeds in the local area or region.

Prepare and serve food safely. If you will be cooking or preparing food, check with the landowner to find an appropriate area and learn what food-safety or other regulations apply. Permits may be required. Charging a fee or asking for donations may not be allowed.

Be present if you provide food or drink. Unattended items and their packaging can harm wildlife that consume them. Unattended items are considered litter and they detract from the wildland character of backcountry environments. .

Restore the site. Leave the site as you found it—don't create a burden for Trail volunteers.

Advertise off-trail. Advertising—even noncommercial—is prohibited on the A.T.

Forgo alcoholic beverages. Don't risk the legality and liability associated with serving minors, over-serving adults, or the safety issues associated with intoxicated hikers.

Be hospitable to all. Be sure to make all trail users and volunteers feel welcome.

For more information, visit ATC's Web site at www.appalachiantrail.org/trailmagic.

The A.T. Guide

SoBo	NoBo	The A.T. Guide	Elev
1153.3	1030.9	White Rock Cliff, view.	1606
1153.1	1031.1	Lambs Knoll 50 yards west to tower, view.	1751
1152.0	1032.0	Lambs Knoll tower road (paved).	1374
1151.5	1032.7	Rocky Run Shelter (0.2W) 24.7◀9.1◀5.0▼7.5▶15.7▶20.6... Left fork on side trail to better water source & old shelter. Right to new shelter.	1011
1150.5	1033.7	Fox Gap, Reno Monument Rd (paved), South Mountain Creamery (2E).	1069
1149.7	1034.5	Dahlgren Backpack Campground. Large tenting area, picnic tables, restrooms; no fee. Note proximity to road.	980
1149.4	1034.8	Turners Gap, US Alt 40, restaurant 0.1E, Boonsboro, MD (2.5W). (pg.102)	1089
1148.1	1036.1	Monument Rd.	1350
1147.8	1036.4	Washington Monument State Park, picnic tables, parking and restrooms adjacent to visitor center.	1379
1147.5	1036.7	Washington Monument (0.1W).	1550
1145.4	1038.8	Boonsboro Mountain Rd, residential area.	1322
1145.1	1039.1	Bartram Hill Trail to west.	1409
1144.6	1039.6	I-70 footbridge, US 40. N39 32.115 W77 36.209 P (pg.102) Parking north end of footbridge 0.1 east.	1267
1144.0	1040.2	Pine Knob Shelter (0.1W), south end of loop trail. 16.6◀12.5◀7.5▼8.2▶13.1▶22.7 Piped spring next to shelter.	1389
1142.4	1041.8	Annapolis Rocks to west, campsite Caretaker on site. Tentsites near outstanding overlook.	1820
1141.4	1042.8	Campsite, Black Rock Cliffs to west.	1819
1141.0	1043.2	Black Rock Creek	1606
1140.8	1043.4	Pogo Memorial Campsite Campsite east of AT, spring 100 yards west. Thurston Griggs Trail to west.	1500
1136.0	1048.2	Wolfsville Rd, MD 17, Smithsburg, MD (1.5W). (pg.102)	1400
1135.8	1048.4	Ensign Cowall Shelter 20.7◀15.7◀8.2▼4.9▶14.5▶16.9...	1415
1135.6	1048.6	Boxed spring, somewhat stagnant, south between shelter & road.	1520
		Powerline.	
1134.5	1049.7	Foxville Rd, MD 77, Smithsburg, MD (1.7W).	1611
1133.3	1050.9	Spring.	1362

SoBo	NoBo	Description	Elev
1133.1	1051.1	Powerline	1384
1132.7	1051.5	Warner Gap Hollow, stream, Warner Gap Rd (gravel, AT to west).	1150
1132.0	1052.2	Little Antietam Creek	1104
1131.9	1052.3	Raven Rock Rd, MD 491.	1083
1131.6	1052.6	Raven Rock Cliff, view 100 yards east.	1304
1130.9	1053.3	Raven Rock Shelter (0.1W), Ritchie Rd (0.6E) 20.6◀13.1◀4.9▶9.6▶12.0▶13.2 New "two story" shelter. Water on opposite side of AT (0.1E)	1682 (16)
1129.1	1055.1	Ends of High Rock Loop Trail 0.2 apart 0.1E from either end to view and parking. N39 41.690 W77 31.394 P	1821
1126.3	1057.9	Pen Mar County Park N39 42.983 W77 30.433 P (pg.103)	1277
1126.0	1058.2	**Cascade, MD** (1.4E), **Waynesboro, PA** (2.1W)	1250
1125.9	1058.3	**MD-PA** border, RR tracks, Mason-Dixon line (no sign) Pen Mar Rd	1240
1125.3	1058.9	Falls Creek, footbridge, campsite	1048
1124.9	1059.3	Buena Vista Rd	1290
1123.7	1060.5	Old PA 16.	1350
1123.4	1060.8	Footbridge, stream, PA 16, N39 44.495 W77 29.422 P ♦ (pg.103)	1200
1123.2	1061.0	**Blue Ridge Summit, PA** (1.2E) Mentzer Gap Rd, NoBo: turn west	1250
1122.8	1061.4	Rattlesnake Run Rd (gravel)	1366
1121.3	1062.9	**Deer Lick Shelters** 22.7◀14.5◀9.6▶2.4▶3.6▶10.2.	1435 (2x5)
1121.0	1063.2	Spring 10 yards north on AT or (0.2E) on blue-blazed trail. Pipeline clearing	1502
1120.4	1063.8	Dirt road.	1395
1119.1	1065.1	Orange-blazed Chickadee Snowmobile Trail	938
1118.9	1065.3	**Antietam Shelter** 16.9◀12.0◀2.4▶1.2▶7.8▶13.4 Water from Old Forge Park 0.1N	911 (6)
1118.8	1065.4	Old Forge Park, Old Forge Rd N39 48.089 W77 28.773 P	916
1117.7	1066.5	**Tumbling Run Shelters** 13.2◀3.6◀1.2▶6.6▶12.2▶19.6 Piped water 75 yards right of shelter.	1089 (8)
1116.4	1067.8	Chimney Rocks, view to east.	1900
1115.5	1068.7	Pipeline clearing	1911
1114.3	1069.9	Powerline	2008
1113.7	1070.5	Snowy Mountain Rd	1706
1113.1	1071.1	Swamp Rd	1560
1112.8	1071.4	PA 233, **South Mountain, PA** 17261 (1.2E) (pg.103)	1613

1034.8   Turners Gap, US Alt 40

¶ ⅋ (0.1W) **Old South Mountain Inn** 301-432-6155
Tu–F 5-9, Sa 4-10, Su brunch 10:30-2, dinner 12-8

Boonsboro, MD 21713 (2.5W)

⌂ M–F 9-1 & 2–5, Sa 9–12, 301-432-6861

¶⌂ **Crawfords** 301-432-2903 M-F 7-6, Sa 7-3, B/L/D.

¶ **Vesta's Pizza** 301-432-6166 Su-Th 11-10, F-Sa 11-11.

¶ **Mountainside Deli** 301-432-6700 M-F 6-8 & Sa 8-8 B/L/D, Su 11-8 L/D. **Potomac Street Creamery** 301-432-5242.

¶ **Palettie Gourmet Bistro** 301-432-0500 W-Su 5-8, hiker special AYCE spaghetti any night $15, closed M-Tu.

¶ **Subway**

⌂ **Cronise Market place** 301-432-7377 M-F 10-7, Sa 9-7, Su 10-6.

⊷ **Boonsboro Veterinarian Hospital** 301-432-7120

⅄ **Marcy's Laundry**

≋⌂ **Boonsboro Free Library** 301-432-5723 M-F 10-7, Sa 10-2.

≋ ¶ **Turn the Page Book Store Café** 301-432-4588

✂ **Pete's Barber Shop**

1039.6   I-70, US 40
                (1.4W) to:

¶ 🅢 **Dogpatch Tavern** 301-791-2844.

⬙ ♦♦ **Greenbrier State Park** 301-791-4767, camping Apr–Oct, pets okay. Camp store open May–Sep, Entrance fee $4PP wkdays; $6PP wkends and holidays, 62+ free entrance, tent sites with showers $25. Lake swimming, row boat and paddle boat rentals.

1048.2   Wolfsville Rd, MD 17

♦ (0.3E) If shelter water source is dry, you may get water from ranger's house. Go 0.1 east (compass south) to a gravel road on left, then 0.2 on gravel road to first house on left.

🛏 ⌂ ⅄⌂⌂ ✉ (0.3W) **The Free State Hiker Hostel** 301-824-2407 ⟨www.freestatehiker.com⟩ bunks $32, shuttles to Smithsburg when available. Open Mar 15-Nov 15, two years only, owned by '06 thru-hiker Ken "Bone Pac" and Jennel Berry, Credit cards accepted. Pizza and Mexican delivery available. Water available from spigot in front. No alcohol and no pets. Maildrops: (non-guest $2) c/o Free State Hiker, LLC 11626 Wolfsville Road, Smithsburg, Maryland 21783.

Smithsburg, MD 21783 (1.5W)

⌂ M–F 8:30–1 & 2–4:30, Sa 8:30–12, 301-824-2828

⌂ **Dollar General Store** 301-824-6940 7 days 8-9.

🏬 **Smithsburg Market** M-Sa 8-7, Su 9-3

🏬 **Food Lion** daily 7-11.

¶ **Rocky's Pizzeria** 301-824-2066, M-F 10:30-10 Sa-Su 10:30-11.

¶ **Vince's New York Pizza** 301-824-3939, Su-Th 11-11, F-Sa 11-12.

¶ **Dixie Eatery** 301-824-5334, closed M, Tu 7-2, W-F 7-8, Sa-Su 7-2.

¶ **Subway** 301-824-3826 24 hrs,

¶ **China 88**

¶ **Carmine's Italian Restaurant**

✚ **Smithsburg Emergency Medical** 301-824-3314.

⊷ **Park Circle Animal Hospital** 301-416-0888.

℞ **Rite Aid pharmacy** 301-824-2211, store 9-9, pharmacy 9-6

⅄ **Laundry**

⌂ **Library** 301-824-7722 M-F 10a-7p, Sa 10a-2p

⊤ **Ace Hardware**

1057.9   Pen Mar County Park

♿🚻☎ Open first Sunday in May to last Sunday in Oct. Vending machines & water fountains; no camping. Restrooms locked when park closed. Pen Mar Rd passes in front of park, east of AT. If intending to walk to town, do so from AT/Pen Mar Rd intersection 0.3N of park. Bobby D's & other pizza places deliver. Most services are in the western edge of Waynesboro, but use the Rouzerville PO which is nearest to the AT. Just beyond the PO, reach Main St (PA 16), and turn left to reach all services listed below. Much more farther into town.

Waynesboro, PA 17214 (2.1W)

🛏🏕🚌📶💻📧 **Burgundy Lane B&B** 717-762-8112 $85-100D w/full breakfast, free laundry & shuttle to trailhead or town stop. Longer shuttles for fee. Maildrops: 128 W Main St, Waynesboro, PA 17268.

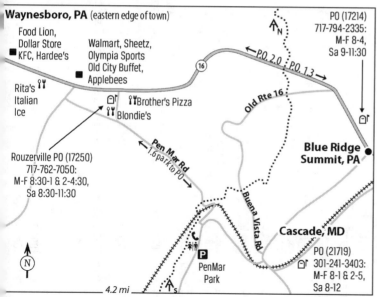

Waynesboro, PA (eastern edge of town)

Food Lion, Dollar Store, KFC, Hardee's

Walmart, Sheetz, Olympia Sports, Old City Buffet, Applebees

Rita's Italian Ice

Brother's Pizza

Blondie's

Rouzerville PO (17250) 717-762-7050; M-F 8:30-1 & 2-4:30, Sa 8:30-11:30

Pen Mar Rd — 1.6 park to PO

PO (17214) 717-794-2335; M-F 8-4, Sa 9-11:30

Old Rte 16

PO 2.0   PO 1.3

16

Blue Ridge Summit, PA

Buena Vista Rd

Cascade, MD

PenMar Park

PO (21719) 301-241-3403; M-F 8-1 & 2-5, Sa 8-12

N

4.2 mi

🏪 **Walmart, Food Lion**

⛽ **Sheetz**

✂ **Cost Cutters Barber Shop**

🍴 **Bobby D's Pizza** 717-762-0388

🍴 **Old City Buffet** American, Chinese, Japanese AYCE L/D.

🍴 **Golden Corral, Mountain Gate** (both offer buffets)

🔧 **Lowe's Hardware**

Also: Olympia Sports large selection of running shoes. 2.5W of post office.

✚ **Waynesboro Hospital** 717-765-4000 501 E Main St.

🐾 **Wayne Heights Animal Hospital** 717-765-9636

🛏🐾📶💻🏕 **Days Inn** 717-762-9113 (5.5W of Walmart) $59S, $69D, $5EAP. Continental breakfast, $10 pet fee, laundry next door.

Cascade, MD (1.4E on Pen Mar/High Rock Rd)

🏪 **Sanders Market** M, W-F 8:30-9, Tu and Sa 8:30-8

🏕 **Cascade coin** 301-241-3831 (1.1 mile from PO).

1060.8   PA 16   *Blue Ridge Summit, PA 17214* (1.2E)
(more services on map)

🍴 **Unique Bar and Grill** 717-794-2565 live music, **Summit Plaza** 717-794-2500 open 7-8, B/L/D.

🏕 **JJ's Laundromat**

🔧 **True Value Hardware**

1071.4   PA 233
South Mountain, MD 17261 (1.2E)

📮 M-F 8:30-1 & 2-4:45, Sa 8:30-11:30, 717-749-5833

(0.1W) 🍴 **South Mountain Tavern**

717-749-3845 M-Sa 9am-2pm, Su 11am-6pm, Su brunch. Mt. Haven Hostel will pickup free from here.

Elev

⚠ *Many springs in PA run dry in June, July & August*

SoBo	NoBo	Feature	Elev
1111.1	1073.1	**Rocky Mountain Shelters** (0.2E) ◗ ♦ ⊏ (8)	1660
		◀10.2 ◀7.8 ◀6.6 ▶5.6 ▶13.0 ▶19.2	
		Piped spring 0.5 mile on trail to road, then right 75 yards.	
1108.1	1076.1	US 30, **Fayetteville, PA** (3.5W) . . . N39 54.352 W77 28.714 ▣ (pg.106)	960
		Overnight parking SW corner of US 30 & Pine Grove Rd, check in at park HQ.	
1107.7	1076.5	Side trail to **Caledonia State Park,** pool area . . . (pg.106)	936
1106.9	1077.3	Locust Gap Rd, Valley Trail to west	1341
1105.5	1078.7	**Quarry Gap Shelters** 13.4◀12.2◀5.6▶7.4▶13.6▶24.5 ◗ ♦ ⊏ (8)	1473
1105.2	1079.0	Footbridge, stream . . . ♦	1547
1104.8	1079.4	Hosack Run Trail to east	1838
1104.0	1080.2	5-way gravel road intersection	2005
1103.2	1081.0	Powerline . . .	1889
1102.8	1081.4	Woods road	2024
1101.5	1082.7	Cross 3 gravel roads about 0.1 apart	2075
1100.9	1083.3	Intersecting gravel roads, campsite to north . . . ♦	1985
1100.5	1083.7	PATC Milesburn Cabin (locked), spring 100 yards west. . . ♦	1704
1100.2	1084.0	Ridge Rd (gravel), campsite north of road	1918
1099.4	1084.8	Rocky Knob Trail (orange-blazed) . . .	1919
1098.8	1085.4	Powerline, campsite to north . . . ♦	1936
1098.1	1086.1	**Birch Run Shelter,** stream 75 yards north on AT . . . ◗ ♦ ⊏ (10)	1811
		19.6◀13.0◀7.4▶6.2▶17.1▶25.2	
1098.0	1086.2	Footbridge, stream . . . ♦	1805
1096.8	1087.4	Shippensburg Rd . . . N39 59.834 W77 24.301 ▣ (pg.106)	2040
1095.7	1088.5	Service road (gravel)	1987
1094.9	1089.3	**AT Midpoint,** Side trail to Michener Cabin (locked) . . . ♦ (0.3E)	1850
1094.3	1089.9	Woods road	1896
1093.0	1091.2	Woodrow Rd (gravel), campsite 0.1N on AT . . . ♦	1807
1092.5	1091.7	Stream. . . ♦	1555

SoBo	NoBo		Elev
1092.0	1092.2	Sunset Rocks Trail to east, rejoins AT to north ⊃●∠(8)	1337
1091.9	1092.3	**Toms Run Shelters**, water behind shelter ●	1319
		19.2◀13.6◀6.2◀▶10.9▶19.0▶37.2	
1091.7	1092.5	Stream ●	1292
1090.7	1093.5	Michaux Rd ●	1334
1089.8	1094.4	Toms Run, footbridge, stream. Sunset Rocks Trail to east. ●	1039
1088.6	1095.6	PA 233 (paved), **AT Museum** . . . . . . N40 01.971 W77 18.291 P (pg.106)	924
		NoBo on road 0.1W, veer right on road into Pine Grove Furnace State Park.	
1087.7	1096.5	Fuller Lake	861
1085.9	1098.3	Campsite ◣	1264
1085.7	1098.5	Pole Steeple Trail to west	1300
1084.7	1099.5	Campsite ◣	1383
1082.5	1101.7	Roadbed	1063
1082.2	1102.0	Trail to **Mountain Creek Campground** (0.7W) signed & steep. . . (pg.106)	1032
1081.1	1103.1	Spring 50 yards west on marked trail ⊃●◣∠(9)	748
1081.0	1103.2	**James Fry (Tagg Run) Shelter** (0.2E), campsite west of AT	719
		24.5◀17.1◀10.9◀▶8.1▶26.3▶33.6 Spring uphill from shelter; water 0.2E farther.	
1080.6	1103.6	Pine Grove Rd (paved)	687
1080.4	1103.8	Stream ●●	663
1080.0	1104.2	⌂ AT turns east, NoBo cross RR tracks ●	660
1079.8	1104.4	PA 34, Hunters Run Rd . . . . . . N40 4.624 W77 11.702 P (0.5S) ⊞	637
		Green Mountain Store (0.2E) 7 days	
1077.8	1106.4	PA 94, **Mt Holly Springs, PA** (2.5W) . . . . (pg.106-107) ⌂⊞†⌂	880
1077.5	1106.7	Sheet Iron Roof Rd, trail to **Deer Run Campground**	786
		(0.4W) 717-486-8168, tentsite $10 w/shower, cabin $62.	
1077.1	1107.1	Footbridge, stream, campsite ●◣	696
1076.8	1107.4	Footbridge, stream ●●	683
1076.4	1107.8	Old Town Rd (gravel) ●	750
1075.8	1108.4	Rock maze	1181
1075.4	1108.8	Rock maze	1092
1075.0	1109.2	Whiskey Spring Rd, reliable water from spring ●	830

⚠ No camping in Cumberland Valley between Alec Kennedy and Darlington Shelters, except at backpackers campsite south of Boiling Springs.

SoBo	NoBo		Elev
1073.0	1111.2	Little Dogwood Run, campsite, orange-blazed trail 1.7E to BSA campground. ◣	884
1072.9	1111.3	**Alec Kennedy Shelter** (0.2E), spring behind shelter is unreliable . . ⊃◊∠(7)	966
		25.2◀19.0◀8.1◀▶18.2▶25.5▶34.1	
1072.0	1112.2	Center Point Knob, original AT midpoint, White Rocks Trail 0.4E to view ▣	1060

1076.1   US 30

1076.5   Side trail to park

♣ ♨ ⊗ ॐ 🕿 **Caledonia State Park** 717-352-2161 Open Mar. 30 - Dec. 10. Pool and snack bar open seven days in summer (Jun. 9 - Labor Day) snack bar 11-7. Phone and vending next to the pool and near office. Campsites with showers, $21 Su-Th, $25 F-Sa, $2 more for campsites that allow pets, $2 less for PA residents. $3 shower only.

♨ (1.5E) **Bobby A's Grill & Bar** 717-352-2252

Fayetteville, PA 17222 (spread out to west, distances given for each service)

(0.4W) ♨ 🕿 **Taormina's Italian Restaurant** 717-352-8503 Tu-Su 11-9, Pizza, Subs, ice cream.

(0.8W) 🏪 **Henicle's Market** deli, 7 days, M-Sa 8-9, Su 9-5.

(2.6W) ⛏ ♨ ✉ **Scottish Inn and Suites** 717-352-2144, 800-251-1962 $55S, $69D, $15 pets. $5 for pickup or return to trail. $10 for ride to Walmart. **Leroy's Original BBQ** on premises. Guest maildrops: 5651 Lincoln Way East, Fayetteville, PA 17222

(2.6W) ♨ **Flamingo Restaurant** excellent large breakfast.

(3.2W) △ **Squeaky Clean Laundry**

(3.2W) 🏧 M-F 8-4:30, Sa 8:30-12, 717-352-2022

(3.2W) ☤ **Rite Aid**

(7W) 🏪 **Walmart** open 24hrs with pharmacy (Chambersburg, PA)

🚍 **Freeman's Shuttle Service** 717-352-2513, 717-658-9185

1087.4   Shippensburg Rd 0.1E to the first dirt road (marked Private Drive), then 0.4 to 5th house on left:

⛏ ॐ △ 🚍 ⊗ ☎ ✉ **High Mountain Haven** 717-352-4686 Bunks $20pp, tenting $10pp, open year-round. Laundry $3, Showers $3 for non-guests. Phone and internet available. For-fee shuttles, kennels for pets, fuel by oz. Maildrops: (hiker name) c/o High Mt. Haven, 2630 Shippensburg Road Lot-L Biglerville, PA 17307.

1095.6   PA 233, Pine Grove Furnace State Park

🏪 **Pine Grove General Store**, open 7 days Labor day to Memorial Day. Foods and cold drinks. Vending machines outside. Home of the *half gallon challenge.*

ℹ **A.T. Museum** Hikers welcome to bring food to eat outside and relax. Artifacts of pioneering hikers, thru-hiker photos from the last 30 years and signs from Springer, Center Point Knob and Katahdin. The museum is open on weekends in the spring and fall and daily from noon-4pm Memorial day to Labor day. **A.T. Hall of Fame Banquet** (Trail Festival) , Jun 8-9, Hike for History fundraiser on Sept. 15.

⛏ ⊗ ☎ ✉ **Ironmasters Mansion Hostel** 717-241-4360 $25 Thru-hiker rate includes bunk, linen, shower, towel, dinner & breakfast. Laundry planned for 2012. Check-in 5-9pm, check-out 9am. Maildrops: Ironmasters Hostel, 1212 Pine Grove Rd, Gardners, PA 17324.

⛏ ♁ 🅿 **Pine Grove Furnace State Park** 5-person campsites $21 weekdays, $25 weekends. $2 off for PA residents. Some dog-allowed sites. Beach/swimming area. Restrooms throughout park. Check in with the park office before leaving a vehicle overnight; vehicles can be left for no more than one week. Closed mid-Dec, opens Apr 1.

1102.0   Side trail to campground

⛏ ♣ 🏪 ॐ △ 🕿 **Mountain Creek Campground** 717-486-7681 Open Apr-Nov, cabins $45D, $5EAP, tent sites $25D, heated pool, camp store.

1106.4   PA 94   *Mt. Holly Springs, PA 17065* (2.5W)

Two intersections about 0.5 mile apart. 5 miles farther to 81 interchange with Walmart and movies at Carlisle Commons.

🏧 M-F 8-1 & 2-4:30, Sa 9-12, 717-486-3468

⛏ ♨ ⊗ **Holly Inn, Restaurant and Tavern** 717-486-3823 $55D $10EAP free ride to/from AT if available, live music.

🏪 **Sheetz, Family Dollar**

♨ **Subway**, **Sicilia Pizza, Laura's** breakfast, lunch, and ice cream.

℞ Holly Pharmacy 717-486-5321
△ Dollie's Laundromat

1115.2   PA 174, ***Boiling Springs, PA 17007*** (more services on map)

🛏🍴△🛜🖥 Allenberry Resort Inn & Playhouse
717-258-3211, 800-430-5468 ⟨www.allenberry.com⟩ Hiker special $40 double cccupancy (a big discount) $6 breakfast buffet, $10 lunch, $15 dinner, $15 theater or $10 matinee, $4 laundry, pool, accepts credit cards.

🛏△🛜🖥✉ Gelinas Manor 717-258-6584
⟨www.gelinasmanor.com⟩ Room with shared bath for $79D/up, no pets, only one room available at this rate. Full breakfast served 8:30. Laundry $6/load. Credit cards accepted. Computer access by request only. Guest maildrops: MUST say "in care of Gelinas Manor", 219 Front Street, Boiling Springs, PA 17007.

⚓ Free hiker campsite with privy south of town.

🍴 Boiling Springs Tavern 717-258-3614 L/D 11:30-2, 5-9:30, closed Su-M. **Anile's Ristorante & Pizzeria** 717-258-5070 L/D subs, pizza, entrees, about 0.5 mile north of Gettys. Su-Th 11-10, F-Sa 11-11,

🍴 Caffe 101 B/L/D.

🍴 Karn's Quality Foods 717-258-1458 Daily 7–10.

🛒 💲 Gettys Food Mart 717-241-6163 ATM inside.

🚶 Yellow Breeches Outfitters 717-258-6752
Primarily a fishing outfitter; limited hiking selection.

🚿 Boiling Springs Pool 717-258-412 Memorial Day-Labor Day, M-Su 11-7, $10 admission, $1 hot shower.

➕ Boiling Springs Family Medical 717-249-8300

🐕 Boiling Springs Animal Hosp. 717-258-4575 M-T 3-7:30, W-F 8-6, Sa 8-1, 1.4W on Park Drive.

🚌 Mike's Shuttle Service 717-497-6022

📶 ATC Mid-Atlantic Regional Office
717-258-5771 Open wkdays 8-3, possibly later. Water faucet on south side of building. Staff and bulletin board provide info on trail conditions, water availability and parking. Small shop with guidebooks and maps. White gas/denatured alcohol for small donation.

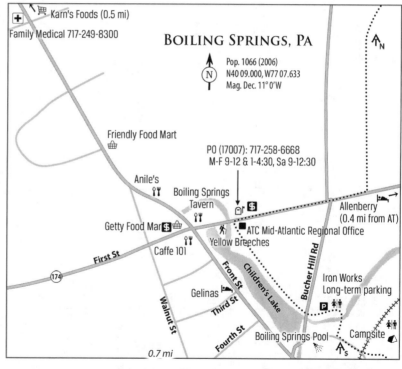

BOILING SPRINGS, PA

Pop. 1066 (2006)
N40 09.000, W77 07.633
Mag. Dec. 11° 0'W

Karn's Foods (0.5 mi)
Family Medical 717-249-8300

Friendly Food Mart

PO (17007): 717-258-6668
M-F 9-12 & 1-4:30, Sa 9-12:30

Anile's

Boiling Springs Tavern

Allenberry (0.4 mi from AT)

ATC Mid-Atlantic Regional Office

Getty Food Mart

Yellow Breeches

Caffe 101

First St

Gelinas

Walnut St

Third St

Front St

Children's Lake

Bucher Hill Rd

Iron Works Long-term parking

Fourth St

Boiling Springs Pool

Campsite

0.7 mi

SoBo	NoBo	The A.T. Guide	Elev
1070.6	1113.6	Cornfield, south end	551
1070.1	1114.1	Leidigh Dr	553
1069.5	1114.7	Backpacker's Campsite	507
1069.2	1115.0	Bucher Hill Rd, Iron Works Parking. N40 8.868 W77 7.445 P	495
1069.0	1115.2	PA 174, First Street, ATC Mid-Atlantic Regional Office (pg.107) **Boiling Springs, PA**	500
1067.5	1116.7	Stone wall	609
1066.9	1117.3	PA 74, York Rd. N40 10.385 W77 7.263 P	568
1065.9	1118.3	Lisburn Rd	542
1065.4	1118.8	Byers Rd	543
1065.3	1118.9	Footbridge, stream	497
1064.9	1119.3	PA 641, Trindle Rd. N40 11.700 W77 6.500 P	540
1063.7	1120.5	Ridge Rd, Biddle Rd. (pg.110)	465
1063.2	1121.0	Old Stonehouse Rd, footbridge, stream	469
1062.5	1121.7	Appalachian Dr	509
1062.2	1122.0	PA Turnpike (I-76) overpass	493
1061.6	1122.6	Railroad tracks	472
1061.0	1123.2	US 11, **Carlisle, PA** (5.0W) (pg.110)	490
1060.1	1124.1	Pass over I-81 on Bernheisel Rd	485
1059.5	1124.7	Fence stile (two)	461
1058.7	1125.5	Conodoguinet Creek, footbridge adjacent to road. N40 15.589 W77 6.221 P **Scott Farm Trail Work Center** Open May–Oct, picnic table, no camping. The AT u-turns, passes under bridge, and heads north.	480
1057.6	1126.6	Sherwood Drive, parking to east. N40 16.439 W77 5.967 P Many footbridges, streams north and south of this road	415
1056.7	1127.5	PA 944 tunnel	480
1055.8	1128.4	Piped spring where AT crosses overgrown dirt road NoBo planning stay at Darlington Shelter consider getting water here.	746
1055.1	1129.1	View	1140
1054.9	1129.4	Darlington Trail, Tuscarora Trail	1274
1054.7	1129.5	**Darlington Shelter** (0.1E) 37.2◄26.3◄18.2◄▶7.3▶15.9▶22.6 ◢ ◊ ⊏ (5) Unreliable water on blue-blazed trail in front of shelter. Taj Mahal privy.	1223
1053.2	1131.0	Gravel road	750
1052.8	1131.4	Millers Gap Rd (paved) N40 19.359 W77 4.260 P	704
1052.5	1131.7	PA 850	690
1051.1	1133.1	Service road	780

SoBo	NoBo	Description	Elev
1049.9	1134.3	Pipeline, view, trail very rocky from here north to PA 274	1335
1048.3	1135.9	Blue-blazed trail 0.4W to service road	1254
1047.4	1136.8	**Cove Mountain Shelter** (0.2E) 33.6◄25.5◄7.3◄▶8.6▶15.3▶33.3 Spring 0.1 mile on steep side trail.	1268
1045.4	1138.8	Hawk Rock, view	983
1044.7	1139.5	⚠ Old trail to west, AT turns east (uphill for NoBo)	444
1044.3	1139.9	Inn Rd	371
1043.8	1140.4	PA 274, pass under US 11/15, trail very rocky from here south to pipeline	385
1043.4	1140.8	**Duncannon, PA**, High St + Broadway (pg.110-111)	383
1041.4	1142.8	Susquehanna River North end of Clarks Ferry Bridge, US 22/322, railroad tracks ... N40 23.759 W77 0.512 P (pg.110)	394
1040.5	1143.7	View	614
1039.1	1145.1	Susquehanna Trail to west.	1156
1038.8	1145.4	**Clarks Ferry Shelter** (0.1E) 34.1◄15.9◄8.6◄▶6.7▶24.7▶38.1 Reliable piped spring just beyond shelter.	1258
1038.5	1145.7	Powerline	1346
1035.9	1148.3	Powerline	1242
1035.0	1149.2	PA 225 ... N40 24.711 W76 55.796 P	1263
1034.4	1149.8	Powerline	1297
1033.0	1151.2	Table Rock, view	1347
1032.1	1152.1	**Peters Mountain Shelter** 22.6◄15.3◄6.7◄▶18.0▶31.4▶35.5. Weak spring 0.1 mile steeply downhill from shelter (300 rock steps).	1188
1031.1	1153.1	Victoria Trail.	1225
1030.5	1153.7	Whitetail Trail.	1363

1120.5 Ridge Rd, Biddle Rd

🛏🏕📶🖥 **Pheasant Field B&B** (0.5W) 717-258-0717 $99/up, laundry free, behaved pets ok. Go 0.25W to Hickory Town Rd, turn left on road, B&B on right.

1123.2 US 11, *Carlisle, PA 17013* (5W)

The AT passes over the highway on a footbridge. Side trails are bushwhacked down to the road on either end. Most businesses listed below are on the outskirts of Carlisle to the west in view from the overpass. Hotels run short of rooms (and go up in price) every other weekend when there is a car show.

🛏🏕📶🖥✉ **Super 8 Motel** 717-249-7000 $54.99S, $59.99D, cont B, $10 pet fee, computer $1/20mins. Guest maildrops: 1800 Harrisburg Pike, Carlisle, PA 17013.

🛏📶🖥🏕 **Hotel Carlisle** 717-243-1717 $64.95, $10 pet fee.

🛏🏕📶✉ **Days Inn** 717-245-2242 $55/up, cont B, $15 pet fee. Maildrops: 1825 Harrisburg Pike, Carlisle, PA 17013.

🛏🏕📶🖥✉ **Red Roof Inn** 717-245-2400 call for rates. Maildrops: 1450 Harrisburg Pike, Carlisle, PA 17015.

🛏📶 **Americas Best Value Inn** 717-249-7775 $49.99/up, cont B, $15 pet fee.

🍴 **Middlesex Diner** 24hrs.

🍴⛪🔪🏕 (0.4E) **Flying J Truckstop** 717-243-6659, 24hrs. Has store, diner, pizza by the slice, showers ($10) and laundry.

Mechanicsburg, PA 17050 (7E)

Large city with many motels, restaurants, and retail.

🛏🍸 **Park Inn** 717-697-0321 Notable due to its two sizeable bars (**Legends Sports Bar & Grille** and **High-energy Nightclub**) and sand volleyball courts.

1140.8 *Duncannon, PA 17020* (more services on map)

🛏🍴🏕🖥✉ **Doyle Hotel** 717-834-6789, $25S, $7.50EAP + tax, bar serves L/D, iso canisters, Coleman/alcohol/oz, accepts Visa/MC/Disc. Maildrops: (USPS/UPS) 7 North Market Street, Duncannon, PA 17020.

🛏🏕🚌 **Motel Stardust** 717-834-3191

🛏📶 **Red Carpet Inn** 717-834-3320 $50S, $65D + tax.

⛺🚌 **Riverfront Campground** 717-834-5252, south of the Clarks Ferry Bridge, sites and shower $3.50PP, shuttles.

🍴 **Zeiderelli's Pizza & Subs** 717-834-3331

🍴 **Sorrento Pizza** 717-834-5167

🍴 **Goodies** B/L/D.

🍴 **Ranch House Restaurant** B/L/D, near Motel Stardust has breakfast and dinner buffet on weekends.

🛒 **Mutzabaugh's Market** 717-834-3121 7 days, pickup/return to Doyle once daily.

💊 **Rite Aid** next door to market.

⛪🍴🔪🏕 **All American Travel Plaza**, $8 showers.

🐾 **Cove Mountain Animal Hospital** 717-834-5534

🏕 **Laundry**

🔧 **Maguire's True Value Hardware** Coleman and Heet.

🚌 **Trail Angel Mary** 717-834-4706 2 Ann St, Duncannon, PA 17020

🚶 **Blue Mountain Outfitters** 717-957-2413

1142.8 Susquehanna River, US 22/322

🛏 **Le-Ellen Motel** 717-921-8715, $35S, $40D, no pets. Can be reached by walking 1.0E alongside railroad tracks.

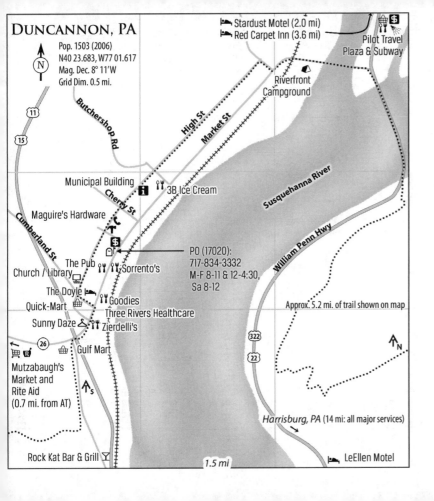

The A.T. Guide

SoBo	NoBo	The A.T. Guide	Elev
1029.4	1154.8	Kinter View	1320
1028.0	1156.2	Shikellimy Trail 0.9E to parking area. N40 26.259 W76 49.185	1215
1027.0	1157.2	Campsite	1408
1025.7	1158.5	Spring 100 yards east on side trail	700
1025.4	1158.8	PA 325, Clarks Creek north of road. N40 27.092 W76 46.574	550
1025.1	1159.1	Spring	616
1025.0	1159.2	Henry Knauber Trail to east	694
1023.7	1160.5	Spring	1297
1022.1	1162.1	Horse-Shoe Trail to east	1650
1021.4	1162.8	Rattling Run.	1548
1018.9	1165.3	Yellow Springs Trail	1417
1018.7	1165.5	Clearing with trail register, camping	1450
		Yellow Springs Village Site, old coal mining settlement (0.7W)	
1017.8	1166.4	Spring	1444
1016.6	1167.6	Sand Spring Trail west to "The General"	1437
1016.4	1167.8	Cold Spring Trail to east	1400
1014.2	1170.0	Spring, campsite	1116
1014.1	1170.1	**Rausch Gap Shelter** (0.3E), no tenting or fires permitted	1094
		33.3◄24.7◄18.0◄▶13.4▶17.5▶32.6	
1013.6	1170.6	AT on gravel road for 0.2 mile, bridge over Rausch Creek	925
1013.3	1170.9	Cemetery to west.	877
1013.1	1171.1	Stony Creek, footbridge	842
1012.0	1172.2	Second Mountain.	1357
1010.3	1173.9	Field	655
1010.0	1174.2	Cross two roads: Greenpoint School Rd, then PA 72	582

SoBo	NoBo		Elev
1009.4	1174.8	Pass under PA 72 and cross PA 443. N40 28.923 W76 33.038 ▣ ◆ ◁	490
		Stream, campsite south of PA 72	
1008.6	1175.6	Campsite ◆ ◁	694
1008.0	1176.2	Swatara Gap, PA 72, **Lickdale, PA** (2.1E) (pg.114)	480
1007.6	1176.6	I-81, AT passes underneath	450
1007.3	1176.9	Gravel road	629
1003.4	1180.8	Abandoned powerline overlook, view ▣	1388
1000.7	1183.5	**William Penn Shelter** (0.1E) ⟩ ◆ ◀ ⊆ (16)	1421
		38.1◄31.4◄13.4◄►4.1►19.2►33.9	
		Water and tent sites 0.1W on blue-blazed trail.	
998.6	1185.6	PA 645, Waggoners Gap Rd N40 30.396 W76 22.609 ▣ (pg.114-115)	1235
		Pine Grove, PA (3.4W)	
997.4	1186.8	Fisher Lookout, view	1286
996.7	1187.5	Kimmel Lookout, view. ▣	1335
996.6	1187.6	PA 501, **501 Shelter** (0.1W) N40 30.75 W76 20.664 ▣ ⟩ ◆ ◁ (pg.114-115)	1473
		35.5◄17.5◄4.1◄►15.1►29.8►38.9 **Pine Grove, PA** (4.2W), **Bethel, PA** (4.1E)	
996.1	1188.1	Trail to Pilger Ruh (Pilgrims Rest), spring to east, ◆ ◁	1450
		Applebee Campsite to west.	
993.5	1190.7	Round Head, Shower Steps Trail, campsite to south on AT. ▣ ◆ ◁	1500
		Side trail to view.	
991.5	1192.7	Overlook, view. ▣	1412
991.1	1193.1	⚠ NoBo: AT turns east, Boulderfield Trail to west (straight ahead). ◆	1294
991.0	1193.2	Hertline Campsite and picnic table ◁	1200
990.3	1193.9	Pipeline, road paralleling pipeline, cross twice, then parallel to AT	1531

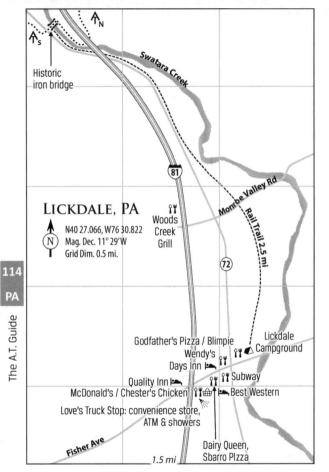

LICKDALE, PA

↑ N40 27.066, W76 30.822
Ⓝ Mag. Dec. 11° 29'W
Grid Dim. 0.5 mi.

Woods Creek Grill

Historic iron bridge

Swatara Creek

81

Monroe Valley Rd

Rail Trail 2.5 mi

72

Lickdale Campground

Godfather's Pizza / Blimpie
Wendy's
Days Inn
Subway
Quality Inn
McDonald's / Chester's Chicken
Best Western
Love's Truck Stop: convenience store, ATM & showers

Dairy Queen, Sbarro PIzza

Fisher Ave

1.5 mi

1176.2   Swatara Gap, PA 72
Lickdale, PA (2.1E) *(more services on map)*

🛏️ ♿ 📶 🖥️ **Days Inn** 717-865-4064 $55/up, cont B, pets $15, jacuzzi.

🛏️ ♿ 📶 🖥️ **Best Western** 717-865-4234 $72.99/up, cont B. Guests get 10% discount at Subway and DQ, indoor heated pool, no pets.

🛏️ ♿ 📶 🖥️ **Quality Inn** 717-865-6600 $109.99 plus tax, cont B, pets $10, pool.

🛏️ ◐ ⌂ ♿ **Lickdale Campground & General Store** 877-865-6411 Open 5-9, 7 days. Tentsite $28/up, cabin sleeps 4 $55/up. Pets okay.

🍴 📶 (1.3E) **Woods Creek Grill** 717-861-4555 11-midnight, closed Mondays. Has hiker specials, live music, serves beer.

⌂ 🍴 💲 ⛽ 📞 **Love's Truckstop** $10 showers, ATM

1185.6   PA 645, **Pine Grove, PA** (3.4W) *(more services on map)*

🍴 **Original Italian Pizza** 570-345-5432 Delivers to 501 shelter.

🍴 ⌂ 💲 ⛽ ♿ **Pilot Travel Center** 570-345-8800, 24hr, other side of 81, **Subway, Dairy Queen** and diner inside, B/L/D, shower $10.

🏪 **Bergers Market** 570-345-3663, open 7 days

🚌 **PA Moneypit** 570-345-1119, or Joyce at 570-345-0474. pamoneypit@yahoo.com, shuttles to most PA towns & airports, $1.50/mile.

     4.8W near intersection of I-81

🛏️ 📶 🖥️ **Comfort Inn** 570-345-8031 $62.50 includes hot breakfast. Hiker friendly, honors flat rate all season, pool, pet fee $10.

🛏️ **Colony Lodge** 570-345-8095 $40-$65, Some pet rooms.

🛏️ 📶 **Econo Lodge** 570-345-4099 $55S, $60-$130, pets $10 in smoking room.

1187.6   PA 501, **Bethel, PA** (4.1E) *(services on map)*

⌂ **501 Shelter** Caretaker house nearby, solar shower, house faucet, no alcohol, no smoking in shelter, pets on leash.

Pine Grove, PA 17963 (4.2W)

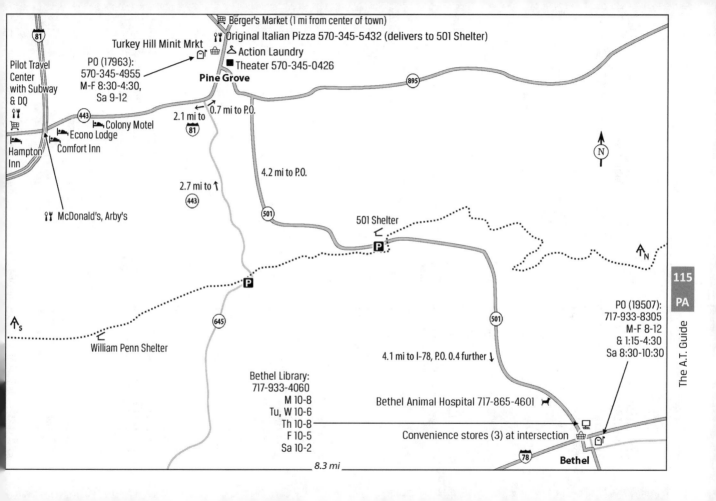

🏬 Berger's Market (1 mi from center of town)
🍴 Original Italian Pizza 570-345-5432 (delivers to 501 Shelter)
Turkey Hill Minit Mrkt
⚒ Action Laundry
🏪 Theater 570-345-0426

PO (17963):
570-345-4955
M-F 8:30-4:30,
Sa 9-12

Pine Grove

895

Pilot Travel
Center
with Subway
& DQ

443

2.1 mi to
81

0.7 mi to P.O.

Colony Motel
Econo Lodge
Comfort Inn

4.2 mi to P.O.

Hampton
Inn

2.7 mi to ↑

N

443

501

🍴 McDonald's, Arby's

501 Shelter

P

115
PA

The A.T. Guide

P

N

Aˢ

645

William Penn Shelter

PO (19507):
717-933-8305
M-F 8-12
& 1:15-4:30
Sa 8:30-10:30

4.1 mi to I-78, P.O. 0.4 further ↓

Bethel Library:
717-933-4060
M 10-8
Tu, W 10-6
Th 10-8
F 10-5
Sa 10-2

Bethel Animal Hospital 717-865-4601 🐾

Convenience stores (3) at intersection

501

💻
🏪 🏠

78

Bethel

8.3 mi

SoBo	NoBo	The A.T. Guide	Elev
987.6	1196.6	Fort Dietrich Snyder Monument ♦ (0.2W)	1482
987.3	1196.9	PA 183, Rentschler Marker on side trail 30 yards north of road	1436
986.8	1197.4	Game Commission road (gravel). N40 31.636 W76 12.888 🅿	1498
986.0	1198.2	Black Swatara Spring 0.3E ♦	1510
983.4	1200.8	Eagles Nest Trail to east	1627
982.2	1202.0	Sand Spring Trail 0.2E to spring ♦	1510
981.5	1202.7	**Eagles Nest Shelter** (0.3W), spring on trail to shelter ☾♦⌐(8) 32.6◀19.2◀15.1◀▶14.7▶23.8▶31.2	1593
979.6	1204.6	Shartlesville-Cross Mtn Rd (pg.119) **Shartlesville, PA** 19554 (3.6E)	1450
976.9	1207.3	Phillips Canyon Spring (unreliable) ◁	1500
974.9	1209.3	State Game Land Rd	1432
974.3	1209.9	Pipeline clearing	1418
972.7	1211.5	Schuylkill Trail 2.4E to Hamburg, parking 0.1N N40 34.774 W76 1.600 🅿	545
972.5	1211.7	**Port Clinton, PA,** Broad St + Penn St (pg.118-119)	419
972.2	1212.0	PA 61, Blue Mtn Rd, **Hamburg, PA** (1.7E) (pg.118-119)	490
969.7	1214.5	Spring to west, campsite ♦◁	1193
968.5	1215.7	Minnehaha Spring, frequently dry ◁	1370

SoBo	NoBo	Description	Elev
967.1	1217.1	Reservoir Rd, stream north on AT . . . N40 35.374 W75 56.659 P♦	888
966.8	1217.4	**Windsor Furnace Shelter** (0.1W) . . . Parking 0.3E only with permission from Hamburg Borough 610-562-7821.)♦⊏(8)	867
966.1	1218.1	33.9◀29.8◀14.7◀▶9.1▶16.5▶26.5 No swimming, creek south of shelter.	990
966.1	1218.1	Blue-blazed trail to **Blue Rocks Campground** (1.5E) . . . (pg.119)	990
965.2	1219.0	Pulpit Rock, 30 yards west to privy at Pulpit Rock Astronomical Park. . .)◙	1582
963.4	1220.8	Yellow-blazed trail to **Blue Rocks Campground** (1.5E) . . . (pg.119)	1590
963.0	1221.2	The Pinnacle, 0.1E to panoramic view, no camping or fires ◙	1615
961.3	1222.9	Furnace Creek Trail to west	1455
961.0	1223.2	Gold Spring, no camping. ♦	1387
960.4	1223.8	Blue-blazed trail 1.5W reconnects with AT near Windsor Furnace Shelter	1427
960.1	1224.1	Pinnacle Spur Trail to west	1408
959.5	1224.7	Panther Spring, dependable ♦	1077
958.6	1225.6	Parking lot 0.4E on side trail . . . N40 37.528 W75 57.208 P	840
957.7	1226.5	Hawk Mountain Rd, **Eckville Shelter** (0.2E) Open May-Sep . .)♦⊏(6) 38.9◀23.8◀9.1◀▶7.4▶17.4▶24.2 Enclosed bunkroom, tent platforms, flush toilet, spigot at side of caretaker's house. 1.6W to Hawk Mountain Sanctuary.	697
957.2	1227.0	Footbridge, stream, campsite north on AT ♦	587
955.8	1228.4	Hawk Mtn Trail to west	1377
954.7	1229.5	Dans Pulpit, trail register. ◙	1597
954.1	1230.1	Dans Spring 0.1E ♦	1565
951.5	1232.7	Tri-County Corner, AT to west.	1532
950.3	1233.9	**Allentown Hiking Club Shelter**)◊♦⊏(8) 31.2◀16.5◀7.4◀▶10.0▶16.8▶33.5 Unreliable spring downhill in front of shelter 0.2 mile, another 0.1 farther.	1500
950.0	1234.2	Springs to east; Blue 100 yards, Yellow 0.3 mi ♦	1344
948.4	1235.8	Fort Franklin Rd (gravel) . . . N40 41.655 W75 50.515 P	1350

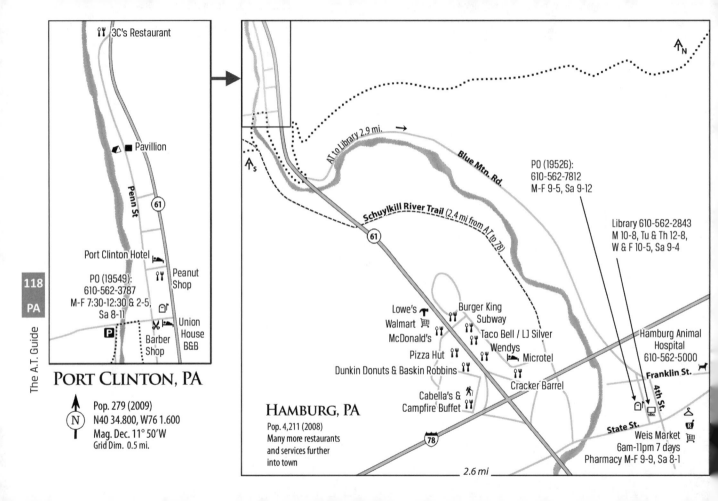

ᵀ𝖸 3C's Restaurant

▲■ Pavillion

Penn St
(61)

Port Clinton Hotel 🛏

PO (19549):
610-562-3787
M-F 7:30-12:30 & 2-5,
Sa 8-11

ᵀ𝖸 Peanut Shop

🏠

✂ Barber Shop

🅿

Union House B&B

PORT CLINTON, PA

Ⓝ Pop. 279 (2009)
N40 34.800, W76 1.600
Mag. Dec. 11° 50'W
Grid Dim. 0.5 mi.

↑N

AT to Library 2.9 mi. →

Blue Mtn. Rd.

↑S

Schuylkill River Trail (2.4 mi from AT to 78)

(61)

PO (19526):
610-562-7812
M-F 9-5, Sa 9-12

Library 610-562-2843
M 10-8, Tu & Th 12-8,
W & F 10-5, Sa 9-4

Lowe's 🪧
Walmart 🛒   Burger King ᵀ𝖸
McDonald's 🍴   Subway
                    Taco Bell / LJ Silver ᵀ𝖸
            Wendys
Pizza Hut ᵀ𝖸   🛏 Microtel
Dunkin Donuts & Baskin Robbins ᵀ𝖸
                    ᵀ𝖸 Cracker Barrel
        Cabella's & 🚶
        Campfire Buffet ᵀ𝖸

Hamburg Animal
Hospital
610-562-5000 🐕

Franklin St.

4th St.

🏠 💻

State St.

△
🛏
Weis Market 🛒
6am-11pm 7 days
Pharmacy M-F 9-9, Sa 8-1

HAMBURG, PA

Pop. 4,211 (2008)
Many more restaurants
and services further
into town

(78)

2.6 mi

1204.6   Shartlesville-Cross Mtn Rd
Shartlesville, PA 19526 (3.6E)
🛏 **Scottish Inn** 610-488-1578 $42/up, pets $5, ATM nearby.

1211.7   Broad St, Penn St
Port Clinton, PA 19549 (more services on map)
🛏 🍴 ⚠ **Union House B&B** ⟨www.union-house.com⟩ 610-562-3155 after 5pm 610-562-4076, open Friday-Sunday.

🛏 🍴 ⚠ **Port Clinton Hotel** 610-562-3354, 888-562-2626 ⟨www.portclintonhotel.net⟩ $49.05S, $62.13D, $10 deposit for room key and towel, limited rooms available. Laundry, dining Tu-Th 11-9, F-Sa 11-closing, Su 11-10, closed Monday, Please shower before use of dining room, Visa/MC accepted.

🏠 💲 **The Peanut Shop** trail mixes, ATM.

🔶 🚶 **Pavillion Tenting** sign in at pavillion, no car camping, no drive-ins.

1212.0   PA 61, Blue Mtn Rd
Hamburg, PA 19526 (1.7E) (more services on map)
🛏 🍴 ⚠ 📶 **Microtel Inn** 610-562-4234 ⟨www.microtelinn.com⟩ $84.50S $92.50 up to 4, reservations recommended, **Pappy T's** pub & lounge on-site

🍴 **Wendy's**, **Burger King**, **Cracker Barrel**

🏃 **Cabela's** 610-929-7000, M-Sa 8-9, Su 9-8

🍴 **Campfire Restaurant** Inside Cabela's with cafeteria-style meals weekdays, AYCE meals on weekends.

🏠 **Turkey Hill Market**

🏥 **Rite Aid** 610-562-9454, **CVS** 610-562-2454

⚠ **Hamburg Coin Laundry**

🐾 **Hamburg Animal Hospital** 610-562-5000 M-Th 9-7, Sa 9-11.

🚌 **Barta Bus Service** 610-921-0601 ⟨www.bartabus.com⟩ Routes within Hamburg $1.95 per boarding, stops at Cabellas.

Pottsville, PA 17901 (15W, compass north of AT on PA 61)
🍺 **Yuengling Brewery** 570-628-4890 America's oldest brewery has three tours daily.

1218.1   Blue-blazed trail to campground
1220.8   Yellow-blazed trail to campground
🛏 🔶 🏠 🚿 ⚠ **Blue Rocks Campground** 610-756-6366 Hiker rate $16 tentsite, $50 cabin accommodates 2 adults, 2 children. Free showers. Open Apr-Nov.

SoBo	NoBo	The A.T. Guide		Elev
946.5	1237.7	Trail 0.2W to restaurant (closer to AT + PA 309)		1367
946.2	1238.0	PA 309, Blue Mountain Summit	N40 42.429 W75 48.516 P (pg.122)	1360
944.3	1239.9	Powerline, New Tripoli Campsite 0.2W.		1445
943.1	1241.1	Knife Edge, view		1553
942.7	1241.5	Bear Rocks, view		1604
941.3	1242.9	Bake Oven Knob Rd (gravel)	N40 44.677 W75 44.314 P	1450
940.9	1243.3	Bake Oven Knob.		1560
940.3	1243.9	**Bake Oven Knob Shelter** 26.5◄17.4◄10.0▼▲6.8▶23.5▶37.3		1404
		Trail in front leads downhill to multiple water sources, more reliable farther down.		
937.9	1246.3	Lehigh Furnace Gap, Ashfield Rd, Comm tower.	N40 46.173 W75 41.649 P	1320
936.7	1247.5	South Mountain Trail 0.3E to view.		1600
935.8	1248.4	South Mountain Trail 0.5E to view.		1591
935.1	1249.1	TV tower, AT is over Lehigh Valley Tunnel		1515
933.7	1250.5	South Mountain Trail to west.		1086
933.5	1250.7	**George W. Outerbridge Shelter**, reliable piped spring 0.1N.		999
		24.2◄16.8◄6.8▲6.8▶16.7▶30.5▶61.7		
933.0	1251.2	Lehigh River south bank, PA 873, **Slatington, PA** (2.0E)	(pg.122)	439
932.5	1251.7	PA 248/145 traffic light, **Walnutport, PA** (2.0E)	(pg.122)	510
932.4	1251.8	Superfund Trailhead, **Palmerton, PA** (1.5W) N40 46.989 W75 36.247 P (pg.123)		520
		Water 0.4W on blue-blazed trail to Palmerton.		
931.5	1252.7	Superfund Detour south end.		1438
928.7	1255.5	Superfund Detour north, powerline		1381
928.0	1256.2	Metallica Spring 0.1W on unmarked trail		1339
927.6	1256.6	Little Gap Rd, **Danielsville, PA** (1.5E)	N40 48.369 W75 32.077 P (pg.124)	1100

	⊙	1356
		1575
	N40 48.551 W75 27.073 🅿 (0.7E)	1580
	◆	1583
	N40 49.530 W75 24.857 🅿 (pg.124)	1540
	☽ ◆ ◑ ⊏ (8)	1477
		1499
		1493
	⊙	1450
	N40 51.639 W75 17.565 🅿 (pg.124-125)	1109 / 980
		1594

6000
5000
4000
3000
2000
1000

SoBo	NoBo	
927.2	**1257.0**	Tower access road (gravel)
924.0	**1260.2**	Dirt road, powerline.
922.8	**1261.4**	Delps Trail to east.
921.2	**1263.0**	Stempa Spring 0.6E
920.3	**1263.9**	Smith Gap Rd (paved)
916.8	**1267.4**	**Leroy A. Smith Shelter** (0.2E). 33.5◀23.5◀16.7◀▶13.8▶45.0▶51.6 Water 0.2 mile down blue-blazed trail; second source 0.2 mile farther. Piped spring 0.5 mile down service road.
916.6	**1267.6**	Powerline
914.9	**1269.3**	Pipeline
913.2	**1271.0**	Hahns Overlook, view.
912.4	**1271.8**	Powerline
912.2	**1272.0**	PA 33, **Wind Gap, PA** (1.0E)
910.1	**1274.1**	Private road (gravel)

SoBo   NoBo   The A.T. Guide

1238.0   PA 309

🛏 🛝 🍴 🚌 ✉ 💧 **Blue Mountain Summit B&B** 570-386-2003, ⟨www.bluemountainsummit.com⟩ In view to west. $95–$125 double occupancy includes breakfast. No pets, ask about camping near restaurant and shuttles. Help yourself to water at outside spigot at southwest corner of building. Dining Th-Sa 11-10, Su 11-8, live music on Fridays. In winter (Nov-Feb), opens at 3pm on Thursday and noon on Friday. All major credit cards accepted. Guest maildrops: 2520 W Penn Pike, Andreas, PA 18211.

1251.2   Lehigh River, PA 873

Slatington, PA 18080 (2E) *(more services on map)*

🛏 🚌 🚿 💻 ✉ **Fine Lodging** 610-760-0700 This is a residency hotel so call ahead. $39/up, access to microwave, limited computer use, alcohol in moderation. $4 shower without stay. Well-behaved, clean pets okay. Free pickup/return from Lehigh Gap when available. Longer shuttles for donation as time permits. Maildrops must have ETA and "C/O Fine Lodging": (USPS/UPS) 700 Main Street, Slatington, PA 18080.

🍴 **Slatington Diner** B/L

🖊 **Bechtel's Pharmacy** 610-767-4121

💻 **Slatington Library** 610-767-6461 M,W: 9-7, Tu 9-3, F 9-5, Sa 8-2.

🪓 **AF Boyer Hardware**

1251.7   PA 248/145 Walnutport, PA 18088 (2E)

🏬 **Pathmark Supermarket** 610-760-8008, M-Sa 6-12pm, Su 6-10.

🏧 🖊 **Kmart** 610-767-1812

🍴 **King Palace Chinese Restaurant** 610-767-0151, AYCE lunch $5.75, also delivers.

🍴 **Valley Pizza Family Restaurant** 610-767-9000 L/D, delivers.

🍴 **Momma's Pizza** 610-767-5560.

✚ **St Luke's Family Practice Center** 610-760-8080

🖊 **Rite Aid Pharmacy** 610-767-9595

🐾 **Blue Ridge Veterinary Clinic** 610-767-4896 Call before coming.

The A.T. Guide

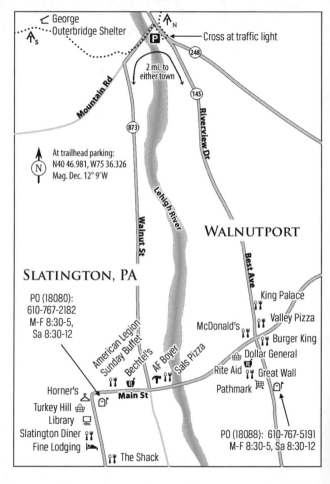

1251.8   Superfund Trailhead
Palmerton, PA 18071 (1.5W)
(more services on map)

Town Ordinance: Pets must be kept on leash.

🛏 **Jail House Hostel** 610-826-2505, 443 Delaware Avenue. Spacious basement of the borough hall was never used as a jail. Hikers stay free; showers available. Check in at the borough office before 4pm on weekdays. Check in at police station after hours and on weekends. 10pm curfew. ID is required. No vehicle assisted hikers. No pets inside, but they can be left tied outside.

🍴 **Palmerton Restaurant** 610-826-5454 Dining M-Th 4-10, F-Su 11-10.

🛒 **5** **Country Harvest Family Market** four blocks from hostel.

🍴💻 **Bert's Restaurant** B/L/D, close to hostel, has internet.

🍴 **Tony's Pizzeria** L/D, no delivery. **Joe's Place** L/D, deli sandwiches. **Simply Something** B/L/D. **Palmerton Pizza, Hunan House Chinese Restaurant**.

✚ **Palmerton Hospital** 610-826-3141

🐾 **Little Gap Animal Hospital** 610-826-2793 (3.5W) from town.

⚖ **Laundromat** across the street from hostel.

PA 248 is fast-moving and shoulderless, and so is not an easy hitch. NoBo intending to go into Palmerton should cross at traffic light and continue on the AT for 0.1 mile, where a clearly marked, level side trail leads 1.5 miles to town. Rocky climb from Lehigh Gap. Deforested ridge due to zinc smelting from 1898-1980. Palmerton Superfund site.

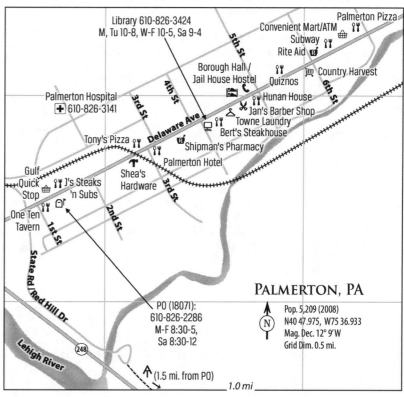

Library 610-826-3424
M, Tu 10-8, W-F 10-5, Sa 9-4

Palmerton Pizza
Convenient Mart/ATM
Subway
Rite Aid

Borough Hall /
Jail House Hostel

Country Harvest

Palmerton Hospital
✚ 610-826-3141

Quiznos
Hunan House
Jan's Barber Shop
Towne Laundry
Bert's Steakhouse

Tony's Pizza
Shipman's Pharmacy

Palmerton Hotel

Gulf
Quick
Stop

J's Steaks
'n Subs

Shea's
Hardware

One Ten
Tavern

PO (18071):
610-826-2286
M-F 8:30-5,
Sa 8:30-12

Delaware Ave
5th St
4th St
3rd St
6th St
2nd St
1st St
3rd St
State Rd. Red Hill Dr
Lehigh River
(248)

PALMERTON, PA

Ⓝ Pop. 5,209 (2008)
N40 47.975, W75 36.933
Mag. Dec. 12° 9'W
Grid Dim. 0.5 mi.

(1.5 mi. from PO)

1.0 mi

The A.T. Guide

1256.6   Little Gap, Little Gap Rd

�11♦ **Slopeside Grill** West 100 yards and 0.3mi up driveway. Hikers welcome to get water from outside spigot. Grill hours: Fri 5-11pm, Sat 2-11pm, Sun 2-9pm.

Danielsville, PA 18038 (1.5E on Blue Mountain Dr, then left on Mountainview Dr to PO and B&B.)

⌂ M-F 8-12 & 1-5, Sa 8-12, 610-767-6882

🛏⛺🚗🛜✉   **Filbert B&B** 610-428-3300 ⟨www.filbertbnb.com⟩ $100S, $150D. Hosted by Kathy in victorian farmhouse includes full country breakfast. Will pickup at Little Gap (no charge). Fee for pickup at Lehigh or Smith Gap. Call ahead for reservations, surcharge for credit cards. Parking for section hikers, ask about shuttles. Italian and Chinese restaurants will deliver. Maildrops: 3740 Filbert Dr, Danielsville, PA 18038.

�11 💲 (0.8E) **Blue Mountain Restaurant & Ice Cream** 610-767-6379.

🏪 (1.0E) **Miller's Market**

1263.9   Smith Gap Rd

♦ 💦 🚗 🅿 (1.0W) Home of John "Mechanical Man" Stempa, eponym of the spring 0.7 mile south. The Stempas (610-381-4606) welcome you to get water from the spigot at rear of the house and to use the outside shower during daylight hours. Pet friendly. Please sign register. This is a safe place to park your car. For-fee shuttles ranging from PA 309 to Delaware Water Gap. Ask about stoves and fuel. No camping.

1272.0   PA 33

🛏 (0.1W) **Gateway Motel** 610-863-4959, $60S $65D, sodas sold at office, free shuttle to town when available, welcome to refill water.

🐾 (4W) **Creature Comforts** 610-381-2287, 24/7 emergency animal care.

Wind Gap, PA 18091 (1E) *(more services on map)*
Bluegrass Festival June 7-10

⌂ M-F 8:30-5, Sa 8:30-12, 610-863-6206

🛏🛜 **Travel Inn** 610-863-4146 Double room $59 weekdays, $69 weekends. Room for 4 $69 weekdays, $79 weekends, pets $10.

🏬 **Giant Food Store** 24hr

🏬 💳 **K-Mart** with pharmacy

🏪 **Turkey Hill Market**

�11 **Beer Stein** L/D, ask about camping

�11 **J&R's Smokehouse** L/D

�11 **Sal's Pizza** 610-863-7565, delivers

�11 **Hong Kong Chinese** L/D buffet,

💳 **CVS** 610-863-5341

✚ **Priority Care** 610-654-5454 Walk-in clinic M-F 8am-8pm, Sa 10am-5pm, Su 10am-4pm.

✚ **Slate Belt Family Practice** 610-863-3019

Also: Gap Theatre 610-863-3094 Movies F-Su.

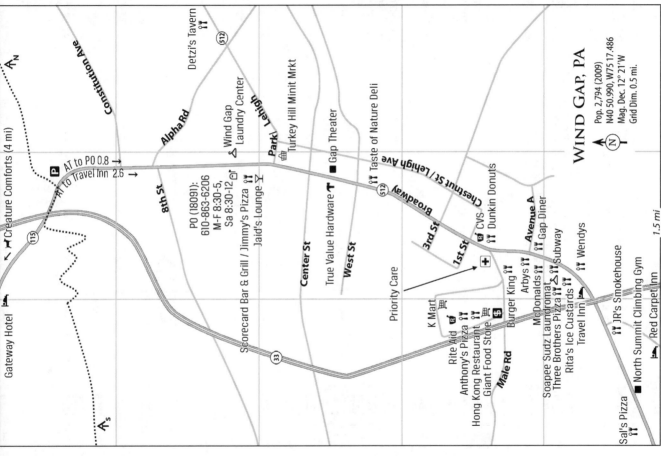

WIND GAP, PA

Pop. 2,794 (2009)
N40 50.990, W75 17.486
Mag. Dec. 12° 21'W
Grid Dim. 0.5 mi.

Constitution Ave

Detzi's Tavern (512)

Alpha Rd

Wind Gap Laundry Center

Turkey Hill Minit Mrkt

Park

Lehigh

Gap Theater

Taste of Nature Deli

AT to PO 0.8 →
AT to Travel Inn 2.6 →

Creature Comforts (4 mi)

P

8th St

PO (18091):
610-863-6206
M-F 8:30-5,
Sa 8:30-12

Scorecard Bar & Grill / Jimmy's Pizza
Jaid's Lounge

True Value Hardware

Center St

West St

Chestnut St / Lehigh Ave

Broadway

(512)

3rd St

1st St

CVS
Dunkin Donuts

Avenue A

Gap Diner

Subway

Wendys

Priority Care

115

Gateway Hotel

33

Priority Care

K Mart

Rite Aid
Anthony's Pizza
Hong Kong Restaurant
Giant Food Store

Male Rd

Burger King
McDonalds
Arbys
Soapee Sudz Laundromat
Three Brothers Pizza
Rita's Ice Custards
Travel Inn

North Summit Climbing Gym

JR's Smokehouse

Red Carpet Inn

Sal's Pizza

1.5 mi

125
PA

The A.T. Guide

SoBo	NoBo	The A.T. Guide	Elev
906.4	1277.8	Campsite	1644
905.8	1278.4	Spring to west	1598
905.3	1278.9	Wolf Rocks, view	1629
903.6	1280.6	Fox Gap, PA 191 (paved). N40 56.126 W75 11.815 P	1400
903.1	1281.1	Powerline **Kirkridge Shelter** 37.3◄30.5◄13.8▼►3.2►37.8► 43.6	1442
903.0	1281.2	Tap 0.1 mile to back left of shelter, off in cold months.	1467
902.7	1281.5	Campsite, view	1505
901.1	1283.1	Totts Gap, gravel road, powerline to south	1300
900.8	1283.4	Pipeline	1384
900.5	1283.7	Roadbed	1405
899.1	1285.1	Mt Minsi	1461
898.1	1286.1	Lookout Rock, view	800
897.9	1286.3	Stream	786
897.3	1286.9	Council Rock	600
897.1	1287.1	Turn east on gravel road	589
896.6	1287.4	Hiker parking lot	520
896.5	1287.7	PA 611, **Delaware Water Gap, PA** N40 58.788 W75 8.518 P (pg.128)	405
896.2	1288.0	**PA-NJ** border, I-80, Delaware River Bridge west bank	307
895.3	1288.9	Kittatinny Visitor Center N40 58.219 W75 7.729 P H	328
		NoBo: cross under I-80 and turn left.	
894.9	1289.3	Parking, water pump. For overnight parking, visitor center is preferred. P	346
		The sign "camping for A.T. through hikers" refers to a site 3.0N on AT.	
894.5	1289.7	Dunnfield Trail to east	502
893.4	1290.8	Holly Spring Trail	950
891.3	1292.9	Backpacker Campsite, Douglas Trail to west, water south of camp.	1327
		No fires, use bear boxes/poles, leash dogs.	
890.5	1293.7	Sunfish Pond south end, no swimming or camping.	1382
889.7	1294.5	Sunfish Pond north end, rock sculptures	1435
889.0	1295.2	Stream	1473
888.3	1295.9	Powerline	1581
888.2	1296.0	Kittatinny Mountain, rocky summit	1534
887.6	1296.6	Kaiser Trail to west	1431

SoBo	NoBo		Elev
885.8	**1298.4**	Camp Rd (gravel), footbridge .... N41 1.977 W75 0.237 P ♦ (pg.128)	1131
		Mohican Outdoor Center (0.3W)	
884.6	**1299.6**	Rattlesnake Swamp Trail, view.	1491
883.7	**1300.5**	Catfish Lookout Tower, picnic table below the tower	1565
883.1	**1301.1**	Rattlesnake Spring on dirt road about 17 yards west of AT.	1260
882.8	**1301.4**	Stream.	1257
882.6	**1301.6**	Millbrook-Blairstown Rd (paved) .... N41 3.567 W74 57.815 P ♦♦	1291
		Millbrook Village (1.1W) historical park with picnic area.	
882.3	**1301.9**	Swamp	1265
882.0	**1302.2**	Powerline	1407
879.9	**1304.3**	Campsite	1522
878.8	**1305.4**	Blue Mtn Lakes Rd .... N41 5.357 W74 54.783 P ♦	1350
		Pump south of road and west of AT, no camping in zone from 0.5 mile of road to one mile north of Crater Lake.	
876.7	**1307.5**	Side trail leads 0.5E to Crater Lake. No camping.	1477
875.7	**1308.5**	Buttermilk Falls Trail, campsites to the north	1574
874.4	**1309.8**	Campsite	1305
874.0	**1310.2**	Rattlesnake Mountain	1492
873.7	**1310.5**	Spring	1358
871.8	**1312.4**	**Brink Road Shelter** (0.2W) 61.7◄45.0◄31.2◄▶6.6▶12.4▶15.3	1234
		Bear box. Close to road. Spring 100 yards to right.	
870.6	**1313.6**	Jacobs Ladder Trail	1376
868.8	**1315.4**	Powerline	1244
868.2	**1316.0**	US 206, Culvers Gap, **Branchville, NJ** (3.4E) (pg.128-129)	935
867.7	**1316.5**	Sunrise Mountain Rd (paved) .... N41 10.780 W74 47.277 P	968
866.3	**1317.9**	Culver Fire Tower	1550

1287.7   PA 611, *Delaware Water Gap, PA 18327*

The Church of the Mountain Hostel 570-476-0345 Bunkroom, showers, overflow tenting, rides to Stroudsburg when available. Donations encouraged. 2-night max. No drive-ins, no parking, no laundry. Phone numbers of persons who can be of assistance are posted in the hostel. Thurs night hot dog dinner.

Pocono Inn 570-476-0000 $55 weekdays, $59 weekends

Deer Head Inn 570-424-2000 $90/up weekdays, $120/up weekends. No pets, no TV. Restaurant & lounge open to all. Live music W-Su, hiker attire okay.

Water Gap Diner B/L/D, **Doughboy's Pizza** open 7 days in summer.

Village Farmer & Bakery 8am-8pm 7 days. Hot dog and slice of pie $2.49. Breakfast sandwich $4.99.

Antelao Restaurant (upscale dining)

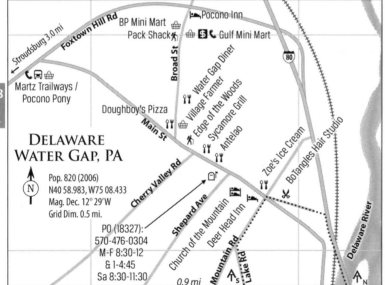

DELAWARE WATER GAP, PA

↑N

Pop. 820 (2006)
N40 58.983, W75 08.433
Mag. Dec. 12° 29'W
Grid Dim. 0.5 mi.

PO (18327):
570-476-0304
M-F 8:30-12
& 1-4:45
Sa 8:30-11:30

0.9 mi

Labels on map: Stroudsburg 3.0 mi, Foxtown Hill Rd, BP Mini Mart, Pocono Inn, Pack Shack, Gulf Mini Mart, Broad St, Water Gap Diner, Village Farmer, Edge of the Woods, Sycamore Grill, Antelao, Martz Trailways / Pocono Pony, Doughboy's Pizza, Main St, Zoe's Ice Cream, BoTangles Hair Studio, Cherry Valley Rd, Shepard Ave, Church of the Mountain, Deer Head Inn, Mountain Rd, Lake Rd, Delaware River, I-80

Edge of the Woods Outfitters 570-421-6681
Full line of gear, trail food, gear repair, Coleman/alcohol/oz. Shuttles from Little Gap to Bear Mtn. Maildrops: (FedEx/UPS only) 110 Main St, Delaware Water Gap, PA 18327.

Pack Shack 570-424-8533 Gear, food, fuel/oz, shuttles and slackpacks. 10-5 M-F, 8-6 weekends.

Pocono Pony 570-839-6862 ⟨gomcta.com⟩ $1.25 each way to Stroudsburg Mall.

Martz Trailways 570-421-3040 $56.50 NYC roundtrip.

Pocono Cab 570-424-2800,

WGM Taxi 570-223-9289.

Stroudsburg, PA 18360 (3.5W)

Large town with all services, including supermarket, motels, laundry, and movie theater.

Dunkleberger's Sports 570-421-7950

Walmart 24hrs

1298.4   Camp Road

Mohican Outdoor Center (0.3W)
908-362-5670 <www.outdoors.org/lodging/mohican/>
Bunkroom $30PP weekdays, $39 weekends, tenting $9, both include shower and a towel. Shower without stay is $5. Campfires only in designated areas. Lobby with microwave open to all guests 8am-8pm. Water available at the lodge or a spigot near the garage on the right. Camp store open 9am-5pm (7pm in peak of summer). Deli sandwiches, sodas, candy, Coleman/alcohol/oz, and limited hiker supplies. Operated by the AMC. Maildrops: 50 Camp Road, Blairstown, NJ 07825.

1316.0   US 206, Culvers Gap *(more services on map)*

Stokes State Park 973-948-3820, Tentsite for up to six persons $20. Cabins $45 (4-person), $85 (8-person), $120 (12-person). Free showers.

⊨ 🛜 ✉ **Forest Motel** 973-948-5456, $57S $68.40D, pets $20. Guest maildrops: 104 Rte 206 N, Branchville, NJ 07826.

⊨ **Cobmin Ridge Motel** 973-948-3459

🍴 **Joe to Go** Leave pack on bench outside.

🍴 **Jumboland Diner** B/L/D, $2.99 breakfast special and Thursday dinner buffet.

🍴 **Jimmy's Pizza & Pasta** closed M,

🏬 (1.5E) **Dale's Market** 973-948-3078

🏬 **Yellow Cottage Deli & Bakery**
    Branchville, NJ 07826 (3.4E)
⏰ M–F 8:30–5, Sa 8:30–1, 973-948-3580

330.3   NJ 23

👫♦🅿✉ **High Point State Park Headquarters** 973-875-4800 Office open year-round, water spigot outside. Maildrops: 1480 State Rte 23, Sussex, NJ 07461.

◗🍴🚿 2.5 mile from headquarters are campsites at Sawmill Pond, swim area, concession stand, grill, and hot showers. $20 night, 6 per site. No pets or alcohol. Open Apr 1 - Oct 31.

⊨△🚌🛜✉ (1.5E) **High Point Country Inn** 973-702-1860 $69.99 weekdays, $79.99 weekends double occupancy. Laundry 7, pets $5, no room phone. Free pick-up/return to trail, longer shuttles for a fee. Guest maildrops: 1328 NJ 23, Wantage, NJ 07461.

Port Jervis, NY 12785 (4.4W)

⊨🛜✉ **Days Inn** 845-856-6611 $65D, $10EAP, cont B, pets $20. Guest maildrops: 2247 Greenville Turnpike, Port Jervis, NY 12771.

🍴 **Village Pizza** 973-293-3364

🍴 **Little Caesars Pizza** 570-491-4436

🖳🛒 **Shop Rite Market**, **Price Chopper**

💊 **Rite Aid** 845-856-8342, **Medicine Shoppe** 845-856-6681

➕ **Bon Secours Community Hospital** 845-858-7000

🐾 **Tri-States Veterinary Medical** 845-856-1914

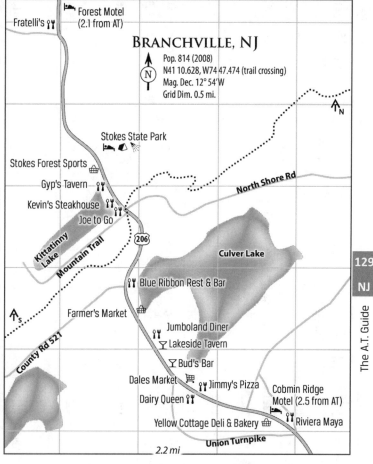

Forest Motel (2.1 from AT)

Fratelli's 🍴

BRANCHVILLE, NJ
Pop. 814 (2008)
N41 10.628, W74 47.474 (trail crossing)
Mag. Dec. 12° 54'W
Grid Dim. 0.5 mi.

Stokes State Park ⊨◗🚿

Stokes Forest Sports 🧺

Gyp's Tavern 🍴

North Shore Rd

Kevin's Steakhouse 🍴🍴
Joe to Go 🍴

Kittatinny Lake

Mountain Trail

206

Culver Lake

🍴 **Blue Ribbon Rest & Bar**

Farmer's Market 🏬

County Rd 521

🍴 Jumboland Diner
🍷 Lakeside Tavern

🍷 Bud's Bar

Dales Market 🏬 🍴 Jimmy's Pizza

Dairy Queen 🍴

Cobmin Ridge Motel (2.5 from AT)

Yellow Cottage Deli & Bakery 🏬   🍴 Riviera Maya

Union Turnpike

2.2 mi

SoBo	NoBo	The A.T. Guide	Elev
865.3	1318.9	Stony Brook	1346
865.2	1319.0	**Gren Anderson Shelter** (0.1W)	1341
		51.6◄37.8◄6.6◄►5.8►8.7►13.0 Spring to left of shelter and downhill 70 yards.	
863.8	1320.4	Tinsley Trail	1443
862.8	1321.4	Sunrise Mountain, no camping at pavilion	1653
862.1	1322.1	Roadbed.	1430
861.1	1323.1	Stream (slow outflow from pond)	1379
859.4	1324.8	**Mashipacong Shelter** 43.6◄12.4◄5.8◄►2.9►7.2►19.6	1431
859.2	1325.0	Spring (0.6N) on red-blazed Iris Trail. Bear box. Close to road.	1336
		Deckertown Turnpike. N41 15.136 W74 41.367	
858.1	1326.1	Three intersections with red-blazed trail	1436
856.5	1327.7	**Rutherford Shelter** (0.4E) 15.3◄8.7◄2.9◄►4.3►16.7►28.2	1451
856.3	1327.9	Spring 100 yards before shelter on connecting trail. Slow stream. Bear box.	1484
		View.	
854.9	1329.3	Intersection with blue-blazed trail.	1619
854.0	1330.2	Iris Trail 0.2E to parking on NJ 23	1524
853.9	1330.3	NJ 23 N41 18.158 W74 40.065 **P** ● (pg.129)	1500
		High Point State Park Headquarters, **Port Jervis, NY** (4.4W)	
852.9	1331.3	Wooden tower, trail 0.3W to beach and concessions	1701
852.7	1331.5	Green-blazed trail 0.3W to 220' tower atop highest point in NJ	1628
852.2	1332.0	**High Point Shelter** (0.1E) 13.0◄7.2◄4.3◄►12.4►23.9►36.0.	1318
		Streams on both sides of shelter. Road to privy to right of shelter. Bear box.	
850.9	1333.3	County 519 (paved)	1100
850.1	1334.1	Courtwright Rd (gravel)	973
849.6	1334.6	Streams	1022
848.9	1335.3	Fergerson Rd (gravel), east 20 yards on road.	876
848.2	1336.0	Gemmer Rd (paved)	738
847.9	1336.3	Footbridge, stream	714
847.5	1336.7	Two footbridges, streams	617
847.2	1337.0	Goodrich Rd (paved)	644
847.0	1337.2	Pond	677
846.8	1337.4	Murray property 0.2W, gravel driveway (pg.132)	663
846.4	1337.8	Goldsmith Lane	680
846.0	1338.2	Unionville Rd (paved), Country Rd 615 (pg.132-133)	610
845.7	1338.5	Quarry Rd	654
845.1	1339.1	Lott Rd, **Unionville, NY** (0.7W) (pg.132-133)	590

SoBo	NoBo			Elev
844.1	1340.1	NJ 284, **Unionville, NY** (0.7W)	N41 17.631 W74 33.369 **P** (pg.132-133)	420
843.7	1340.5	Lower Rd (Oil City Rd).		530
843.1	1341.1	Carnegie Rd, NoBo: follow road 0.2W		415
842.9	1341.3	State Line Rd, NoBo: follow road 0.5E		420
842.6	1341.6	Wallkill River, parking.	N41 17.005 W74 31.562 **P**	410
842.3	1341.9	AT + State Line Rd north end. NoBo: turn east into Wallkill Reserve		406
841.5	1342.7	90 degree turn on Wallkill perimeter		393
841.1	1343.1	90 degree turn on Wallkill perimeter		413
840.3	1343.9	Liberty Corners Rd (paved).		440
840.2	1344.0	Water to west.	◖	591
839.8	1344.4	**Pochuck Mtn. Shelter** (0.1W) 19.6◄16.7◄12.4◄▶11.5▶23.6▶37.9.	◖ ⌂ ⌐(6)	901
		Bear box. Spigot at vacant house at foot of Pochuck Mountain.		
839.0	1345.2	View.	▣	1132
838.3	1345.9	Pochuck Mountain	▣	1154
837.7	1346.5	Lovemma Lane (gravel).	◖	887
837.6	1346.6	Stream.	◖	798
837.1	1347.1	County Rd 565, **Glenwood, NJ** (1.1W), stream south of road	◖ (pg.132)	720
836.4	1347.8	Roadbed.		766
835.6	1348.6	Country Rd 517, **Glenwood, NJ** (1.1W)	N41 14.142 W74 28.830 **P** (pg.132)	443
834.9	1349.3	Pochuck Creek suspension footbridge.		407
		Boardwalk over swamp for (0.6S) and (0.2N) of footbridge.		
834.2	1350.0	Canal Rd.	N41 13.597 W74 28.137 **P**	410
833.9	1350.3	Footbridge, Wawayanda Creek.	◖	417
833.3	1350.9	NJ 94, **Vernon, NJ** (2.4E)	N41 13.160 W74 27.306 **P** (pg.132)	450
832.2	1352.0	Spring.	◖	1052
831.9	1352.3	Pinwheels vista 0.1W, Wawayanda Mountain, side trail 0.8E to views	▣	1340
831.0	1353.2	Footbridge, stream	◖	1003
830.2	1354.0	Barrett Rd (paved), **New Milford, NY** (1.8W).	(pg.132)	1140
829.1	1355.1	Cross stream on Iron Mountain Rd	Water from park 0.1N and 0.2E.	1060
828.3	1355.9	**Wawayanda Shelter** (0.1W) 28.2◄23.9◄11.5◄▶12.1▶26.4▶31.7	◖ ⌂ ⌐(6)	1214
828.2	1356.0	Wawayanda State Park (0.2E)	N41 11.883 W74 23.847 **P** ⛹ ◖	1182
827.8	1356.4	Warwick Turnpike.	N41 12.085 W74 23.497 **P** (pg.132)	1140
827.3	1356.9	Footbridge, stream.	◖	1134
826.5	1357.7	Long House Dr / Brady Rd	N41 11.732 W74 22.290 **P**	1138

⚠ *Hitchhiking is illegal in NY; camp only in designated sites; fires only in campsite fire rings.*

SoBo	NoBo			Elev
825.3	1358.9	Long House Creek, footbridge	◖	1085
824.5	1359.7	Ernest Walter Trail (yellow-blazed) to east		1368

1337.4   Trail to Murray property (Privately owned cabin)
⚡🏠💧🚿🌙 Long distance hikers may stay or get water. Cabin, tenting, well water, shower & privy. No drugs, alcohol or groups.

1338.2, 1339.1, 1340.1
            Unionville, NY 10988 (see map)

1347.1   County Rd 565
1348.6   County Rd 517 (0.9W to PO and Pochuck Valley Farm)
            Glenwood, NJ 07418 (1.1W from either road)
🏠 M-F 7:30-5, Sa 10-2, 973-764-2616
🛏🛜✉ **Apple Valley Inn** 973-764-3735 $145-$160, includes country breakfast, no pets, shuttles to County Roads 517 & 565 with stay. Guest maildrops: PO Box 302, Glenwood, NJ 07418.
🍴🛒👫 **Pochuck Valley Farm**   Sandwiches, produce, bakery. Water spigot and restroom. Open daily M-F 5-6:30, Sa-Su 5-6.

1350.9   NJ 94
🛒 (0.1W) **Heaven Hill Farm** 973-764-5144 7 days, 9-5, until 7 in summer (6 on Sundays) ice cream, bakery, fresh fruit & vegetables.
🛏🛜 (1.8E) **Appalachian Motel** 973-764-6070 $69-150, pets $20.
            Vernon, NJ 07462 (2.4E)
🏠 M-F 8:30-5, Sa 9:30-12:30, 973-764-9056
🛏🚿⛺🖥 Located in **St. Thomas Episcopal Church** $10PP donation, capacity 12. Stay one night only, longer by permission. No pets inside. Shower/towel, fridge, micro, & cooking in kitchen by permission. Hikers may have to share space with other groups and are expected to help w/cleanup. No alcohol permitted. Hikers welcome to attend Sunday services.
🍴 **Rigatoni's, Mixing Bowl, Place By the Tracks, Long Spring Chinese Restaurant, Burger King**
🛒 **A&P Food Store**
➕ **Vernon Urgent Care** 973-209-2260 1.1 miles beyond hostel,

M-F 8-8, Sa-Su 9-5. **Newton Memorial Hospital** 973-383-2121
🐾 **Vernon Veterinary Clinic** 973-764-3630
💊 **Rite Aid**
🧺 **K&C Washer**
🖥 **Dorothy Henry Library** M/W/F 9-5, Tu/Th 9-8:30.

1354.0   Barrett Rd
            New Milford, NY 10959 (1.8W)
🏠 M-F 8:30-12:30 & 2-4:30, Sa 9-11:30, 845-986-3557

1356.4   Warwick Turnpike
            Warwick, NY 10990
            2.7W to intersection with NY 94:
🛏🧺🖥🅿🛜🖥 **Meadow Lark Farm B&B** 845-651-4286 ⟨www.meadowlarkfarm.com⟩ Weeknight rate $75S/D or $99 for 3-person room, includes breakfast. Rate is higher on Fri-Sa nights. Tenting on lawn $15 includes shower and breakfast. All major CC, pets welcome. Shuttles $1 per round-trip mile; free parking for section hikers. Maildrops: 180 Union Corners Road, Warwick, NY 10990.
🛒 **Shop Rite Supermarket, Price Chopper**
💊 **Rite Aid**
🍴 **Pronto Pizza, Pennings Farm Market** Harvest Grill, ice cream
Also: Warwick Drive-In Theatre 845-986-4440 $8 adults, $5 kids and seniors, no credit cards.
            1.5 miles farther north on NY 94 to downtown Warwick where there are many restaurants and the post office and library.
🏠 M-F 8:30-5, Sa 9-4, 845-986-0271
🐾 **Orchard Grove Animal Hospital** 845-986-9399
➕ **St Anthonys Community Hospital** 845-986-2276
🧺 **South Street Wash & Fold, Warwick Laundry Center**
🖥 **Albert Wisner Public Library** 845-986-1047, M-Th 9-8, F-Sa 9-5, Su 12-4.

The A.T. Guide

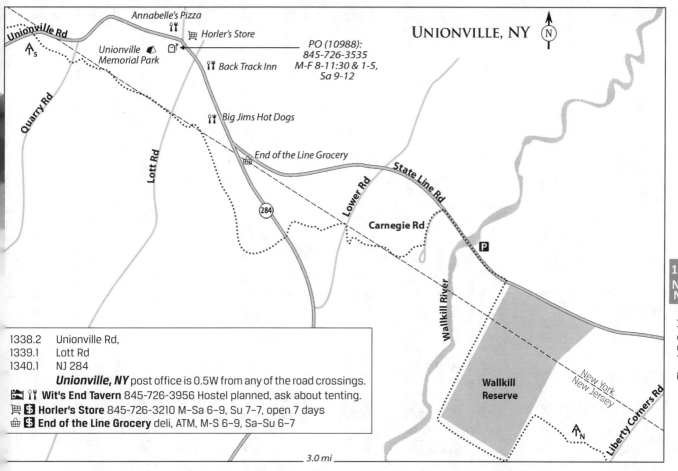

Annabelle's Pizza

Horler's Store

UNIONVILLE, NY N

Unionville
Memorial Park

Back Track Inn

PO (10988):
845-726-3535
M-F 8-11:30 & 1-5,
Sa 9-12

Unionville Rd

Quary Rd

Lott Rd

Big Jims Hot Dogs

End of the Line Grocery

284

State Line Rd

Lower Rd

Carnegie Rd

P

Wallkill River

New York
New Jersey

Wallkill
Reserve

Liberty Corners Rd

1338.2	Unionville Rd,
1339.1	Lott Rd
1340.1	NJ 284

Unionville, NY post office is 0.5W from any of the road crossings.

Wit's End Tavern 845-726-3956 Hostel planned, ask about tenting.

Horler's Store 845-726-3210 M-Sa 6-9, Su 7-7, open 7 days

End of the Line Grocery deli, ATM, M-S 6-9, Sa-Su 6-7

— 3.0 mi —

SoBo	NoBo	The A.T. Guide	Elev
824.2	1360.0	**NJ-NY** border, State Line Trail 1.0E to **Lakeside, NJ**.	1385
823.8	1360.4	0.1N on AT is Zig Zag Trail to west. Prospect Rock, highest point on AT in NY. Views of Greenwood Lake to east.	1433
822.9	1361.3	Furnace Brook	1153
822.6	1361.6	Ladder.	1290
821.2	1363.0	Cascade Brook	1166
820.4	1363.8	Village Vista Trail, 0.8E to Greenwood Lake	1263
818.8	1365.4	Powerline	1175
818.3	1365.9	NY 17A, **Bellvale, NY** (1.6W). N41 14.658 W74 17.216 **P** (pg.136-137) **Greenwood Lake, NY** (2.0E)	1153
817.6	1366.6	Pipeline clearing	1225
817.0	1367.2	Eastern Pinnacles, short bypass trail to west	1206
816.8	1367.4	Brook	1058
816.5	1367.7	Cat Rocks, view	1076
816.2	1368.0	**Wildcat Shelter** (0.2W) Water on trail to shelter. 36.0◀23.6◀12.1◀▶14.3▶19.6▶22.7	1086
814.9	1369.3	Highlands Trail	771
814.7	1369.5	Lakes Rd (paved), 0.1N powerline, footbridge and stream	680
814.3	1369.9	Fitzgerald Falls	756
813.1	1371.1	Allis Trail, Sterling Fire Tower 5.0E	1265
812.4	1371.8	Mombasha High Point	1280
811.3	1372.9	Boardwalk, pond	927
811.2	1373.0	West Mombasha Rd, stream just north on AT N41 16.159 W74 12.876 **P**	947
810.3	1373.9	Buchanan Mountain	1142
809.5	1374.7	East Mombasha Rd (paved)	840
809.2	1375.0	Little Dam Lake, footbridge.	742
808.0	1376.2	Orange Turnpike. N41 16.167 W74 10.862 **P** ◆ (0.5E)	802
807.4	1376.8	Arden Mountain	1180
807.1	1377.1	Sapphire Trail	1158
806.6	1377.6	View. (pg.136)	1027
806.3	1377.9	NY 17, **Southfields, NY** (2.1E), **Harriman, NY** (3.7W)	550
805.8	1378.4	AT on Arden Valley Rd for 0.4 mile, N41 15.893 W74 9.261 **P** Passes over NY State Thruway 87.	635
804.6	1379.6	Island Pond Rd (gravel) 0.1E to pond	1029
804.0	1380.2	Lemon Squeezer, Arden-Surebridge Trail to east	1150
803.7	1380.5	Island Pond Mountain	1319

SoBo	NoBo		Elev
803.3	1380.9	New York Long Path 52.0E to Manhattan	1079
802.6	1381.6	Surebridge Brook	1111
802.0	1382.2	AT joins Red Dot Trail (south end)	1350
801.9	1382.3	**Fingerboard Shelter** 37.9◀26.4◀14.3◀▶5.3▶8.4▶40.6 ◊⌂(8)	1368
		Spring downhill to left unreliable. Water at Lake Tiorati 0.5E on Hurst Trail.	
801.3	1382.9	Fingerboard Mountain	1328
800.7	1383.5	Arden Valley Rd (paved) ⋯ N41 16.542 W74 5.286 P 🛉	1201
		(0.3E) Lake Tiorati Circle, restrooms, showers, vending machines. Open summer.	
800.0	1384.2	Woods road	1040
798.7	1385.5	Footbridge, stream	857
798.6	1385.6	Seven Lakes Dr	850
796.6	1387.6	**William Brien Memorial Shelter** 31.7◀19.6◀5.3◀▶3.1▶35.3▶44.3 ◊⌂(8)	1080
		Unreliable spring-fed well 80 yards down blue-blazed trail to right of shelter.	
		Yellow-blazed Menomine Trail to east.	
795.7	1388.5	AT joins Red Dot Trail (north end)	940
795.3	1388.9	Black Mountain, views, can see NY City skyline	1212
794.5	1389.7	Palisades Parkway, busy 4-lane divided highway	696
		Visitor center in median 0.4W, soda & snack machines. NY City 34E.	
794.2	1390.0	Beechy Bottom Brook, footbridge, parking 0.8W	627
793.5	1390.7	**West Mountain Shelter** (0.6E) 22.7◀8.4◀3.1◀▶32.2▶41.2▶49.0 ⌂(8)	1186
792.7	1391.5	Views from ridge of West Mountain	1136
792.1	1392.1	Fawn Trail to west	683
791.7	1392.5	Seven Lakes Dr	610
790.5	1393.7	Perkins Memorial Dr	838
789.3	1394.9	Bear Mountain, Perkins Memorial Tower, view NYC skyline.	1305
		Vending machines.	
788.4	1395.8	Perkins Memorial Dr (crossed three times)	1147
787.2	1397.0	Bear Mountain Recreation Area, Hessian Lake . N41 18.670 W74 0.434 P (pg.140)	173
787.0	1397.2	Tunnel under US 9, Trailside Museum, bear cage is lowest point on AT . (pg.140)	166
786.5	1397.7	Bear Mountain Bridge, Hudson River, **Fort Montgomery, NY** (1.8W) . (pg.140)	200
785.9	1398.3	NY 9D, Bear Mountain Bridge north end	192
785.2	1399.0	Camp Smith Trail, 0.6E to Anthonys Nose, views of Hudson River	730
784.3	1399.9	Hemlock Springs Campsite	550
784.1	1400.1	Manitou Rd (gravel). N41 19.776 W73 57.195 P	460
783.1	1401.1	Osborne Loop Trail to west (blue-blazed)	800

1365.9   NY 17A

�water ☎ (0.3W) **Bellvale Farms** Ice cream, water from hose, can use phone, ask about parking.
Bellvale, NY 10912 (1.6W)
🍴 **Mamma's Boy Pizza** 845-986-1802, deli sandwiches, 7 days.

🚶 **Gear To Go Outfitters** 718-399-7848, Free delivery to any trailhead in NY state with a $75 minimum order.

Minimize Campfire Impacts

•Use stoves for cooking – if you need a fire, build one only where it's legal and in an existing fire ring. Leave hatchets and saws at home – collect dead and downed wood that you can break by hand. Burn all wood to ash.

•Do not try to burn trash, including foil, plastic, glass, cans, tea bags, food, or anything with food on it. These items do not burn thoroughly. They create noxious fumes, attract wildlife like skunks and bears, and make the area unsightly.

•Where campfires are permitted, leave the fire ring clean by removing others' trash and scattering unused wood, cold coals, and ashes 200 feet away from camp after the fire is cold and completely out.

Read more of the Leave No Trace techniques developed for the A.T.: www.appalachiantrail.org/LNT

Greenwood Lake, NY 10925 (2E)
🛏🍴⛺🚐📶🖥✉ **Anton's on the Lake** 845-477-0010 800-754-8935 ⟨www.antonsonthelake.com⟩ thru hikers $80S/D Sunday through Thursday, $125/up Friday and Saturday. All major CC, rooms with whirlpool available, no pets, no smoking, laundry small loads only, swimming, offers free shuttles and slackpacking w/stay, longer shuttles for a fee. Open year round, very hiker friendly. Maildrops for guests: (USPS) PO Box 1505 or (FedEx/UPS) 7 Waterstone Road, Greenwood Lake, NY 10925.

🛏🍴💲📶✉ **Breezy Point Inn** 845-477-8100 ⟨www.breezypointinn. com⟩ Open May 1 - Nov 1. $85/up, no pets, no smoking, L/D dining 7 days. Guest maildrops: 620 Jersey Ave, Greenwood Lake, NY 10925.

🍴 **Subway**, **Sing Loong Kitchen**, **Ashley's Pizzeria & Café**, **Delicious Deli**, **Doc's Pizza & Steak**

🏪 **Country Grocery**, **Cumberland Farms** deli sandwiches, 24/7.

📷 **CVS Pharmacy**

🖥 **Greenwood Lake Public Library** M/F 9-5, Tu-Th 9-9, Sa 10-4, Su 11-3.

🚐 **Greenwood Lake Taxi** 845-477-0314

🔧 **Greenwood True Value Hardware**
Warwick, NY 10990
4.5W to downtown area
3.1W to 🛏⛺📶 **Warwick Motel** 845-986-6656 $79/up, continenta breakfast, pool.

1377.9   NY 17
Southfields, NY 10975 (2.1E)
🏤 M–F 8:30–12 & 1–5, Sa 8:30–11:30, 845-351-2628
🛏 **Tuxedo Motel** 845-351-4747 $49.50S, 54.50D, $10EAP, no pets accepts Visa/MC.
Harriman, NY 10926 (3.7W)
Lodging, groceries, restaurants, and laundromats.

GREENWOOD LAKE, NY

Pop. 3,419 (2009)
N41 13.360, W74 17.650
Mag. Dec. 13° 4'W
Grid Dim 0.5 mi.

N

PO (10925):
845-477-7328
M-F 8-5, Sa 9-12

↑ 1.8 mi. ↑ **17A**

Bagel Express

Friendly Beer & Soda

17A

Village Vista Trail
0.8 mi. from park to ↑

Subway

CVS

Star's Dog House

Cumberland Farms
(Open 24/7)

210

Citgo

Planet Pizza

Linden Motel

Sunrise
Diner

Village
Farmer

Lion's
Field

Walnut St

Lake
Lodging

Elm St

Village Buzz Cafe

O'Hare's Pub

Linden Ave

Ten Eyke Ave

Breezy Point Inn
0.5 mi.

Murphy's

Latin Cuisine

Sing Loong Kitchen

Jersey Ave

Ashley's Pizza

Library:
845-477-8377
M & F 9-5
Tu-Th 9-9,
Sa 10-4,
Su 11-3

Country
Grocery

True Value Hardware

Waterstone Rd.

137

NY

NJTransit.com
973-275-5555
(bus to NYC
M-F @ $14)

Windermere Ave

Anton's on
the Lake

Sterling Rd

The A.T. Guide

0.9 mi

SoBo	NoBo	The A.T. Guide	Elev
782.8	1401.4	Curry Pond Trail to west (yellow-blazed)	881
781.7	1402.5	Osborne Loop Trail to west (blue-blazed)	890
781.3	1402.9	Carriage Connector Trail to west (yellow-blazed)	543
780.7	1403.5	US 9 + NY 403, **Peekskill, NY** (4.5E) (pg.140)	400
780.4	1403.8	Old Highland Turnpike (paved)	493
780.1	1404.1	Franciscan Way (paved), **Graymoor Spiritual Life Center** (0.4E) (pg.141)	565
779.9	1404.3	Two gravel roads	489
778.2	1406.0	Blue-blazed trail 0.1W to Denning Hill	900
777.4	1406.8	Old Albany Post Rd (gravel), Chapman Rd.	607
776.4	1407.8	Canopus Hill.	829
775.8	1408.4	Brook (pg.141)	412
775.7	1408.5	Canopus Hill Rd (paved)	420
774.7	1409.5	South Highland Rd (paved), stream north side of road.	570
773.9	1410.3	Stream.	705
773.2	1411.0	Catfish Loop Trail (red-blazed)	970
772.0	1412.2	Dennytown Rd (paved), Three Lake Trail to west . N41 25.234 W73 52.135 P	860
		Water on side of pump building, open late-Apr-Oct.	
771.8	1412.4	Catfish Loop Trail to east (red-blazed)	835
770.4	1413.8	Sunken Mine Rd (gravel), stream to north.	800
769.2	1415.0	Three Lakes Trail	985
768.3	1415.9	NY 301, Canopus Lake, **Clarence Fahnestock State Park** (1E) (pg.141)	920
767.7	1416.5	Fahnestock Trail to west	1097
766.3	1417.9	Blue-blazed trail east to lake	999
765.5	1418.7	Stream	1030
764.1	1420.1	Shenandoah Mountain, view, painted 911 Memorial Flag.	1282
763.7	1420.5	Long Hill Rd (gravel)	1100
763.2	1421.0	Powerline	1045
762.6	1421.6	Shenandoah Tenting Area 0.1W, hand pump	900

SoBo	NoBo			Elev
762.2	1422.0	Brook	◆	773
761.4	1422.8	Bridge over brook.	◆	367
761.3	1422.9	Hortontown Rd, N41 30.843 W73 47.509 P (one car)) ◆ ⊏ (6)		377
		RPH Shelter (1982) 40.6◀35.3◀32.2◀▶9.0▶16.8▶25.6 Shelter open Apr-mid-Nov, grounds available year-round. Iron water pump to left of shelter (treat).		
760.9	1423.3	Footbridge, stream, Taconic State Pkwy underpass	◆	552
759.2	1425.0	Hosner Mountain Loop Trail to west		970
758.0	1426.2	Hosner Mountain Loop Trail to west		736
757.8	1426.4	Hosner Mountain Rd, footbridge, stream	◆	500
756.2	1428.0	NY 52, **Stormville, NY** (1.9W) (pg.141)		800
755.7	1428.5	Stream	◆	892
755.0	1429.2	AT on Old Stormville Mountain Rd for 0.1 mile		1023
754.8	1429.4	AT on Stormville Mountain Rd for 0.1 mile crosses over I-84		950
754.6	1429.6	Grape Hollow Rd		980
753.4	1430.8	Side trail 0.6W to Indian Pass		1203
752.4	1431.8	Mt Egbert	) ◆ ⊏ (6)	1329
752.3	1431.9	**Morgan Stewart Shelter** 44.3◀41.2◀9.0◀▶7.8▶16.6▶20.6		1307
751.2	1433.0	Depot Hill Rd N41 34.288 W73 40.840 P		1230
749.3	1434.9	Railroad track, Whakey Lake Stream	◆	688
749.1	1435.0	Old Route 55		707
749.0	1435.2	NY 55, **Poughquag, NY** (3.1W) N41 35.380 W73 39.551 P (0.1W) (pg.141)		720
748.7	1435.5	Beekman Uplands Trail to west		787
748.1	1436.1	Footbridge, stream (more streams in this area)	◆	723
747.8	1436.4	Nuclear Lake south end, loop trail to east (yellow-blazed).		770
746.9	1437.3	Nuclear Lake north end, loop trail to east		794
746.4	1437.8	Beekman Uplands Trail to west		870
745.4	1438.8	Footbridge, swampy area	◆	1057
745.1	1439.1	Penny Rd		1139
744.8	1439.4	West Mountain		1200
744.5	1439.7	**Telephone Pioneers Shelter** (0.1E) shelter trail crosses stream) △ ⊏ (6) 49.0◀16.8◀7.8◀▶8.8▶12.8▶21.2 If dry, get water from residence 0.7N.		1058
743.8	1440.4	County Rd 20, West Dover Rd, **Pawling, NY** (3.1E) (pg.141)	◆	650
741.8	1442.4	Footbridge, stream, farm.	◆	477

1397.0 Bear Mountain Recreation Area
Bear Mountain, NY 10911
⌂ M–F 8–10, 845-786-3747 Limited hours not good for maildrop.
🍴 Concessions & vending near Hessian Lake.

1397.2 Trailside Museum and Zoo
Open 10-4:30; no charge for hikers passing through. Dogs not allowed. Lowest elevation on the AT, 124' above sea level, is within the park. If you have a dog, or if the zoo is closed, use bypass (see map).

1397.7 Bear Mountain Bridge, ***Fort Montgomery, NY 10922*** (1.8W)
🛏 ✉ **Bear Mountain Bridge Motel** 845-446-2472 $69S, $75D, no pets, accepts Visa/MC, pickup/return to trail (zoo) with stay. Guest maildrops: PO Box 554, Fort Montgomery, NY 10922.
🛏 ⚥ 🛜 🖥 ✉ **Holiday Inn Express** 845-446-4277 $120D, $10EAP. Continental breakfast, indoor pool & sauna, coin laundry, 24-hour business center. Guest maildrops: 1106 Route 9 W, Fort Montgomery, NY 10922-0620.
🛏 🛜 **Overlook Lodge** 845-786-2731 $119/up, continental breakfast, some pet rooms. Same contact number for **Bear Mountain Inn** (see map), which is under renovation but may re-open in 2012.

🛏 **Victorian Riverview Inn** 845-446-5479 $175.
🛏 🍴 **The Garrison House** 845-446-2322 $139/up. Ask for hiker rate.
🛏 🛜 **Econo Lodge** 845-446-9400 $75D, continental breakfast. Pets $10.
🍴 **Bagel Café** ATM, **Tony's Pizzeria** 845-446-4000, **Dunkin' Donuts**, **Fox's Country Deli**
🏪 **Food Mart**
🖥 **Highland Falls Library** 845-446-3113 M 10-5, Tu 10-7, W-F 10-5, Sa 10-2.

1403.5 US 9, NY 403
🍴 🏪 ⚬ **Appalachian Market** at trailhead. Open 24hrs, deli serves B/L/D. Water from spigot on north side of building.
  Peekskill, NY 10566 (4.5E) large town with all services
⌂ M–F 9–5, Sa 9–4, 914-737-6437

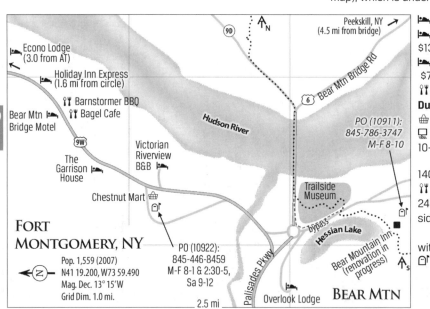

Peekskill, NY (4.5 mi from bridge)

9D

↑N

Bear Mtn Bridge Rd

🛏 Econo Lodge (3.0 from AT)

🛏 Holiday Inn Express (1.6 mi from circle)

6

🍴 Barnstormer BBQ
🍴 Bagel Cafe

Bear Mtn 🛏 Bridge Motel

9W

Hudson River

PO (10911): 845-786-3747 M-F 8-10

The Garrison House 🛏

Victorian Riverview B&B 🛏

Chestnut Mart 🏪

Trailside Museum

FORT MONTGOMERY, NY
Pop. 1,559 (2007)
N41 19.200, W73 59.490
Mag. Dec. 13° 15'W
Grid Dim. 1.0 mi.

PO (10922): 845-446-8459 M-F 8-1 & 2:30-5, Sa 9-12

Palisades Pkwy

bypass

Hessian Lake

Bear Mountain Inn (renovation in progress)

↑S

🛏 Overlook Lodge

BEAR MTN

2.5 mi

1404.1   Franciscan Way

⌐◊☽ ♪ **Graymoor Spiritual Life Center** (0.4E) 800-338-2620 Hikers permitted to sleep at monastery's ball field picnic shelter which has water, privy, and shower during warm months. Open all season and free. Follow signs and blue-blazes; stay to the left at both forks in the road.

1407.8   Canopus Hill Rd

⌂ 🆂 (1.6E) **Putnam Valley Market** 845-528-8626 Directions: (0.3E) on Canopus Hill Rd, (0.1S) on Canopus Hollow Rd, (1.2W) on Sunset Hill Road. Pizza, hot food from the grill, phone, ATM, open M-Sa 6–9, Su 6-7.

1415.9   NY 301, Canopus Lake

◖👬🌿 📞 (1E) **Clarence Fahnestock State Park** 845-225-7207, 800-456-2267 Open mid-Apr to mid-Dec. Thru-hikers get one free night of camping. Phone across street at Pelton Pond.

1428.0   NY 52

⌂ 🍴🆂◊📞 (0.4E) **Mountaintop Market Deli** 845-221-0928 Open daily 6–8, ATM and pay phone inside, welcome to water from faucet on side of building.
🍴 **Danny's Pizzeria** pizza by the slice.

   Stormville, NY 12582 (1.9W)
⌂ M-F 8:30–5, Sa 9–12, 845-226-2627
🍴 **Stormville Pizza**

1435.2   NY 55

🛒🍴📞 (1.5W) Pleasant Ridge Plaza with **Poughquag Central Market**, **Pleasant Ridge Pizza** L/D.
⌕ (1.2W) **CVS**
🍴 **R's Gulf Quickmart & Deli** 845-452-4040

Poughquag, NY 12570 (3.1W)
⌂ M-F 8:30–5, Sa 8:30–12:30, 845-724-4763
🛏 **Pine Grove Motel** 845-724-5151 $65S $70D, no pets, accepts Visa/MC.
🍴 **Great Wall**, **Clove Valley Deli & Café**
⌕ **Total Care Pharmacy, Beekman Pharmacy**
🐕 **Beekman Animal Hospital** 845-724-8387

1440.4   County Rd 20, West Dover Rd
Dover Oak north side of road, largest oak tree on AT. Girth 20' 4" and estimated to be over 300 years old. Spigot on fence post at purple house 100 yards east of the trail. Please help yourself, they would prefer that you do not interrupt them to ask permission.
   Pawling, NY 12564 (3.1E)
⌂ M-F 8:30–5, Sa 9–12, 845-855-2669
◖👬📞 **Edward R. Murrow Memorial Park** Town allows hikers to camp in park for one night only. One mile from the center of Main Street, park offers lake swimming, no pets.
🍴 **Great Wall II Take Out Chinese** 845-855-9750
🍴 **Hong Kong Chinese Kitchen**
🍴 **Mama Pizza II** 845-855-9270
🍴 **Vinny's Deli & Pasta**
🍴 **Gaudino Pizzeria**
🍴 **McKeever's Restaurant** L/D
🍴 **Chris's Deli**
🛒⌕ **Hannaford Supermarket & Pharmacy** (2S) on NY 22.
🛒⌕ **A&G Food Market** (3.4S) on NY 22.
⌂ **Family Quick Stop**
⌕ **CVS**
🛁 **Laundromat**
🖳 **Pawling Free Library** Tu-Th 10-8, F-Sa 10-4.
🚆 **MTA Metro-North Railroad** 212-532-4900 Train service to NYC.

SoBo	NoBo	The A.T. Guide	Elev
741.4	1442.8	**Appalachian Trail Railroad Station**, trash cans. (pg.144) P — N41 35.629 W73 35.224	480
741.2	1443.0	NY 22, **Wingdale, NY** (4.0W), deli 0.6E	480
740.4	1443.8	Hurd Corners Rd, wooden water tower	588
		Stream to west	
739.7	1444.5	Hammersly Ridge	1065
739.5	1444.7	Red Trail	1011
739.1	1445.1	Yellow Trail to east	949
738.7	1445.5	Red Trail to east.	980
738.6	1445.6	Green trail west, Red Trail east.	993
737.7	1446.5	Pawling Nature Reserve to east	910
736.7	1447.5	Stream	803
736.1	1448.1	Leather Hill Rd (gravel), stream to south	750
735.7	1448.5	**Wiley Shelter**, pump 0.1N, treat water 25.6◄16.6◄8.8◄▶4.0▶12.4▶19.7	724
735.5	1448.7	Duell Hollow Rd	620
735.2	1449.0	Footbridge, stream	432
734.5	1449.7	NY-CT border, Hoyt Rd	400
734.1	1450.1	Side trail to parking, brook to north — N41 38.508 W73 31.248 P	459
733.9	1450.3	CT 55, **Gaylordsville, CT** (2.5E)	460
		Wingdale, NY (3.3W) — N41 38.679 W73 31.155 P (pg.144)	
732.7	1451.5	Ten Mile Hill, Herrick Trail to east	1000
731.7	1452.5	**Ten Mile River Shelter** (0.1E) 20.6◄12.8◄4.0◄▶8.4▶15.7▶25.7	300
		Water to left. Group campsites across river and up trail to left.	
731.6	1452.6	Ten Mile River, Ned Anderson Memorial Bridge	280
730.2	1454.0	Bulls Bridge Rd (paved) + Schaghticoke Rd — N41 40.535 W73 30.610 P (pg.144)	381
		AT on Schaghticoke Rd (gravel) 0.3 mile	
729.2	1455.0	*CT-NY Campfires prohibited in CT. Camping only in designated sites.*	1048
728.6	1455.6	View	1213
727.2	1457.0	NY-CT, stream to north	1258
726.5	1457.7	Indian Rocks, view to east.	1020
726.3	1457.9	Schaghticoke Mountain Campsite to west, stream on AT	931
725.4	1458.8	Stream.	984
724.4	1459.8	Thayer Brook	969
723.3	1460.9	**Mt Algo Shelter** 21.2◄12.4◄8.4◄▶7.3▶17.3▶29.6	636
723.0	1461.2	CT 341, Schaghticoke Rd, **Kent, CT** (0.8E) (pg.144-145)	350
722.9	1461.3	Macedonia Brook	384
722.4	1461.8	Numeral Rock Trail to east	839

SoBo	NoBo	Description	Elev
720.2	1464.0	Skiff Mountain Rd (paved), stream to south	850
719.5	1464.7	Calebs Peak	1142
719.3	1464.9	St. Johns Ledges, steep stone steps down to Housatonic River	902
718.3	1465.9	River Rd south end, NoBo: turn west on road for 0.8 mile	480
717.5	1466.7	Kent Rd to west	436
717.4	1466.8	River Rd north end	403
716.0	1468.2	**Stewart Hollow Brook Shelter** (0.1W)	415
		19.7◄15.7◄7.3▲▶10.0▶22.3▶29.8 Footbridge over SH Brook.	
715.4	1468.8	Stony Brook, campsite to west	423
713.9	1470.3	Footbridge, stream	435
713.6	1470.6	River Rd N41 48.342 W73 23.697 **P**	460
713.4	1470.8	Dawn Hill Rd (paved)	566
712.7	1471.5	Silver Hill Campsite 0.1E, water from pump	914
711.9	1472.3	CT 4, Guinea Brook, **Cornwall Bridge, CT** (0.9E) (pg.146)	700
711.7	1472.5	High water bypass east on CT 4, then left on unpaved Old Sharon Rd for 0.5 mi. / Old Sharon Rd (gravel)	785
711.6	1472.6	Breadloaf Trail 0.1E, view	954
710.5	1473.7	Hatch Brook	880
710.3	1473.9	Pine Knob Loop Trail 1.0E to Housatonic Meadows State Park	972
709.7	1474.5	Another intersection with Pine Knob Loop Trail to east.	1032
709.3	1474.9	Caesar Rd, Caesar Brook Campsite, stream to north.	796
707.9	1476.3	Stream.	874
707.2	1477.0	Carse Brook, footbridge	810
707.1	1477.1	West Cornwall Rd, **West Cornwall, CT** (2.2E), **Sharon, CT** (4.7W) (pg.146)	880
706.8	1477.4	Pass through cracked boulder similar to Lemon Squeezer.	1175
706.0	1478.2	**Pine Swamp Brook Shelter**	1107
		25.7◄17.3◄10.0▲▶12.3▶19.8▶21.0	
705.1	1479.1	Sharon Mountain Rd	1150
704.2	1480.0	Woods road	1286
703.6	1480.6	Sharon Mountain Campsite 0.1W, stream nearby.	1200
700.7	1483.5	Belters Campsite 0.2W, view.	780

1442.8   **Appalachian Trail Railroad Station,** NY 22

🔌 👬 🚿 ✉ **Native Landscapes & Garden Center** 845-855-7050 Open daily 7-5, Owner Pete Muroski is hiker-friendly. Allows camping on site, use of restrooms, shower. Maildrops: 991 Route 22, Pawling, NY 12564.

🚈 **Metro-North Railroad** 212-532-4900 ⟨www.mta.info\mnr\index.html⟩ Runs only on weekends to NYC Grand Central Station. The trip requires a transfer, costs $14 one-way, and takes about two hours. Must pay in cash when boarding at the trailhead; can purchase round trip and pay with credit card if your trip originates at Grand Central Station.

Departures from AT station	Departures from Grand Central
2:44pm	7:48pm
4:44pm	9:48pm
6:35pm	

🍴 🏪 👬 📞 (0.6E) **Tony's Deli** sandwiches, salads, soda machine outside. Open daily 5-midnight.

Wingdale, NY 12594 (4W)

🏠 M-F 8-5, Sa 8-12:30, 845-832-6147

🛏🏕📶 **Dutches Motor Inn** 845-832-6400 $65S/D ($73 if using MC/Visa/AmEx), guest laundry $7, pets allowed.

🍴 **Adam's Diner** 24 hrs, **Big W's Roadside Barbeque**, **Jacye's Bar & Grill**, **Peking Kitchen**

🏪 **Wingdale Supermarket**

🏪 **Ben's Store** deli, hot foods.

🔧 **Wingdale Hardware**

💻 **Dover Plains Library** M-F 10-8, Sa 10-4.

1450.3   CT 55, *Gaylordsville, CT 06755* (2.5E)

🏠 M-F 8-1 & 2-5, Sa 8-12, 860-354-9727

🏪 💲 📞 **Gaylordsville Country Store** deli

🍴 **Gaylordsville Diner**, **Alfredo's**, **White Peach** W-Th 5:30-9, F-Sa 5:30-10, Su 12-9, Closed M-Tu.

Wingdale, NY (3.3W) listed above

🍴 (1.4W) **Buttonwood Café** M/W 9-3, Th-F 9-5, Sa-Su 9-5, bakery serving B/L and ice cream.

1454.0   Bulls Bridge Rd

📷 (0.4E) To covered bridge with view of the Housatonic cascading down the backside of a dam. The one-lane bridge was built in 1842. Wooden bridges are covered to protect the wood deck and trusswork from the elements.

0.2 beyond bridge:

🏪 💲 **Country Market** Fruit, ice cream, sodas and more. M-Sa 5:30-7, Sunday 6:30-7

🍴 **Bulls Bridge Inn** 860-927-1000 Serves dinner $10-20, M-F 5-9:30, Sa 5-10, Su 4-9, American cuisine, casual atmosphere, bar.

1461.2   CT 341, Schaghticoke Rd

Kent, CT 06757 (0.8E) *(more services on map)*

🛏 🍴 ✉ **Fife 'n Drum Inn & Restaurant** 860-927-3509 ⟨www.fifendrum.com⟩ hiker room rates include tax $116D wkdays, $140D wkends, $25EAP + tax, no pets. Call for reservations, front desk closed Tu. Guest maildrops: (USPS) PO Box 188 or (FedEx/UPS) 53 N Main Street, Kent, CT 06757.

🛏 🚗 📶 ✉ **Cooper Creek B&B** 860-927-4334 Hiker rate Su-Th $90D. (2.5N) of town via US 7. Shuttles to/from trail head and town with stay. Maildrops: 230 Kent Cornwall Road, Kent, CT 06757.

🛏 **Starbuck Inn** 860-927-1788 $198D/up + tax, includes full breakfast & afternoon tea. Sometimes discounted mid-week. Credit cards accepted, no pets.

🚶🍴🚌📶✉ Backcountry
Outfitters 860-927-3377

⟨www.bcoutfitters.com⟩ M–Sa 9–6, Su 10–4. In summer hours extended till 8pm weekdays, 9pm Fri & Sat, 6pm Sunday. Fuel/oz, iso-butane, backpacking gear and supplies. Farmer's market F 4-7.

Annie Bananie ice cream & grill inside serving hot dogs, coffee, snacks, barrels of candy. Shuttles anywhere. Maildrops: 5 Bridge Street, Kent, CT 06757.

🏠🍴 JP Gifford

Breakfast sandwiches, salads, bakery, coffee and supplies.

⚖ **Kent Landromat** Near PO, open 6am-11pm 7days. Hikers may use outlets to charge phones, please read & observe posted rules.

Also:

Sundog Shoe 10% hiker discount on footwear (Merrel, High-Tech, Keen), socks, and footbeds (Superfeet, Power Step).

House of Books UPS services, open daily 10-5:30.

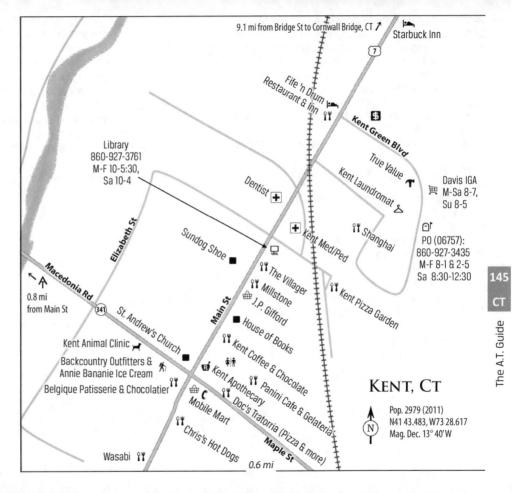

9.1 mi from Bridge St to Cornwall Bridge, CT ↗

Starbuck Inn

Fife 'n Drum Restaurant & Inn

Kent Green Blvd

True Value

Kent Laundromat

Davis IGA M-Sa 8-7, Su 8-5

Library 860-927-3761 M-F 10-5:30, Sa 10-4

Dentist

Kent Med/Ped

Shanghai

PO (06757): 860-927-3435 M-F 8-1 & 2-5 Sa 8:30-12:30

Elizabeth St

Sundog Shoe

The Villager

Millstone

J.P. Gifford

Kent Pizza Garden

← ↗
0.8 mi from Main St

Macedonia Rd

341 St. Andrew's Church

Main St

House of Books

Kent Animal Clinic

Backcountry Outfitters & Annie Bananie Ice Cream

Belgique Patisserie & Chocolatier

Kent Coffee & Chocolate

Kent Apothecary

Panini Cafe & Gelateria

Doc's Tratorria (Pizza & more)

Mobile Mart

Chris's Hot Dogs

Wasabi

Maple St

0.6 mi

KENT, CT

N

Pop. 2979 (2011)
N41 43.483, W73 28.617
Mag. Dec. 13° 40'W

145
CT

The A.T. Guide

1472.3   CT 4, **_Cornwall Bridge, CT 06754_** (0.9E)
🏠 M–F 8–1 & 2–5, Sa 9–12, 860-672-6710

🚣 🚿 **Housatonic Meadows State Park** Primitive camping one mile north of town on US 7. Campsite $13 (1–4) $2EAP, 6 per site, open mid-Apr to Sep, registration at main cabin by gate, no alcohol.

🛏🏕✉ **The Amselhaus** 860-248-3155 $65PP shared room hiker rate includes laundry, use of full kitchen and rides to town. Located behind package store. Maildrops: C/O Tyler, 7 River Road South, Cornwall Bridge, CT 06754.

🛏🏕🚐✉ **Hitching Post Motel** 860-672-6219 $65S, $75D, weekends $95/up, pets $10, laundry $5, shuttle when available. Maildrops: 45 Kent Road, Cornwall Bridge, CT 06754.

🛏🚐📶 **Cornwall Inn** 860-672-6884 Su–Th $90D, includes breakfast, shared bath, pickup/return to trailhead.

🍴 **Jim's Tall Order** Hamburgers and hot dogs, located in lot of package store.

🍴🛒💲📞 **Cornwall General Store** M-Sa 6am-7pm, Su 6-6 Hiker-friendly store with groceries, deli, ice cream and ATM. Deli serves breakfast and sandwiches.

⛽ **Citgo Xtramart**

🏃 **Housatonic River Outfitters** 860-672-1010 ⟨www.dryflies.com⟩ Some hiker gear, Aqua-Mira, white gas/alcohol/oz (no canisters).

🐾 **Housatonic Veterinary Care** 860-672-4948 closed Su & W.

🔨 **Northwest Lumber & Hardware**

Also: Cornwall Package Store 860-672-6645 closed Su, water spigot outside. Stopping to sign their register can be refreshing.

1477.1   West Cornwall Rd
West Cornwall, CT 06796 (2.2E)
🏠 M–F 8:30–1 & 2–4:30, Sa 9–12, 860-672-6791

🍴 **Wandering Moose Café** 860-672-0178

🍴 **Buck's Ice Cream**
Sharon, CT 06069 (4.7W)
🏠 M–F 8:30–4:30, Sa 9:30–12:30, 860-364-5306

🍴 **Country Corner Restaurant**

🛒 **Sharon Farm Market**

➕ **Sharon Hospital** 860-364-4141

💊 **Sharon Pharmacy**

🧺 **Queen B Cleaner** 7 days 7-9.

Gary Monk (trail name "Blaze") counted every white blaze he passed during his 2002 northbound thru-hike. There were 80,900. I wouldn't tell anyone about getting lost.

Leave What You Find

•Leave plants, cultural artifacts and other natural objects where you found them for others to enjoy.

•Don't build structures or dig trenches around tents.

•Do not damage live trees or plants; green wood burns poorly. Collect only firewood that is dead, down, and no larger than your wrist. Leave dead standing trees and dead limbs on standing trees for the wildlife.

•Consider using rubber tips on the bottom of your trekking poles to avoid scratch marks on rocks, "clicking" sounds, and leaving holes along the trail.

•Avoid introducing or transporting non-native species by checking your boots, socks, packs, tents, and clothing for non-native seeds that you could remove before hitting the trail.

Read more of the Leave No Trace techniques developed for the A.T.: www.appalachiantrail.org/LNT

About the Author

David Miller (Awol) thru-hiked the AT in 2003, and is the author of ***Awol on the Appalachian Trail.*** David is a member of the Appalachian Trail Conservancy (ATC), American Long Distance Hiking Association (ALDHA), and American Hiking Society (AHS).

SoBo	NoBo	The A.T. Guide	Elev
700.4	1483.8	US 7, CT 112 N41 55.928 W73 21.840 P	520
699.8	1484.4	US 7 bridge, Housatonic River	587
699.4	1484.8	Mohawk Trail 0.5E to view	594
698.8	1485.4	Warren Turnpike, footbridge, stream to north	564
697.9	1486.3	Water St parking. AT to west over Iron Mtn Bridge. **Falls Village, CT** 0.3E N41 57.352 W73 22.056 P (pg.150)	530
697.0	1487.2	Housatonic River Rd, AT crosses road twice 0.2 mi. N41 57.736 W73 22.442 P In between are two short trails east to views of great falls.	653
696.3	1487.9	Spring	829
694.4	1489.8	Mt Prospect	1475
693.7	1490.5	**Limestone Spring Shelter** (0.5W), road 0.25 farther. 29.6◀22.3◀12.3◀▶7.5▶8.7▶17.5	1321
693.6	1490.6	Rands View (field)	1250
693.2	1491.0	Giants Thumb	1279
692.4	1491.8	Stream	1027
690.3	1493.9	AT on US 44 for 0.2W	700
689.9	1494.3	AT on Cobble Rd 0.2E, **Salisbury, CT** (0.5W) (pg.150-151)	710
689.6	1494.6	Undermountain Rd (paved) N41 59.645 W73 25.615 P (pg.150-151) **Salisbury, CT** (0.8W)	720
689.3	1494.9	Stream	833
688.2	1496.0	Streams (multiple)	1129
687.3	1496.9	Lions Head Trail 0.5W to Bunker Hill Rd	1518
687.0	1497.2	Lions Head, view, bypass trail to west	1742
686.2	1498.0	**Riga Shelter,** tent platform behind shelter 29.8◀19.8◀7.5◀▶1.2▶10.0▶10.1	1661
685.7	1498.5	Ball Brook Campsite, stream	1738
685.0	1499.2	**Brassie Brook Shelter,** stream 20 yards north on AT 21.0◀8.7◀1.2◀▶8.8▶8.9▶23.2	1751
684.5	1499.7	Undermountain Trail 1.9E to CT 41	1825
684.3	1499.9	Bear Mountain Rd to west	1920
683.6	1500.6	Bear Mountain, rock observation tower, view	2316
683.2	1501.0	Unmarked trail 0.6W to Mt Washington Rd	1822
683.0	1501.2	Paradise Lane Trail to east, **CT-MA** border 50 yards north (not marked)	1702
682.8	1501.4	Sages Ravine Campsite to west	1544
682.4	1501.8	Sages Ravine, AT parallel to stream for 0.3 mile, Misplaced border sign at footbridge.	1489
681.1	1503.1	Laurel Ridge Campsite 0.1W, spring to south	1617
680.8	1503.4	Stream	1681

SoBo	NoBo	Feature		Elev
679.1	1505.1	Mt Race, views along ridgeline for 0.6S.	⊡	2365
678.0	1506.2	Race Brook Falls Trail 0.3E to campsite	☽ ◣	1950
677.3	1506.9	Mt Everett	⊡	2602
676.6	1507.6	Guilder Pond Picnic Area, Mt Everett Rd.	☽	2107
676.2	1508.0	The Hemlocks Shelter (0.1E) 17.5◄10.0◄8.8►0.1►14.4►19.7	☽ ◣ ⊏ (10)	1935
676.1	1508.1	Glen Brook Shelter (0.1E) 10.1◄8.9◄0.1►14.3►19.6►21.4	☽ ◣ ⊏	1962
675.5	1508.7	Elbow Trail 1.5E to MA 41 near **Racebrook Lodge**	(pg.151)	1766
674.5	1509.7	Mt Bushnell		1860
673.4	1510.8	Jug End, view	⊡	1470
672.6	1511.6	Jug End Rd, reliable piped spring 0.2E N42 8.665 W73 25.893 **P**	◣	882
671.8	1512.4	MA 41, **South Egremont, MA** (1.2W)	(pg.151)	810
670.8	1513.4	Footbridge, stream (2 close together)	◣	718
670.2	1514.0	Footbridge, stream	◣	695
670.0	1514.2	South Egremont Rd, Shays Rebellion Monument N42 8.828 W73 23.200 **P**	◣	700
669.1	1515.1	Gravel road		750
668.8	1515.4	West Rd (paved)		704
668.2	1516.0	US 7, RR track to south, **Great Barrington, MA** (3.0W)	(pg.152)	687
667.9	1516.3	Footbridge, stream	◣	677
667.3	1516.9	Housatonic River, cross on Kellogg Rd Bridge N42 8.637 W73 21.572 **P**		720
666.8	1517.4	Boardman St		715
665.5	1518.7	June Mtn		1237
665.3	1518.9	Homes Rd (paved)		1150
664.5	1519.7	Footbridge, spring at bottom of cleft		1507
663.9	1520.3	East Mountain, view	⊡	1800
663.5	1520.7	Woods road		1785
661.8	1522.4	Ice Gulch, **Tom Leonard Shelter** 23.2◄14.4◄14.3►5.3►7.1►21.1 Campsite overlooking ravine north of shelter. Stream 0.2 on path to left or 0.3 on path to right. N42 10.471 W73 17.639 **P**	⊡ ☽ ◣ ⊏ (10)	1574
660.7	1523.5	Lake Buel Rd (paved), parking area with kiosk N42 10.471 W73 17.639 **P**		1150
659.8	1524.4	MA 23 (paved), **East Mountain Retreat Center** (1.0W) N42 11.065 W73 17.444 **P**	(pg.153)	1050

SoBo   NoBo   The A.T. Guide

149
MA

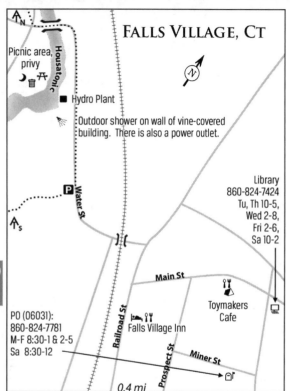

FALLS VILLAGE, CT

Picnic area, privy

Housatonic

Hydro Plant

Outdoor shower on wall of vine-covered building. There is also a power outlet.

Library
860-824-7424
Tu, Th 10-5,
Wed 2-8,
Fri 2-6,
Sa 10-2

Water St

Main St

Railroad St

Prospect St

Toymakers Cafe

PO (06031):
860-824-7781
M-F 8:30-1 & 2-5
Sa 8:30-12

Falls Village Inn

Miner St

0.4 mi

1486.3　Water Street Parking Area
Falls Village, CT 06031 (_more services on map_)
¶♦ **Toymakers Café** 860-824-8168 B/L, Th-F 7-2, Sa-Su 7-4, free tent sites, hiker friendly, knock on upstairs door if closed.
¶ **Falls Village Inn** Rooms 199/up, also has restaurant & bar.

1494.3　Lower Cobble Rd (0.5W)
1494.6　Undermountain Rd (0.8W)
Salisbury, CT 06068 (_more services on map_)
🏠🚌✉ **Maria McCabe** offers rooms in her home, 860-435-0593, $35P includes shower, use of living room, shuttle to coin laundry/store, cash only, Grove Street.
🏠△✉ **Vanessa Breton** offers rooms in her home, 860-435-9577, cell 86 671-1457 four beds $40PP, laundry $5. Guest maildrops: 7 The Lock Up Roa Salisbury, CT 06068.
¶ **Chaiwalla** 860-435-9758 W-Su 10-6. Hiker friendly tea room.
🚶✉ **Peter Becks Village Store**
860-596-4217 ⟨www.peterbecks.com⟩ M & W-Sa 10-6:30, Su 11-4, closed gear, Coleman/denatured alcohol/oz and canisters. Maildrops: 19 Main Stre Salisbury, CT 06068.
🛒¶ **La Bonne Epicure Market** M-Sa 8-7, Sunday until 6pm. Grocery, de bakery, pizza by the slice.
ℹ **Town Hall** 860-435-5170 M-F 8-4 Inside bathrooms & phone, local calls on
Lakeville, CT
(_2.0 mi. south of Salisbury_)
🛏 **Inn at Iron Masters** 860-435-9844 On US44 1.0 south of of Town Hall. $13 up, cont B, all non-smoking, pet rooms available.
¶ **Boathouse** Sports bar/restaurant
¶ **Mizza's Pizza**
△ **Washboard Laundromat** Behind Mizza's

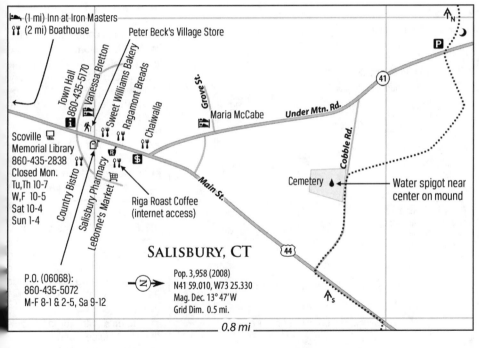

(1 mi) Inn at Iron Masters
(2 mi) Boathouse

Peter Beck's Village Store

Town Hall
860-435-5170

Vanessa Bretton
Sweet Williams Bakery
Ragamont Breads
Chaiwalla

Grove St.

Maria McCabe

Under Mtn. Rd.

Cobble Rd.

P

41

Scoville
Memorial Library
860-435-2838
Closed Mon.
Tu,Th 10-7
W,F 10-5
Sat 10-4
Sun 1-4

Country Bistro
Salisbury Pharmacy
LeBonne's Market

Riga Roast Coffee
(internet access)

Main St.

Cemetery

Water spigot near
center on mound

44

P.O. (06068):
860-435-5072
M-F 8-1 & 2-5, Sa 9-12

SALISBURY, CT

N

S

Pop. 3,958 (2008)
N41 59.010, W73 25.330
Mag. Dec. 13° 47'W
Grid Dim. 0.5 mi.

0.8 mi

1508.7   Elbow Trailhead on MA 41

Racebrook Lodge 413-229-2916 ⟨www.rblodge.com⟩ $85–$170 Rates lowest off-season (Nov-May). M-Th $105-$170, F-Su $115-245. Stay includes breakfast. Pets $15/night. **Stagecoach Inn** on-site open Th-Sa for dinner. Accepts all major CC, open year-round. Guest maildrops: 864 S Undermountain Road, Sheffield, MA 01257.

1512.4   MA 41

South Egremont, MA 01258 (1.2W)

M-F 8:15–12 & 12:30–4, Sa 9–11:30, 413-528-1571

(0.1W) **ATC New England Regional Office** 413-528-8002 in Kellogg Conservation Center.

Country Market deli

Mom's Country Cafe Breakfast/Lunch restaurant open 6:30-3 every day. Breakfast all day, free refills on coffee, outdoor water spigot, hikers welcome.

The A.T. Guide

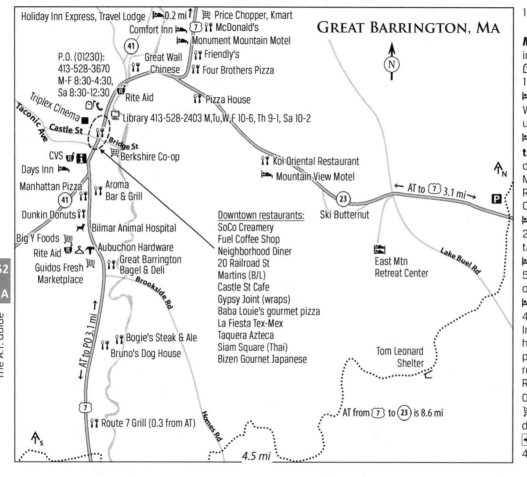

GREAT BARRINGTON, MA

1516.0   US 7, Railroad tracks

***Great   Barrington,
MA 01230*** (3W) Lodging prices
increase on F-Sa nights.
🏤 M–F 8:30–4:30, Sa 8:30–
12:30, 413-528-3670

🛏🛜 **Days Inn** 413-528-3150
Weekdays $79, weekends $99/
up, includes continental b'fast.

🛏🛀🛜✉ **Monument Moun-
tain Motel** 413-528-3272 weekdays $50S $65D, coin laundry.
Maildrops: 247 Stockbridge
Road, Rt 7, Great Barrington, MA
01230

🛏🛀🛜 **Travel Lodge** 413-528-
2340 hiker rate Su-Th $60D +
tax, $10EAP, cont B, coin laundry.

🛏🛜 **Mountain View Motel** 413-
528-0250 $55S, $10EAP, higher
on weekends.

🛏🛀🖥✉ **Comfort Inn**
413-644-3200 Prices seasonal.
Includes full breakfast, indoor
heated pool and hot tub, no
pets. Maildrops with advance
reservation: 249 Stockbridge
Rd, Rt 7, Great Barrington, MA
01230.

🛒 **Guido's** with organic produce, cold juices, and more.

➕ **Fairview Hospital**
413-528-0790

1524.4   MA 23

🏕️ ✉️ (1W) **East Mountain Retreat Center** 413-528-6617 ⟨www.eastretreat.org⟩ left 1.0 mile, blue sign on left and 0.5 mile on driveway, $10PP donation suggested, shower, pizzeria delivers to hostel, 10pm curfew and 8:30am checkout, cash only, Maildrops: (FedEx/UPS) 8 Lake Buel Road, Great Barrington, MA 01230.

Great Barrington, MA (4W) (see above)

1535.5   Jerusalem Rd (0.6W to town)
1536.6   Main Rd (0.9W to town)
Tyringham, MA 01264
🏤 M–F 9–12:30 & 4–5:30, Sa 8:30–12:30, 413-243-1225
📶🖥️ **Library** Adjacent to P.O. Tuesday 3-5, Saturday 10-12
🛏️ **Cobble View B&B** 413-243-2463 $110/up, includes cont B, no pets, no smoking, Visa/MC accepted.

1543.5   **Upper Goose Pond Cabin** (0.5W)
⌐(14)🍂🌢🌙 On side trail north of pond. Fireplace, covered porch, bunks with mattresses. Swimming and canoeing. Open daily Memorial Day-late-Sep & weekends late-Oct. During summer, caretaker brings water; otherwise, pond is water source. Tent platforms. When caretaker not in residence, hikers may camp on porch or tent platforms. Donations requested.

1545.1   US 20
🛏️📶🖥️✉️🌢 (0.1E) **Berkshire Lakeshire Lodge** 413-243-9907 Weekdays $55-85D, $65-95 four person room. Higher on weekends, no pets. Hikers welcome to get water from outside spigot. No services nearby but you can get pizza and Chinese food delivered. Maildrops: 3949 Jacob's Ladder Rd, Rt 10, Becket, MA 01223.

Lee, MA 01238 (5W)
🏤 M–F 8:30–4:30, Sa 9–12, 413-243-1392
Lodging busy on wkends in Jul-Aug with Tanglewood Music Festival.

🛏️ **Super 8** 413-243-0143
🛏️📶 **Americas Best Value Inn** 413-243-0501 ⟨www.bestvalueinn.com⟩ Su-Th $60-79, F-Sa $110-$195, cont B.
🛏️📶 **Roadway Inn** 413-243-0813 Jul-Aug $79-159S/D, other months $59S/D, cont B.
🛏️⛺📶 **Pilgrim Inn** 413-243-1328 Su-Th $95D, F-Sa $225D, cont B.
🍴 **Dunkin Donuts, Athena's Pizza House, Friendly's, Joe's Diner, McDonalds**, and many more.
🏪 **Price Chopper Supermarket** 413-528-2408
☒ **Rite Aid**
🐾 **Valley Veterinary Clinic** 413-243-2414
⚖ **Lee Coin-Op Laundry**

1554.6   Washington Mtn Rd
🍂🌢�✉️ Home of the "**Cookie Lady**" 100 yards east 413-623-5859 Water spigot near the garage door, please sign register on the steps. Homemade cookies often available; pick your own blueberries at reasonable rates, soda, ice cream and boiled eggs. Camping allowed, ask permission first. Shuttle range from Hoyt Rd. in NY to Manchester Center, VT. Maildrops: Roy & Marilyn Wiley, 47 Washington Mountain Road, Becket, MA 01223.

Becket, MA 01223 (5E)
🏤 M–F 8-4, Sa 9-11:30, 413-623-8845
🛏️📶🖥️ (6E) **Becket Motel** 413-623-8888 $70-120, includes shuttle from/to trailhead. Maildrops: 29 Chester Road, Becket, MA 01223.

SoBo	NoBo	The A.T. Guide	Elev
658.6	1525.6	Blue Hill Rd (paved), Stony Brook Rd	1550
657.8	1526.4	Beartown Mtn Rd, Benedict Pond, 0.5W on blue-blazed trail to	1623
657.6	1526.6	Beartown State Forest, beach, picnic area, phone, tent sites $10.	1639
657.2	1527.0	Benedict Pond Loop Trail to west, footbridge and stream east of AT	1820
		The Ledges	1835
656.5	1527.7	Mt Wilcox South Shelters 19.7◄19.6◄5.3◄▶1.8▶15.8▶24.6 Old shelter 0.1E (6), newer shelter 0.2E (12).	1838
655.5	1528.7	Pond, Swann Brook outlet at south end.	2084
654.7	1529.5	Mt Wilcox North Shelter (0.3E) 21.4◄7.1◄1.8◄▶14.0▶22.8▶31.6	1856
654.0	1530.2	Motorcycle path	1810
653.8	1530.4	Beartown Mountain Rd, NoBo: turn east	1726
653.5	1530.7	East Brook, footbridge, more streams north and south	
650.9	1533.3	Fernside Rd / Jerusalem Rd (gravel)	1200
650.7	1533.5	Shaker Campsite to east; platforms, bear box, water north on AT	883
649.0	1535.2	Cobble Hill	1254
648.7	1535.5	Jerusalem Rd (paved), Tyringham, MA 01264 (0.6W) (pg.153)	1105
		Water 0.1W on left side of road (treat), water also outside of P.O. 0.6W.	
648.3	1535.9	Three streams crossed by footbridges	979
647.6	1536.6	Main Rd (paved), Tyringham, MA (0.9W) N42 14.125 W73 11.667 [P] (pg.153)	993
		Water, parking to west.	
646.0	1538.2	Baldy Mtn	1881
645.8	1538.4	Webster Rd (gravel)	1800
645.2	1539.0	Knee-Deep Pond to west.	1669
644.2	1540.0	Spring on unmarked side trail 0.1W	1775
643.4	1540.8	Goose Pond Rd (gravel) N42 16.459 W73 11.025 [P] (0.1E)	1650
643.0	1541.2	Cooper Brook, footbridge.	1573
642.5	1541.7	Signed trail junction NoBo: this is not the side trail to Upper Goose Pond Cabin.	1738
641.4	1542.8	Higley Brook, footbridge, Upper Goose Pond to west	1512
640.8	1543.4	Old chimney	1499
640.7	1543.5	Upper Goose Pond Cabin (0.5W) 21.1◄15.8◄14.0◄▶8.8▶17.6▶34.5 (pg.153)	1570
639.5	1544.7	MA Turnpike I-90	1400
639.2	1545.0	Greenwater Brook, footbridge	1387
639.1	1545.1	US 20, Lee, MA (5.0W), hotel 0.1E N42 17.577 W73 9.684 [P] (0.1W) (pg.153)	1400

SoBo	NoBo	Description	Elev
638.7	1545.5	Powerline, stream to north	1589
638.3	1545.9	Tyne Rd / Becket Rd, stream to south	1804
637.8	1546.4	Becket Mountain	2180
636.8	1547.4	Walling Mountain	2230
636.2	1548.0	Finerty Pond	1959
634.4	1549.8	Washington Mountain Brook	1788
633.8	1550.4	County Rd (gravel)	1881
633.5	1550.7	Bald Top	2040
631.9	1552.3	**October Mountain Shelter,** intermittent stream, cables. ♦ ◊ ⏚ (12) 24.6◀22.8◀8.8◀▶8.8▶25.7▶32.3	1923
631.2	1553.0	West Branch Rd (gravel)	1960
629.6	1554.6	AT joins dirt road and crosses N42 22.618 W73 9.044 P (pg.153) Washington Mtn Rd (paved), **Becket, MA** 01223 (5.0E)	2015
627.6	1556.6	Streams ♦	1855
626.5	1557.7	Blotz Rd (paved), small parking lot on north side N42 24.561 W73 9.017 P	1850
625.8	1558.4	Warner Hill	2050
624.2	1560.0	Tully Mountain	2090
623.4	1560.8	Powerline ☽ ♦ ⏚ (10)	1944
623.1	1561.1	**Kay Wood Shelter** (0.2E) 31.6◀17.6◀8.8◀▶16.9▶23.5▶33.4	1775
622.8	1561.4	Grange Hall Rd	1651
622.6	1561.6	Barton Brook, footbridge	1565
621.2	1563.0	Woods road	1366
620.6	1563.6	Railroad tracks, Housatonic St + Depot St	1241
620.1	1564.1	MA 8 & 9, **Dalton, MA** (pg.156)	1200
619.1	1565.1	AT on Gulf Rd / High St for 1.0 mile N42 28.909 W73 10.695 P	1180

BRTA Commuter bus connects *Great Barrington*, *Dalton*, *Cheshire*, *North Adams*, *Adams*, *Williamstown*, *Pittsfield*, *Lee* and *Berkshire Mall*. Buses run M-F and Sa until 6pm. Fares $1.25/town up to $4.40. Drivers cannot make change. Flag bus anywhere on the route. For routes call: 800-292-2782.

EMS 413-445-4967, **Regal Cinema 10** 413-445-4967, and many other stores are in **Berkshire Mall**, on St. Rd. 8, 4 mi. north of Dalton & 7 mi. south of Cheshire.

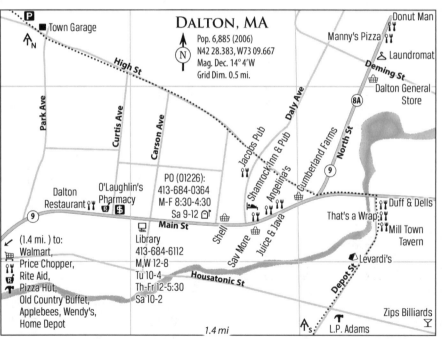

DALTON, MA
Pop. 6,885 (2006)
N42 28.383, W73 09.667
Mag. Dec. 14°4'W
Grid Dim. 0.5 mi.

Town Garage

High St

Park Ave

Curtis Ave

Carson Ave

Jacobs Pub

Shamrock Inn & Pub

Angelina's

Daly Ave

Cumberland Farms

North St

8A

Donut Man

Manny's Pizza

Laundromat

Deming St

Dalton General Store

PO (01226):
413-684-0364
M-F 8:30-4:30
Sa 9-12

Dalton Restaurant

O'Laughlin's Pharmacy

9

Shell

Main St

Sav More

Juice & Java

That's a Wrap

Duff & Dells

Mill Town Tavern

Levardi's

Library
413-684-6112
M,W 12-8
Tu 10-4
Th-Fr 12-5:30
Sa 10-2

Housatonic St

Depot St.

Zips Billiards

L.P. Adams

(1.4 mi.) to:
Walmart,
Price Chopper,
Rite Aid,
Pizza Hut,
Old Country Buffet,
Applebees, Wendy's,
Home Depot

1.4 mi

1564.1 MA 8 & 9
Dalton, MA 01227

Thomas Levardi 413-684-3359, 413-212-9691. 83 Depot Street, allows hikers to use water spigot outside and provides the hospitality of his front porch and back yard for tenting (with permission).

Shamrock Village Inn 413-684-0860 Tax included hiker rates Su-Th are $70.17 for room with a double bed or $72.67 for a room with 2 doubles or 1 queen bed. Fri&Sat $91.53/$100.68 respectively. These rates will be reduced 10% for AT hikers. From Memorial Day through Labor Day a free continental breakfast on Sat & Sun. Well-behaved pets allowed with $75 deposit. Coin laundry, free use of computer and WiFi.

Depot Diner B/L, closed Su. **That's a Wrap** sandwiches, **Angelina's Subs** with veggie burgers, **Dalton Restaurant** serves D Th–Sa with live entertainment.

Dalton Laundry closed Su.

LP Adams Coleman/denatured alcohol.

1572.9 Main St, School St
1573.5 MA 8 (4.0E)
Cheshire, MA 01225 (more services on map)

St. Mary of the Assumption Church Check in with Father David Raymond (west side door near the mailbox). Two hiker rooms, use of restrooms and outside cooking area No laundry or showers. Welcome to attend service in hiker attire. Please donate. Maildrops: 159 Church Street, Cheshire, MA 01225.

🛏🚶📶🖥✉ **Harbour House Inn Bed & Breakfast** 413-743-8959 ⟨www.harbourhouseinn.com⟩ $85 hiker rate Su-Thurs, includes breakfast, no pets, no smoking, shuttle to trail with stay. Operated by Eva. Guest maildrops: 725 North State Rd, Cheshire, MA 01225.

🚶 **AT Bicycle Works & Outfitters** 413-822-5357 ⟨www.atbicycleworks.com⟩ Some hiker supplies, Coleman/alcohol

by ounce and iso-butane, owner 2005 thru hiker Larry "Draggin" Dragon. No regular hours, call and he will open shop for you.

🍴 **Cobble View Pub & Pizzeria** T–Su 11-10

🍴 **Diane's Twist** M–Su 11:30–9, deli sandwiches, soda, ice cream.

🏬 **HD Reynolds** a general store, hiker snacks and Coleman fuel.

🚌 **BRTA** stops across the street from the post office.

     East from MA 8:

🚶 (2.2E) **Berkshire Outfitters** 413-743-5900 ⟨www.berkshireoutfitters.com⟩ M-F 10-6, Sa 10-5, Su 11-4, Full service outfitter, Coleman/alcohol/oz, freeze-dried foods, minor equipment repairs.

     Adams, MA 01220 (4.2E)

⌂ M-F 8:30–4:30, Sa 10–12, 413-743-5177

🛏🚶📶 **Mount Greylock Inn** 413-743-2665 ⟨www.mountgreylock-inn.com⟩ Accepts major CC, open year round.

🛒 **Big Y Foods Supermarket**

💊 **Rite Aid, Medicine Shop**

🐕 **Adams Veterinary Clinic** 413-743-4000

🧺📞 **Thrifty Bundle Laundromat**, **Waterworks**, many fast-food outlets

1581.3 Mt Greylock (3,491') is Massachusetts's highest peak. Veterans War Memorial Tower is on the summit. There are views of the Green, Catskill, and Taconic mountain ranges and surrounding towns. No camping or fires on summit.

🛏🏠🍴🚿📶 **Bascom Lodge** on summit 413-743-1591 private rooms $125/up, bunkroom $35. Bunkroom includes use of shower and continental breakfast. Shower & towel w/o stay $5, some snacks in gift shop, restaurant serves B/L/D.

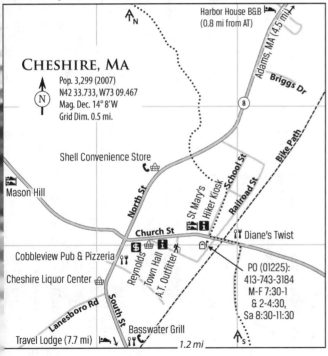

CHESHIRE, MA
Pop. 3,299 (2007)
N42 33.733, W73 09.467
Mag. Dec. 14° 8'W
Grid Dim. 0.5 mi.

Harbor House B&B
(0.8 mi from AT)

Adams, MA (4.5 mi.)

Briggs Dr

8

Bike Path

Shell Convenience Store

Mason Hill

North St

School St

Railroad St

St Mary's

Hiker Kiosk

Church St

Cobbleview Pub & Pizzeria

Reynolds

Town Hall

A.T. Outfitter

Cheshire Liquor Center

PO (01225):
413-743-3184
M-F 7:30-1
& 2-4:30,
Sa 8:30-11:30

Diane's Twist

Lanesboro Rd

South St

Basswater Grill

Travel Lodge (7.7 mi)

1.2 mi

SoBo	NoBo	The A.T. Guide		Elev
616.9	1567.3	Spring	◆	1927
616.0	1568.2	Powerlines		1911
615.9	1568.3	Crystal Mountain Campsite 0.2E, water on AT just north of side trail	☽ ◆ ⬳ (5)	1964
615.1	1569.1	Gore Brook, outlet of Gore Pond	◆	2038
614.0	1570.2	Stream	◆	1987
613.5	1570.7	Stream	◆	1843
612.9	1571.3	The Cobbles, outcroppings of marble with view of Hoosic. River Valley, Mt Greylock, and the town of Cheshire.	▣	1820
611.8	1572.4	Furnace Hill Rd (south end)	◆	1052
611.3	1572.9	Main St + School St, **Cheshire, MA** (pg.156-157)		986
610.7	1573.5	MA 8, **Cheshire, MA, Adams, MA** (4.0E) (pg.156-157)		1007
609.7	1574.5	Outlook Ave (paved), stream and powerline to north	◆	1330

> ✱ **Touch-Me-Not** – Also known as "jewelweed". Trumpet-shaped flowers with a short curled tail hang horizontally like a bug in flight. Yellow with splotches of orange. Salve from crushed stems is a folk remedy for poison ivy's itch.

SoBo	NoBo	The A.T. Guide		Elev
607.1	1577.1	Old Adams Rd (dirt)		2350
606.2	1578.0	**Mark Noepel Shelter** (0.2E), spring to right of shelter 34.5◄25.7◄16.9 ▼ 6.6►16.5►23.7 Spring stronger the farther you go.	☽ ◆ ⬳ (10)	2843
605.7	1578.5	Jones Nose Trail to west		3252
603.9	1580.3	Rockwell Rd / Summit Rd to west	N42 37.864 W73 10.696 🅿	3037
603.5	1580.7	Cross Rockwell Rd twice, side trails to east		3158
602.9	1581.3	Mt Greylock, highest peak in MA (pg.157) 🏛		3491
602.5	1581.7	Thunderbolt Trail and Bellows Pipe Trail, 75 yards apart, both to east.		3126
600.9	1583.3	Bernard Farm Trail		2799
600.6	1583.6	Mt Williams		2971
599.8	1584.4	Notch Rd (paved)		2336
599.6	1584.6	**Wilbur Clearing Shelter** (0.3W) On Money Brook Trail	☽ △ ◆ ⬳ (8)	2300
		32.3◄23.5◄6.6 ▼ 9.9►17.1►23.0. Intermittent stream.		
599.3	1584.9	Mt Prospect Trail to west.		2523
597.8	1586.4	Pattison Rd (paved)	N42 41.256 W73 9.586 🅿 ◆	1027

Elevation chart (x-axis: 1000–6000)

SoBo	NoBo		Elev
597.1	**1587.1**	Phelps Ave (south end), on road 0.5 mile	732
596.6	**1587.6**	MA 2, Hoosic River. . . . . N42 41.941 W73 9.208 P (0.1E) (pg.160-161)	660
		footbridge and RR tracks, **Williamstown, MA** (west), **North Adams, MA** (east)	
596.5	**1587.7**	Massachusetts Ave, NoBo: east on road for 0.1 mile	666
596.2	**1588.0**	Footbridge, stream	748
595.0	**1589.2**	Sherman Brook Campsite to west; blue-blazed trail bypasses boulder	1353
		field north of campsite; Petes Spring at junction of AT and blue-blazed trail.	
593.9	**1590.3**	Pine Cobble Trail to west	2119
593.8	**1590.4**	'98 Trail to west	2140
592.5	**1591.7**	**MA-VT** border, southern end of Long Trail (LT)	2330
		The AT and LT are concurrent northbound for the next 105.2 miles.	
592.1	**1592.1**	Spring, stream to north	2189
590.0	**1594.2**	Stream	2092
589.7	**1594.5**	**Seth Warner Shelter** (0.2W)	2243
		33.4◄16.5◄9.9◄▶7.2▶13.1▶ 21.6 Brook 0.1 left of shelter, known to dry up.	
589.4	**1594.8**	Country Rd, Powerline	2290
587.7	**1596.5**	Powerline	2888
586.8	**1597.4**	Roaring Branch, pond	2491
584.5	**1599.7**	Woods road, Stamford Stream	2251
584.1	**1600.1**	Stream	2200
583.6	**1600.6**	Pond	2213
583.2	**1601.0**	Woods road	2217
582.5	**1601.7**	**Congdon Shelter**	2104
		23.7◄17.1◄7.2◄▶5.9▶14.4▶18.7	
581.7	**1602.5**	Stream	2242
580.4	**1603.8**	Footbridge, stream	2228
580.0	**1604.2**	Harmon Hill	2325
579.5	**1604.7**	Spring	2115
578.2	**1606.0**	VT 9, **Bennington, VT** (5.1W) . . . . . N42 53.104 W73 6.920 P (pg.162-163)	1366

1587.6   MA 2, Hoosic River

Williamstown, MA 01267 (2.6W) *(more services on map)*
Williams College ranked as top liberal arts college in 2010 by US News & World Report.

🛏🖥✉ **Williamstown Motel** 413-458-5202 $59 wkdays, $69 wkends, includes cont B. Will pickup at Route 2. Major CC accepted. Maildrops: 295 Main Street, Williamstown, MA 01267.

🛏🖥✉ **Willows Motel** 413-458-5768, $69-129, cont B, no pets. Maildrops: 480 Main Street, Williamstown, MA 01267.

🛏 **Maple Terrace** 413-458-9677 $78/up.   Includes continental breakfast. Heated pool; all rooms non-smoking.

🛏 **Redwood Motel** 413-664-4351 ⟨www.redwood-motel.com⟩ $85-129, major CC accepted.

🛏🖥✉ **Howard Johnson** 413-458-8158, $69-$119, 5% hiker discount, cont B. Maildrops: 213 Main Street, Williamstown, MA 01267.

🛏✉ **River Bend Farm** 413-458-3121 $120D includes breakfast. Unique experience in an authentic 1770 colonial farmhouse. Free pickup & return when available.

🛏🚿 **Williams Inn** 413-458-9371 $180D/up, but $6 gets you a shower, swim and sauna, $1 towel.

🚶🔦✉ **The Mountain Goat** 413-458-8445 ⟨www.mountaingoat.com⟩ open 7 days, backpacking gear and supplies, Coleman/alcohol by the once, camping allowed behind the store with permission for up to 5 people, 2 days maximum, no fires. Maildrops: 130 Water St, Williamstown, MA 01267.

🍴 **Spice Root Indian Cuisine** 10% hiker discount.

✉ **Nature's Closet** Apparel & footwear. Maildrops: 61 Spring St, Williamstown, MA 01267.

🖥 **Milne Public Library** M-F 10-5:30, W 10-8, Sa 10-4

🚌 **Greyhound Bus Service**

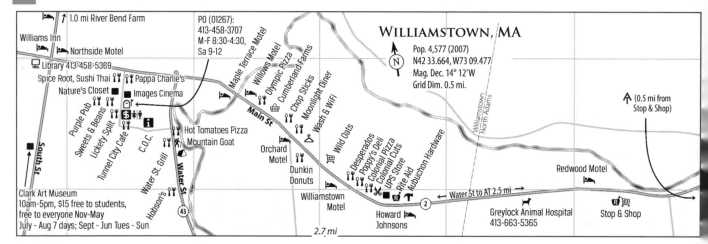

North Adams, MA 01247 (east) *(more services on map)*

🛏🍴👕📶🖥**Holiday Inn** 413-663-6500 Average summer rate $169.99. Pool, hot tub. **Richmond Grill** on-site.

🍴 **Oriental Buffet**, AYCE L/D buffet

➕ **North Adams Regional Hospital** 413-664-5000

🐾 **Greylock Animal Hospital** 413-663-5365, M-Th 8-7, F 8-5, Sa 8-3, Su 9-1

🚌 **David Ackerson** 413-346-1033 daveackerson@yahoo.com Shuttles to trailheads ranging from Bear Mtn Bridge to Hanover, and to/from area airports.

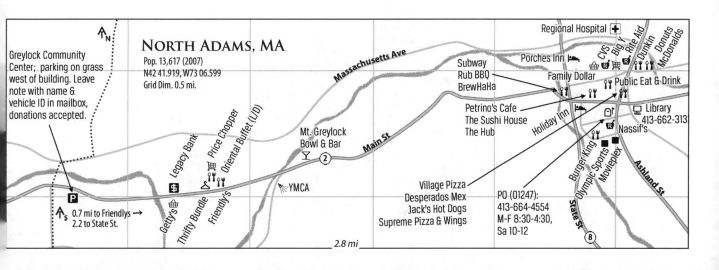

NORTH ADAMS, MA
Pop. 13,617 (2007)
N42 41.919, W73 06.599
Grid Dim. 0.5 mi.

Greylock Community Center; parking on grass west of building. Leave note with name & vehicle ID in mailbox, donations accepted.

0.7 mi to Friendlys →
2.2 to State St.

Massachusetts Ave

Legacy Bank
Price Chopper
Oriental Buffet (L/D)

Mt. Greylock Bowl & Bar
Main St

Getty's
Thrifty Bundle
Friendly's
YMCA

2.8 mi

Regional Hospital ➕
Porches Inn
Subway
Rub BBQ
BrewHaHa
Family Dollar

CVS
Big Y
Rite Aid
Dunkin Donuts
McDonalds

Public Eat & Drink

Petrino's Cafe
The Sushi House
The Hub

Holiday Inn

Library
413-662-313

Nassif's

Village Pizza
Desperados Mex
Jack's Hot Dogs
Supreme Pizza & Wings

Burger King
Olympic Sports
Movieplex

PO (01247):
413-664-4554
M-F 8:30-4:30,
Sa 10-12

State St
Ashland St

8

The A.T. Guide

Hampton Inn
Hannaford
Chili's
Home Depot
China Wok
279

BENNINGTON, VT

N

Pop. 9,037 (2007)
N42 52.700, W73 11.819
Mag. Dec. 14° 11'W
Grid Dim. 1.0 mi.

Best Western
Price
Chopper
Walmart
Pizza House
Movie Theater
Dairy Bar
Wendys
Dunkin Donuts
Pizza Hut

67A

Knotty Pine Motel
Super Shoe Store
CVS
Aldi
McDonalds
Taco Bell & KFC

Park St.

Rec Center

Kocher Dr.

Burger King
Quiznos
Chamber of
Commerce

Benmont Ave.

Bennington Battle
Monument

7

Jensen's Home Cooking

Blue Benn Diner

Rattlesnake
Cafe

Laundry

Kirkside

Rite Aid

Family Dollar

Greenberg Hardware

Elm St.

Izabella's

South St Cafe

Visitor Center

Subway & Dunkin' Donuts
Spice & Nice Natural Foods
The Pharmacy
Lil' Britain
Your Belly's Deli
Madison Brew Co. & Bennington Pizza House
Lucky Dragon

County Rd.

Benner's Bagels, Pizza
Ryan's
Peppermill
Gimme Pizza
Laundromat

Main St.

Autumn Inn
Papa Pete's

9

3.4 mi.
from
edge of
map

Bakery

Henry's
Market

Mt. Anthony Veterinary
Hospital 802-442-4324

9

Ramunto's

Library

Carmody's
Friendly's

P.O. (05201):
802-442-2421
M-F 8-5, Sa 9-2

SW Vermont Med. Center 802-442-6361

2.8 mi

Catamount Motel

Bennington, VT 05201 (5.1W)

(more services on map)

🛏🏕🚗📶🖥✉ **Autumn Inn Motel** 802-447-7625 $55S $65D, $10 for pickup and return to trail head. Guest maildrops: 924 Main Street, Bennington, VT 05201.

🛏📶 **Kirkside Motor Lodge** 802-447-7596, $79/up, prices seasonal.

🛏📶🖥✉ **Knotty Pine Motel** 802-442-5487 ⟨www.knottypinemotel.com⟩ ⟨kpine@sover.net⟩ 6.5 miles from the AT on VT 9, $80/up, includes cont B, pets free, pool. Maildrops (guests only): 130 Northside Drive, Bennington, VT 05201.

🛏📶 **Catamount Motel** 802-442-5977, $55D/up, prices seasonal.

🍴 **Lil' Britain** Fish and chips.

🚌 **Green Mountain Express** 802-447-0477 ⟨www.greenmtncn.org⟩

🚌 **Bennington Taxi** 802-442-9052

Also: Movie theater, shoe repair.

Travel and Camp on Durable Surfaces

•Stay on the trail; never shortcut switchbacks. Take breaks off-trail on durable surfaces, such as rock or grass.

•Restrict activities to areas where vegetation is already absent.

•Avoid expanding existing trails and campsites by walking in the middle of the trail, and using the already-impacted core areas of campsites.

•If tree branches block the trail, move them off if possible, rather than going around and creating new trails.

•Wear gaiters and waterproof boots, so you may walk through puddles instead of walking around them and creating a wide spot in the trail.

Read more of the Leave No Trace techniques developed for the A.T.: www.appalachiantrail.org/LNT

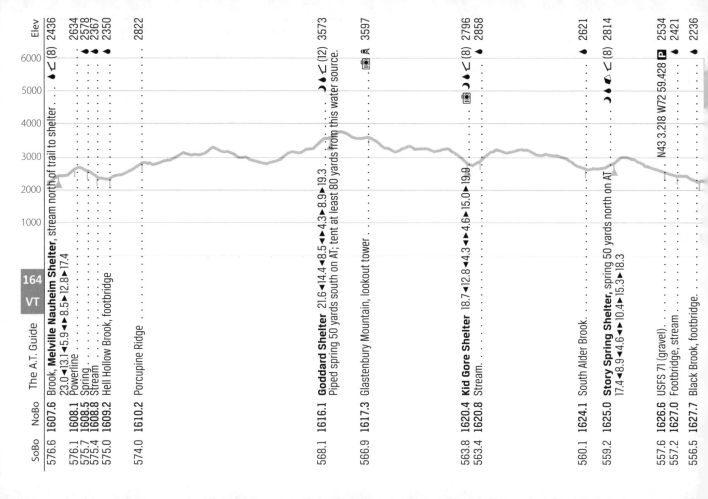

SoBo	NoBo	The A.T. Guide	Elev
576.6	**1607.6**	Brook, **Melville Nauheim Shelter**, stream north of trail to shelter. ◆ ⊏ (8) 23.0◀13.1◀5.9▶8.5▶12.8▶17.4	2436
576.1	**1608.1**	Powerline	2634
575.7	**1608.5**	Spring	2578
575.4	**1608.8**	Stream	2367
575.0	**1609.2**	Hell Hollow Brook, footbridge	2350
574.0	**1610.2**	Porcupine Ridge	2822
568.1	**1616.1**	**Goddard Shelter** 21.6◀14.4◀8.5▶4.3▶8.9▶19.3 ⟩◆⊏(12) Piped spring 50 yards south on AT; tent at least 80 yards from this water source.	3573
566.9	**1617.3**	Glastenbury Mountain, lookout tower	3597
563.8	**1620.4**	**Kid Gore Shelter** 18.7◀12.8◀4.3▶4.6▶15.0▶19.9 ⟩◆⊏(8)	2796
563.4	**1620.8**	Stream.	2858
560.1	**1624.1**	South Alder Brook.	2621
559.2	**1625.0**	**Story Spring Shelter**, spring 50 yards north on AT ⟩◆⊏(8) 17.4◀8.9◀4.6▶10.4▶15.3▶18.3	2814
557.6	**1626.6**	USFS 71 (gravel). N43 3.218 W72 59.428 P	2534
557.2	**1627.0**	Footbridge, stream	2421
556.5	**1627.7**	Black Brook, footbridge.	2236

SoBo	NoBo			Elev
555.6	**1628.6**	Stratton-Arlington Rd (gravel) . . . . N43 3.663 W72 58.083 **P** ●		2230
		NoBo: east on road across Deerfield River. Daniel Webster Monument 0.3E.		
554.1	**1630.1**	Woods road		2640
551.8	**1632.4**	Stratton Mountain, lookout tower, caretaker cabin, no camping . . . . . 📷🔭		3936
		Summit on which Benton MacKaye conceived the idea for the AT.		
551.6	**1632.6**	Spring to east. ●		3854
549.3	**1634.9**	Footbridge, stream . . . . ☽♦⊂(16)		2479
548.8	**1635.4**	**Stratton Pond Shelter** (0.2W)		2655
		19.3◄15.0◄10.4◄4.9►7.9►12.7 Overnight fee, no tenting, no fires.		
548.7	**1635.5**	Lye Brook Trail to west . . . . ♦		2586
548.6	**1635.6**	Stratton Pond, North Shore Trail 0.5W to campsite. ◿		2596
547.9	**1636.3**	Stream. ●		2534
547.3	**1636.9**	Stream. ●		2475
546.8	**1637.4**	Winhall River, footbridge, stream ●		2302
545.3	**1638.9**	Stream. ●		2246
543.9	**1640.3**	**William B. Douglas Shelter** (0.5W) . . . . . . ☽⊂(10)		2304
		19.9◄15.3◄4.9►3.0►7.8►15.9 Spring to left of shelter.		
543.0	**1641.2**	Prospect Rock to west, view. . . . . 📷		2150
540.9	**1643.3**	**Spruce Peak Shelter** (0.1W) 18.3◄7.9◄3.0◄4.8►12.9►17.6. . . . ☽⊂(14)		2247
540.5	**1643.7**	Spruce Peak 0.1W.		2040
540.1	**1644.1**	Stream, powerline . . . . ●		1838
539.9	**1644.3**	Stream. . . . . ●		1894
538.6	**1645.6**	Powerline, footbridge, stream . . . . ●		1726
538.1	**1646.1**	VT 11 & 30 . . . . N43 12.409 W72 58.243 **P** (pg.168-169)		1840
		Manchester Center, VT (5.4W)		
537.2	**1647.0**	Footbridge, stream . . . . ●		2161
536.1	**1648.1**	**Bromley Shelter** 12.7◄7.8◄4.8►8.1►12.8►14.3 . . ●♦(4)⊂(12)		2605

SoBo	NoBo	The A.T. Guide	Elev
535.5	**1648.7**	Ski slope	3106
535.1	**1649.1**	Bromley Mountain, view five states from tower, no tenting or fires	3260
532.6	**1651.6**	Mad Tom Notch, USFS 21 (gravel), water from pump	2446
531.0	**1653.2**	Styles Peak	3394
529.3	**1654.9**	Peru Peak	3429
528.4	**1655.8**	Spring	2820
528.0	**1656.2**	**Peru Peak Shelter** 15.9◄12.9◄8.1◄►4.7►6.2►6.4 Fee	2616
527.7	**1656.5**	Footbridge, stream (two).	2590
527.5	**1656.7**	Griffith Lake Tenting Area.	2600
		Camping only at designated sites within 0.5 mile of Griffith Lake.	
527.2	**1657.0**	Old Job Trail to east, Griffith Lake Trail to west	2641
525.4	**1658.8**	Baker Peak, Baker Peak Trail to west	2664
523.3	**1660.9**	**Lost Pond Shelter**	2210
		17.6◄12.8◄4.7◄►1.5►1.7►5.0 Overnight fee.	
522.8	**1661.4**	Spring	1975
521.8	**1662.4**	Old Job Trail to **Old Job Shelter** (1.0E), Lake Brook is water source	1544
		14.3◄6.2◄1.5◄►0.2►3.5►8.3	
521.6	**1662.6**	**Big Branch Shelter** 6.4◄1.7◄0.2◄►3.3►8.1►13.2.	1512
		Close to road; heavy weekend use. Water source is Big Branch. Privy uphill.	
520.5	**1663.7**	Danby-Landgrove Rd. N43 22.362 W72 57.764 **P** (pg.168)	1539
		Big Black Branch Bridge, **Danby, VT** (3.5W)	
519.9	**1664.3**	Footbridge, stream	1667
518.4	**1665.8**	Homer Stone Brook Trail to west.	1880
518.3	**1665.9**	**Little Rock Pond Shelter & Tenting Area.**	1852
		5.0◄3.5◄3.3◄►4.8►9.9►13.6 Water source is at the caretaker's platform.	
		Overnight fee. Tenting restricted to designated sites.	
517.2	**1667.0**	Footbridge, stream	1955

SoBo	NoBo	Feature	Elev
514.0	1670.2	Trail to White Rocks Cliff 0.2W	2294
513.5	1670.7	Greenwall Shelter (0.2E) 8.3◀8.1◀4.8▶5.1▶8.8▶14.6. ⟅ △ ⊏ Spring 0.1 mile on side trail behind shelter, prone to fail in dry seasons.	2114
512.8	1671.4	Bully Brook, Keewaydin Trail to west. ●	1443
512.1	1672.1	Sugar Hill Rd (gravel)	1245
512.0	1672.2	VT 140, footbridge, stream . . . N43 27.404 W72 55.972 (0.2E) P ● (pg.168) **Wallingford, VT** (2.8W)	1160
511.0	1673.2	View on short side trail to west	1691
510.3	1673.9	Bear Mountain	2247
509.4	1674.8	Patch Hollow	1779
509.0	1675.2	Footbridge, stream (3)	1664
508.8	1675.4	Lake Trail loop to west (yellow blazed) 100 yards north, red-blazed tr to east	1668
508.4	1675.8	**Minerva Hinchey Shelter** 13.2◀9.9◀5.1▶3.7▶9.5▶16.3 ⟅ ● ⊏ (10) spring 75 yards in front of shelter.	1631
506.5	1677.7	View to Rutland Airport.	1385
505.8	1678.4	Clarendon Gorge, suspension bridge, swimming holes in Mill River	836
505.7	1678.5	VT 103, restaurant 0.5W . . . . . N43 31.286 W72 55.550 P ● (pg.168 & 172) **North Clarendon, VT** (4.2W) **Rutland, VT** (8.0W)	860
505.2	1679.0	View, north end of rock scramble	1339
504.7	1679.5	**Clarendon Shelter** (0.1E) 13.6◀8.8◀3.7▶5.8▶12.6▶14.5 ⟅ ● ⊏ (10)	1264
504.2	1680.0	Beacon Hill	1740
503.9	1680.3	Lottery Rd (gravel), powerline	1690
503.4	1680.8	Hermit Spring to east (unreliable) △	1825
502.3	1681.9	Stream.	1614
502.1	1682.1	Keiffer Rd (gravel) ●	1550
501.8	1682.4	Cold River Rd / Lower Rd (paved) Nobo east on road 75 yards ⊞ **W.E. Pierce Groceries** in North Shrewsbury (2.4E)	1416
501.0	1683.3	Gould Brook to west, AT parallel for 0.5 miles ●	1480
500.3	1683.9	Upper Cold River Rd (gravel)	1630
499.6	1684.6	Gravel road, Robinson Brook. ●	1745
498.9	1685.3	**Governor Clement Shelter** 14.6◀9.5◀5.8▶6.8▶8.7▶10.6 ⟅ ● ⊏ (12)	1920
498.4	1685.8	AT on gravel road 0.3 miles of shelter	2069
494.7	1689.5	Shrewsbury Peak Trail to east, marked with blue diamond	3512

✿ **Clintonia** – Foot-tall plant with plastic-looking blue berries atop long stems.

1646.1   VT 11 & 30

🛏🏕🚗📶✉ **Bromley Sun Lodge** (2.1E) 800-722-2159 $80/up, pets $20, tavern, indoor pool, game room, shuttle to and from trail head with stay. Maildrops: (non-guests $5) 4216 VT 11, Peru, VT 05152.

🏪✉ **Bromley Market** (2.5E) Maildrops: 3776 VT 11, Peru, VT 05152.

🛏🍴🚗📶✉ **Johnny Seesaw's Lodge** 802-824-5533 ⟨www.johnnyseesaw.com⟩ wkdays $50, wkends $100, pets $10, restaurant serves B/D, lounge, shuttle to trailhead with stay. Maildrops: 3574 VT 11, Peru, VT 05152.

🛏🚗📶✉ **Bromley View Inn** (3.0E) on VA 30, 877-633-0308 ⟨www.bromleyviewinn.com⟩ $85D/up, includes hot breakfast, call for shuttle to and from VT 11/30 trailhead with stay. Maildrops: 522 VT 30, Bondville, VT 05340.

Manchester Center, VT (5.4W) *(more services on map)*

🛏🏕✉ **Avalanche Motel** (3.5W) En-route to town, 802-362-3333, $69-$89, Pets $15. Maildrops: 2187 Depot St, Manchester Center, VT 05255.

🛏📶✉ **Sutton's Place** 802-362-1165, $60S, $70D, $87(room for 3), no pets allowed but can stay on porch. Accepts MC/Visa. USPS Maildrops: (USPS) PO Box 142 or (UPS) 55 School St, Manchester Center, VT 05255.

🛏📶 **Carriage House** 802-362-1706 $68D, no pets.

🛏📶 **Palmer House** 802-362-3600, ask for hiker discount, $2.50 for cont B, no pets, indoor and outdoor pool.

🏃 **EMS** 802-366-8082, 7 days 10-6, full service outfitter, Coleman/alcohol/oz, maintains list of shuttle providers and places to stay.

Also: **Northshire Bookstore**

1663.7   Danby-Landgrove Rd
           Danby, VT 05739 (3.5W)
🏤 M-F 7:15-12 & 1:15-4, Sa 7:30-10:30, 802-293-5105

🛏🍴🚗📶✉ **Silas Griffith Inn B&B** 802-293-5567 ⟨www.silasgriffith.com⟩ $99/up, includes breakfast, no smoking, restaurant Th-Su by reservation. Shuttles to/from trail (USFS 10) with stay. Hiker friendly, family friendly, pet friendly. Guest maildrops: 178 South Main St,

Danby, VT 05739.

🚿🍴🚗🅿✉ **Otter Creek Campground** 802-293-5041 Two miles north of USFS 10 in Danby on US 7, tent sites $18, pets on leash, Coleman fuel, small selection of food items and camping supplies, shuttles and long-term parking for fee. USPS/UPS Maildrops: 1136 US 7, Danby, VT 05739.

🍴 **White Dog Tavern** with dinner menu.

🏪 **Mt. Tabor Country Store** 802-293-5641 M-Sa 5-8, Su 5-7

🏪 **Nichols Store & Deli**

📖 **Silas Griffith Library**

🔧 **Crosby Hardware**

1672.2   VT 140 **Wallingford, VT 05773** (2.8W)
🏤 M-F 8-4:30, Sa 9-12, 802-446-2140

🍴 **Mom's Country Kitchen** 802-446-2606 B/L, closes at 2.
Sal's Italian Restaurant & Pizza

🏪 **Wallingford Country Store & Deli**, **Cumberland Farms**

🔧 **Nail It Down Hardware**

📖 **Gilbert Hart Library** 802-446-2685 Su-M closed, Tu 10-5, W 10-8, Th-F 10-5, Sa 9-12.

1678.5   VT 103 🍴 (0.5W) **Whistle Stop Restaurant** 802-747-7070 Closed Mondays. Tu-Sa 6:30am-7pm, Su 7-7, pizza, ice cream, $15 minimum for credit card purchases. Bus stop nearby goes to Rutland.

🐾 (0.5W) **Cold River Veterinary Center** 802-747-4076

🏪📞 (1W) **East Clarendon General Store** 802-786-0948, M-Su 6:30-7, call ahead for maildrop information.

           North Clarendon, VT 05759 (4.2W)
🏤 M-F 8-1 & 2-4:30, Sa 8-10, 802-773-7893

🏪 **Mike's Country Store**

           Rutland, VT (8W from VT 103) *(See page 172)*

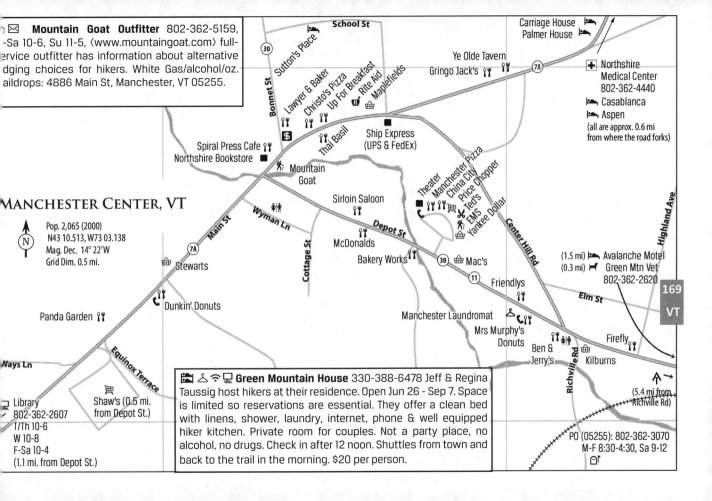

Mountain Goat Outfitter 802-362-5159, ‑Sa 10-6, Su 11-5, ⟨www.mountaingoat.com⟩ full-service outfitter has information about alternative ‑dging choices for hikers. White Gas/alcohol/oz. aildrops: 4886 Main St, Manchester, VT 05255.

School St

Carriage House
Palmer House

Sutton's Place

(30)

Bonnet St

Lawyer & Baker
Christo's Pizza
Up For Breakfast
Rite Aid
Maplefields

Ye Olde Tavern
Gringo Jack's

(7A)

Northshire
Medical Center
802-362-4440

Casablanca

Aspen
(all are approx. 0.6 mi.
from where the road forks)

Spiral Press Cafe
Northshire Bookstore

Thai Basil

Ship Express
(UPS & FedEx)

Manchester Pizza
China City
Price Chopper
Ted's
EMS
Yankee Dollar

Mountain
Goat

Theater

MANCHESTER CENTER, VT

Pop. 2,065 (2000)
N43 10.513, W73 03.138
Mag. Dec. 14° 22'W
Grid Dim. 0.5 mi.

Wyman Ln

Main St

Sirloin Saloon

Depot St

Highland Ave

169
VT

(7A)

Stewarts

Cottage St

McDonalds

Bakery Works

(30)

Mac's

(11)

Friendlys

(1.5 mi) Avalanche Motel
(0.3 mi) Green Mtn Vet
802-362-2620

Elm St

Panda Garden

Dunkin' Donuts

Manchester Laundromat

Mrs Murphy's
Donuts

Firefly

Ways Ln

Equinox Terrace

Library
802-362-2607
T/Th 10-6
W 10-8
F-Sa 10-4
(1.1 mi. from Depot St.)

Shaw's (0.5 mi.
from Depot St.)

Green Mountain House 330-388-6478 Jeff & Regina Taussig host hikers at their residence. Open Jun 26 - Sep 7. Space is limited so reservations are essential. They offer a clean bed with linens, shower, laundry, internet, phone & well equipped hiker kitchen. Private room for couples. Not a party place, no alcohol, no drugs. Check in after 12 noon. Shuttles from town and back to the trail in the morning. $20 per person.

Ben &
Jerry's

Kilburns

Richville Rd

Center Hill Rd

(5.4 mi from
Richville Rd)

PO (05255): 802-362-3070
M-F 8:30-4:30, Sa 9-12

SoBo	NoBo	The A.T. Guide	Elev
492.1	1692.1	**Cooper Lodge Shelter** 16.3◀12.6◀6.8◀▶1.9▶3.8▶5.7 ☾●⛺☪(16)	3928
		Spring 60 yards north on AT. Trail behind shelter to top of Killington 0.2 mile.	
491.8	1692.4	Bucklin Trail to west	3806
490.2	1694.0	**Pico Camp** (0.5E) 14.5◀8.7◀1.9◀▶1.9▶3.8▶11.9 ●⛺☪(4)	3482
		Shelter on Sherburne Pass Tr where it leaves the Long Tr/AT south of Pico summit.	
489.0	1695.2	Spring	3153
488.3	1695.9	**Churchill Scott Shelter** (0.1W) 10.6◀3.8◀1.9◀▶1.9▶10.0▶19.9 ☾△☪	2620
		Composting privy, unreliable water source at southern spur from shelter, no fires.	
488.2	1696.0	Stream.	2436
487.8	1696.4	Stream. △	2076
487.3	1696.9	US 4, **Rutland, VT** (10.0W) N43 39.996 W72 50.997 **P** (pg.172)	1880
487.2	1697.0	Stream.	1916
486.4	1697.8	Maine Junction, **Tucker-Johnson Shelter** (0.4W) ☾●⛺☪(8)	2259
		5.7◀3.8◀1.9◀▶8.1▶18.0▶29.6 ⚠ White-blazed Trail to west is the Long Trail	
486.2	1698.0	Spring, Deer Leap Trail to east	2303
485.1	1699.1	Deer Leap Trail 0.3E to view	2434
485.0	1699.2	Sherburne Pass Trail 0.5E to **Inn at Long Trail** (pg.173)	2440
484.3	1699.9	Spring	1850
484.0	1700.2	**Gifford Woods State Park**, coin-op showers	1653
483.9	1700.3	US 4 / VT 100, **Killington, VT** (0.6E) N43 40.455 W72 48.578 **P** (pg.173)	1612
483.3	1700.9	Kent Pond, sdie trail to **Killington, VT** (0.4E) (pg.173)	1558
482.3	1701.9	Thundering Brook Rd (gravel)	1405
482.1	1702.1	Thundering Falls to west.	1241
481.9	1702.3	River Rd (gravel)	1269
480.8	1703.4	Quimby Mountain	2525
480.4	1703.8	Powerline, boulder to sit on, view to Pico slopes.	2341
480.1	1704.1	Gravel road	2338
478.3	1705.9	**Stony Brook Shelter** (0.1E) 11.9◀10.0◀8.1◀▶9.9▶21.5▶30.3 ☾●⛺☪(8)	1779
		Tent sites behind shelter. Water from stream 0.1N on AT.	
477.7	1706.5	Stony Brook Rd (gravel), Stony Brook and footbridge. ●	1368
475.3	1708.9	Stream, woods roads before and after ●	2032

SoBo	NoBo		Elev	
473.8	1710.4	Chateauguay Rd (gravel), Mink Brook	2022	♦
473.4	1710.8	Locust Creek	2160	♦
471.0	1713.2	The Lookout, 0.1W to cabin and tower	2384	🏠
468.4	1715.8	**Winturri Shelter** (0.2W) 19.9◄18.0◄9.9◄▶11.6▶20.4▶27.7	2082	☾♦⊂(8)
467.7	1716.5	Woods road	1770	
466.1	1718.1	Ascutney Mountain	1487	📷
465.0	1719.2	VT 12, Barnard Gulf Rd (paved)	877	P♦(pg.174)
		Gulf Stream south of road crossing. **Woodstock, VT** (4.2E) N43 39.309 W72 33.972		
464.3	1719.9	Dana Hill	1532	
463.1	1721.1	Woodstock Stage Rd, Barnard Brook	820	♦(pg.174)
462.8	1721.4	Stream	1022	
462.3	1721.9	Totman Hill Rd, footbridge, stream.	1003	
461.5	1722.7	Bartlett Brook Rd (gravel), footbridge, stream	1009	
460.9	1723.3	Pomfret Rd (paved), Pomfret Brook south of road crossing, powerline..	980	♦
460.5	1723.7	View	1549	📷
459.7	1724.5	View	1724	📷
459.1	1725.1	Cloudland Rd (gravel), **Cloudland Market** (0.2W) closed M & Su	1370	⌂
458.6	1725.6	Previous AT shelter (Cloudland) now on private land (0.5W).	1630	
		Facility available at landowner's discretion.		
457.3	1726.9	Thistle Hill	1959	☾♦⊂(8)
456.8	1727.4	**Thistle Hill Shelter** (0.2E), stream 0.1 further	1774	
		29.6◄21.5◄11.6◄▶8.8▶16.1▶25.6		
456.5	1727.7	Dimick Brook	1520	♦
455.5	1728.7	Joe Ranger Rd (gravel)	1309	
454.9	1729.3	Bunker Hill Rd (dirt).	1417	

❋ Queen Anne's Lace – White flower cluster in disk shaped doily 3–5" wide on hairy stem.

1696.9   US 4

🛏🔋⛺🍴⛺✉ (0.8E) **The Inn at Long Trail** 802-775-7181 or 800-325-2540 ⟨www.innatlongtrail.com⟩ Hiker rooms and free camping reservations recommended on weekends. Some pet rooms. Rooms include full breakfast. Coin laundry, outside water spigot. Closed mid-April through early June. **McGrath's Irish Pub** L/D 11:30-9pm, live music Fri & Sat. Maildrops: (FedEx/UPS) 709 US 4, Killington, VT 05751.

Rutland, VT (11W)
US 4 (0.8E to Inn)

🛏🍴⛺✉ **Hikers Hostel at 23 Center Street and Yellow Deli** 802-775-9800 ⟨www.hikershostel.org⟩ Suggested donation $20. Kitchenette, coin laundry, some hiking supplies at adjacent shop. No pets, no alcohol or smoking on property. ATM across the street. Guest maildrops: Hiker Hostel, 23 Center Street, Rutland, VT 05701.

🛏🍴⛺📶🖥✉ (1.5W)**Mendon Mountain View Resort Lodge** 802-773-4311 or 800-368-4311 ⟨www.mendonmountainview.com⟩ $49D/up, higher in fall, pet rooms available. Pool, game room, hot tub, saunas, laundry $6 per load, and restaurant serving B/D. On bus route. Maildrops: 5654 US Rt 4, Mendon, VT 05701.

🧍 **Mountain Travelers Outdoor Shop** 802-775-0814, M–S=F 10–6, Sa 10-4. Backpacking equipment and supplies, Coleman/alcohol/oz.

🏪 **Rutland Area Food Co-op** 802-773-0737 7 days

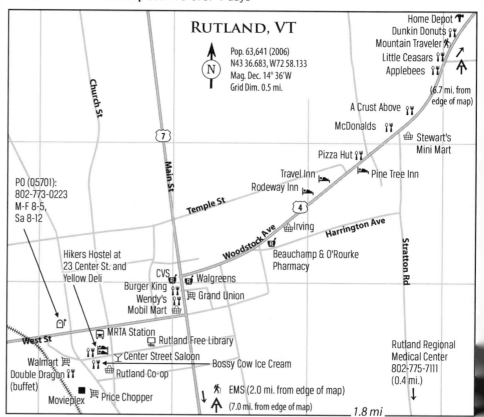

RUTLAND, VT

Pop. 63,641 (2006)
N43 36.683, W72 58.133
Mag. Dec. 14° 36'W
Grid Dim. 0.5 mi.

Home Depot
Dunkin Donuts
Mountain Traveler
Little Ceasars
Applebees
(6.7 mi. from edge of map)

A Crust Above
McDonalds
Stewart's Mini Mart
Pizza Hut
Travel Inn
Pine Tree Inn
Rodeway Inn

Church St

Main St

Temple St

7

4

Woodstock Ave
Irving
Harrington Ave
Beauchamp & O'Rourke Pharmacy
Stratton Rd

PO (05701):
802-773-0223
M-F 8-5,
Sa 8-12

Hikers Hostel at 23 Center St. and Yellow Deli

CVS
Walgreens
Burger King
Wendy's
Mobil Mart
Grand Union

West St

MRTA Station
Rutland Free Library
Center Street Saloon
Bossy Cow Ice Cream

Walmart
Double Dragon (buffet)
Rutland Co-op

Movieplex
Price Chopper

Rutland Regional Medical Center
802-775-7111
(0.4 mi.)

🧍 EMS (2.0 mi. from edge of map)
(7.0 mi. from edge of map)

1.8 mi

Rutland Veterinary Clinic 802-773-2779 24/7

Amtrak 800-872-7245 Provides daily train service from Rutland to New York and many other cities.

Rutland Taxi 802-236-3133

Rutland Airport South of Rutland on US 7

1699.2   Sherburne Pass Trail
⊨ ◐ ¶↑ ⚲ ✉ (0.5E) **The Inn at Long Trail** (See US 4)

1700.3   US 4, VT 100
◐ ♙↑ ≋ The AT passes thru **Gifford Woods State Park** with shelters, $21 tent sites, $4 tent sites for AT hikers in special hiker section, coin-op showers, water spigot. Fills up quickly in fall.

Killington, VT 05751 (0.6E)
♙ ✉ **Base Camp Outfitters** 802-775-0166, M-F 9:30-5:30, Sa 9-6, Su 9-5. (Summer hour: 9-6 every day) Full service outfitter, alcohol/oz and iso-butane. Maildrops: 2363 Route 4, Killington VT 05751.

⊨ ⌂ **Greenbrier Inn** 802-775-1575 $100D/ up, no pets.

Pittsfield, VT 05762 (7W)
⌂ M-F 8-12, 2-4:30, Sa 8:30-11:30, 802-746-8953

⊕ ¶↑ 💲 **Original General Store** B/L/D

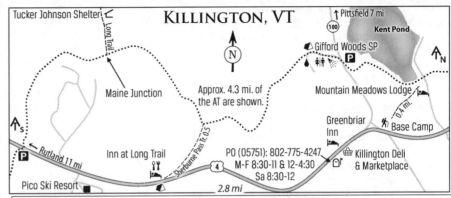

KILLINGTON, VT

Tucker Johnson Shelter
Long Trail
↑ Pittsfield 7 mi
(100)
Kent Pond
Gifford Woods SP
P
N
Maine Junction
Approx. 4.3 mi. of the AT are shown.
Mountain Meadows Lodge
0.4 mi.
↑ N
S
Greenbriar Inn
Base Camp
P
Rutland 11 mi
Inn at Long Trail
Sherburne Pass Tr. 0.5
PO (05751): 802-775-4247
M-F 8:30-11 & 12-4:30
Sa 8:30-12
Killington Deli & Marketplace
4
Pico Ski Resort
2.8 mi

🚌 **Marble Valley Regional Transit District** "The Bus" 802-773-3244, ext 117 M-F. ⟨www.thebus.com⟩ Red & white bus can be flagged down; they will stop if it is safe to do so.

Manchester to Rutland: ($2PP) Loops from downtown Rutland to Manchester Center, passing through Clarendon, Wallingford, and Danby. Stops of note include Rutland Airport and Shaws in Manchester Center.

Rutland Killington Commuter (RKC) ($2PP) Continuous loop from downtown Rutland to Killington, passing AT on US 4. Hikers can board eastbound (toward Killington) at the Pico Ski area 0.4E of AT or westbound at The Inn at Long Trail. Schedule subject to change; bus loops nearly every hour from 8am till 11pm.

1700.9   Kent Pond
⊨ ◐ ¶↑ ⚲ P ⌂ 📺 ✉ **Mountain Meadows Lodge** 802-775-1010 ⟨www.mountainmeadowslodge.com⟩ AT crosses property. Room $59, tent/hammock site $10/PP. Lunch or dinner $10. No pets inside; barn & woodshed available. Outdoor pool, hot tub, and sauna. Parking for section hikers. Open year round. Lodging not available most weekends & events. Maildrops: 285 Thundering Brook Road, Killington, VT 05751.

0.4E side trail to **Base Camp Outfitters** (listed above)

1719.2   VT 12, Barnard Gulf Rd

🏠 **On The Edge Farm** (0.2W) 802-457-4510 Open daily in summer M-F 10-5:30, Sunday 10-5. Fall hours Th-Monday 10-5. Pies, fruit, smoked meats and cheese, cold drinks.

Woodstock, VT 05091 (4.2E)

🏤 M-F 8:30-5, Sa 9-12, 802-457-1323

Tourist town with several motels and restaurants.

🛏 **Shire River View Motel** 802-457-2211 $138/up

🛏🛜 **Braeside Motel** 802-457-1366 $98-168, no pets.

🛏 **Pond Ridge Motel** 802-457-1667 $79S/up, $99D/up.

🍴 **Bentley's**, **Pizza Chef**

🏠 **Cumberland Farms**, **Gillingham FH & Sons**

🧪 **Woodstock Pharmacy**

🐕 **Woodstock Veterinary Hospital** 802-457-2229

🖥 **Norman Williams Public Library** 802-457-2295 M-F 10-5

Also: Movie theater, bookstore, salon.

1721.1   Woodstock Stage Rd

South Pomfret, VT 05067 (1E)

🏤 M-F 8-1 & 2-4:45, Sa 8:30-11:30, 802-457-1147

🏠 **Teago's General Store** 802-457-1626, 7 days, PO inside store.

The A.T. Guide

1. Plan Ahead and Prepare
2. Travel and Camp on Durable Surfaces
3. Dispose of Waste Properly
4. Leave What You Find
5. Minimize Campfire Impacts
6. Respect Wildlife
7. Be Considerate of Other Visitors

leave no trace

This copyrighted information has been reprinted with permission from the Leave No Trace Center for Outdoor Ethics: ⟨www.LNT.org⟩

Trail Etiquette

The AT is probably better without rigid rules of behavior, and definitely better without hikers who harangue others with such rules. Act as a civil person would in any public place. For more on etiquette, visit backpacking websites.

Avoid using a cell phone anywhere within the trail corridor, especially in shelters or within earshot of other hikers. Turn ringer off.

When hikers approach one another on the trail, the uphill hiker has the right-of-way, but the rule is irrelevant. If a hiker is approaching, look for an opportunity to step aside, regardless of your position, doing your best not to trample the last living patch of rock gnome lichen. Be aware of hikers approaching from behind, and step aside so that they may pass.

Take only as much shelter space as you need to sleep. Shelter spaces cannot be reserved for friends who have yet to arrive. If you bring alcohol to a shelter or campsite, do so discreetly. Soon after dark is bedtime for most hikers.

The AT is liberating, and outlandish behavior is part of AT lore. Be considerate; boisterous and erratic behavior may be unsettling to strangers stuck in the woods with you. Conversely, hikers seeking a serene experience should be aware that AT hiking is, for many, a social experience. Be tolerant. Stay flexible and be prepared to move on rather than trying to convince others to conform to your expectations.

Town Etiquette

Ask permission before bringing a pack into a place of business.

Don't expect generosity, and show appreciation when it is offered. If you are granted work-for-stay, strive to provide service equal to the value of your stay.

Assume that alcohol is not permitted in hostels & campsites until told otherwise.

Respect hotel room capacities; hotel owners should know how many people intend to stay in a room. Try to leave hotel rooms as clean as a car traveler would. If a shower is available, use it.

The A.T. Guide

SoBo	NoBo	The A.T. Guide	Elev
452.5	1731.7	Stream	541
452.3	1731.9	Quechee West Hartford Rd, NoBo west on road 0.4 mi, cross White River.	479
452.0	1732.2	VT 14, White River, **West Hartford, VT** (pg.179)	395
		NoBo: turn west, on road 0.3 mile, P0 to east.	
451.6	1732.6	Tigertown Rd, NoBo: turn east, on road 0.4 mile N43 43.250 W72 24.793 P	398
451.3	1732.9	I-89 underpass	557
450.6	1733.6	Podunk Rd (gravel), Podunk Brook N43 43.006 W72 24.013 P	860
450.1	1734.1	Woods road	1050
449.7	1734.5	Woods road, stream	1004
448.0	1736.2	**Happy Hill Shelter** (0.1E) 30.3◄20.4◄8.8►7.3►16.8►22.5 ◗ ◊ ⊂ (8)	1426
		Brook near shelter, known to run dry.	
447.7	1736.5	Tucker Trail 3.1W to Norwich	1337
446.4	1737.8	Woods road	1149
445.2	1739.0	Powerline	1193
444.7	1739.5	Stream	857
444.6	1739.6	Elm Street, NoBo: turn east, on road 1.0 mile	861
443.6	1740.6	Main St, **Norwich, VT**, NoBo: turn east, on road 1.4 miles (pg.178-179)	544
442.7	1741.5	**VT-NH** border, Connecticut River	380
442.1	1742.1	**Hanover, NH**, Dartmouth College N43 42.391 W72 16.656 P (pg.180-181)	552
		NoBo: turn east on SR 10.	
441.4	1742.8	NH 120, trailhead near convenience store.	533
440.7	1743.5	**Velvet Rocks Shelter** (0.2W) 27.7◄16.1◄7.3►9.5►15.2►21.9 ◗ ◗ ⊂ (6)	925
		Spring on northern access to shelter.	
440.1	1744.1	North shelter loop trail (0.2W)	974
438.4	1745.8	Pond, boardwalk	808
437.7	1746.5	Trescott Rd (paved)	939
436.4	1747.8	Footbridge, stream (2)	850
436.3	1747.9	Etna-Hanover Center Rd (paved), **Etna, NH** (0.8E) (pg.181)	845
		Cell phone reception at cemetery to west	
433.8	1750.4	Three Mile Rd (gravel) N43 43.077 W72 10.559 P	1426
433.6	1750.6	Mink Brook, footbridge	1357

SoBo	NoBo	Description	Elev
432.0	1752.2	Moose Mountain south peak.	2290
431.2	1753.0	**Moose Mountain Shelter** (0.1E) 25.6◀16.8◀9.5◀▶5.7▶12.4▶17.7 Loop trail to shelter, water at AT and northern leg intersection, tenting on northern leg of loop. ☽ ◊ ♦ ⊂ (8)	2131
429.9	1754.3	Moose Mountain north peak.	2315
428.4	1755.8	South fork of Hewes Brook.	1059
428.2	1756.0	Goose Pond Rd (paved)	963

�# **Cattail** – A tall (head-high) plant that grows in swampy areas. Characteristic part of the plant looks like a fuzzy cigar impaled lengthwise on a spear.

SoBo	NoBo	Description	Elev
426.1	1758.1	Holts Ledge, precipitous drop-off, views ◉	1937
425.5	1758.7	**Trapper John Shelter** (0.2W), privy behind shelter 0.1 mile. 22.5◀15.2◀5.7◀▶6.7▶12.0▶27.7 ☽ ♦ ⊂ (6)	1517
424.6	1759.6	Grafton Turnpike(paved), Dorchester Rd N43 47.400 W72 6.000 P ♦ (pg.182) **Lyme Center, NH** (1.3W) **Lyme, NH** (3.2W) ⚠ Nobo east on wedge of land between fork in road, side trail to Bill Ackerly home 0.1 north of intersection.	880
423.2	1761.0	Grant Brook	1228
422.9	1761.3	Concrete milepost	1143
422.6	1761.6	Lyme-Dorchester Rd (gravel). N43 47.400 W72 6.176 P	1124
420.9	1763.3	Lamberts Ridge. ◉	2369
419.3	1764.9	Smarts Ranger Trail to east	2731
418.8	1765.4	Smarts Mountain, fire tower ◉ ⚑ ◊ ♦ ⊂ (12) Tenting and spring south of summit. **Fire Wardens Cabin** north of summit, west of AT. Spring in front of shelter. Clark Pond Loop Trail to east. 21.9◀12.4◀6.7◀▶5.3▶21.0▶27.9	3237
414.9	1769.3	South Jacobs Brook ♦	1450
414.3	1769.9	Eastman Ledges ◉	1894
413.9	1770.3	North Jacobs Brook. ♦	1934
413.5	1770.7	**Hexacuba Shelter** (0.3E) 17.7◀12.0◀5.3◀▶15.7▶22.6▶31.6 ☽ ◊ ♦ (2) ⊂ (8) Shelter on steep side trail, unreliable stream at intersection with side trail.	2071

SoBo   NoBo   The A.T. Guide

Plan Ahead and Prepare

•Check Appalachian Trail (A.T.) guidebooks and maps for guidance and note that camping regulations vary considerably along the Trail. Travel in groups of 10 or fewer. If you are traveling in a group of more than 5, avoid using shelters, leaving them for lone hikers and smaller groups.

•Bring a lightweight trowel or wide tent stake to dig a hole for burying human waste.

•Bring a piece of screening to filter food scraps from your dishwater and pack them out with you.

•Bring a waterproof bag and at least 50 feet of rope to hang food and other scented articles. Or, carry a bear-resistant food container ("bear canister") to store these items.

•Repackage food in resealable bags to minimize waste.

•Prepare for extreme weather, hazards, and emergencies – especially the cold – to avoid impacts from searches, rescues, and campfires.

•Learn when areas are most crowded and try to avoid those times. If you are planning a northbound thru-hike, avoid starting on March 1, March 15, the first day of spring, or April 1.

Read more of the Leave No Trace techniques developed for the A.T.: www.appalachiantrail.org/LNT

The A.T. Guide

1732.2   VT 14, White River
West Hartford, VT 05084

Ask at general store or library about places to stay. Post office 0.2E from bridge on VT 14.

🏢 M–F 7:30–4:30, Sa 7:30–10, 802-295-6293

🏠 🍴 💲 **West Hartford Village Store and Full Belly Deli**
Thru-hiker specials, big breakfast, open until 8pm in summer. Water from spigot outside.

🚌 **Twin State Taxi** 802-295-7878

💻 **West Hartford Public Library** 802-295-7992, M, Tu & W 2-7, till 7:30 in summer, F 12-7, Sa 9-2, closed Th & Su. Friday night movies 7-9pm.

1740.6   Main St
Norwich, VT 05055 *(more services on map)*

🛏 🍴 📶 💻 ✉ **Norwich Inn** 802-649-1143 ⟨www.norwichinn.com⟩ $99 includes a free beer, rooms for pets, no smoking, reservations recommended. Restaurant Tu–Su B/L/D, pub serves dinner 7 days, microbrewery. Maildrops for guests: PO Box 908, Norwich, VT 04055.

🏪💻 **Dan & Whits General Store** 7 days 7-9, 0.1W on Main St. Hikers get free day old sandwiches when available.

💻 **Norwich Library** 802-649-1184, M 1-8, Tu-W-F 10-5:30, Th 10-8, Sa 10-3.

Also: The Massage Center 802-649-1149 Across from Dan & Whits. 30 min foot soak & massage $25.

ℹ The Hanover area Friends of the AT and Chamber of Commerce work to make Hanover a hiker-friendly town. They produce a brochure with complete coverage of hiker services in Norwich and Hanover. They are available at the PO, libraries, and many more places in town.

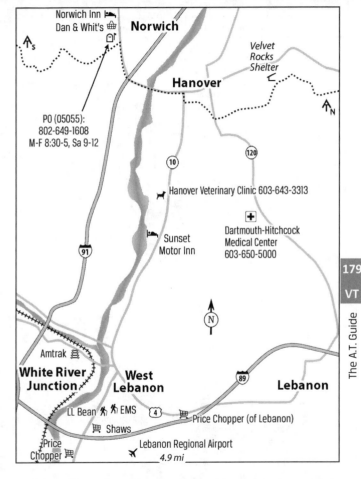

Norwich Inn
Dan & Whit's
Norwich

Velvet Rocks Shelter

Hanover

PO (05055):
802-649-1608
M-F 8:30-5, Sa 9-12

10

120

Hanover Veterinary Clinic 603-643-3313

Dartmouth-Hitchcock
Medical Center
603-650-5000

91

Sunset
Motor Inn

N

Amtrak

White River
Junction

West
Lebanon

89

Lebanon

LL Bean   EMS

4

Price Chopper (of Lebanon)

Shaws

Price
Chopper

Lebanon Regional Airport
4.9 mi

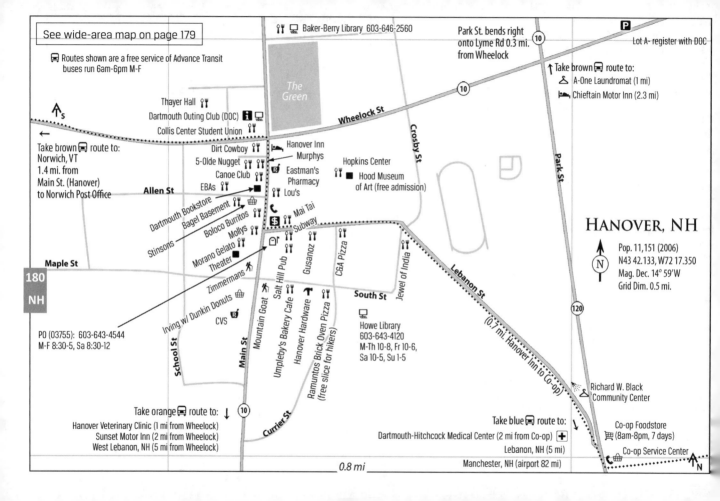

See wide-area map on page 179

Routes shown are a free service of Advance Transit buses run 6am-6pm M-F

Baker-Berry Library 603-646-2560

Park St. bends right onto Lyme Rd 0.3 mi. from Wheelock

Lot A- register with DOC

Take brown route to:
A-One Laundromat (1 mi)
Chieftain Motor Inn (2.3 mi)

The Green

Thayer Hall
Dartmouth Outing Club (DOC)
Collis Center Student Union

Wheelock St

Crosby St

Park St

Take brown route to:
Norwich, VT
1.4 mi. from
Main St. (Hanover)
to Norwich Post Office

Dirt Cowboy
5-Olde Nugget
Canoe Club
EBAs

Hanover Inn
Murphys

Eastman's Pharmacy
Lou's

Hopkins Center
Hood Museum of Art (free admission)

Allen St

Dartmouth Bookstore
Bagel Basement
Boloco Burritos
Stinsons
Mollys
Morano Gelato
Theater

Mai Tai
Subway

Maple St

HANOVER, NH

Pop. 11,151 (2006)
N43 42.133, W72 17.350
Mag. Dec. 14° 59'W
Grid Dim. 0.5 mi.

N

Zimmermans

Irving w/ Dunkin Donuts
CVS

Mountain Goat
Salt Hill Pub
Umpleby's Bakery Cafe
Hanover Hardware
Gusanoz

CGA Pizza

Jewel of India

South St

Lebanon St

120

PO (03755): 603-643-4544
M-F 8:30-5, Sa 8:30-12

Ramuntos Brick Oven Pizza
(free slice for hikers)

Howe Library
603-643-4120
M-Th 10-8, Fr 10-6,
Sa 10-5, Su 1-5

(0.7 mi. Hanover Inn to Co-op)

Richard W. Black
Community Center

School St

Main St

Take orange route to:
Hanover Veterinary Clinic (1 mi from Wheelock)
Sunset Motor Inn (2 mi from Wheelock)
West Lebanon, NH (5 mi from Wheelock)

10

Currier St

Take blue route to:
Dartmouth-Hitchcock Medical Center (2 mi from Co-op)
Lebanon, NH (5 mi)
Manchester, NH (airport 82 mi)

Co-op Foodstore
(8am-8pm, 7 days)

Co-op Service Center

N

0.8 mi

1742.1   Dartmouth College
Hanover, NH 03755 (more services on map)

ℹ️ 📶 💻 🚲 **Dartmouth Outing Club (DOC)** 603-646-2428 In Robinson Hall. Not available during Dartmouth orientation (first two weeks of Sept. Unsecured room in basement for hikers to store gear while in town, cannot be left overnight. Computers for free internet use. There are no hiker accommodations on campus.

🅿️ Overnight parking on Wheelock Street (Lot A), register with DOC. No parking near bridge over Connecticut River.

🛏🚿📶💻📧 **Sunset Motor Inn** 603-298-8721, open 8-11, Call ahead. Will shuttle when bus is not running, free laundry before 6pm, quiet after 10pm, $10 pet fee. Maildrops: 305 N Main Street, West Lebanon, NH 03874.

🛏📶 **Chieftain Motor Inn** 603-643-2550, 2 miles north on NH 10, $75–$100, cont B, pets allowed, shuttle in summer when available.

🛏 **Hanover Inn** 603-643-4300 High-priced rooms, discount sometimes available.

🍴 **EBA's** $6.99 pizza buffet M, Tu, & Th 5-9pm

🍴 **Jewel of India** buffet Su 11:30-2:30

🛒 **Hanover Food Co-op** open daily, large selection. Please use member # 7000 at checkout to help fund Hiker FAQs brochure.

🛍🍴 **Stinson's** Convenience store offers $5 hiker lunch special: deli sandwich, can of soda, and small bag of chips.

🥾📧 **Mountain Goat** 603-676-7240 Full line of backpacking gear, freeze dried foods, fuel/oz. Maildrops: 68 S Main Street Hanover, NH 03755.

🚿🛁 **Richard W. Black Recreation Center** 603-643-5315 M-F 9am-5pm, offers shower w/soap $3, load of laundry w/soap $2, last call for either 4:30pm, after Aug 28 open wkends.

⛏ **Hanover Hardware** Coleman/alcohol/oz

🚌 **Advance Transit**, 6-6 M-F, offers FREE bus service throughout Hanover, to medical center listed below, White River Junction, Lebanon and West Lebanon.

🚌 **Apex Transportation** 603-252-8294 Steve "Stray Kat" Lake.

🚌 **Dartmouth Coach** 603-448-2800

✈️ **Hanover Veterinary** 603-643-3313

🛁 **A-One Laundromat** 603-643-1514 (1.0N) on Lyme Road. Can take Advance Bus, get off at police station. M-F 7-8, Sa-Su 8-5.

White River Junction, VT

🚆 **Amtrak** 800-872-7245 Vermonter line travels north as far as St. Albans, VT, and south through New York, Philadelphia, Baltimore and Washington, DC. There is no ticket office at this station, but you can reserve on the phone and pay when you board.

West Lebanon, NH

🏃 **EMS** 603-298-7716, **LL Bean**

🛒 **Shaw's** 603-298-0388 7am-10pm, 7-9 Sunday

🛒 **Price Chopper** 603-298-9670 24hrs

Lebanon, NH

🛒 **Price Chopper** 603-448-3970

1747.9   Etna-Hanover Center Rd, **Etna, NH 03750** (0.8E)

🛏🚿🛁 **Tiggers Tree House** 603-643-9213 Private home; not a party place. Call from trailhead, Etna General Store (they will let you use their phone) or Dartmouth Outing Club for pickup, pets allowed, donations accepted or buy laundry soap or work for stay. Advance notice ensures a place to stay. Can arrange rides to grocery store, Walmart, EMS.

🛍🍴 (0.8E) **Etna General Store** 603-643-1655, M-F 6-7, Sa, Su 8-7. Deli, hot meals, open 7 days. Denatured alcohol/oz.

1759.6   Grafton Turnpike, Dorchester Rd, Dartmouth Skiway
Bill Ackerly Welcomes hiker visits. Help yourself to water, rest, chat and play a game of croquet.

Lyme Center, NH 03769 (1.3W)
⌂ M-F 8-12 & 2:30-4:45, Sa 8-11:30, 603-795-2688

Lyme, NH 03768 (3.2W)
⌂ M-F 7:45-12 & 1:30-5:15, Sa 7:45-12, 603-795-4421

🍴 ☎ **Stella's Italian Kitchen & Market** 603-795-4302
⟨www.stellaslyme.com⟩, M-Th 10-9, F-Sa 10-10, Su closed.

🛏🐾📶🖥 **Dowd's Country Inn B&B** 603-795-4712
⟨www.dowdscountryinn.com⟩ starting at $85S $100D mid week through Sep, breakfast and afternoon tea included. Pets allowed in some rooms. Call in advance; pickup sometimes available.

⛪🍴☎ **Lyme Country Store** (3.3W) ice cream, produce, deli, open 7 days.

✈ **Lyme Veterinary Hospital** (2.8W) bear right onto High St and hospital is 50 yards up on the left, 603-795-2747.

Appalachian Mountain Club (AMC) 603-466-2727
The club maintains the AT from Kinsman Notch, NH to Grafton Notch, ME. AMC offers hikers overnight accommodations at eight huts, 14 shelters and tentsites, Joe Dodge Lodge at Pinkham Notch and the Highland Center at Crawford Notch.
Huts have bunk space for 30-90 people. There is no road access, heat, or showers. They use alternative energy sources and composting toilets. Overnight stay includes bunk, dinner & breakfast, and the per-person cost starts at $85 (discount for AMC members). Reservations recommended. Enviable work-for-stay for the first 2 thru-hikers; 4 at Lakes of the Clouds Hut. WFS hikers get floor space for sleeping and feast on leftovers. Don't count on hut stays without reservations, and camping is not allowed near most of the huts.

🚌 **AMC Hiker Shuttle** operates June 2 - Sept 12 with stops at Crawford Notch, Pinkham Notch, and Gorham.

White Mountain National Forest (the "Whites")

Passage through the Whites should be planned carefully. It is one of the more heavily visited sections of the AT, and campsites are limited. The trail is rugged, so your pace may be slowed. Weather is dynamic, adding to the dangers of hiking on stretches of trail above treeline.

Take adequate cold-weather gear, check weather reports whenever possible, carry maps, and know your options for overnighting. The Appalachian Mountain Club (AMC) and Randolf Mountain Club (RMC) maintain camps, which are detailed in the following pages. Most of these have fees. Have cash on hand even if you do not plan to use them; your plans may change.

There are many trails in the Whites. The AT is the only white-blazed trail, but blazes are farther apart than they are elsewhere on the AT. Mileages on trail signs may be outdated. The AT is always coincident with another named trail, and the other trail name may be the one you see on signs.

Wherever the AT changes from one trail to another, there is an entry of the form: "AT: Town Line Tr◄►Glencliff Tr." This shorthand notation means that the AT to the south of this point is coincident with the Town Line Trail; to the north, the AT joins the Glencliff Trail.

The area within a quarter mile of all AMC and RMC facilities and everything above treeline (trees 8' or less) are part of the Forest Protection Area (FPA). Trails are often marked where they enter or leave the FPA. Do not camp within a FPA, and camp at least 200' from water and trails. Rocks aligned to form a trail boundary (scree walls) are an indication that you should not leave the treadway. Doing so damages fragile plant life.

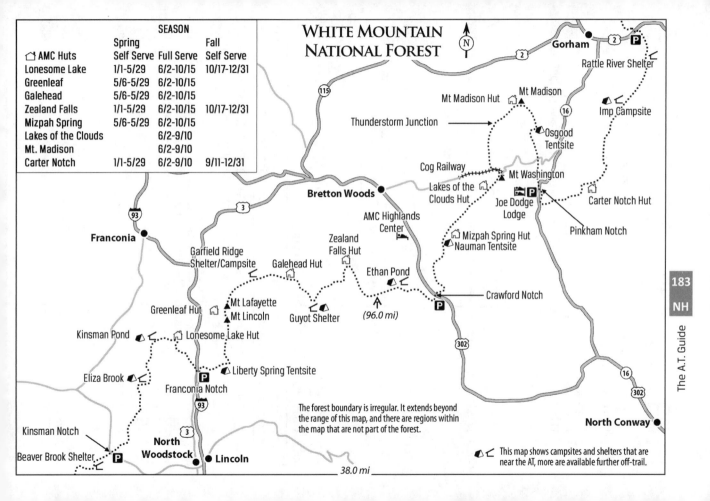

WHITE MOUNTAIN NATIONAL FOREST

⌂ AMC Huts	SEASON		
	Spring		Fall
	Self Serve	Full Serve	Self Serve
Lonesome Lake	1/1-5/29	6/2-10/15	10/17-12/31
Greenleaf	5/6-5/29	6/2-10/15	
Galehead	5/6-5/29	6/2-10/15	
Zealand Falls	1/1-5/29	6/2-10/15	10/17-12/31
Mizpah Spring	5/6-5/29	6/2-10/15	
Lakes of the Clouds		6/2-9/10	
Mt. Madison		6/2-9/10	
Carter Notch	1/1-5/29	6/2-9/10	9/11-12/31

N

Gorham

Rattle River Shelter

Mt Madison Hut   Mt Madison

Thunderstorm Junction

Imp Campsite

Osgood Tentsite

Cog Railway

Lakes of the Clouds Hut   Mt Washington

Joe Dodge Lodge

Carter Notch Hut

Bretton Woods

AMC Highlands Center

Pinkham Notch

Mizpah Spring Hut
Nauman Tentsite

Franconia

Garfield Ridge Shelter/Campsite

Galehead Hut

Zealand Falls Hut

Ethan Pond

Crawford Notch

Greenleaf Hut   Mt Lafayette
Mt Lincoln

Guyot Shelter

(96.0 mi)

183

NH

The A.T. Guide

Kinsman Pond

Lonesome Lake Hut

Liberty Spring Tentsite

Eliza Brook

Franconia Notch

Kinsman Notch

North Woodstock

Lincoln

North Conway

Beaver Brook Shelter

The forest boundary is irregular. It extends beyond the range of this map, and there are regions within the map that are not part of the forest.

◣◿ This map shows campsites and shelters that are near the AT, more are available further off-trail.

38.0 mi

SoBo	NoBo	The A.T. Guide	Elev
411.9	1772.3	Mt Cube south peak, cross Rivendell Trail to west	2911
411.8	1772.4	Side trail 0.3W to Mt Cube north peak.	2892
410.2	1774.0	Brackett Brook	1482
409.3	1774.9	Stream.	1307
409.1	1775.1	Woods road	1206
408.6	1775.6	NH 25A (paved) Nobo east on road 100 yards. N43 54.078 W71 59.029 P (pg.186) Wentworth, NH (4.8E)	923
406.7	1777.5	Cape Moonshine Rd (gravel) . . . . N43 54.950 W71 57.876 P (pg.186)	1439
406.0	1778.2	AT northbound joins Ore Hill Trail. Ore Hill Campsite (shelter destroyed by fire in 2011) Muddy spring 100 yards downhill from tentsites.	1889
404.0	1780.2	Ore Hill.	1832
403.3	1780.9	NH 25C, Warren, NH (4.0E) . . . . N43 57.220 W71 56.690 P (pg.186) AT on road past parking area & power lines, Ore Hill Brook north of road.	1547
401.3	1782.9	Mt Mist.	2200
400.9	1783.3	View.	1876
400.7	1783.5	Webster Slide Trail 0.7W to summit, view.	1685
398.7	1785.5	NH 25, stream north of road . . . . N43 59.395 W71 53.971 P (pg.186)	1056
397.8	1786.4	AT: Ore Hill Tr ◆► Wachipauka Pond Tr, Glencliff, NH (0.5E), Warren, NH (5.0E) Jeffers Brook Shelter, Jeffers Brook, footbridge 0.1 south	1330
		27.7◄21.0◄15.7◄►6.9►15.9►19.9	
397.7	1786.5	Long Pond Rd (gravel) NoBo: 0.1E on road.	1352
		AT: Wachipauka Pond Trail ◆► Town Line Trail	
397.5	1786.7	High St (paved) NoBo: 0.2W on road. AT: Town Line Trail ◆► Glencliff Trail	1365
397.2	1787.0	Stream.	1522
396.9	1787.3	Hurricane Trail to east	1684
396.0	1788.2	Stream.	2511
395.5	1788.7	Spring	3033
393.2	1791.0	Mt Moosilauke, Gorge Brook Trail to east	4802
392.8	1791.4	AT: Glencliff Trail ◆► Beaver Brook Trail, Benton Trail to west	4588

The notation "AT: Ore Hill Tr ◆► Wachipauka Pond Tr" indicates that the AT to the south is coincident with the Ore Hill Trail; the AT to the north joins the Wachipauka Pond Tr.

SoBo	NoBo	Description	Elev
391.3	1792.9	Ridge Trail to east	4066
390.9	1793.3	**Beaver Brook Shelter** 27.9◄22.6◄6.9◄▶9.0▶13.0▶28.1	3749
		Shelter on Beaver Brook trail. Beaver Brook on way to shelter.	
389.6	1794.6	Beaver Brook, footbridges, streams	1907
389.4	1794.8	NH 112, Kinsman Notch . . . N44 2.389 W71 47.525 P (pg.187-189)	1870
		North Woodstock, NH (5.0E), **Lincoln, NH** (6.0E)	
388.7	1795.5	AT: Beaver Brook Trail ◄▶ Kinsman Ridge Trail	2686
		Dilly Cliff Trail to east	
386.1	1798.1	Gordon Pond Trail to east	2687
384.8	1799.4	Mt Wolf east peak, summit to east	3478
382.9	1801.3	Reel Brook Trail to east	2634
382.5	1801.7	Powerline	2613
381.9	1802.3	**Eliza Brook Shelter** 31.6◄15.9◄9.0◄▶4.0▶19.1▶24.6	2408
381.1	1803.1	Eliza Brook, parallel to AT for 0.8 mi	2872
380.4	1803.8	Harrington Pond	3412
379.4	1804.8	South Kinsman Mountain	4358
378.5	1805.7	North Kinsman Mountain	4293
378.1	1806.1	Mt Kinsman Trail to west.	3858
377.9	1806.3	**Kinsman Pond Shelter** 19.9◄13.0◄4.0◄▶15.1▶20.6▶29.6	3763
		Caretaker, fee $8PP. Treat pond water. Kinsman Ridge Tr to west, Kinsman Pond Tr to east. AT: Kinsman Ridge Trail ◄▶ Fishin' Jimmy Trail	
377.1	1807.1	Stream.	2835
376.1	1808.1	Lonesome Lake Hut. (see AMC notes, pg.182-183)	2758
		AT: Fishin' Jimmy Tr ◄▶ Cascade Brook Tr (east), many other trail intersections	
375.1	1809.1	Kinsman Pond Trail to east.	2319
374.6	1809.6	Cascade Brook	2106
373.6	1810.6	Whitehouse Brook	1645
373.2	1811.0	US 3, I-93, At underpass. Town east on US 3; better to take side trail (next entry)	1472
373.1	1811.1	Franconia Notch . . . N44 6.014 W71 40.952 P (pg.187)	1428
		Paved trail to Flume parking (1.0E). **North Woodstock, NH** (1.0E) left from parking area on US 3. **Lincoln, NH** (4.8S) of North Woodstock.	
		AT: Cascade Brook Trail ◄▶ Liberty Springs Trail	
372.4	1811.8	Flume side trail to east.	1835
371.9	1812.3	Streams	2063

1775.6   NH Rte 25A, Gov. Meldrim Thomson Scenic Hwy

⌂ ◑ **Mt Cube Sugar Farm** (1.9W) 603-353-4709 Owned and operated by the Thomson family, for whom the road is named. The farm is on the original route of the AT and hosted Grandma Gatewood on her hikes. The fruit stand, open 8:30–dusk, offers homemade snacks, maple products, sodas, seasonal fruits and vegetables. Hikers may be allowed to stay in the sugar house or tent outside. The sugar house has stove, microwave and restrooms.

Wentworth, NH 03282 (4.3E on NH 25A, then right 0.5 on NH 25)

⌂ M–F 7–1 & 3–5, Sa 7:15–12, 603-764-9444

⌸ ℂ **Shawnee's General Store** 603-764-5553, Su–Th 6–9, F–S 6–9.

1777.5   Cape Moonshine Rd.

◑ ⚿ **Dancing Bones Intentional Community** Hot outdoor showers, open-air kitchen, tent platforms, composting toilets and good conversation. This is a residential community, so please be respectful when using shared facilities. Smoking is permitted in designated areas. Pets are welcome on a case by case basis.

1780.9   NH 25C

Warren, NH 03279 (4E)

⌂ M–F 7:30-1 & 2:30-5, Sa 7:30-12, 603-764-5733

🍴 **Calamity Jane's Restaurant** 603-764-5288, M-Su 6-8

🍴 **Sticky Fingers** ice cream M-Su 12-8

🍴 **Greenhouse Restaurant** 603-764-5708 Th,F,M 3-11pm, Sa-Su noon-11pm, open mic Thursdays, band on Fridays.

⌸ ℂ **Warren Village Market** produce/deli

⚠ **Laundry** M-Su 8:30-8:30

🔧 **Trust Worthy Hardware**

✚ **Mt Moosilauke Health Center** 603-764-5704, M, 8-6, Tu-Th 8-5, F 8-4, located past the Warren Village Market on the right.

1785.5   NH 25

Glencliff, NH 03238 (0.5E)

⌂ ℂ M-F 7-10 & 2-5, Sa 7-1, 603-989-5154

🛏 ◑ ⚿ ⚠ 🚐 🖥 **Hikers Welcome Hostel** 603-989-0040 Bunk ($15) and camping ($10) includes shower. Shower only w/ towel $2.50, laundry $2.50 wash, $2.50 dry. Snacks, sodas, and ice cream. Slackpacking & shuttles (5 miles to resupply in Warren). Coleman/alcohol/oz. Tools to help with gear repair, and selection of used gear available, particularly winter wear.

Warren, NH (5E) see entry above

1794.8   NH 112, Kinsman Notch

⋔ ⌇ Lost River Gorge (0.5E) 603-745-8031 A tourist attraction featuring a boulder jumble similar to Mahoosuc Notch. Has a grill serving short-order lunch menu and a gift store with snacks.

◭⛽ ⚡ ⚘⌂⌇ ✉ Lost River Valley Campground (3.0E) 603-745-8321, 800-370-5678 〈www.lostriver.com〉 cabin $59S, 69D, camping primitive sites $20, pets allowed but not in cabins. Showers, coin laundry, pay phone, open mid-May to Columbus Day 8-9, quiet 10pm-8am, owner Jim Kelly. Maildrops: 951 Lost River Road, North Woodstock, NH 03262.

North Woodstock, NH (5E), **Lincoln, NH** (6E)
(See pages 188-189)

1811.1   Franconia Notch

⋔⛽ ⌇ ✉ (0.7E) **Flume Visitor Center** with snack bar, restaurant open daily early May–late Oct, 9–5. Maildrops: Flume Gorge, 9 Franconia Notch State Park, Franconia, NH 03580.

◭⛺⚘⌇✉ (2.1W) **Lafayette Campground** 603-823-9513, tent sites $25D, limited store, no pets, quiet 10pm. Open mid-May-mid-Oct. Maildrops: Franconia State Park, Lafayette Campground, Franconia, NH 03580.

🛏📶✉ (1.2E) **Profile Motel & Cottages** 603-745-2759 〈www.profilemotel.com〉 weekday $59S $69D, weekend $72S $79D, fridge and microwave in room, grills and tables outside, open 7-10. Closed in winter. Maildrops: 391 US 3, Lincoln, NH 03251.

🛏🖥✉ (1.5E) **Mt. Liberty Motel** 603-745-3600 〈MtLibertyMotel.com〉 $60D mid-May - mid-Oct, no pets, ask about shuttles. Closed in winter. Maildrops: 10 Liberty Road, PO Box 422, Lincoln, NH 03251.

North Woodstock, NH (see pages 188-189)

Randolph Mountain Club (RMC)

The Randolph Mountain Club became the 31st AT maintaining club by joining in 2010. They maintain the section of the AT from Edmands Col to Madison Hut.

The club also maintains four shelters in the Northern Presidentials. Per-person fees are: Gray Knob - $12.00, Crag Camp - $12.00, The Perch - $7.00, and Log Cabin - $7.00. Fees must be paid in cash for stays at Gray Knob, Crag Camp and The Perch. Persons without cash will be directed to stay at the Log Cabin and will receive a receipt to mail in their fee. There is a caretaker year-round at Gray Knob if you need assistance or have questions. During the summer months, a second caretaker is in residence at Crag Camp. A caretaker visits Crag Camp and The Perch every evening, throughout the year.

All are open year-round. The camps are busy on weekends. Reservations are not accepted at any of the shelters; usage is first-come, first-served. If space is not available, be prepared to camp. Camping is not permitted within a quarter mile of RMC shelters.

There is no trash disposal; carry in, carry out. Please keep noise to a minimum after 10pm. The use of cell phones and portable TVs is not permitted. Group size is limited to ten. There is no smoking inside RMC facilities. When a camp is full, all guests are asked to limit their stay to two consecutive nights. Outdoor wood campfires are not allowed at any of the camps. Dogs are allowed at RMC's facilities, but they should be under voice control at all times.

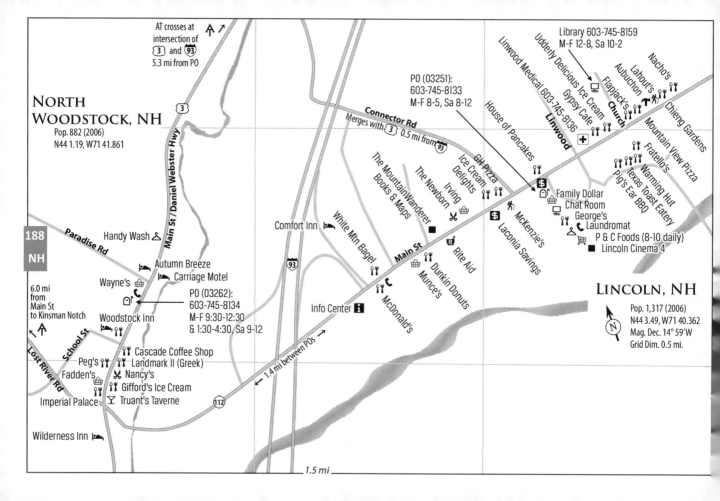

NORTH WOODSTOCK, NH
Pop. 882 (2006)
N44 1.19, W71 41.861

AT crosses at intersection of ③ and ⑨³ 5.3 mi from PO

Connector Rd
Merges with ③ 0.5 mi from ⑨³

PO (03251):
603-745-8133
M-F 8-5, Sa 8-12

Library 603-745-8159
M-F 12-8, Sa 10-2

Udderly Delicious Ice Cream
Linwood Medical 603-745-8136
Gypsy Cafe
Flapjack's
Aubuchon
Lahout's
Nacho's
Chieng Gardens
Church
Linwood
House of Pancakes

GH Pizza
Ice Cream Delights
Irving
The Newborn
The Mountain Wanderer Books & Maps

Family Dollar
Chat Room
George's
Laundromat
P & C Foods (8-10 daily)
Lincoln Cinema 4

Mountain View Pizza
Fratello's
Warming Hut
Texas Toast Eatery
Pig's Ear BBQ

McKenzie's
Laconia Savings

Comfort Inn
White Mtn Bagel
Main St
Rite Aid
Dunkin Donuts
Munce's
Info Center
McDonald's

**188
NH**

Paradise Rd
Handy Wash

Autumn Breeze
Carriage Motel
Wayne's
PO (03262):
603-745-8134
M-F 9:30-12:30
& 1:30-4:30, Sa 9-12
Woodstock Inn

6.0 mi from Main St to Kinsman Notch

School St
Lost River Rd

Cascade Coffee Shop
Peg's
Landmark II (Greek)
Fadden's
Nancy's
Gifford's Ice Cream
Imperial Palace
Truant's Taverne
Wilderness Inn

1.4 mi between POs

LINCOLN, NH
Pop. 1,317 (2006)
N44 3.49, W71 40.362
Mag. Dec. 14° 59'W
Grid Dim. 0.5 mi.

N

1.5 mi

North Woodstock, NH (4.8S) (more services on map)

🛏️🍴📶🖥️ **Woodstock Inn** 603-745-3951, 800-321-3985 ⟨www.woodstockinnnh.com⟩ 10% discount for thru-hikers, prices seasonal, stay includes full breakfast, no pets. Two restaurants and a micro-brewery on-site.

🛏️📶 **Autumn Breeze** 603-745-8549 ⟨www.autumnbreezemotel.com⟩ summer rates $70-90, rooms have kitchenettes, no pets.

🛏️✉️ **The Carriage Motel** 603-745-2416 ⟨www.carriagemotel.com⟩ (2011 prices) $64D, $10EAP, no pets, game room, pool, gas grills. Closed in winter. Maildrops: 180 Main Street, North Woodstock, NH 03262.

🛏️📶✉️ **Wilderness Inn B&B** 603-745-3890, 888-777-7813 ⟨www.thewildernessinn.com⟩ Rates starting from $70S $80D. One four-person room. Includes full breakfast. No pets, no smoking. Free shuttle from Kinsman or Franconia Notch with stay as time permits. Maildrops: 50 Courtney Rd, North Woodstock, NH 03262.

⛪ **Fadden's General Store** ice cream, fudge and more.

🚌 **The Shuttle Connection** 508-889-8515 ⟨www.shuttleconnection.com⟩ Shuttles between town and trail or to bus terminals and airports ranging from Portland, ME to NY. Can handle large groups.

North Woodstock, NH (5.8S) (more services on map)

🥾 **Lahout's Summit Shop** ⟨www.lahouts.com⟩ 603-745-2882 M-F 9:20-5:30, Sa 9-5:30, Su 9-5, full service outfitter, Coleman/alcohol/oz.

🖥️ **Chat Room/Books** M-Th 10-6, F-Sa 10-8.

Franconia, NH 03580 (10W of Franconia notch)

🏤 M-F 8:30-1 & 2-5, Sa 9-12, 603-823-5611

🛏️⛺📶🖥️✉️ **Gale River Motel** 603-823-5655, 800-255-7989 info@galerivermotel.com ⟨www.galerivermotel.com⟩ $50–$200, pets with approval, laundry wash $1, dry $1, Coleman/alcohol/oz. Free pickup/return to trail with stay, longer shuttles for a fee, open year-round. Maildrops: 1 Main Street, Franconia, NH 03580.

🥾 **Franconia Sport Shop** 603-823-5241 Some gear, clothing and boots.

🛒 **Mac's Market**

⛪🍴 **Franconia Village Store** deli

🖥️ **Abbie Greenleaf Library**

Also: AMC shuttle stop, Bus service, hardware.

190
NH

SoBo	NoBo	The A.T. Guide	Elev
370.4	1813.8	Liberty Spring Campsite. Overnight fee $8PP, caretaker, 7S and 3D platforms.	3886
370.2	1814.0	AT: Liberty Springs Tr ◀ ▶ Franconia Ridge Tr to west. Franconia Ridge Trail above treeline for 2.0 miles.	4267
368.4	1815.8	Little Haystack Mountain, Falling Waters Trail to west	4800
367.7	1816.5	Mt Lincoln, Franconia Ridge	5089
366.8	1817.4	Mt Lafayette, Greenleaf Hut (1.1W). Greenleaf Hut visible from summit of Mt Lafayette. Located down steep Greenleaf Trail. AT: Franconia Ridge Trail ◀ ▶ Garfield Ridge Trail	5259
366.0	1818.2	Skookumchuck Trail to west	4729
363.9	1820.3	Garfield Pond	3860
363.2	1821.0	Mt Garfield	4500
363.0	1821.2	Garfield Trail to west	4258
362.8	1821.4	**Garfield Ridge Shelter/Campsite,** reliable water source 28.1◀19.1◀15.1◀ ▶5.5 ▶14.5 ▶56.5 Overnight fee $8PP, caretaker.	3951
362.3	1821.9	Franconia Brook Trail to east goes steeply down to 13 Falls Campsite.	3450
360.7	1823.5	Gale River Trail to west.	3420
360.1	1824.1	Frost Trail to Galehead Hut ◀ ▶ Twinway Trail. AT: Garfield Ridge Trail ◀ ▶ Twinway Trail	3800
359.3	1824.9	South Twin Mountain, North Twin Spur Trail to west	4902
357.3	1826.9	**Guyot Shelter** 0.7E on Bondcliff Tr, plus 0.3 left on spur trail. 24.6◀20.6◀5.5◀ ▶9.0 ▶51.0 ▶57.1 Overnight fee $8PP, caretaker.	4534
357.2	1827.0	Mt. Guyot, view to east.	4597
356.2	1828.0	Trail west to summit of Zeacliff Ridge	4056
354.9	1829.3	Zeacliff Pond to east	3807
354.5	1829.7	Zeacliff, Zeacliff Trail to east.	3774
354.3	1829.9	View to east.	3681
353.8	1830.4	Whitewall Brook, many streams leading to falls	3213
353.4	1830.8	Lend-A-Hand Trail to west	2686
353.3	1830.9	Zealand Falls Hut, next to falls	2635
353.0	1831.2	Ethan Pond Trail to west, AT: Twinway Trail ◀ ▶ Ethan Pond Trail	2481
351.7	1832.5	Zeacliff Trail to east.	2461
350.8	1833.4	Stream, Thoreau Falls to east	2483
350.6	1833.6	Footbridge, stream	2483
350.3	1833.9	Stream, Shoal Pond Trail to east	2528

SoBo	NoBo	Description	Elev
349.6	**1834.6**	Footbridge, stream. ♦	2644
348.3	**1835.9**	**Ethan Pond Campsite,** Ethan Pond, inlet brook to pond ☽ ♦ ⌂ (10)	2874
		29.6◄14.5◄9.0◄►42.0►48.1►61.8	
		Overnight fee $8PP, caretaker, 2S and 2D platforms.	
347.2	**1837.0**	Willey Range Trail to west, stream north on AT ♦	2634
347.0	**1837.2**	Kedron Flume Trail to west.	2468
345.9	**1838.3**	Ripley Falls 0.5E	1566
345.7	**1838.5**	RR tracks, parking, AT: Ethan Pond Trail ♦► road walk. N44 10.627 W71 23.167 🅿	1443
		AT follows paved parking driveway 0.3 to US 302.	
345.4	**1838.8**	Crawford Notch, US 302. AT: road walk ◄► Webster Cliff Trail (pg.192)	1277
345.3	**1838.9**	Saco River, Saco River Trail to east, Sam Willey Trail to west ♦	1265
344.6	**1839.6**	Stream. ♦	1931
343.0	**1841.2**	Webster Cliffs, views from many spots along 0.5 mile traverse 📷	3280
342.1	**1842.1**	Mt Webster, Webster Jackson Trail to west, NoBo: AT to east 📷	3910
340.7	**1843.5**	Mt Jackson, Webster Jackson Trail to west 📷	4052
339.0	**1845.2**	Mizpah cutoff to west, Mizpah Spring Hut to east, Nauman Campsite ⌂ ♦	3800
		Tent site next to hut, overnight fee $8PP.	
338.2	**1846.0**	Mt Pierce (Mt Clinton) 📷	4312
338.1	**1846.1**	AT: Webster Cliff Trail ◄► Crawford Path	4259
336.8	**1847.4**	Mt Eisenhower Loop Trail west to summit. 📷	4446
336.2	**1848.0**	Mt Eisenhower Loop Trail west to summit. 📷	4459
336.0	**1848.2**	Mt Eisenhower Trail to east	4488
335.4	**1848.8**	Mt Franklin 📷	5004
334.9	**1849.3**	Mt Monroe Loop Trail west to summit 📷	5069
334.3	**1849.9**	Mt Monroe Loop Trail west to summit 📷	5094
334.2	**1850.0**	Lakes of the Clouds Hut ⌂ ♦ ☽	5048
		Four trails intersect near hut. AT stays on Crawford Path.	
333.5	**1850.7**	Davis Path to east, Westside Trail to west	5593
332.9	**1851.3**	Mt Washington, AT: Crawford Path ◄► Trinity Heights Connector 📷 (pg.192)	6288
332.5	**1851.7**	Cog Railroad (AT is just north), AT: Trinity Heights Connector ◄► Gulfside Trail	5942
332.1	**1852.1**	Westside Trail to west	5507
331.7	**1852.5**	Mt Clay Loop Trail to west.	5445
331.2	**1853.0**	Mt Clay Loop Trail to east, Sphinx Trail to east	5252
330.2	**1854.0**	Mt Jefferson Loop Trail, summit 0.3W 📷	5408
329.4	**1854.4**	Six Husband Trail 0.4W to Mt Jefferson 📷	5335
SoBo	NoBo	The A.T. Guide	Elev

1838.8   Crawford Notch, US 302

🍴☕ (1W) **Willey House** Snack bar, open daily mid-May to mid-Oct, 9–5.

🔺🚿⛰☕ (1.8E) **Dry River Campground** 603-374-2272 ⟨www.nhstateparks.com/crawford.html⟩ Tent sites $25 for 2 adults and up to 4 children. Pets allowed, coin laundry & showers, ask about shuttles, all major CC, quiet 10pm-7am.

🛏🏠🍴♿🚿🚌📶✉ (3.5W) **AMC's Highland Center** 603-278-4453 ⟨www.outdoors.org⟩ Lodge $80PP/up includes dinner and breakfast. Shapleigh Bunkhouse $40/up includes breakfast. No pets, no smoking. Coin shower for non-guests. Shuttles daily Jun-mid to Columbus Day (Oct 8, 2012), afterwards only weekends and holidays. Shuttle costs $10 for rides less than 10 minutes, $17 for all other stops on route. Restaurant open to all: Lunch short-order menu, breakfast buffet $13, $12 for AMC members; family style dinner $27, $23 for AMC members. Store sells snacks, sodas, some clothing and canister fuel. Maildrops ($5 fee): Route 302, Bretton Woods, NH 03574.

♿ (E3.3) **Crawford Notch General Store** ⟨www.crawfordnotchcamping.com⟩

🚐 **John Bartlett** 508-330-4178 ⟨jbclimbs@comcast.net⟩ Based in Conway, shuttle range from Kinsman Notch to Pinkham Notch. Advance notice helpful.

1851.3   Mt Washington

🍴♿🚻☕ Second highest peak on the AT. **Summit House** open 8am-8pm Memorial Day-Columbus Day. Snack bar open 9am-6pm.

Respect Wildlife

•Bears inhabit or travel through nearly every part of the A.T. Sightings have increased at shelters and campsites and even small food rewards teach bears to associate humans with food. When that happens, they often have to be killed to protect human safety. Dropped, spilled, or improperly stored food also attracts rodents to shelters. Even a few noodles or pieces of granola are a large meal for mice. Clean up spills completely and pack out all food scraps.

•Store your food according to local regulations. Store all food, trash, and scented articles (toothpaste, sunscreen, insect repellent, water purification chemicals, balm, etc.) out of reach of bears and other animals. A safe distance is 12 feet from the ground and 6 feet from a limb or trunk.

•Protect wildlife by keeping a respectful distance so as not to cause a change in their behavior. If you are hiking with a dog, keep it on a short leash. Do not follow or approach animals. Particularly avoid wildlife during sensitive times, i.e., when mating, nesting, raising young, or during winter.

Read more of the Leave No Trace techniques developed for the A.T.: www.appalachiantrail.org/LNT

American Hiking Society

Founded in 1976, American Hiking Society is the only national organization dedicated to promoting and protecting America's hiking trails, their surrounding natural areas and the hiking experience.

To learn more about American Hiking Society and our programs such as National Trails Day, National Trails Fund, and Volunteer Vacations, visit AmericanHiking.org or call (800) 972-8608.

SoBo	NoBo	The A.T. Guide	Elev
329.4	1854.8	Edmands Col, Gulfside Spring 50 yards east, **(pg.196)**	4938
328.7	1855.5	Edmands Col cutoff to east, Randolph Path & Mt Jefferson loop to west.	5280
		Israel Ridge Path to RMC Perch Shelter (0.9W), $7 fee.	
328.1	1856.1	Thunderstorm Junction **(pg.196)**	5500
327.5	1856.7	Airline Trail, King Ravine Trail to west	5149
327.2	1857.0	Madison Spring Hut, Valley Way Trail 0.6W to VW Tent Site, no fee	4800
326.7	1857.5	AT: Gulfside Trail ◀▶ Osgood Trail	5366
		Mt Madison, Watson Path to west.	
326.4	1857.8	Howker Ridge Trail to east.	5117
326.1	1858.1	Parapet Trail to east, Daniel Webster Trail to west	4875
324.2	1860.0	Osgood Tent Site to west, no fee. AT: Osgood Trail	2535
323.9	1860.3	Stream.	2521
323.5	1860.7	AT: Osgood Cutoff ◀▶ Great Gulf Trail to east.	2317
323.5	1860.7	Parapet Brook, AT: Great Gulf Trail ◀▶ Madison Gulf Trail to west	2312
323.4	1860.8	West branch of Peabody River, suspension bridge. Great Gulf Tr to east.	2300
322.9	1861.3	Stream.	2386
322.0	1862.2	Stream.	2562
321.5	1862.7	Lowes Bald Spot 0.1W	2825
321.4	1862.8	Mt Washington Auto Rd N44 16.892 W71 15.203 **P**	2715
321.2	1863.0	AT: Madison Gulf Trail ◀▶ Old Jackson Rd	2658
320.4	1863.8	Nelson Crag Trail and Raymond Path to east	2560
320.1	1864.1	George's Gorge Trail to west.	2258
		Peabody River, four other trails cross the AT from here to Pinkham Notch	
319.4	1864.8	**Gorham, NH** (10.7W), AT: Old Jackson Rd ◀▶ Lost Pond Trail	2050
		NH 16, Pinkham Notch N44 15.416 W71 15.158 **P (pg.196-197)**	
318.4	1865.8	AT: Lost Pond Trail ◀▶ Wildcat Ridge Trail	2006
318.0	1866.2	View.	2838
317.4	1866.8	Rocky crevasse, stairs.	3242
316.7	1867.5	Wildcat Mountain peak E.	4044
316.4	1867.8	Wildcat Mountain peak D, observation tower, ski gondola 0.1N.	3990
		Gondola rides to/from the AT, $12 round trip, restaurant at base, open Jul–Oct.	
315.3	1868.9	Wildcat Mountain peak C.	4263
314.4	1869.8	Wildcat Mountain peak A.	4422
313.9	1870.3	Spring	3688
313.6	1870.6	AT: Wildcat Ridge Trail ◀▶ Nineteen Mile Brook Trail to east	3360
313.2	1871.0	AT: Nineteen Mile Brook Trail ◀▶ Carter Moriah Trail, Carter Notch Hut (0.1E).	3898
312.9	1871.3	Spring to west	4319
312.3	1871.9	Carter Dome, Rainbow Trail to east	4832
311.9	1872.3	Black Angel Trail to east, Carter Dome Trail to west.	4627
311.4	1872.8	Mt Hight, view.	4671
310.9	1873.3	Zeta Pass, two Carter Dome trailheads to west	3890

SoBo	NoBo	Description	Elev
308.8	1875.4	Middle Carter Mountain, view	4610
308.2	1876.0	North Carter Mountain, North Carter Trail to west, just south of summit	4539
306.3	1877.9	**Imp Campsite** (0.2W) 56.5◄51.0◄42.0◄▶6.1▶19.8▶25.0 Overnight fee $8PP, caretaker, composting privy.	3344
305.6	1878.6	Stony Brook Trail to west, Moriah Brook Trail to east	3143
304.2	1880.0	Mt Moriah, summit to west. △ AT: Carter Moriah Trail ◆▶ Kenduskeag Trail	3991
302.9	1881.3	△ AT: Kenduskeag Trail ◆▶ Rattle River Trail	3387
302.5	1881.7	Stream.	2871
301.8	1882.4	Rattle River	2022
300.4	1883.8	East Rattle River, multiple streams	1349
300.2	1884.0	**Rattle River Shelter** 57.1◄48.1◄6.1◄▶13.7▶18.9▶23.3 No fee. Water source is Rattle River. Gently sloping trail from shelter to US 2.	1279
298.9	1885.3	Stream.	973
298.3	1885.9	AT 0.1W on US 2, **Gorham, NH** (3.6W) N44 24.048 W71 6.589 P (pg.196-197)	780
298.2	1886.0	AT east on North Rd.	803
297.6	1886.6	AT west on Hogan Rd (gravel) N44 24.386 W71 7.009 P	793
296.7	1887.5	Brook	1238
294.7	1889.5	Mt Hayes, Mahoosuc Trail to west	2555
293.1	1891.1	View.	2351
292.5	1891.7	Cascade Mountain	2631
291.4	1892.8	Trident Col Campsite to west, no fee, spring 0.2 on side trail	2020
291.1	1893.1	Spring.	1936
290.4	1893.8	Page Pond.	2248
289.8	1894.4	Wocket Ledge, view.	2664
289.3	1894.9	Stream.	2615
288.7	1895.5	Dream Lake	2639

1854.8 Edmands Col
1856.1 Thunderstorm Junction
🏚 **Crag Camp Cabin** (1.1W) on Spur Trail, **Gray Knob Cabin** (1.2W) on Lowe Path. Camp at least 0.25 from either cabin.

1864.8 NH 16, Pinkham Notch
🏚 ⅋ 🚹 🌾 🚌 📞 📨 **Pinkham Notch Visitor Center and Joe Dodge Lodge** 603-466-2721 ⟨www.outdoors.org⟩ Open year round. Cafeteria with B/L/D buffets. Coin-op $1 shower available 24hrs, $1 towel rental. Bunkroom prices seasonal, usually $80PP in summer includes breakfast and dinner. No pets. Meals available to non-guests; AYCE breakfast served 6:30-8:30, a la carte lunch, family-style dinner 6pm. Vending machines, Coleman/alcohol/iso-butane/oz. Shuttle 8am daily $17. Accepts major credit cards. Maildrops: AMC Visitor Center, c/o Front Desk, 361 Rte. 16, Gorham, NH 03581.
Gorham, NH (10.7W from Pinkham Notch)

1885.9 US 2 *(more services on map)*
(on AT) **White Mountains Lodge and Hostel** *(see map)*
(1.8W) **White Birches Camping Park** *(see map)*
 Gorham, NH 03581 (3.6W from US 2)
⌂♂ ID required; all packages should include your legal name.
🛏 ⅋ 🀙 🖥 (2.9W) **Town and Country Inn** 603-466-3315 ⟨www.townandcountryinn.com⟩ $58-90, pets $6. Breakfast 6-10:30, dinner 5-10, cocktails. Indoor pool, sauna.
🛏 🏚 ⅋ 🛆 🚌 **Hiker's Paradise** at Colonial Fort Inn 603-466-2732, 800-470-4224 ⟨www.hikersparadise.com⟩ bunks $21 with linen, tub/shower, kitchen. Private rooms available. No pets or maildrops. Coin laundry for guests. Restaurant serves breakfast. Coleman/alcohol/oz. Free shuttle with stay from/to Route 2, other limited shuttles.
🛏 🏚 🛆 📨 **The Barn** also the **Libby House B&B** 603-466-2271, bunks $20. B&B room for two with breakfast $100.

Coleman/alcohol/oz, kitchen, stove microwave, refrigerator for use, no pets, laundry $5, Visa MC accepted, shuttles as time permits. Guest maildrops: 55 Main Street, Gorham, NH 03581. $15 maildrop fee for non-guests.
🛏 ⅋ 🛆 🀙 **Royalty Inn** 603-466-3312 ⟨www.royaltyinn.com⟩ $49-150, a/c, indoor pool.
🛏 🛆 🀙 **Top Notch Inn** 603-466-5496 ⟨www.topnotchinn.com⟩ Pool, a/c, pets allowed, no smoking, all major credit cards accepted.
🛏 **Northern Peaks Motor Inn** 603-466-3374 ⟨www.northernpeaksmotorinn.com⟩, a/c, pool, pets $5, no smoking, all major credit cards accepted, hiker friendly.
🚶 🏪 **Gorham Hardware and Sports** 603-466-2312 Open 8-5:30. Gear, hiking food, Coleman/alcohol/oz and iso-butane. Accepts Visa/MC/Disc.
🏪 **Jackson's General** 603-466-5050 Coleman/alcohol/oz. Leki pole repair. Ships UPS.
🚌 **Arthur Jolin** 603-466-2127 Short and long distance shuttles anywhere from VT through Katahdin and off-trail locations like Boston or Portland airports.
🚌 **Concord Coach** 800-639-3317 Bus service stops daily at Irving store. Routes to Pinkham Notch NH, Manchester NH, and more.
🛆 **Laundry Basket** 7 days 5:30-11.
 Berlin, NH 03570
➕ **Androscoggin Valley Hospital** 603-752-2200

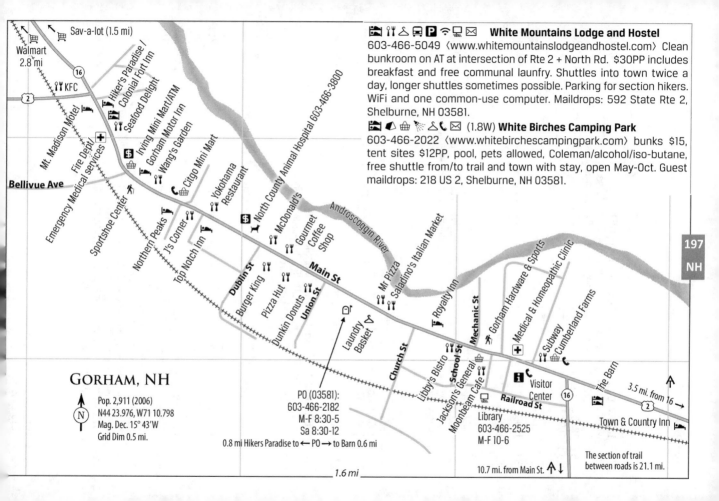

🏠 🍴 ⛺ 🚐 🅿 📶 🖥 ✉ **White Mountains Lodge and Hostel**
603-466-5049 ⟨www.whitemountainslodgeandhostel.com⟩ Clean bunkroom on AT at intersection of Rte 2 + North Rd. $30PP includes breakfast and free communal launfry. Shuttles into town twice a day, longer shuttles sometimes possible. Parking for section hikers. WiFi and one common-use computer. Maildrops: 592 State Rte 2, Shelburne, NH 03581.

🏠 🧺 ⛲ 🐾 🚿 ⛽ ✉ (1.8W) **White Birches Camping Park**
603-466-2022 ⟨www.whitebirchescampingpark.com⟩ bunks $15, tent sites $12PP, pool, pets allowed, Coleman/alcohol/iso-butane, free shuttle from/to trail and town with stay, open May-Oct. Guest maildrops: 218 US 2, Shelburne, NH 03581.

197
NH

Sav-a-lot (1.5 mi)

Walmart 2.8 mi

KFC

Hiker's Paradise / Colonial Fort Inn

Mt. Madison Motel

Seafood Delight

Irving Mini Mart/ATM

Gorham Motor Inn

Wang's Garden

Citgo Mini Mart

Bellivue Ave

Fire Dept/ Emergency Medical services

Yokohama Restaurant

North County Animal Hospital 603-466-3800

Sportshoe Center

Northern Peaks

J's Corner

McDonald's

Gourmet Coffee Shop

Androscoggin River

Saladino's Italian Market

Mr Pizza

Top Notch Inn

Dublin St

Burger King

Pizza Hut

Union St

Main St

Royalty Inn

Mechanic St

Gorham Hardware & Sports

Medical & Homeopathic Clinic

Dunkin Donuts

Laundry Basket

Church St

Libby's Bistro

School St

Jackson's General

Moonbeam Cafe

Subway

Cumberland Farms

The Barn

3.5 mi. from 16 →

PO (03581): 603-466-2182 M-F 8:30-5 Sa 8:30-12

0.8 mi Hikers Paradise to ← PO → to Barn 0.6 mi

Visitor Center

Railroad St

Library 603-466-2525 M-F 10-6

Town & Country Inn

GORHAM, NH

Ⓝ Pop. 2,911 (2006)
N44 23.976, W71 10.798
Mag. Dec. 15° 43'W
Grid Dim 0.5 mi.

10.7 mi. from Main St.

The section of trail between roads is 21.1 mi.

1.6 mi

SoBo	NoBo	The A.T. Guide	Elev
286.5	1897.7	**Gentian Pond Shelter/Campsite** (0.2E) ☽ ♦ ⌂ ⊂ (14) 61.8◀19.8◀13.7◀▶5.2▶9.6▶14.7 Junction of Mahoosuc Trail (AT) and Austin Brook Trail, inlet brook of Gentian Pond. 3S and 1D platforms.	2181
285.5	1898.7	Stream . . . . ♦	2269
285.1	1899.1	Stream . . . . ♦	2526
283.7	1900.5	Mt Success . . . . 🄿	3565
283.1	1901.1	Success Trail to west.	3188
281.8	1902.4	**NH-ME** border	2972
281.3	1902.9	**Carlo Col Shelter and Campsite** (0.3W), on Carlo Col Trail ☽ ♦ ⌂ ⊂ (8) 25.0◀18.9◀5.2◀▶4.4▶9.5▶16.4 Platforms 3S and 2D bear box, no fee.	3210
280.9	1903.3	Mt Carlo	3565
279.5	1904.7	Goose Eye Mountain west peak, Goose Eye Mtn Trail to west	3797
279.1	1905.1	Goose Eye Mountain east peak . . . . 🄿	3790
278.9	1905.3	Wright Trail to east . . . . 🄿	3467
277.9	1906.3	Goose Eye Mountain north peak. . . . . 🄿	3680
276.9	1907.3	**Full Goose Shelter and Campsite** ☽ ⊂ (12) 23.3◀9.6◀4.4◀▶5.1▶12.0▶15.5 No Fee, stream behind shelter.	2966
276.4	1907.8	Fulling Mill Mountain south peak	3395
275.4	1908.8	Mahoosuc Notch south end, Mahoosuc Notch Trail to west. ♦ Most difficult or fun mile of the AT. Make way through jumbled pit of boulders.	2498
274.1	1910.1	Mahoosuc Notch north end, Bull Branch, campsite . . . . ♦◣	2163
273.1	1911.1	Spring . . . . ♦	3288
272.7	1911.5	Mahoosuc Arm	3770
272.0	1912.2	Speck Pond brook . . . . . ♦	3425
271.8	1912.4	**Speck Pond Shelter & Campsite.** ☽ ♦ ⌂ ⊂ (8) 14.7◀9.5◀5.1◀▶6.9▶10.4▶20.9 Overnight fee $8PP, caretaker. Spring down Speck Pond Trail just beyond caretaker's yurt.	3438
270.7	1913.5	Grafton Loop Trail, Old Speck Trail to Old Speck Mtn 🄿 🗼 with small observation tower.	4038
268.4	1915.8	Eyebrow Trail to west . . . . ♦	2525
268.1	1916.1	Stream. . . . . ♦	2406

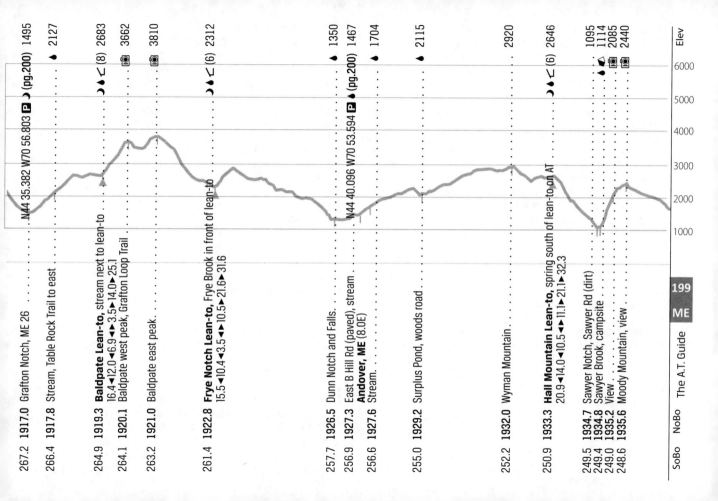

SoBo	NoBo		Elev
267.2	1917.0	Grafton Notch, ME 26 . . . . N44 35.382 W70 56.803 **P** ☽ (pg.200)	1495
266.4	1917.8	Stream, Table Rock Trail to east . . . ♦	2127
264.9	1919.3	**Baldpate Lean-to,** stream next to lean-to . . . ☽♦⊏(8)	2683
		16.4◄12.0◄6.9▼►3.5►14.0►25.1	
264.1	1920.1	Baldpate west peak, Grafton Loop Trail . . . 📷	3662
263.2	1921.0	Baldpate east peak. . . . 📷	3810
261.4	1922.8	**Frye Notch Lean-to,** Frye Brook in front of lean-to . . . ☽♦⊏(6)	2312
		15.5◄10.4◄3.5◄►10.5►21.6►31.6	
257.7	1926.5	Dunn Notch and Falls. . . . ♦	1350
256.9	1927.3	East B Hill Rd (paved), stream . . . N44 40.096 W70 53.594 **P** ♦ (pg.200)	1467
		Andover, ME (8.0E)	
256.6	1927.6	Stream. . . . ♦	1704
255.0	1929.2	Surplus Pond, woods road . . . ♦	2115
252.2	1932.0	Wyman Mountain. . . .	2920
250.9	1933.3	**Hall Mountain Lean-to,** spring south of lean-to on AT . . . ☽♦⊏(6)	2646
		20.9◄14.0◄10.5◄►11.1►21.1►32.3	
249.5	1934.7	Sawyer Notch, Sawyer Rd (dirt) . . . ♦	1095
249.4	1934.8	Sawyer Brook, campsite . . . ♦	1114
249.0	1935.2	View. . . . 📷	2085
248.6	1935.6	Moody Mountain, view . . . 📷	2440

1917.0   Grafton Notch, ME 26

🛏️ ⚠️ 🚪 ✉️ (4.5E) **Mahoosuc Mountain Lodge** 207-824-2073 ⟨www.mahoosuc.com⟩ Bunkrooms $35PP with towel, linen extra. Full kitchen, laundry $5 wash, $3 dry. No dogs. Shuttles $10 from Grafton Notch, call from top of Old Speck. Other shuttles when available. Maildrops: 1513 Bear River Rd, Newry, ME 04261.

🛶 ⚠️ 🚿 ⚠️ 🛜 ✉️ (12.8E) **Stony Brook Recreation and Camping** 207-824-2836 ⟨www.stonybrookrec.com⟩ tent site $25 for 4, lean-to $28 for 4. Shuttles from Grafton Notch for a fee. Pool, miniature golf, rec room, convenience store, Coleman fuel. Located 12 miles east on Hwy 26, then left 0.8 mile on Route 2. Maildrops: 42 Powell Place, Hanover, ME 04237.

Bethel, ME 04217 (12E to Rt 2, right 5 miles on Rt 2)
📮 M-F 9-4, Sa 10-12:30, 207-824-2668

🛏️ ⚠️ ✉️ **Chapman Inn** 207-824-2657 ⟨www.chapmaninn. com⟩ Bunk space $35 in bunkroom includes shower and full breakfast, $25 without breakfast. Rooms $69/up include breakfast. Kitchen privileges, $4 laundry. Maildrops: PO Box 1067, Bethel, ME 04217.

🍴 **Pat's Pizza** 7 days 11-9

🍴 **Sudbury Inn Restaurant & Pub**, Tu-Su 5:30-9, pub 7 days 4:30-9.

🛒 **Bethel Shop 'n Save**

🥾 🚪 **True North Adventurewear** 207-824-2201 Full service outfitter, open 7 days 10-6. Shuttles possible by appointment. Leki repair, Coleman/alcohol/oz and iso-butane, freeze-dried foods.

🐕 **Bethel Animal Hospital** 207-824-2212

Also: Casablanca Cinema 4

1927.3   East B Hill Rd

Andover, ME 04216 (8E)
📮 M-F 8:30-1:30 & 2-4:30, Sa 8:15-12:15, 207-392-4571

🛏️ 🛏️ 🚿 ⚠️ 🚪 🛜 🖥️ ✉️ **Pine Ellis Lodging** 207-392-4161 ⟨www.pineellislodging.com⟩ Bunks $20PP, private rooms $50 & $60 one to three persons. Kitchen privileges, laundry $4. Per-person fee for trailhead pickup. For-fee shuttles; slackpack Grafton Notch to Rangeley, and also shuttles to Rumford, Bethel, airport and bus station. No dogs. Resupply includes items for on-trail snacks and meals. Coleman/denatured/oz and canister fuel. Prices subject to change. Guest maildrops: (USPS) PO Box 12 or (UPS) 20 Pine Street, Andover, ME 04216.

🛏️ ⚠️ 🚪 ✉️ **The Cabin** (3E) 207-392-1333 ⟨www.thecabininmaine.com⟩ $20PP includes linens, kitchen use. Shuttles available. Guest maildrops: (USPS) PO Box 55 or (UPS) 497 East Andover Rd, East Andover, ME 04226.

⚙️ 🍴 🏧 📞 **Andover General Store** 207-392-4172 Deli serves short-order food and pizza, open M-Sa 5-8, Su 6-8.

🍴 **Little Red Hen** Breakfast & lunch M-Sa

Also: Massage therapist, Donna Gifford, 207-357-5686, call for rates. Free pickup/return to Andover.

1937.4   South Arm Rd

🛶 ⚙️ 🚿 ⚠️ ✉️ (3.5W) **South Arm Campground** 207-364-5155 ⟨www.southarm.com⟩ Tent sites, camp store, no credit cards, open May 1-Oct 1. Maildrops: PO Box 310, Andover, ME 04216.

Andover, ME (9E) (see above)

1950.1   ME 17

Oquossoc, ME 04964 (11W)
📮 M-F 8-1 &1:30-4:15, Sa 9-12, 207-864-3685

⚙️ 📞 **Oquossoc Grocery** deli, bakery, Coleman fuel

🍴 **Gingerbread House** serves B/L/D, vegetarian specials.

🍴 **Four Seasons Café** 7 days 11-9 L/D vegetarian specialties.

1963.8   ME 4 **Rangeley, ME** (9W)
        (more services on map)

🛏📶✉ **Town & Lake Motel** 207-864-3755 $85S $99D $10EAP, pets $5. Maildrops: PO Box 43, Rangeley, ME 04970.

🛏🍴📶 **Saddleback Motor Inn** 207-864-3434 $95, pets $10, pool. **Sunset Grill** on-site serves lunch and dinner, closed M and Tu.

🛏🍴📶 **Rangeley Inn** 207-864-3341 〈www.rangeleyinn.com〉 High-end resort may give discount on low-demand nights. **Pour House** on-site.

🛏🍴📶 **North Country Inn B&B** 207-864-2440 〈www.northcountrybb.com〉 $99-149, includes three course breakfast, specials in low/off season.

🍴 **The Shed BBQ** L/D 7 days Memorial-Columbus Day.

🍴 **Sarge's Sports Pub & Grub** L/D and bar, 7 days 11-1, house bands on Friday and Saturday.

🛒💲 **IGA Supermarket** ATM 7 days 7-8.

🥾🏠🚐 **Ecopelagicon** 207-864-2771 Hiker friendly nature store has white gas/alcohol/oz, canister fuel, freeze-dried foods, water filters, clothes, Leki poles and does warranty work. Ask about shuttles.

🥾 **Alpine Shop** 〈www.alpineshoprangeley.com〉 207-864-3741   M-S 9-7:30, Su 10-4, some hiking gear, Coleman/alcohol/oz.

🥾 **Back Woods** 207-864-2335 Gear, clothes.

➕ **Rangeley Health Center** 207-864-4397

💊 **Rangeley Pharmacy** 207-864-3984 M-F 9-5.

🛁 **Village Scrub Board** 7 days 7-7

        Oquossoc, ME (7W from Rangeley)

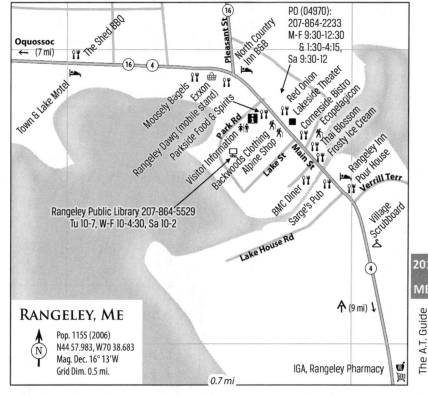

RANGELEY, ME

Ⓝ Pop. 1155 (2006)
N44 57.983, W70 38.683
Mag. Dec. 16° 13'W
Grid Dim. 0.5 mi.

0.7 mi

The A.T. Guide

1965.6   **Piazza Rock Lean-to** There are two side trails north of the shelter, to the west; 100 yards north: To Piazza Rock, overhanging rock bluff; 0.1 north: To "The Caves", blue-blazed route through a labyrinth of boulders and caves.

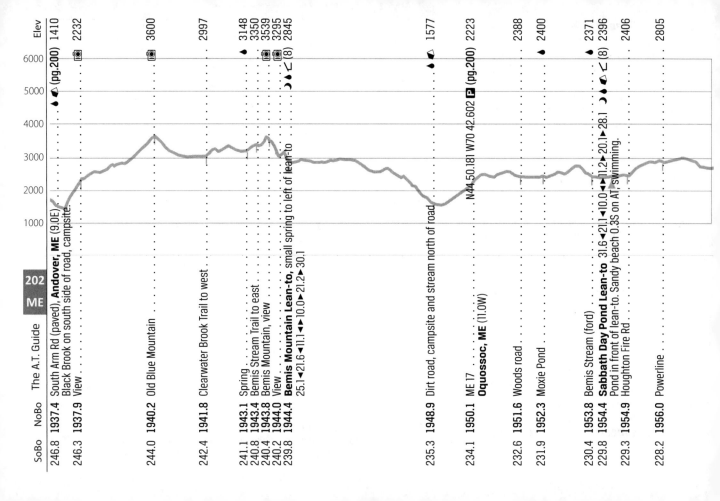

SoBo	NoBo	The A.T. Guide	Elev
246.8	1937.4	South Arm Rd (paved), **Andover, ME** (9.0E)	1410
246.3	1937.9	Black Brook on south side of road, campsite. View.	2232
244.0	1940.2	Old Blue Mountain	3600
242.4	1941.8	Clearwater Brook Trail to west	2997
241.1	1943.1	Spring	3148
240.8	1943.4	Bemis Stream Trail to east	3350
240.4	1943.8	Bemis Mountain, view	3539
240.2	1944.0	View	3295
239.8	1944.4	**Bemis Mountain Lean-to,** small spring to left of lean-to 25.1◀21.6◀11.1◀▶10.0▶21.2▶30.1	2845
235.3	1948.9	Dirt road, campsite and stream north of road	1577
234.1	1950.1	ME 17 **Oquossoc, ME** (11.0W) N44 50.181 W70 42.602 **P** (pg.200)	2223
232.6	1951.6	Woods road	2388
231.9	1952.3	Moxie Pond	2400
230.4	1953.8	Bemis Stream (ford)	2371
229.8	1954.4	**Sabbath Day Pond Lean-to** 31.6◀21.1◀10.0◀▶11.2▶20.1▶28.1 Pond in front of lean-to. Sandy beach 0.3S on AT, swimming.	2396
229.3	1954.9	Houghton Fire Rd	2406
228.2	1956.0	Powerline	2805

202
ME

SoBo	NoBo	Feature	Elev
225.2	**1959.0**	Little Swift River Pond Campsite	2460
		Spring house next to pond.	
224.0	**1960.2**	Chandler Mill Stream, pond	2199
222.9	**1961.3**	Stream.	2328
222.5	**1961.7**	South Pond	2174
220.4	**1963.8**	ME 4, **Rangeley, ME** (9.0W) N44 53.213 W70 32.431 **P** (pg.201)	1635
220.2	**1964.0**	Sandy River, footbridge	1687
219.7	**1964.5**	Old County Rd (gravel)	1889
218.9	**1965.3**	Stream	1998
218.6	**1965.6**	**Piazza Rock Lean-to**, stream through campsite ◐ ◖ ⬦ ⊏ (8) (pg.201)	2109
		32.3◄21.2◄11.2◄▶8.9▶16.9▶35.5 Two-seat privy and cribbage board.	
217.8	**1966.4**	Ethel Pond	2386
217.6	**1966.6**	Saddleback Stream	2473
216.8	**1967.4**	Ethel Pond, woods road passes near north bank, no camping near pond	2662
214.7	**1969.5**	Saddleback Mountain, trail 2.0W to ski lodge.	4120
213.1	**1971.1**	The Horn.	4037
212.4	**1971.8**	Redington Campsite to west, water 0.2W on side trail. ◖ ⬦ (8)	3172
211.1	**1973.1**	Saddleback Junior	3655
210.8	**1973.4**	Stream.	3221
209.7	**1974.5**	**Poplar Ridge Lean-to** (196l) ◐ ◖ ⬦ ⊏ (6)	2968
		30.1◄20.1◄8.9▶8.0▶26.6▶36.8	
		Some tenting at lean-to, more on knoll to the north. Stream in front.	
207.0	**1977.2**	Orbeton Stream (ford)	1550
206.9	**1977.3**	Woods road, NoBo: turn east on road	1654
206.2	**1978.0**	Sluice Brook.	2106

The A.T. Guide

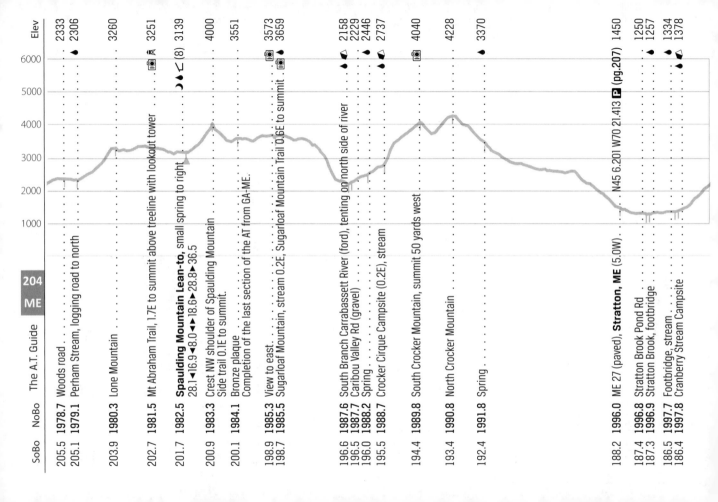

Elev	SoBo	NoBo	The A.T. Guide
2333	205.5	1978.7	Woods road
2306	205.1	1979.1	Perham Stream, logging road to north
3260	203.9	1980.3	Lone Mountain
3251	202.7	1981.5	Mt Abraham Trail, 1.7E to summit above treeline with lookout tower
3139	201.7	1982.5	**Spaulding Mountain Lean-to**, small spring to right 28.1◄16.9◄8.0◄▶18.6▶28.8▶36.5
4000	200.9	1983.3	Crest NW shoulder of Spaulding Mountain Side trail 0.1E to summit.
3551	200.1	1984.1	Bronze plaque Completion of the last section of the AT from GA-ME.
3573	198.9	1985.3	View to east.
3659	198.7	1985.5	Sugarloaf Mountain, stream 0.2E, Sugarloaf Mountain Trail 0.6E to summit
2158	196.6	1987.6	South Branch Carrabassett River (ford), tenting on north side of river
2229	196.5	1987.7	Caribou Valley Rd (gravel)
2446	196.0	1988.2	Spring
2737	195.5	1988.7	Crocker Cirque Campsite (0.2E), stream
4040	194.4	1989.8	South Crocker Mountain, summit 50 yards west
4228	193.4	1990.8	North Crocker Mountain
3370	192.4	1991.8	Spring
1450	188.2	1996.0	ME 27 (paved), **Stratton, ME** (5.0W) N45 6.201 W70 21.413 **P** (pg.207)
1250	187.4	1996.8	Stratton Brook Pond Rd
1257	187.3	1996.9	Stratton Brook, footbridge
1334	186.5	1997.7	Footbridge, stream
1378	186.4	1997.8	Cranberry Stream Campsite

SoBo	NoBo	Description	Elev
185.3	1988.9	Cranberry Pond 0.2W.	2322
185.0	1999.2	Bigelow Range Trail to west	2400
183.9	2000.3	View to east	3376
183.3	2000.9	Horns Pond Trail	3200
183.1	2001.1	**Horns Pond Lean-tos** 35.5◄26.6◄18.6◄►10.2►17.9►27.9 ⊂(16)	3183
182.7	2001.5	Trail 0.2W to North Horn	3704
182.6	2001.6	South Horn	3831
180.5	2003.7	Bigelow Mountain west peak	4145
180.1	2004.1	Avery Memorial Campsite, spring 0.2N on AT, Fire Wardens Trail to east	3825
179.8	2004.4	Avery Peak.	4090
178.6	2005.6	View.	2805
177.9	2006.3	Safford Brook Trail to west	2260
177.8	2006.4	Safford Notch Campsite 0.3E	2238
175.6	2008.6	View.	2949
174.6	2009.6	Little Bigelow Mountain, view	3010
172.9	2011.3	**Little Bigelow Lean-to** 36.8◄28.8◄10.2◄►7.7►17.7►27.4 ⊂(8)	1812
		Plenty of tent sites at lean-to. Swimming in "the Tubs" along AT.	
171.5	2012.7	East Flagstaff Rd, AT east on road for 0.1 mile	1200
171.3	2012.9	Bog Brook Rd, Flagstaff Lake outlet, footbridge N45 8.073 W70 10.283 P (0.1W)	1182
170.6	2013.6	Hemlock Trail to east.	1253
170.3	2013.9	East Flagstaff Lake tentpads, 2 beaches, 2 firepits (9)	1210
169.8	2014.4	Two intersections with Hemlock Trail	1255
168.7	2015.5	Long Falls Dam Rd (paved).	1225
168.6	2015.6	Jerome Brook.	1265
165.2	2019.0	**West Carry Pond Lean-to** 36.5◄17.9◄7.7◄►10.0►19.7►28.7 ⊂(8)	1345
		Swimming in pond. Water at spring house to left of lean-to or at West Carry Pond.	

Equipment Manufacturers and Retailers

AntiGravityGear	910-794-3308	GoLite	888-546-5483
Arc'Teryx	866-458-2473	Gossamer Gear	512-374-0133
Asolo/Lowe Alpine	603-448-8827	Granite Gear	218-834-6157
Backcountry.com	800-409-4502	Gregory	877-477-4292
Big Agnes	877-554-8975	Hi-Tec	800-521-1698
Black Diamond	801-278-5552	Hyperlite Mountain Gear	800-464-9208
CamelBak	800-767-8725	Jacks 'R' Better	757-643-8908
Campmor	888-226-7667	JanSport	800-552-6776
Camp Trails	800-345-7622	Katadyn/PUR	800-755-6701
Cascade Designs	800-531-9531	Keen	866-676-5336
(MSR/Therm-a-Rest/Platypus)		Kelty	866-349-7225
Cedar Tree (Packa)	276-780-2354	Leki	800-255-9982
Columbia	800-547-8066	Limmer	603-694-2668
Dana Designs	888-357-3262	LL Bean	800-441-5713
Danner	877-432-6637	Marmont	888-357-3262
Eagle Creek	800-874-1048	Merrell	800-288-3124
Eastern Mountain Sports	888-463-6367	Montbell	877-666-8235
Etowah Outfitters	770-975-7829	Montrail	800-826-1598
Eureka!	800-572-8822	Mountain Hardwear	800-953-8398
Ex Officio	800-644-7303	Mountainsmith	800-551-5889
Feathered Friends	206-292-2210	Mystery Ranch	406-585-1428
First Need	800-441-8166	NEMO	800-997-9301
Frogg Toggs	800-349-1835	North Face	866-715-3223
Garmin	800-800-1020	Osprey	866-314-3130
Garmont	800-943-4453	Outdoor Research	888-467-4327

Patagonia	800-638-6464
Peak 1/Coleman	800-835-3278
Petzl	877-807-3805
Photon	877-584-6898
Primus	307-857-4700
Princeton Tec	800-257-9080
REI	800-426-4840
Royal Robbins	800-587-9044
Salomon	800-654-2668
Sierra Designs	800-736-8592
Sierra Trading Post	800-713-4534
Six Moon Designs	503-430-2303
Slumberjack	800-233-6283
SOTO Outdoors	503-314-5119
Speer Hammocks	252-619-8289
Suunto	800-543-9124
Tarptent / Henry Shires	650-587-1548
Tecnica	800-258-3897
Teva	800-367-8382
The Underwear Guys	570-573-0209
ULA	435-753-5191
Vasque	800-224-4453
Warmstuff/Adventurelite	570-573-0209
Western Mountaineering	408-287-8944
Zip Stove	800-594-9046

STRATTON, ME

N

Pop. 368 (2006)
N45 8.450, W70 26.617
Mag. Dec. 16° 20'W

PO (04982):
207-246-6461
M-F 8:30-1 & 1:30-4,
Sa 8:30-11

Stratton Diner
Fotter's Market
Stratton Plaza

Maine Roadhouse
(5.0 mi)

Stratton Motel & Hostel

Northland General Store

White Wolf Inn & Restaurant

Main St

Old Mill Laundry

School St

16   27

0.4 mi

(5.0 mi from PO)
Spillover Motel (0.6 mi from PO)

Stratton Plaza Hotel $90 room with 2 queen beds. L/D Tu-Sa 11-10. Karaoke, music on weekends.

Northland Cash Supply 207-246-2376 Open 7 days 5-10, pizza, hiker box, Coleman/alcohol by ounce. Hiker friendly owner (Mark) provides rides back to the trail for free when he's available. Maildrops: 152 Main Street, Stratton, ME 04982.

Fotter's Market 207-246-2401 ATM, Deli, Coleman/alcohol/oz, M-Th 8-7, F-Sa 8-8, Su 9-5.

1996.0   ME 27

(2E) **Mountainside Grocers** 207-237-2248, open 7:30-6 May-Oct, 7:30-8 in winter.
   Stratton, ME 04982 (5W) *(more services on map)*

Stratton Motel 207-246-4171 ⟨www.thestrattonmotel.com⟩ $20 bunk, $50 private room, $5 laundry, free long distance calling, credit cards accepted. Shuttles as far as Bangor, Portland, or Monson. Canister fuel Maildrops for both the Motel and Maine Roadhouse: PO Box 284, Stratton, ME 04982.

Maine Roadhouse 207-246-2060 ⟨www.maineroadhouse.com⟩ (5W) on route 16. Bunkroom $20pp, semiprivate rooms $40S, $50D, free laundry, free long-distance, satellite TV, hiker kitchen and use of outdoor grill. Free shuttles to and from Route 27 and PO. Maildrops same as Stratton Motel.

White Wolf Inn 207-246-2922 $48S/D, $10EAP, pets $10, restaurant serves L/D. Breakfast on weekends. Wednesday is Italian, Friday is Fish Fry, closed Tuesday, does not accept Amex. Maildrops: Main Street, PO Box 590, Stratton, ME 04982.

Spillover Motel 207-246-6571 $59S, $79D. Senior discount (55+) $5. Pets okay for a $20 deposit and $5 charge, cont B. Full kitchen available for use by guests. Maildrops: PO Box 427, Stratton, ME 04982.

207

ME

The A.T. Guide

SoBo	NoBo	The A.T. Guide	Elev
164.5	**2019.7**	Arnolds Point 0.5W	1336
162.7	2021.5	Gravel road, AT to west over Sandy Stream	1279
161.8	2022.4	Gravel road	1287
161.5	2022.7	East Carry Pond, beach at north end	1256
159.5	2024.7	Scott Rd (gravel)	1319
158.7	2025.5	North branch of Carrying Place Stream	1200
155.2	**2029.0**	**Pierce Pond Lean-to,** east bank of Pierce Pond. ☽♦⊏ (6) 27.9◀17.7◀10.0◀▶9.7▶18.7▶22.8	1224
155.1	**2029.1**	Wooden dam, outlet of Pierce Pond ♦	1157
154.8	**2029.4**	Trail 0.3E to Harrison's Pierce Pond Camps, boat landing to west. (pg.212)	1100
154.6	**2029.6**	Otter Pond Rd (gravel)	1077
154.1	**2030.1**	Pierce Pond Stream Falls 0.1E	1000
154.0	**2030.2**	Waterfall 0.1E	974
153.5	**2030.7**	Otter Pond Stream, footbridge ♦	888
151.6	**2032.6**	Kennebec River. Do not ford. Use ferry service. ♦ (pg.212)	517
151.2	**2033.0**	US 201, **Caratunk, ME** (0.3E). N45 14.302 W69 59.777 **P** (pg.212)	520
150.9	**2033.3**	Woods road	698
148.6	2035.6	Holly Brook ♦	926
147.2	2037.0	Grove Rd (gravel)	1242
146.7	2037.5	Holly Brook ♦	1315
146.0	2038.2	Boise-Cascade Logging Rd to west (gravel), Pleasant Pond Rd to east.	1449
145.5	**2038.7**	**Pleasant Pond Lean-to** 27.4◀19.7◀9.7◀▶9.0▶13.1▶22.0 ☽♦⊏ (6)	1391
		Stream on path to lean-to and pond. Beach 0.2 on side trail beyond lean-to.	
145.3	**2038.9**	Pleasant Pond Beach to east	1355
144.2	**2040.0**	Pleasant Pond Mountain	2470

Blueberries – Abundant on open summits like Pleasant Pond Mountain.

SoBo	NoBo		Elev
139.7	2044.5	Stream.	1058
139.3	2044.9	Moxie Pond south end (ford), road, powerlines N45 14.984 W69 49.857 ▣	970
139.1	2045.1	Baker Stream	995
138.8	2045.4	Powerline	1037
136.5	2047.7	**Bald Mountain Brook Lean-to** ☾●⊏ (8)	1329
		28.7◄18.7◄9.0◄►4.1►13.0►25.0	
		Bald Mountain Brook in front of lean-to.	
135.1	2049.1	Summit bypass trail to west.	2163
134.5	2049.7	Moxie Bald Mountain.	2629
134.2	2050.0	Summit bypass trail to west.	2428
133.5	2050.7	Trail to Moxie Bald north peak (0.5W)	2227
132.4	2051.8	**Moxie Bald Mountain Lean-to** ☾●⊏ (8)	1242
		22.8◄13.1◄4.1◄►8.9►20.9►28.3	
		Bald Mountain Pond in front of lean-to.	
131.3	2052.9	Gravel road	1278
130.8	2053.4	Gravel road	1251
130.4	2053.8	Bald Mountain Stream ●	1234
126.9	2057.3	Marble Brook and jeep road	1003
126.5	2057.7	**West Branch of Piscataquis River (ford)**	982
		River normally knee-deep. During heavy rain periods, fording can be dangerous.	

SoBo	NoBo	The A.T. Guide	Elev
123.5	2060.7	**Horseshoe Canyon Lean-to** 22.0◄13.0◄8.9◄▶12.0▶19.4▶24.1.. ⟍♦⟋(8)	794
		On blue-blazed trail. Stream at northern AT junction or river in front and below.	
123.1	2061.1	Stream. ♦	763
121.2	2063.0	East Branch of Piscataquis River (ford)	650
120.9	2063.3	Gravel road	778
120.8	2063.4	Shirley-Blanchard Rd (paved) . . . N45 17.072 W69 35.223 **P**	850
119.7	2064.5	AT on woods road for 0.5 mile	1013
119.3	2064.9	Gravel road	927
117.8	2066.4	Historic AT route near Lake Hebron. . . . N45 17.442 W69 31.995 **P** (pg.212)	900
		0.2E on old roadbed to Bray Rd and parking, then left 1.6 mi to **Monson, ME.**	
117.4	2066.8	Dirt road.	1050
115.9	2068.3	Side trail to Doughty Ponds (0.1W)	1239
115.8	2068.4	Stream.	1261
115.2	2069.0	Gravel road	1392
114.5	2069.7	ME 15 (paved), **Monson, ME.** (4.0E) N45 19.856 W69 32.122 **P** (pg.212-213)	1215
114.4	2069.8	South end of 100-Mile Wilderness. / Spectacle Pond outlet, footbridge	1183
113.6	2070.6	Old Stage Rd (dirt)	1306
113.3	2070.9	Bell Pond	1278
112.6	2071.6	Lily Pond	1130
111.5	2072.7	**Leeman Brook Lean-to** 25.0◄20.9◄12.0◄▶7.4▶12.1▶16.1 Stream in front of lean-to.	1077
110.7	2073.5	North Pond outlet	1035
110.4	2073.8	North Pond Tote Rd	1112
109.3	2074.9	Mud Pond	1060
108.5	2075.3	Bear Pond Ledge	1228
108.5	2075.7	James Brook	981
108.1	2076.1	Woods road	979
108.0	2076.2	Little Wilson Falls, west 30 yards	876
107.7	2076.5	Little Wilson Stream (ford), campsite	750
107.3	2076.9	Follow gravel road for 100 yards, pond	959
105.4	2078.8	Big Wilson Tote Rd	585
105.2	2079.0	Thompson Brook	584
104.8	2079.4	Big Wilson Stream (ford)	600
104.5	2079.7	Railroad tracks	898
104.1	2080.1	**Wilson Valley Lean-to** (1993). 28.3◄19.4◄7.4◄▶4.7▶8.7▶15.6 Spring on opposite side of AT. ⟍♦⟋(6)	972
103.4	2080.8	Woods road	1198

SoBo	NoBo	Feature	Elev
102.1	2082.1	Stream	942
101.8	2082.4	Stream	941
100.9	2083.3	Wilber Brook (ford)	614
100.7	2083.5	Vaughn Stream	633
100.2	2084.0	Bodfish Farm, Long Pond Tote Rd (gravel), Long Pond Stream north of road	659
99.4	2084.8	**Long Pond Stream Lean-to** 24.1◀12.1◀4.7▶4.0▶10.9▶20.8	950
99.2	2085.0	Trail 0.8E to Otter Pond parking	1075
98.3	2085.9	Barren Slide to east, view	1983
98.1	2086.1	Barren Ledges	2016
96.3	2087.9	Barren Mountain	2660
95.4	2088.8	Side trail to **Cloud Pond Lean-to** (0.4E) 16.1◀8.7◀4.0▶6.9▶16.8▶24.0 Cloud Pond is water source.	2501
93.9	2090.3	Fourth Mountain, bog.	1953
93.3	2090.9	Fourth Mountain	2380
91.8	2092.4	Third Mountain Trail to west	1810
90.9	2093.3	Third Mountain, Monument Cliff	2086
90.2	2094.0	Trail 0.1W to West Chairback Pond, stream crosses AT north of side trail	1770
89.3	2094.9	View	2156
88.9	2095.3	Columbus Mountain, outlet stream from West Chairback Pond	2325
88.5	2095.7	**Chairback Gap Lean-to** 15.6◀10.9◀6.9▶9.9▶17.1▶20.7 Unreliable small spring 13 yards downhill and 25 yards north.	1979
88.0	2096.2	Chairback Mountain	2180
85.9	2098.3	0.2W to East Chairback Pond	1689
85.3	2098.9	Spring	1460
84.7	2099.5	Katahdin Ironworks Rd (gravel) N45 28.632 W69 17.107 P (0.4E)	788
84.2	2100.0	West Branch Pleasant River (ford). Wide ford with slick rocky bottom. Campsites to south; no camping/fires for 2.0N.	672
83.3	2100.9	Stream.	769
82.8	2101.4	Gulf Hagas Trail to west, 5.2 mile loop trail whose ends intersect the AT 0.7 mile apart. Features narrow, deep gorge with many waterfalls.	950

2029.4   Trail to camp

🛏 🍴 **Harrison's Pierce Pond Camps**
207-672-3625, 207-612-8184 May-Nov, 7 days. Bed, shower, and 12-pancake breakfast $40. If you only want breakfast ($9-12 served 7-7:30am), reserve a seat the day before. Cash only. Okay to get water at camp and dispose of trash.

2032.6   Kennebec River
The ferry is the official AT route (do not ford); the current is strong and unpredictable due to an upstream dam. Ferry service 7 days:

Before May 1	No service
May 1 - May 19	time & weather permitting, call in advance
May 20 - July 15	9am-11am
July 16 - Sept 30	9am-11am and 2pm-4pm
Oct 1 - Oct 8	9am-11am
Oct 15 - Oct 31	time & weather permitting, call in advance
After Oct 31	No service

🚌 **Fletcher Mountain Outfitters** 207-672-4879 David Corrigan provides ferry service. Shuttles service available when not operating ferry. Some resupply on-hand.

The A.T. Guide

2033.0   US 201
Caratunk, ME 04925 (0.3E)
🏠 ✆ M–F 7:30–11:30 & 12–3:45, Sa 7:30–11:15, 207-672-3416 Across 201 and up Main St 0.3 mile. Accepts debit cards with limited cash back.

🛏 ⛺ ✉ (1E) **The Sterling Inn** 207-672-3333 ⟨www.mainesterlinginn.com⟩ $45-$72 includes breakfast and free pickup from trailhead or from PO. Kids under 12 stay free with parents. Cash only. Address: 1041 Route 201. Maildrops: PO Box 129, Caratunk Maine 04925.

🛏 ◐ 🍴 💲 ⛺ 🛜 🖥 ✉ (2W) **Northern Outdoors** 800-765-7238 ⟨www.northernoutdoors.com⟩ Hiker rate for lodge rooms $73/up, holds up to 6, cabin tents $12PP/up, tenting $8PP. Coin laundry,

hot tub, ATM. No pets allowed in campsites, cabin tents or lodge rooms. B/L/D, free shuttle to/from trail coinciding with ferry schedule. Also offer rafting trips (class IV), food and ale in **Kennebec River Pub & Brewery**. Maildrops: 1771 US 201, The Forks, ME 04985.

🏪 **Berry's General Store** (7.5W) 207-663-4461 Food, and some hardware. 5am-7pm 7 days, year-round. Open till 8 in summer.

2066.4   Historic AT route, side trail 0.2E to hostel,
          1.6 further to *Monson*
🛏 🏠 ◐ 🛒 🖥 ✉ **100 Mile Wilderness Adventures and Outfitters**
207-991-7030 ⟨www.100milewilderness.info⟩ Bunkhouse, private cabins and tenting open mid-May through Mid November. Thru-hiker specials. Good selection of hiker foods, fuel, and gear. Slackpacking, shuttles, and mid-wilderness resupply. Parking for section hikers. Pets welcome. Maildrops for guests: PO Box 47, Bray Road, Monson, ME 04410.

2069.7   ME 15
          Monson, ME 04464 (4E) *(more services on map)*
Strickly enforced: *No stealth camping in town*
🛏 🏠 ◐ 🍴 🛒 🚿 ⛺ 🖥 🛜 🖥 ✉ **Lakeshore House Lodging & Pub**
207-997-7069, 207-343-5033 ⟨www.lakeshorehouse.com⟩ Bunkroom $25PP, private rooms $40S/$55D w/shared bath, tenting $8. Well-behaved dogs okay. Reservations appreciated but not required; check-in anytime, packs out of room by 11am. Accepts credit cards; pay lodging bill in cash to receive free beverage in Pub. WFS possible (3hrs). Free for guests: trailhead pickup & return, loaner laptop, Wifi, kayaks, paddleboats, water trampoline, vehicle parking. Laundromat 24hrs. Coin operated shower for nonguests. Hiker store with long-term resupply, hours vary. Statewide shuttles/slackpack/food drops. $20 "bucket" food drop 30 miles into the 100-mile wilderness. No charge for leaving a vehicle. Pub hours: Tu-Sa 12-9, Su 12-8, bar open later, closed M. AYCE specials W and F, live music Su 2-5pm. Guests welcome at Shaws for breakfast. Maildrops: PO Box 215, Monson, ME 04464.

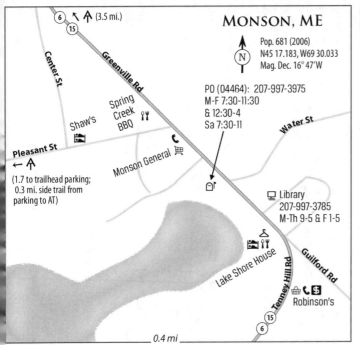

Pop. 681 (2006)
N45 17.183, W69 30.033
Mag. Dec. 16° 47'W

PO (04464): 207-997-3975
M-F 7:30-11:30
& 12:30-4
Sa 7:30-11

(3.5 mi.)

(1.7 to trailhead parking;
0.3 mi. side trail from
parking to AT)

Library
207-997-3785
M-Th 9-5 & F 1-5

Robinson's

0.4 mi

Shaw's Lodging 207-997-3597
shawslodging@gmail.com ⟨www.shawslodging.com⟩ Mid-May-mid-Oct.
$24 bunks, $35 private room, $28 semi-private, $12 tenting. Free pickup/
return with stay. $8 AYCE breakfast, $5 laundry, $5 shower and towel
(w/o stay), internet available. Food drops, slackpacking and shuttles
all over Maine, Coleman/alcohol/oz, canister fuel & AquaMira. No credit
cards. Maildrops (non-guests $5): PO Box 72 or 17 Pleasant St, Monson,
ME 04464.

Buddy Ward 207-343-2564 buppyx4@midmaine.com.
Shuttling anywhere in state of Maine and into NH, slackpacks
the 100-mile wilderness. Voicemail available.

Sydney Pratt 207-997-3221 pielady13@myfairpoint.net
known as "The Pie Lady", will shuttle from Stratton to Katahdin.

Monson General Store 207-997-3964 10-6 7 days. Deli &
bakery, long-term supply including protein bars, wraps, tuna
fish, Lipton sides, granola and trail mixes in bulk. Coleman/
alcohol/oz. Friday night jams held in the store.

🏧 **A.E. Robinson's** 5am-10pm 7 days. ATM fee $2.

Spring Creek Bar-B-Q 207-997-7025
Th-Sa 10am-8pm, Sunday 9am-5pm BYOB.

✉ **Kathy Preble** 207-965-8464 chair_back_mt@yahoo.com
Food drops and shuttles in the 100 mile wilderness, make
arrangements well in advance. Maildrops: (USPS) PO Box 284 or
(UPS) 191 Main Rd, Brownville, ME 04414

Greenville, ME 04485 (14W from ME 15)

Indian Hill Motel 207-695-2623 $72pp

Kelly's Landing 207-695-4438 7 days 7-9, Su AYCE breakfast.

The Black Frog 207-695-1100 Restaurant and pub offers
pizza.

Dairy Bar 207-695-2921 ice cream

Harris Drug Store w/ soda fountain counter and seating.

Indian Hill Trading Post & Supermarket 800-675-4487

Jamieson's Store convenience store w/pizza and subs.

Northwoods Outfitters 207-695-3288
⟨www.maineoutfitter.com⟩ Full service outfitter with fuel/oz and
canister fuel. Expresso bar, pastries, internet. 7 days, 8-5.

✚ **Charles Dean Memorial Hospital** 207-695-5200

Also: two banks with ATMs

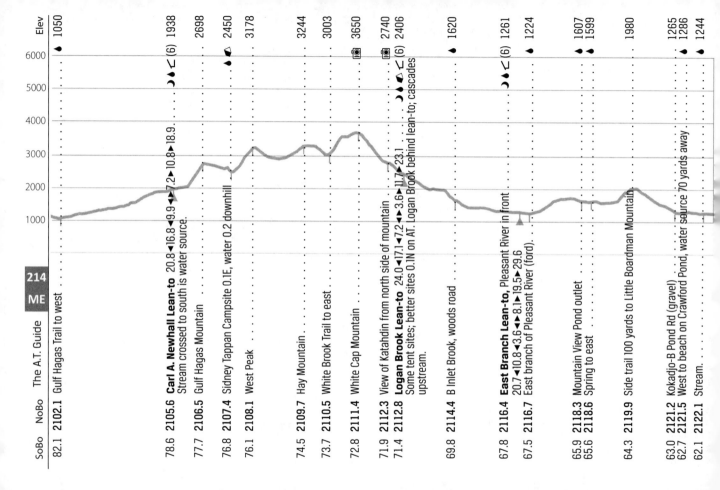

Elev		
1050		
1938		
2698		
2450		
3178		
3244		
3003		
3650		
2740		
2406		
1620		
1261		
1224		
1607		
1599		
1980		
1265		
1286		
1244		

214
ME

SoBo	NoBo	The A.T. Guide
82.1	2102.1	Gulf Hagas Trail to west
78.6	2105.6	**Carl A. Newhall Lean-to** 20.8◄16.8◄9.9▲►7.2►10.8►18.9. ☽♦⊏(6) Stream crossed to south is water source.
77.7	2106.5	Gulf Hagas Mountain
76.8	2107.4	Sidney Tappan Campsite 0.1E, water 0.2 downhill ◁
76.1	2108.1	West Peak
74.5	2109.7	Hay Mountain
73.7	2110.5	White Brook Trail to east
72.8	2111.4	White Cap Mountain 📶
71.9	2112.3	View of Katahdin from north side of mountain 📶
71.4	2112.8	**Logan Brook Lean-to** 24.0◄17.1◄7.2▲►3.6►11.7►23.1 ☽♦◁⊏(6) Some tent sites; better sites 0.1N on AT. Logan Brook behind lean-to; cascades upstream.
69.8	2114.4	B Inlet Brook, woods road
67.8	2116.4	**East Branch Lean-to,** Pleasant River in front 20.7◄10.8◄3.6▲►8.1►19.5►29.6 ☽♦⊏(6)
67.5	2116.7	East branch of Pleasant River (ford).
65.9	2118.3	Mountain View Pond outlet
65.6	2118.6	Spring to east
64.3	2119.9	Side trail 100 yards to Little Boardman Mountain
63.0	2121.2	Kokadjo-B Pond Rd (gravel)
62.7	2121.5	West to beach on Crawford Pond, water source 70 yards away . ♦
62.1	2122.1	Stream. ♦

SoBo	NoBo		Elev
60.2	2124.0	Cooper Brook	1025
59.7	2124.5	**Cooper Brook Falls Lean-to** 18.9◀11.7◀8.1◀▶11.4▶21.5▶29.6 ⌒◆⌂(6)	946
		Brook, falls, swimming hole in front of lean-to. Privy across trail and up hill.	
59.1	2125.1	Large tributary to Cooper Brook	835
56.0	2128.2	Jo-Mary Rd N45 39.087 W69 1.900 P ◆ (pg.216)	625

✻ **Indian pipe** – A type of fungus that grows in moist duff. Translucent white candy cane shape 3-4" tall, grows in clusters. Scale-like leaves/petals.

SoBo	NoBo		Elev
53.5	2130.7	Footbridge, side trail 0.2E to north shore of Cooper Pond	533
53.1	2131.1	Mud Pond to west, footbridge over Mud Brook	508
51.8	2132.4	Antlers Campsite	500
		Campsites on edge of Jo-Mary Lake. Fort Relief two seat privy.	
50.3	2133.9	Potaywadjo Ridge Trail 1.0W (no sign)	539
50.1	2134.1	East to sandy beach on lower Jo-Mary Lake	580
48.3	2135.9	**Potaywadjo Spring Lean-to** (1995) ⌒◆⌂(8)	655
		23.1◀19.5◀11.4◀▶10.1▶18.2▶29.7 Potaywadjo Spring to right.	
47.7	2136.5	Twitchell Brook, footbridge. 📷	513
		Side trail 75 feet to Pemadumcook Lake southwest shore, view of Katahdin.	
46.5	2137.7	Deer Brook	523
45.8	2138.4	Woods road	530
45.7	2138.5	Mahar Tote Rd (dirt) (pg.216)	529
45.6	2138.6	Blue-blazed trail 0.9E to White House Landing boat dock (hostel).	520
45.1	2139.1	Tumbledown Dick Stream (ford)	516
44.5	2139.7	High water trail to west	530
44.0	2140.2	Ford branch of the Nahmakanta Stream	530
		Nahmakanta Stream Campsite	600
42.0	2142.2	Stream.	634

2128.2   Jo-Mary Rd
Very little traffic on road, connects with ME 11 (12.0E).

🛶 ⛺ (9.0E) **Jo-Mary Campground** 207-723-8117   Campsites $16, pets welcome, coin operated showers and laundry.

2138.5   Mahar Tote Rd
🛏 🏠 🍴 ⚰ 🚿 (0.9E) **White House Landing Wilderness Camps** 207-745-5116 MemDay-Oct10. Use air horn to be picked up by boat; no pickups after dark. In the morning you will be returned to a point closer to the trail. $39PP bunk, sleeps 18, $49PP private, includes AYCE breakfast. Meals available only during meal hours (breakfast 8am, lunch 11-1, dinner 5-6). Dinner for guests only. Very adequate items for resupply; hiker foods, Coleman/alcohol/oz and canister fuel. Visa/MC accepted for small fee, shuttles can be arranged.

The A.T. Guide

National Weather Service Wind Chill Chart

		Temperature (°F)												
		35	30	25	20	15	10	5	0	-5	-10	-15	-20	-25
Wind (mph)	5	31	25	19	13	7	1	-5	-11	-16	-22	-28	-34	-40
	10	27	21	15	9	3	-4	-10	-16	-22	-28	-35	-41	-47
	15	25	19	13	6	0	-7	-13	-19	-26	-32	-39	-45	-51
	20	24	17	11	4	-2	-9	-15	-22	-29	-35	-42	-48	-55
	25	23	16	9	3	-4	-11	-17	-24	-31	-37	-44	-51	-58
	30	22	15	8	1	-5	-12	-19	-26	-33	-39	-46	-53	-60
	35	21	14	7	0	-7	-14	-21	-27	-34	-41	-48	-55	-62
	40	20	13	6	-1	-8	-15	-22	-29	-36	-43	-50	-57	-64

Baxter State Park

For information and reservations, call 207-723-5140 8am-4pm. When you are in the area, even as far as Medway, you can tune to AM 1610 for the most recent reports. On the web: ⟨http://www.baxterstateparkauthority.com/hiking/thru-hiking.html⟩

The hiking season is approximately May 15 through October 15. Dates vary based on weather, and the park can be closed any day of the year due to weather. Katahdin ascents may be disallowed even when the park is open. Weather reports are posted at **Katahdin Stream Campground** (KSC) at 7:00am every morning, along with one of these ratings:

Class 1: Open, conditions favorable for day use and climbing.
Class 2: Open, but hiking above treeline not recommended.
Class 3: Hiking above treeline not recommended; specified trails closed.
Class 4: Mandatory closure of all trails at trailhead.

Consequences for hiking when the trail is closed includes fines, equipment seizure and loss of park visitation privileges.

All hikers intending to climb Katahdin must sign in at KSC and sign out when leaving. Hikes to Baxter Peak must be started by noon in June and July, 11am in August, 10am in September, and 9am in October. All AT hikers are welcome to leave their backpack at KSC. Loaner daypacks are available at no charge from the KSC ranger's station. Northbound thru-hikers completing their hike in late summer or early fall usually have an easy time hitching from KSC into Millinocket.

There are fees for nonresidents entering the park by car and fees for use of campsites by residents and nonresidents. Fees must be paid in cash; no credit cards and no work-for-stay.

There are 2 shelters and one tentsite at **The Birches** near KSC that are open to long distance hikers traveling either north on the AT or south on the IAT who have hiked 100 continuous miles immediately prior to entering the Park. Stay is limited to a single night. The fee is $10 per person.

All other AT hikers who wish to overnight in the Park should make reservations in advance. Common options, listed in order of their proximity to KSC are **Abol Campground**, **Daicey Pond Campground** (cabins $55D/up) and **Foster Field Group Area**, just north of Katahdin. Note that Abol Campground in the Park, Abol Pines at Abol Bridge and the privately run Abol Bridge Campground are three distinct entities.

If you are driving to Baxter: gates open 6am weekdays, 5am weekends. Maine residents enter for free; $14 per vehicle for non-residents. KSC parking is limited to 25 cars. This limit is often reached on weekends. Parking can be reserved at KSC, Abol Campground or Roaring Brook Campground by calling up to three weeks in advance, for a $5 fee. There is no long-term parking in Baxter.

Cell phone reception is unlikely anywhere in the park other than on Katahdin, so do not count on calling for a ride from KSC. Even where there is reception, do not place calls from the summit or within earshot of other hikers. Please use a cell phone only if there is an emergency.

Pets are not allowed in the park.

Connie McManus 207-723-6795 Privately run kennel service; pickup/drop off at Abol Bridge.

Elev
679
677
717
812
1520
1186
1031
980
904
685
972
1023
1109
1071
1100
1079
1123
1144
1083
1517

SoBo	NoBo	The A.T. Guide
39.9	2144.3	Prentiss Brook
38.6	2145.6	Side trail east to sand beach on shore of Nahmakanta Lake
38.2	2146.0	**Wadleigh Stream Lean-to,** stream can be dry during summer
		29.6◀21.5◀10.1◀▶8.1▶19.6▶33.0
37.2	2147.0	Spring
36.3	2147.9	Nesuntabunt Mountain, short side trail east to view of Katahdin,
		16 mile line-of-sight distance to Katahdin summit from here.
35.6	2148.6	View
34.8	2149.4	Wadleigh Pond Rd (gravel)
33.9	2150.3	Crescent Pond west end
33.2	2151.0	Pollywog Gorge, side trail overlooking gorge
32.3	2151.9	Pollywog Stream N45 46.774 W69 10.320 **P**
		Cross stream on logging road bridge.
30.6	2153.6	Outlet stream from Murphy Pond
30.1	2154.1	**Rainbow Stream Lean-to,** baseball bat floor
		29.6◀18.2◀8.1◀▶11.5▶24.9▶ 0.0
		Tenting on hill behind lean-to. Excellent swimming hole upstream.
28.2	2156.0	West to Rainbow Lake dam
28.0	2156.2	Stream.
26.3	2157.9	Rainbow Lake Campsite, spring west 30 yards.
25.1	2159.1	Stream.
24.8	2159.4	Unmarked trail leads 0.2W to Rainbow Lake Camps (private)
24.5	2159.7	Trail 0.7E to Rainbow Mountain
22.9	2161.3	Side trail 0.1E to Little Beaver Pond
21.1	2163.1	Rainbow Ledges, view of Katahdin

SoBo	NoBo	Description		Elev
18.6	2165.6	**Hurd Brook Lean-to,** baseball bat floor	☽ ♦ ⊏ (6)	720
		29.7◄19.6◄11.5▼▲13.4▲0.0►0.0		
18.1	2166.1	Small spring.	♦	791
15.9	2168.3	Bog bridge		624
15.4	2168.8	Golden Rd (paved), Nobo east on road. **Millinocket, ME** (19E).....(pg.220)		609
15.1	2169.1	Abol Bridge crosses west branch .... N45 50.111 W68 58.158 P 📷 (pg.220)		578
		of Penobscot River. Parking on east side of road between bridge and trailhead.		
14.7	2169.5	End of Golden Rd, Nobo veer left on dirt road.		620
14.5	2169.7	Abol Stream Trail to east, footbridge. Baxter State Park Boundary	♦	606
14.2	2170.0	Information board, Abol Pond Trail east, registration for The Birches Campsites.		595
14.0	2170.2	Footbridge, Katahdin Stream, Foss and Knowlton Trail to east	♦	591
13.1	2171.1	Foss and Knowlton Brook, footbridge.	♦♦	598
10.4	2173.8	Lower fork of Nesowadnehunk Stream	♦	626
9.4	2174.8	Upper fork of Nesowadnehunk Stream	♦	808
8.6	2175.6	Short side trail to view of Big Niagara Falls	📷♦	951
8.3	2175.9	Side trail west to Toll Dam and Little Niagara Falls	♦	1054
7.5	2176.7	Daicey Pond Nature Trail to west, parking area and privy north of trailhead P	☽	1096
6.7	2177.5	Tracy and Elbow Pond Trails to west, Daicey Pond Nature Trail to east	♦	1119
6.1	2178.1	Grassy Pond Trail to west (two intersections).		1082
5.7	2178.5	Footbridge, stream	♦	1059
5.2	2179.0	Perimeter Rd		1090
5.1	2179.1	Katahdin Stream Campground	♦ ⊏ (16)	1106
		The Birches Lean-tos & Campsite (0.2E) thru-hikers only, $10PP pay at KSC		
		ranger station or info board (9.1S). 33.0◄24.9◄13.4◄►0.0►0.0►0.0		
3.9	2180.3	Owl Trail to west, footbridge, stream	♦	1569
3.8	2180.4	Katahdin Stream Falls	☽	1654
2.9	2181.3	Spring	♦	2411
2.6	2181.6	Pass "The cave" small slab cave		2864
1.6	2182.6	The Gateway, The Tableland		4538
1.0	2183.2	Thoreau Spring, Abol Trail to east	♦	4620
0.0	2184.2	**Katahdin,** Baxter Peak, Northern Terminus of the AT ...(pg.220-221)		5268

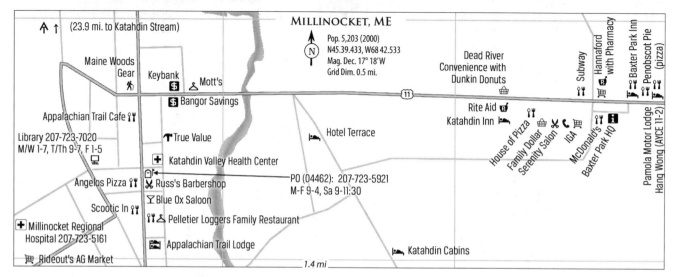

MILLINOCKET, ME

Pop. 5,203 (2000)
N45.39.433, W68 42.533
Mag. Dec. 17° 18'W
Grid Dim. 0.5 mi.

A ↑ (23.9 mi. to Katahdin Stream)

Maine Woods Gear

Keybank

Mott's

Appalachian Trail Cafe

Bangor Savings

Library 207-723-7020
M/W 1-7, T/Th 9-7, F 1-5

True Value

Katahdin Valley Health Center

PO (04462): 207-723-5921
M-F 9-4, Sa 9-11:30

Angelos Pizza

Russ's Barbershop

Blue Ox Saloon

Scootic In

Pelletier Loggers Family Restaurant

Millinocket Regional Hospital 207-723-5161

Appalachian Trail Lodge

Rideout's AG Market

Hotel Terrace

Katahdin Cabins

1.4 mi

Dead River Convenience with Dunkin Donuts

Rite Aid
Katahdin Inn
House of Pizza
Family Dollar
Serenity Salon

IGA

McDonalds

Baxter Park HQ

Subway

Hannaford with Pharmacy

Baxter Park Inn

Penobscot Pie (pizza)

Pamola Motor Lodge
Hang Wong (AYCE 11-2)

2168.8, 2169.1 Golden Rd, Abol Bridge

Abol Bridge Campground & Campstore, Open 7am-7pm all months except December and April. Campsites $16.20S, $21.40D includes shower, $3.50 for shower only. Prepared foods (B/L/D) include subs and burgers. Store sells sandwiches, sodas, ice cream, snacks, white gas/oz and Heet. Visa/MC accepted.

Abol Pines $9+tax ($4+tax ME residents) self-register tent sites and shelters across the street from Abol Bridge Campstore, south of Golden Road. Provided by Maine Department of Conservation.

2184.2 Katahdin, Baxter Peak

Millinocket, ME 04462 (20E) *(more services on map)*

Trail's End Festival September 14-16 with vendors, food, and entertainment. Hardcore trail work on Friday.

The Appalachian Trail Lodge and Cafe
207-723-4321 ⟨www.appalachiantraillodge.com⟩ One-stop hiker service run by Paul (OleMan) & Jaime (NaviGator) Renaud. Bunkroom $25, private room $35S, $55D, family suite call for rates. Showers for nonguests $3. Coin laundry. Fuel, some hiking supplies. Free daily shuttle from Baxter park, from Sept 1, till Oct 15, between 3pm – 4:30pm. Licensed and insured shuttle service for hire to and from bus in Medway, into 100-mile wilderness or Monson, food drops. Slackpack in 100-mile wilderness, other shuttles by arrangement, free parking. No pets, credit cards accepted.

SoBo special: pickup in Medway, bed in bunkroom, breakfast at AT Cafe', and shuttle to KSC. $70pp. By reservation. Maildrops for guests: 33 Penobscot Avenue, Millinocket, ME 04462.

🛏🍴 **Hotel Terrace & Ruthie's Restaurant** 207-723-4545
$59.95S, $65.95D, $6EAP. Ruthie's serves B/L/D.

🛏🍴⚿ **Katahdin Inn** 207-723-4555 $60S, $70D +tax, $10EAP, restaurant and bar on site.

🛏🍴📶✉ **Pamola Motor Lodge** 800-575-9746 $59S $69D, cont. breakfast. **Hang Wong** Chinese restaurant on site with AYCE lunch buffet. Pets $10. Maildrops: 973 Central Street, Millinocket, ME 04462.

🛏✉   **Katahdin Cabins** 207-723-6305 ⟨www.katahdincabins. com⟩ $60 small cabin sleeps 2-3, $80 5-person cabin, cont B, no smoking, cabins have TV, DVD, frig & micro, gas grill, bikes free for use, community room, 20% off for hikers and family, accepts all CC/ cash/checks, owners Skip and Nicole Mohoff. Maildrops: 181 Medway Road, Millinocket, ME 04462.

🛏 **Baxter Park Inn** 207-723-9777 $84S, $10EAP, pets $10, hot tub, pool.

◣ **Hidden Springs Campground** 207-723-6337, Tent sites $12PP, pool, shower.

🍴⚿ **Pelletier Loggers Family Restaurant** 207-723-6100 Open 5am-9pm. Laundry adjacent.

🚌   **Town Taxi** 207-723-2000, 207-447-3474 Shuttles from bus station in Medway to Millinocket $16, from Millinocket to Abol Bridge $45, Millinocket to Katahdin Stream (The Birches) $55.

🚌 **Maine Quest Adventures** 207-746-9615 ⟨www.mainequestadventures.com⟩ pick up at Medway bus station and drop off at Katahdin Stream or Abol Bridge $55/two persons, $5EAP. If late in the afternoon, stay at base camp and tent on lawn for free. Shuttles to Monson and parts of the 100 Mile Wilderness.

✈ **Katahdin Air** 866-359-6246 ⟨www.KatahdinAir.com⟩ One-way flights to a number of trailheads from White House Landing to Monson. $55-120 per person, includes shuttle from Abol Bridge to seaplane base.

Getting to Katahdin

Most routes to Katahdin are through Bangor, Maine, which has an airport and bus terminal. Bangor is 91 miles from Baxter SP. Shuttle services will pick you up in Bangor, but it is more economical to take **Cyr Bus Lines** to Medway, 31 miles from Baxter State Park. Hikers often layover in Millinocket, 24 miles from Katahdin Stream Campground, the closest parking area to Katahdin.

Bangor, ME - Medway, ME

🚌 **Cyr Bus Lines** 800-244-2335 ⟨www.cyrbustours.com⟩
Routes connecting Bangor and Medway. Most one-way routes are $11.50, cash only.
Medway (station at Irving store) - Bangor departs 9:30am
Bangor (Greyhound hub) - Medway departs 6:00pm
Bangor (Concord Trailways hub) - Medway departs 6:30pm

🚌 **Concord Trailways** 207-945-4000
⟨www.concordtrailways.com⟩ Hub near Bangor airport, service as far south as South Station in Massachusetts.

🚌 **Greyhound Bus Service**   800-231-2222 ⟨www.greyhound. com⟩ Bangor hub (207-945-3000) 158 Main St .

🚌 **The Appalachian Trail Lodge, Town Taxi, and Maine Quest Adventures** All listed in Millinocket, provide transportation from Medway to Millinocket and Katahdin.

The A.T. Guide

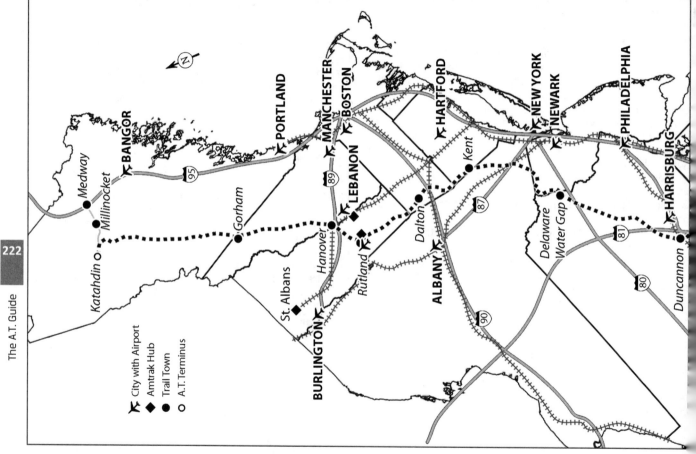

The A.T. Guide

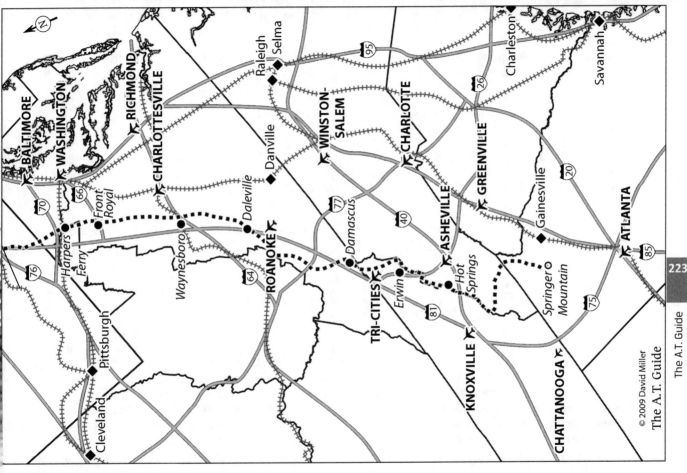

223

The A.T. Guide

© 2009 David Miller

January

Su	M	Tu	W	Th	F	Sa
1	2	3	4	5	6	7
8	9	10	11	12	13	14
15	16	17	18	19	20	21
22	23	24	25	26	27	28
29	30	31				

Full Moon

1 New Year's Day (obsv. Monday)
16 Martin Luther King Jr. Day

February

Su	M	Tu	W	Th	F	Sa
			1	2	3	4
5	6	7	8	9	10	11
12	13	14	15	16	17	18
19	20	21	22	23	24	25
26	27	28	29			

14 Valentine's Day
20 President's Day

March

Su	M	Tu	W	Th	F	Sa
			1	2	3	
4	5	6	7	8	9	10
11	12	13	14	15	16	17
18	19	20	21	22	23	24
25	26	27	28	29	30	31

11 Daylight Saving Time Begins
20 First day of Spring

April

Su	M	Tu	W	Th	F	Sa
1	2	3	4	5	6	7
8	9	10	11	12	13	14
15	16	17	18	19	20	21
22	23	24	25	26	27	28
29	30					

8 Easter

May

Su	M	Tu	W	Th	F	Sa
		1	2	3	4	5
6	7	8	9	10	11	12
13	14	15	16	17	18	19
20	21	22	23	24	25	26
27	28	29	30	31		

13 Mother's Day
28 Memorial Day

June

Su	M	Tu	W	Th	F	Sa
					1	2
3	4	5	6	7	8	9
10	11	12	13	14	15	16
17	18	19	20	21	22	23
24	25	26	27	28	29	30

17 Father's Day
20 Summer Begins

July

Su	M	Tu	W	Th	F	Sa
1	2	3	4	5	6	7
8	9	10	11	12	13	14
15	16	17	18	19	20	21
22	23	24	25	26	27	28
29	30	31				

4 Independence Day

August

Su	M	Tu	W	Th	F	Sa
			1	2	3	4
5	6	7	8	9	10	11
12	13	14	15	16	17	18
19	20	21	22	23	24	25
26	27	28	29	30	31	

12 Perseids Meteor Shower

September

Su	M	Tu	W	Th	F	Sa
						1
2	3	4	5	6	7	8
9	10	11	12	13	14	15
16	17	18	19	20	21	22
23	24	25	26	27	28	29
30						

3 Labor Day
22 Autumn Begins

October

Su	M	Tu	W	Th	F	Sa
	1	2	3	4	5	6
7	8	9	10	11	12	13
14	15	16	17	18	19	20
21	22	23	24	25	26	27
28	29	30	31			

8 Columbus Day
31 Halloween

November

Su	M	Tu	W	Th	F	Sa
				1	2	3
4	5	6	7	8	9	10
11	12	13	14	15	16	17
18	19	20	21	22	23	24
25	26	27	28	29	30	

4 Daylight Saving Time Ends
11 Veterans Day (obsv. Monday)

December

Su	M	Tu	W	Th	F	Sa
						1
2	3	4	5	6	7	8
9	10	11	12	13	14	15
16	17	18	19	20	21	22
23	24	25	26	27	28	29
30	31					

21 First day of Winter
25 Christmas

Jan 13-16   *Southern Ruck* Nantahala Outdoor Center (pg.22)

Jan 27-29   *PA Ruck* Bears Den Trail Center, Bluemont, VA (pg.93)

Mar 3-4   *Backpacking Clinic & Celebration* Amicalola Falls SP (pg.6)

Mar16-18   *Dahlonega Trail Fest,* Dahlonega, GA

Mar31-Apr 1   *Hiker Fool Bash* Sapphire Inn, Franklin, NC (pg.18)

Apr 6-7   *Founder's Bridge AT Festival* Bryson City, NC (pg.22)

Apr 20-21   *Trailfest* Hot Springs, NC (pg.33)

May 18-20   *Trail Days* Damascus, VA (pg.51)

Jun 2   *National Trails Day*®, Everywhere - (AHS, pg.87)

Jun 8-9   *AT Hall of Fame Banquet* Pine Grove Furnace SP (pg.119)

Sep 14-16   *Trail's End Festival* Millinocket, ME (pg.220)

Oct 12-14   *The Gathering* (ALDHA) Concord Univ., Athens, WV